CHINESE VIEWS
OF
FUTURE
WARFARE

CHINESE VIEWS OF FUTURE WARFARE

Michael Pillsbury
Editor

National Defense University Press

WASHINGTON, DC

National Defense University Press Publications

To increase general knowledge and inform discussion, the Institute for National Strategic Studies, through its publication arm the NDU Press, publishes *Strategic Forums*; McNair Papers; proceedings of University- and Institute-sponsored symposia; books relating to U.S. national security, especially to issues of joint, combined, or coalition warfare, peacekeeping operations, and national strategy; and a variety of other works designed to circulate contemporary comment and offer alternatives to current policy. The Press occasionally publishes out-of-print defense classics, historical works, and other especially timely or distinguished writing on national security.

NDU Press publications are sold by the U.S. Government Printing Office. For ordering information, call (202) 512-1800 or write to the Superintendent of Documents, U.S. Government Printing Office, Washington, DC 20402.

Library of Congress Cataloging-in-Publication Data
Chinese views of future warfare / Michael Pillsbury, editor
     p. cm.
    1. China—Defenses—Forecasting. 2. Military art and
science—Forecasting. 3. Twenty-first century. I. Pillsbury, Michael.
UA835.C5437   1996
355.02'0951—dc21   96-47553
                                                      CIP

First Printing, March 1997

ISBN 1-57906-035-8

Contents

PART ONE:
THE STRATEGIC THOUGHT
OF DENG XIAOPING

PART TWO:
FUTURE SECURITY TRENDS

PART THREE:
MODERNIZING FOR LOCAL WAR

PART FOUR:

THE REVOLUTION IN MILITARY AFFAIRS

x

Photographs

A view of China's national defense headquarters overlooking Beihai Park

Foreword

The United States, while increasing military-to-miltary contacts with the Chinese, has also been urging China to improve its transparency about military matters. China has now taken several steps in this regard. For example, my counterpart, the President of China's National Defense University, agreed in late 1996 to expand the exchange program between our two institutions, thereby further enhancing a program already working well since 1985.

Another positive sign has been the opening of China's professional military literature to outsiders. It is now possible to purchase Chinese books and subscribe to Chinese military journals that were not publicly available before. Taking advantage of this welcome development, and working directly with the Chinese, the editor of this volume introduces to the West the works of authoritative and innovative Chinese authors whose writings focus on the future of the Chinese military. Although this material is now officially available to foreigners, it is in practice difficult to come by. So the carefully selected, representative essays published in this volume make Chinese military thinking even more accessible to Western readers.

This volume reveals, for example, China's keen interest in the Revolution in Military Affairs. Western specialists may be surprised to learn how far Chinese strategic thinking has advanced beyond the funadamental concepts of Sun Tzu and Chairman Mao. Western readers will even detect differences among writers on specific issues, although there are no raging debates on major issues like those one might find in Western literature. However, Chinese military transparency, although growing, has far to go to reach Western standards. Western analysts and scholars must, for instance, still rely on secondary sources for information on Chinese force size, structure, military budgets, and weapons systems. Continued Chinese secrecy makes it impossible to know with confidence what China's doctrines or programs for the future may actually be. But this volume—done in full cooperation with the Chinese and disclosing heretofore guarded information—is a step in the right direction and an important starting point for understanding China's future military modernization.

ERVIN J. ROKKE
Lieutenant General, USAF
President, National Defense University

The Academy of Military Science in Beijing hosts a delegation from the Atlantic Council of the United States, March 1995

Lieutenant General Ervin J. Rokke, President, NDU, congratulates his Chinese counterpart, Lieutenant General Xing Shizhong, after signing the Memorandum of Cooperation and Reciprocal Relations, October 18, 1996.

Preface

This collection of articles was made possible through a process that began in March 1995, when the President of the Chinese Academy of Military Science hosted a delegation of the Atlantic Council of the United States in Beijing. Over 4 days, our delegation met with more than 50 Chinese strategic experts including Defense Minister General Chi Haotian. This unprecedented visit provided the opportunity to obtain 100 Chinese military books and professional military journals. One journal, *China Military Science*, published by the Academy of Military Science, is the source of most of the articles in this collection. The remaining articles are from the *Liberation Army Daily* newspaper and several books published by the Chinese military press. *China Military Science* features articles by authors with many different approaches to thinking about future warfare. In fact, the journal's editor told me in Beijing that he selects a variety of articles for each issue from many schools of thought. Interestingly, he even publishes several articles in each issue about the continuing relevance of ancient strategic theories.

Most of this collection of articles about future warfare by senior Chinese military authors first appeared in 1994 to 1996. They were selected within certain strict Chinese rules that China places on foreign access to military publications. During four trips to the Academy of Military Science in Beijing, 10 Chinese senior military officers were interviewed regarding Chinese views of future warfare and queried about China's most insightful or most authoritative military authors for me to translate for the National Defense University Press. I explained that China's best professional military writing about the future ought to become better known in the United States where, by default, the perception exists that China lacks a vision of the nature of future warfare.

Early on, several Chinese military officers frankly told me that 15 or so of China's best military strategists never publish openly. For security reasons, no generals in China can openly publish about current military issues. However, there is greater latitude for Chinese military authors to speculate in *China Military Science* about the nature of future warfare. Because of Chinese limitations about publication of current military issues, I had no choice but to limit my selection of articles and authors to the subject of future warfare. However, this restriction proved to be serendipitous when I discovered a previously neglected community of Chinese military experts on the future. I was introduced to 30 authors who belong to organizations like the Society for the Study of Future Warfare and the Institute for Grand Strategy and who serve at the National Defense University, the Academy of Military Science, and other parts of the People's Liberation Army.

I have arranged the articles by subject:

- Part One: Deng's doctrine of future types and causes of warfare
- Part Two: China's future threats or security environment
- Part Three: Short-term future challenges for possible Local War
- Part Four: Long-term future warfare and the Revolution in Military Affairs.

Over the past decade, a small group of Western professors and government analysts has published a few books and many articles about Chinese views on defense strategy and military modernization. The sources for these publications are largely U.S. Government translations provided by the Foreign Broadcast Information Service's *Daily Report China* and occasional interviews the authors have had in China with PLA officers and other defense experts. The following significant and recent studies provide extensive bibliographies for further reading :

Kenneth W. Allen, Glenn Krumel, Jonathan D. Pollack, *China's Air Force Enters the 21st Century* (Santa Monica, CA: The Rand Corporation, 1995).

Thomas J. Christensen, *Useful Adversaries: Grand Strategy, Domestic Mobilization, and Sino-American Conflict, 1947-1958* (Princeton: Princeton University Press, 1996).

Bates Gill and Taeho Kim, *China's Arms Acquisitions from Abroad: A Quest for "Superb and Secret Weapons"* (Oxford: Oxford University Press, 1995).

Alastair Iain Johnston, *Cultural Realism: Strategic Culture and Grand Strategy in Chinese History* (Princeton: Princeton University Press, 1995).

C. Dennison Lane, Mark Weisenbloom and Dimon Liu, eds., *Chinese Military Modernization* (London: Kegan Paul International, 1996).

"Special Issue: China's Military in Transition.," ed. David Shambaugh, *The China Quarterly* (June 1996).

Michael D. Swaine, *The Role of the Chinese Military in National Security Policymaking* (Santa Monica, CA: The Rand Corporation, 1996).

Robert Sutter with Peter Mitchener, *China's Rising Military Power and Influence: Issues and Opinions for the U.S.* (Washington, DC: Congressional Research Service, January 1996).

Senior Colonel Deng Xiaobao receives a copy of the English translations from Michael Pillsbury, editor of this volume. As Editor in Chief of the the prestigious China Military Science, *Colonel Deng is responsible for selecting a wide variety of articles for each quarterly issue. The publisher of the journal is the Academy of Military Science.*

Summaries of the Articles

The articles in Parts One and Two are necessarily a bit more general and abstract because of their subject matter. Those in Parts Three and Four tend to be more specific and concrete.

Part One: Articles on Deng Xiaoping's Strategic Thought

The six authors in this part quote Deng's speeches extensively on future warfare, the future security environment and Deng's "Local War" concept. Western readers who do not subscribe to Marxist-Leninism may find these doctrinal articles peculiar. After all, what is important to Western observers is that Deng radically replaced the strategic thought of Chairman Mao. Yet what China's military authors must dutifully show is that Deng "modified" Mao's thought, and therefore Mao's strategic thought remains valid and relevant for future warfare. This formulation continues in the articles in Parts Two and Three, but is largely dropped from the articles in Part Four on the Revolution in Military Affairs.

Senior Colonel Peng Guangqian, author of "Deng Xiaoping's Strategic Thought," praises several features of Deng's thought:

- "Deng Xiaoping's strategic thought constitutes a scientific system with a rich content."
- "Deng Xiaoping's strategic thoughts are innately consistent with Mao Zedong's strategic thoughts."

In "Deng Xiaoping's Theory of Defense Modernization," General Zhao Nanqi, former President, Academy of Military Science, provides details on Deng's military recommendations for future warfare.

- Many comrades were concerned about the danger of war, but each year Deng would say that "war would not break out in 5 to 10 years."
- Deng believes that People's War is still a magic weapon to defeating enemies, and Mao Zedong's thoughts on People's War can put us "in an invincible position."

"Deng Xiaoping's Theory of War And Peace," by Colonel Hong Baoxiu, quotes extensively from Deng's writings, including the following "new points":

- "Though the United States has become the only superpower, it lacks the economic power to dominate the world."
- "The world's multipolar process has created a situation whereby various forces are increasingly balancing each other."
- Deng Xiaoping believes, "World war can be postponed, but accidental incidents and local circumstances are not entirely predictable."
- "It was the viewpoint of Marx and Engels that private ownership and the existence of classes were the root cause of war. Lenin raised the point that 'modern wars grow out of imperialism.'"

In his article "Deng Xiaoping's Perspective on National Interest," Colonel Hong Bin suggests that Deng's theory of national interest affected China's approach to the future by justifying short term losses: "We should be willing to pay the price and suffer some losses. It is certain that we will suffer some losses for the present. But we should not be afraid of that, so long as it is beneficial in the long run."

In his article, "Adhere to Active Defense And Modern People's War," Senior Colonel Wang Naiming sums up Deng's modifications of Mao's views:

- World war may be postponed or avoided, but local wars and regional conflicts are far from over.
- Deng Xiaoping has established "active defense" and People's War under modern conditions as the fundamental guiding policy for our national defense force development. "We should still adhere to the strategic policy of active defense, and this is because the policy reflects the objective law of war and is the most vital essence of Marxist military theory and Mao Zedong's military thought."

In "Defense Policy in the New Era," Colonel Fang Ning of the Department of military systems at the Academy of Military Science makes the following points:

- Technology "has in no way reduced the role and functions of people's warfare in future anti-aggression wars."
- "Future people's warfare must also adapt to the characteristics of modern wars."
- People's War under modern conditions "relies on the masses of people."
- "Future anti-aggression wars will mainly be fought on Chinese territory."

Part Two: Articles on the Future Security Environment

The five articles in this part describe the future threat environment China will face. It is one of crises, better armed neighbors, religious wars, and the growing military threat of Japan. The first article is a speech given by Chinese Defense Minister Chi Haotian at the National Defense University in Washington, DC, on December 10, 1996, which focuses on the United States.

Military Improvements by Major Powers

In "The International Military Situation in the 1990s," Major General Yu Qifen, now the Director of the Strategy Department of the Academy of Military Science, points out more than 30 features of the future security environment. A significant trend General Yu sees is the improvement of weapons and soldiers by the major powers:

- "The Americans believe that the key to a deterrent force lies in technological advantage during peacetime. . . .The U.S. Defense Department put forward in 1990 the program on key technology exploration, to include the following seven fields: global reconnaissance and telecommunication, accurate strike, air superiority and defense, marine control and submarine superiority, advanced combat vehicles on the ground, computers and electronic equipment, and software engineering."
- "Countries such as India, the ASEAN nations and some Middle Eastern countries have spent several hundred billion dollars on the purchase of modern weapons and equipment."
- "Western European countries widely believe that the 'true military academy' relies on military maneuvers. It is an all-round test of training for soldiers in military, politics, educational, psychological and physical ability."

- "The U.S. army has reopened the annual 'Louisiana Exercises' and has set up six combat labs to develop low-cost experimental sample training systems of high efficiency so as to improve troop quality and competence. In Britain, there are 3 big military training centers for special battle training. In France, there are as many as thirteen big training centers."

China's Weapons: Inferior to Japan, Russia, USA, India, ASEAN, and Taiwan

One of China's best "connected" civilian analysts is Gao Heng, a research fellow at the Institute of World Economics and Politics of the Academy of Social Science in Beijing. Gao publishes frequently in a variety of Chinese journals on the subject of the future security environment. Among the many organizations with which he is affiliated, Gao was one of the organizers of the Institute for Grand Strategy which studies the future strategies of the major powers.

Gao writes, "After the Cold War, China faced a less severe military threat from the major powers. But, in the future, the gap between China and other major powers will be wider" because:

- China's "military expenditure per capita is extremely low."
- This gap will not close "within a short period of time."
- China's advanced military equipment is "still in the embryonic stage."
- "Chinese soldiers' educational level can not meet the needs of modern war."
- The weapons of India, ASEAN countries, Taiwan, Japan, Russia and United States are superior to China's nuclear and conventional weapons.
- This "quality gap" is expanding rapidly.

Another problem for China will be Japan. Gao writes, "Because of pressure from home and abroad, Japan dared not to voice publicly its goal of becoming a military superpower." Gao cites Japanese officials about the following points:

- "Japan possesses nuclear fuels and technology to produce 1000 to 2000 atom bombs."
- "Japan can make intercontinental missiles (It successfully launched the H2 rocket)."

- Japan's navy "is on the top of the list for its capability in East Asia."
- Japan "has in fact given up its 'three nonnuclear principles.'"
- "Japan has trampled on its Peace Constitution and passed a law authorizing a Japanese military role in peacekeeping operations."
- Japan is the world's second largest in military expenditures after the United States.
- Japan advocates "a new nationalism" in order to become a military superpower.

Future Asian Religious Conflicts

Senior Colonel Yao Youzhi and Colonel Liu Hongsong are analysts in the Strategy Department of the Academy of Military Science. Their article "Future Security Trends in the Asian-Pacific Region," asserts, "Compared to other regions in the world, the current security situation in the Asia-Pacific region is relatively stable." However, they anticipate that there will be conflicts in the region's future. One cause will be religion: "Religious issues have become an important factor in Asian-Pacific security and conflicts. The Asian-Pacific region is one of the three big birth-places for religion in the world, as well as the meeting place for all kinds of cultures. There exist big differences in religions and religious parties, and contradictions and conflicts that are hard to reconcile."

Managing Local War Crises

In his article, "Managing China's Future Security Crises," Zheng Jian, a research analyst in the Strategy Department of the Academy of Military Science provides a checklist of principles by which China should manage future "National Defense Security Crises" (NDSC). Crises could be caused by:

- Multiple opponents stronger or weaker than China
- External offensives seizing opportunities of our internal disturbances
- "Chain reactions from many directions"
- Opponents' using comprehensive threats
- Intervention by "indirectly concerned countries or international organizations"
- Local crisis not endangering our country's overall security"

- Enduring conflicts repeated over a long period of time.

Zheng's many recommendations include:

- Forecasting the crisis situations scientifically
- Combining fighting with negotiation
- Fighting "even if the opponent is more powerful than us"
- Controlling the rhythm of the action properly
- Preventing the opponent from escalating through prevention.

Zheng concludes, "Actions should be controlled according to the stage of the crisis. The aim in doing so is to give an opponent enough time to exchange information with us, judge the state of affairs, take actions to contribute to the easing of the situation, and react to our suggestions." However, if an opponent tries to escalate the conflict, "we should strive to contain it ahead of time."

Part Three: Articles on Modernizing for Local War

These papers reflect China's current focus on near-term modernization. The focus is a term translated as "Local War." I selected Local War authors who have held some of the most important leadership positions in China's defense complex, including articles by the Chief of the General Staff, the Chairman of the coordinating commission for all of China's defense industries, the sole military member of the Standing Committee of the Politburo, and four generals who were responsible (at the time they wrote) for armor, artillery, logistics, and the strategic rocket forces or Second Artillery. Two of these authors have served as the presidents of the Academy of Military Science, whose focus on future warfare is in the near term decade ahead, not the first three decades of the 21st century. They call for modernization of armor, artillery, logistics, and nuclear forces and more reliance on science and technology.

What is remarkable about the Local War school's writing is that the ideas contained in the articles on the Military Revolution are never explicitly criticized or even mentioned. For example, despite their high positions as Chief of the General Staff and Politburo Standing Committee member, neither General Fu Quanyou nor General Liu Huaqing has apparently never mentioned the "military revolution" or the kinds of future operations and future weapons that dominate the writing of the Military Revolution school of thought found in the articles in Part Four.

Deng's concept of Local War loses a great deal in translation. The Chinese ideograph for "local" (*ju bu*) can mean regional, partial, sectional or local, all at the same time. For clarity, I have translated it differently in this collection depending on the context. The definition of Local War refers mainly to the scale of a war rather than its location.

The Politburo's General Liu Huaqing on Local War and the Navy

General Liu Huaqing, who is over 80 years old, is China's highest ranking military officer as a member of the Politburo Standing Committee and Vice Chairman of the Central Military Commission. His article commemorates the 100th anniversary of Sino-Japanese War by listing the military challenges China faces. General Liu does not want China to repeat this historical humiliation, so he advocates, "It is quite necessary to concentrate our efforts on the issue of how to enhance the building up of our country's coastal defense. History tells us that whether one has maritime sense and can pay attention to the building of coastal defense is supremely important to the rise or decline and the honor or disgrace of a nation." He adds, apparently to China's ground force officers, "Comrades in our army must have an even deeper understanding of the importance of enhancing our coastal defense."

The PLA Chief of Staff on Logistics and Local War

"Future Logistics Modernization," General Fu Quanyou's article, extensively quotes Deng Xiaoping about the great importance of logistics modernization for Local War. General Fu sees merit in using China's civilian economy. Fu writes, "We should use specially designated civilian enterprises to supply the set amount of military materials at agreed upon times, and let society shoulder more responsibility. We should have various and useful ties with the large and medium-size commercial enterprises and establish stable channels of supply."

Nuclear Weapons

In his article on the development of Chinese strategic nuclear weapons, Major General Yang Huan traces the history of China's strategic rocket forces or "second artillery" since 1958. He proposes that future work should focus on the following three areas:

- First, China must improve the survival ability of its strategic nuclear weapons. He writes, "We should strengthen research on small, solid fuel and highly automated mobile missiles" as well as on stealth technology in order to strengthen the survival ability of missiles before launch and in the course of their flight.
- Second, he believes that China should improve the striking power of its strategic nuclear weapons, "to increase the credibility of limited nuclear deterrence, we should work to improve accuracy," and our new generation should have higher striking capability.
- Third, General Yang advocates that China should improve the penetration ability of its strategic weapons. He explains, "In an era when space technology is developing rapidly and a defense system with many methods and many layers is appearing, we should pay special attention to the study of technology."

In "Nuclear Shadows on High-Tech Warfare," Major General Wu Jianguo reports that "the possibility of using nuclear weapons cannot be ruled out." He suggests several scenarios.

Armor

In his article "Research and Development of Armor," Major General Chen Benchan states that the development of future Chinese armor takes place when "there is a new technological revolution going on." He warns, "We should go our own way and not follow the footsteps of others." He lays out five principles for the future development of tanks and armored vehicles:

- Increase the survivability and fire power
- Upgrade current weapons in a planned way
- Take better account of terrain and weather conditions
- Establish a complete set of armored vehicles with higher standardization
- Strive for advanced, reliable, economical and easier to operate armor weapons.

General Chen concludes that armor weapons by the year 2000 must meet the requirements of future warfare which are "the ability to strike deep, react fast, and coordinate well with the air force." He advocates "priority to the development of new types of main battle tanks, infantry fighting vehicles, automatic battle command complexes, and antiaircraft vehicles."

COSTIND Director on Requirements for Local War

General Ding Henggao is China's highest ranking officer in charge of defense industry, as the Chairman of COSTIND, the Commission on Science, Technology and Industry. General Ding's article, "Reforming Defense Science, Technology, and Industry," is therefore authoritative. Like other members of the Local War school, however, he focuses narrowly on the near term future. General Ding writes, "in high-tech local war, we have to

- Speed up the research and development of new weapons
- Develop our national defense science and technology to reach an advanced world level."

General Ding points out that "defense science, technology and industry are important symbols of our comprehensive national power." He writes, "One of the reasons that we are not looked down upon in the world is that we have built a relatively complete defense industry, and we have been able to research and manufacture various types of conventional and strategic nuclear weapons. Deng Xiaoping said, 'If China did not have atom bombs and hydrogen bombs, and had not launched satellites since the 60s, then China would not be called an important, influential country and would not enjoy the international status that it does today'."

General Ding sees a need to use both foreign technology and China's growing civilian economy. He writes, "Defense and commercial products are becoming more and more compatible. While we emphasize the conversion of defense technology into commercial use, we must study defense-commercial dual-purpose technology and possible transfers from commercial technology to defense use."

Artillery

"China's Artillery Development," by Major General Zi Wuzheng, emphasizes that "compared with the advanced level of foreign artillery, we face serious challenges." For future warfare, General Zi suggests, "I believe that in the development of artillery weapons it is preferable to have fewer but better products." He stresses that:

- Prototypes should be used to strengthen advanced research
- Technology should leap forward
- We should "Eliminate Soviet models features but not blindly copy Western models."

Logistics

In his article, "Logistics Support for Regional Warfare," Major General Yang Chengyu focuses on "how to improve the logistic support ability of our army." Like General Fu Quanyou, General Yang stresses that advanced technology and "the extraordinary fierceness of the rear defense struggle" will "create the requirements for logistic support of our armed forces" in the following ways:

- Improve rapid mobile operations: "Speed is precious in war."
- Rapid-reaction troops will depend on logistics.
- Improve sustainment capability for continuous attack operations.
- Local war's consumption rate decides the course and the outcome of war.
- U.S. troops used four times more daily per man in the Gulf War than in Vietnam.

According to General Yang, "Our country is large and still undeveloped. With our supply and demand problems not well solved, how can we strengthen logistics development for preparedness against war and improve continuous support capability for war time?" He answers:

- "First of all. . . .Only when our national economy has been developed can the national defense development rest on a solid material base. Then logistics support can be provided continuously from the rear of the country.
- "It is necessary to give priority to . . . the preparation of battlefields in the directions and areas where the operations will occur, and the development of new equipment for war.
- "Storing and acquiring materials for war must be nationally coherent with structural improvements concentrated at the main positions.
- "We must firmly foster the idea of overall rear service for a People's War . . . the system of powerful support by both soldiers and civilians as a whole. . . . Thus, we can transfer latent support

capability into actual support strength immediately when war breaks out.

- "It is a very important aspect of operations to destroy the enemy's support system."

State Planning—Integrating Civil-Military Production

Shun Zhenhuan, a civilian analyst on the State Planning Commission in Beijing, has contributed an authoritative article, "Reform of China's Defense Industry." He admits, "China's defense industry system after 1949 was basically modeled on the plan in the former Soviet Union. It has been a highly centralized system since the first 5-year plan." In the future, he states, "The ultimate aim of restructuring our defense industry is to build an integrated system of defense/commerical production."

Shun suggests that civilian economic progress will be crucial because "A national industrial census indicates that advanced equipment makes up only 3 percent of all equipment in the military sector, whereas it is 12.9 percent in the commercial sector. About 40 percent of equipment used in some old military factories is over 20 years old, and some of it dates to World War II." Shun describes in detail how the State Planning Commission recommends that military and civilian industries be integrated in the future for their mutual benefit.

A Former Academy of Military Science President on "Military Science"

In a chapter from his book on Chinese military science, Lieutenant General Zheng Wenhan, a former President of the Academy of Military Science, defines Chinese military science to be "a system of knowledge about war, laws for guiding wars, and principles of war preparations and combat operations. Military science plays an important role in guiding force development, and provides theoretical methods of fighting and winning a war. The objects of the study of military science are wars and other activities of military practice," which include:

- "The causes of wars, the nature of wars, the relationships between war and politics, economics, science, and geography, and exploring the law of emergence of wars and development, so as to lay the foundations for directing wars correctly."

- New subjects, such as military operational analysis, war mobilization science, future warfare science, the science of military law and so on.

General Zheng writes that the main fields that form military science are military thought, military operational art, force development, military technology, military history, and military geography. "In 1959, the President of the Academy of Military Science, Marshall Ye Jianying said military science could be divided into three parts, namely military thought, military art and military technology."

Defeating a Superior Enemy by Surprise Air Attack

In "Dialectics of Defeating the Superior with the Inferior," Professor Shen Kuiguan of the Air Force Command Institute in Beijing provides a history of this concept and applies it to future warfare in a fashion which suggests the value of large, surprise air attack on a distracted or unsuspecting enemy, such as the Israeli attacks that destroyed the Egyptian air force in 1967. Shen begins by noting, "The concept of defeating a powerful opponent with a weak force, or defeating the enemy even when outnumbered was continually been put forward by people from the Yin, Zhou, Ming, and Qing Dynasties. . . . Altering the overall balance of combat factors between two belligerents is the practical foundation of defeating the superior with the inferior." The principle even applies to the outcome of the Gulf War, according to Professor Shen: "A comprehensive understanding and analysis of the Gulf War is needed in order to avoid the erroneous conclusion that it is impossible for a weak force to defeat the powerful opponent in a high-tech war."

One way "to defeat a powerful opponent with a weak force in a high-tech war is to bring the overall function of its operational system into full play [and] to persevere in defeating the superior with the inferior in crucial battles."

Shen outlines several ways to defeat a superior enemy. In one example, he writes, a "superior strategy is significant to defeating the powerful opponent with a weak force. In the Third Middle East War, Israel was obviously in a disadvantageous position in the prewar period, but its successful use of superior strategies led to Egypt's erroneous judgement in operational orientation. With Egypt's focus turned to the Gulf, Israel launched a surprise attack on Egypt and destroyed most of its air force."

General Li Jijun: Cherish Mao, But Use Statistics

Lieutenant General Li Jijun is well known in China for his experimental field work on the doctrine of Local Warfare in the 1980s while he served as Commander of the 38th Group Army. He then served as Director of the General Office of the powerful Central Military Commission, and since 1994 has been the Vice-President of the Academy of Military Science. In his article, "Notes on Military Theory and Military Strategy," he advises how to analyze future warfare.

- First, he suggests the study of Mao Zedong because "he was a great strategist of rare gifts and bold vision. Take the war to resist the United States and assist Korea for example. At that time, New China was just founded, there was big flood in southern China, hungry people were anxiously waiting to be fed, and industries were still in shambles. It took unusual strategic daring and resolution to dare to fight against the number one power in the world." In Korea in 1950 he writes, "If you counted the enemy's aircraft carriers and actual forces, the enemy strength was several times our own. . . .To fight against a superior force and win victory is the highest honor for our army."
- Second, he emphasizes Mao's defeat of the United States. "Mao Zedong's brilliance in military strategic thought is even acknowledged by our enemy. From the end of the Second World War to the Gulf War, the United States fought two local wars, the Korean War and the Vietnam War, and in both suffered defeat. In both, its opponent was China. In the Korean War, it was the direct opponent, and in the Vietnam War, it was the indirect opponent."

Aside from knowing Mao's military thought, General Li suggests that analysis of future warfare should employ several different methods—cause-and-effect or historical analysis, statistical analysis, and systems analysis.

- Statistical analysis is needed. Dupuy of the United States has suggested that the "coefficient of dispersion of soldiers has increased 4,000 times" in the last 400 years. "The Soviet Army stipulated that an artillery battalion's salvo could suppress the center of resistance by a platoon, and that infantry density of fire should be eight bullets per minute per meter. These statistics from the Second World War raised the level of theoretical understanding."

- Systems analysis can show "the intrinsic links and changes of the various factors of war. For instance, the development of technology and its application in the war could cause changes in military equipment, and could in turn cause changes in strategies, battles and tactics."

In "Chinese Modern Local War and U.S. Limited War," Chen Zhou cites American political scientists to suggest several differences between the practice of these two types of war, including his view that the Chinese approach has been more successful.

Part Four: Articles on the Revolution in Military Affairs

The "Military Revolution" authors advocate taking seriously a potential Revolution in Military Affairs (RMA). These authors seem so focused on the implications for China of a revolution in military affairs that they often neglect to even mention the subject of modernization for Local War and People's War. One author approvingly quotes the views of Andrew W. Marshall on an RMA, and another states that Secretary William Perry established a senior steering group on the RMA in the Pentagon. Others mention Russian views of the RMA. Many of these "RMA authors" serve at the Academy of Military Science, an institution of more than 500 officers (with few students) modeled largely on the General Staff Academy in Moscow, which also has written about the future implications of a potential RMA.

China's interest in how the revolution in military affairs will develop seems destined to continue. For example, late in 1996, two young officers at the Academy of Military Science, Zhu Xiaoli and Zhao Xiaozhu, authored a book, *America, Russia and the Revolution in Military Affairs* (Academy Press). In their preface, Zhu and Zhao thank their mentors at the Academy, who include many authors featured in this volume such as Generals Li Jijun and Wang Pufeng. Zhu and Zhao trace the history of American and Russian military writing about the revolution in military affairs. They conclude with an interesting warning: "Those who believe that the current revolution in military affairs will be under the control of the United States or can develop only according to the speed and directions set by the United States are extremely wrong and quite dangerous." Zhu and Zhao assert four reasons why the United States will fall behind after a decade and yield leadership to others:

- Exploiting a future RMA will not depend on having the largest defense budget and "sometimes it is exactly the opposite."
- Other nations may develop new operational concepts before the United States because the U.S. military is too confident to innovate radically.
- Information technology, which is decisive for the RMA, is developing in the commerical sector available to all nations.
- Several developing nations have started to participate in the "RMA competition" and are using new "measures of effectiveness" to determine the weapons they intend to acquire.

The articles in Part 1 on Deng Xiaoping's strategic thought asserted that the current world power structure in which the United States is the sole superpower will be transformed to a world of equal multipolar powers in two decades. The articles in Part 4 on the RMA similarly emphasize that some China's military authors doubt that the supremacy of U.S. military technology can be preserved in the early 21st century.

COSTIND'S Beijing Institute of Systems Engineering

In "Weapons of the 21st Century," Mr. Chang Mengxiong suggests that "we are in the midst of a new revolution in military technology" and that in the 21st century both weapons and military units will be "information-intensified." Chang describes these future weapons, then proposes that China's leaders use a new set of "measures of effectiveness" to support decisions to determine what future weapons to acquire.

Chang's former institute has no equivalent in the United States because Chinese defense industries are government owned and controlled through COSTIND on the model of the Defense Industries (VPK) in the former USSR. To find an equivalent to Chang, an American would have to imagine that the U.S. Defense Under Secretary for Acquisition actually owned and controlled the budgets and planning of all major defense corporations like Northrop-Grumman, Lockheed-Martin, and General Dynamics, as well as government defense plants, and further imagine that at the top of this structure a group of analysts like Chang Mengxiong provided long-term assessments about what weapons systems merit increased investment or cancellation.

How does Chang see the 21st century? He asserts that

- Weapons and soldiers will both be "information-intensified" by the years 2010-2020.
- Soldiers will carry GPS direction finding, night vision, IFF, and other systems.
- Soldiers will request launching of information-intensified weapons by remote control.
- Soldier's clothing will have "adjustable temperature, color" and for some permit flying.
- Individual soldiers will be able to receive orders directly from division commanders.

Chang also discusses the potential for the robot troops about which there is much discussion both in China and abroad, which will include:

- "Information-intensified combat platforms"
- "Robot sentries, robot engineers, robot infantrymen, and . . . unmanned smart tanks"
- Robot troops arrayed in large numbers.

One of Chang's most vivid metaphors states, "Information-intensified combat methods are like a Chinese boxer with a knowledge of vital body points who can bring an opponent to his knees with a minimum of movement."

Chang discusses some specific new concepts for weapons:

- High performance microwave weapons to "destroy the opponent's electronic equipment"
- Information superiority is more important than air and sea superiority
- We will "have to gain air and sea superiority, but even more important, we will have to win information superiority first of all"
- Information deterrence will be a new operational concept
- Virtual reality for training, planning, and analysis.

Like nuclear deterrence, "information deterrence" will be vital, especially if "the power with a weaker information capability can deliver a crippling attack on the information system of the power with a stronger information system." In a very important point, Chang stresses, "Even if two adversaries are generally equal in hard weapons, unless the party with a weaker information capability is able effectively to weaken the information capability of the adversary, it has very little possibility of winning the war."

Virtual reality technology will be used "for designing and producing prototype machines and manufacturing weapons; troop training and war preparations; drawing up joint combat doctrine; drafting emergency plans; post-mortem evaluations; and historical analysis." Virtual reality "will help create a relatively smooth transition from virtual (imaginary) weapons and virtual (imaginary) battlefields to real weapons and real battlefields, and thus have far-reaching effects on military activities."

Chang believes that the measures of effectiveness and the criteria used to make weapons acquisition decisions will have to be changed to reflect the 21st century future warfare.

- Measures are obsolete that focus on firepower lethality, mobility, and logistics.
- Future weapons must be based on the information-intensity gap.
- Information-intensity gaps "translate into a gap in combat capabilities."

21st-Century Naval Warfare

In the first of two articles on "21st-Century Naval Warfare," Captain Shen Zhongchang and his coauthors from the Chinese Navy Research Institute suggest that "certain cutting-edge technologies [are] likely to be applied first to naval warfare." Direct attacks on naval battlefields will become possible from outer space, high altitudes and remote land bases because "naval battle space is going to expand unprecedentedly." They argue that the essential forms of future naval warfare will be:

- Long-range precision strikes by warships, carrier-based aircraft, and missiles
- Submarines will make missile attacks on air targets
- "The submarine will rise in status to become a major naval warfare force"

- Anti-submarine warfare will restrict submarines in shallow water zones
- "Underwater aircraft carriers and undersea mine-laying robots."

Shen writes that the "mastery of outer space" will be a prerequisite "for naval victory with outer space becoming the new commanding elevation for naval combat." Ships at sea will carry out anti reconnaissance strikes against space satellites and other space systems. "The side with electromagnetic combat superiority will make full use of that invisible 'killer mace' to win naval victory."

With new technology, they believe:

- "The sea bed [will be] an ideal place to build military bases."
- Tactical laser weapons will be used first in antiship missile defense systems.
- Naval ships and cruise missiles will become stealth capable.
- Long range combat, missile combat, and air force cover will be crucial.
- "Tactics will change sharply."
- "Remote grappling" and over-the-horizon strikes will be key to future battles.
- "Speed against speed will become the crux of future naval victory."
- Naval battles will be mostly of medium and small scale.
- Lasers, particle beams and microwave beams will have precision and lethality.
- "Lightning attacks and powerful first strikes will be more widely used."
- There will be no "grand scenes of decisive fleet engagements."
- "The future naval warfare force organization will grow ever smaller and more multifunctional."

Shen and his co-authors emphasize that future naval rivalry over "electromagnetic space" will be more important than land, sea, and air space. A foreign study weighed technology factors affecting combat capability. Eight criteria were examined. The conclusion was that electronic warfare technology had the most impact. Thus, "the 'electromagnetic' advantage will become the focus of rivalry between opponents. Naval C^3I systems "will be the 'nerve center' and 'force multiplier' in future naval warfare."

Dominant Role of Submarines

In their second article, "The Military Revolution in Naval Warfare," Captain Shen Zhongchang and his co-authors list new technologies in nuclear propulsion, space, shipbuilding, microelectronics, satellites, air cushion effects, surface effects, and materials as the "materials base for the new military revolution" which will also influence naval combat doctrine and operational concepts. They conclude that "There is no doubt that during the revolution, combat theory and concepts will be largely modified." They describe several points:

- Concentrations of ships will be replaced by small formations and single vessels.
- Vessels will be distributed "evenly" in the sea.
- Underwater strikes will be another important combat mode for the navy.
- "The role of submarines in future information warfare will be very important."
- There will be digitization of sea warfare to connect platforms and all arms of the services.
- The opponent's information network will be an important target.

Quoting Alvin Toffler, Captain Shen describes the Gulf War as a "trial of strength" between Third Wave coalition forces and the Iraqis, who were reduced to a Second Wave force because of the destruction of their C^3I system. Protection of C^3I is now so important that "the U.S. Defense Department has invested $1 billion in establishing a network to safeguard its information system."

However, the opponent's system may not be so safe from attack. Captain Shen writes, "There are many ways to destroy information systems," such as:

- "Attacking radar and radio stations with smart weapons"
- "Jamming an enemy's communication facilities with electronic warfare"
- "Attacking communication centers, facilities and command ships"
- "Destroying an enemy's electronic system with electromagnetic pulse weapons"
- "Destroying computer software with a computer virus"

- Developing directed energy weapons and electromagnetic pulse weapons.

Shen believes, "All nations" will give attention to developing submarine forces. "China's neighboring countries are already forcusing on purchasing and developing submarines—for instance, Korea will buy 11 submarines from Germany. Indonesia will increase the number of its submarines from 3 to 5, and Australia plans to build 6 submarines. Malaysia, Singapore and Thailand are also establishing submarine forces." Shen adds, "During the First World War, the dominant vessel was the battleship, and in the Second World War, it was the aircraft carrier. In future global wars, the most powerful weapon will be the submarine."

In conclusion, Captain Shen suggests that information warfare will be a naval requirement. Ships will have to be designed with this in mind. He explains, "During the development of modern vessels, soft systems, especially communication facilities, target determining installations, and electronic warfare systems" will have to "become compatible with the C³I system of the air and land forces."

Control of Outer Space

In his article "21st-Century Air Warfare," Colonel Ming Zengfu of the Air Force Command Institute argues that "the air battlefield will become decisively significant" in future warfare. He too stresses the growing significance of smart munition, intelligent operational platforms, and integrated automatic C³I systems. Colonel Ming predicts "more and more stealth planes will be rushing into the air battlefields of the 21st century, and stealth penetration bombing will be more commonly applied." He adds that an air force must be able to "take down" the enemy's operational system by "striking the seams and ripping the fabric."

Air Power: Trigger of the Revolution in Military Affairs

In "The Military Revolution in Air Power," Major General Zheng Shenxia and Senior Colonel Zhang Changzhi make a case that the Revolution in Military Affairs will strengthen aerospace forces more than any others. They emphasize the growing importance of precision strike, stealth, night vision, longer range attacks, lethality of smart munitions, increased C³I capability, and electronic warfare. They were deeply impressed by the U.S. capability in the Gulf War to capture "all the high frequency and ultrahigh frequency radio signals of the Iraqi army," store the information "gathered by the 34 reconnaissance satellites, 260 electronic reconnaissance planes and 40 warning aircraft" and then "destroy the Iraqi communication system." They conclude that "information is the key to victory."

According to General Zheng, however, after the Gulf War the United States "gradually increased research centered on information combat." U.S. Defense Secretary Perry "put forward the proposal of 'military revolution' in early 1994, which officially confirmed the existence of the revolution." General Zheng suggests that "The application of air power in *Desert Storm*" was "the 'trigger' of the new military revolution."

General Zheng believes that air power can "start and stop operations easily" which is "definitely what military decision makers want to apply in today's conflicts, in which no one wants to escalate the conflicts but everyone is eager to restrain the other." In future warfare, "the ultimate goal of the parties involved is not to occupy the other's territory but to check the enemy country and take initiative at the negotiation table. Because an air force can achieve such a goal without escalating the conflict, it has more opportunities to be employed."

Zheng concludes with a message to China's ground force officers: "a former U.S. Air Force Chief of Staff said before the Gulf War, the only way to avoid excessive blood-shedding by the army was to use the air force."

Finally, General Zheng states that the air force must be "linked" to space forces. He suggests that not only is it correct that "he who controls outer space controls the Earth," but also " to maintain air superiority one must control outer space."

21st-Century Army Operations

In their article, "21st Century Land Operations," Colonel Xiao Jingmin and Major Bao Bin, both of the Strategy Department, Academy of Military Science, forecast there will be "profound changes in the operational concept" in 21st-century land operations because of the military revolution. Xiao and Bao believe that:

- Battle space will be extended to hundreds or several thousand kilometers.
- "The front and rear of the battlefield will be attacked simultaneously."

- "The strategic rear area might be the first target of attack."
- "Time and speed will have new meanings."
- Enemy C^3I systems and high threat weapons will be the main targets.
- Information attacks and firepower will be combined.
- The destruction of numerous enemy forces will no longer be the primary task.

Like other authors, Xiao and Bao use the term "informationize" to characterize the whole process of combat. For example, the "armed forces will use satellites, high altitude aircraft, helicopters, and unmanned flying equipment and sensors to collect and process information" and use "digital communication techniques to transmit computer data within the information network." Future warfare cannot be carried out by "a simple adjustment in the structure of the army" but will be "a network formed by the land, sea, air and space forces."

Xiao and Bao stress that a "network" among various units of the armed forces will be able to:

- "Carry out long-range and accurate strikes"
- "Every soldier will have the information and firepower support of the whole digital information network"
- "Every unit will be in contact with the enemy force on the battlefield, and there will be no front lines."

Information Warfare with Chinese Characteristics

In his article, "The Challenge of Information Warfare," Major General Wang Pufeng quotes Andrew W. Marshall of the U. S. Defense Department, with whom he agrees that "the information era will touch off a revolution in military affairs, just as the cannon in the 15th century and the machine in the past 150 years of the industrial era touched off revolutions." General Wang concludes, "Information warfare will control the form and future of war" and sees it "as a driving force in the modernization of China's military and combat readiness. . . . We have much work to do to shrink this gap."

He emphasizes three points.

- First, "establish a strategic reconnaissance warning and air defense system."

- Second, develop information weapons systems such as "air defense weapons systems, offensive tactical guided missile attack systems, . . .electronic warfare equipment systems, and underwater mine laying systems. These will give China over the horizon, high precision, concealed, sudden defensive attack capability and a stronger survival capacity and make the enemy terrified and worried, providing an effective threat."
- Third, build information networks to bring all branches into a single combat network.

General Wang raises the question of how China can use "our inferior position in information" and suggests four approaches.

- False intelligence and false targets to "muddle the opponents perceptions, and inspire false assessments," and "to blind or even destroy the opponent's reconnaissance."
- Resist jamming of communication by using many channels.
- Resist viruses by protection.
- Use information counterattacks.

General Wang advocates the basic warfare style that Mao Zedong taught, "you do your fighting and I'll do mine." He mentions specific ideas for Chinese forces such as to:

- "Carry out raids on enemy operation platforms and bases"
- "Damage and foil the enemy's offensive"
- Organize "sabotage operations"
- "Make continuous raids to exhaust and wear down the enemy"
- Organize special warfare troops with information technology weapons.

Almost poetically, General Wang concludes about the RMA that "those who perceive it first will swiftly rise to the top and have the advantage of the first opportunities. Those who perceive it late will unavoidably also be caught up in the vortex of this revolution. Every military will receive this baptism. This revolution is first a revolution in concepts."

"Informationized" Armies in 2040

In their article on information warfare, Wang Baocun and Li Fei state in the *Liberation Army Daily* in June 1995 that the essence of information warfare has not been defined authoritatively and the redefinitions are "imperfect and even somewhat biased." They themselves use a broad definition to include computer virus warfare, precision strike warfare and stealth warfare. Quoting U.S. Army experts they agree that while tanks were the major weapons of the 20th century, the computer will be the key weapon of the 21st century. Therefore, computer viruses to alter or destroy a computer's normal operating programs with "rapid contagion, long standing latency, and active and continuous encroachment" will be able to severely disrupt not only the C³I system and smart weapons but the entire combat potential of a nation.

America's military digitization will take several decades. In the first stage, the U.S. Army will digitize some units by installing "digitized communications equipment, second-generation, forward-looking infrared, radar, identification friend-or-foe equipment, and the global positioning system." In the second stage, after 2010 the army will be linked digitally to the navy and air force and write information war doctrine. This will require about three decades and be completed by 2040. One reason for the delays is that the weapons development cycle takes 15 years and the conversion of the military structure from one to another will take roughly two decades. Wang and Li conclude, "So it is obvious that by midcentury, the United States probably will have built the world's first completely smart military."

Wang and Li believe that some effects of information warfare can be forecast:

- First, attacks will be on "brain centers" which will "submit very quickly."
- Second, jointness. Smart anti-tank missiles "fired from friendly naval submarines."
- Third, "force concentrations will occur faster, more precisely, and more often."
- Fourth, units will be "smaller, more integrated and more multifunctional."

Wang and Li believe that weapons acquisition decisions will be affected in the future. The current trend is toward "more research and new technology and less production and arms purchases." They state that the United States, Germany, Japan, and France all aim to develop smart weapons, smart platforms, and C³I systems.

Innovation Through Doctrine Pushing or Technology Pushing?
In his article "Future Trends of Modern Operations," Major General
Wu Guoqing, Director of the Department of Operations and Tactics,
Academy of Military Science, describes the "profound reforms of
concepts, modes, and tactics in modern operational doctrine." He lists:

- Operational Concepts — Warfare will have more "jointness,"
be of smaller scale than World War II, be shorter in duration,
involve deep attacks on rear areas and the C^3I systems, change the
definition of "battlefield dominance" to mobile or maneuver
warfare by leapfrogging.
- Operational Methods—"Large quantities of high-tech
weapons" will "accelerate a series of revolutionary changes in
concepts." For example, "opposing sides may not necessarily face
each other in battles. Instead, they will launch attacks hundreds
or even thousands of kilometers away by fully employing air
assaults and missile weapons."
- "Precision all weather targeting, stealth weapons, precision
guidance, night fighting" means that "operations will most likely
become 'combination boxing,' the combination of various
operational modes and patterns."
- "Air strikes are no longer only attacks by the air force. Naval
and army air forces can also play very important roles. Missile
attacks can be either from aircraft, cruise missiles, or by land;
information war, electronic wars and psychological war are
usually combined actions of all services together."
- Advances in simulation technology will improve "deception
warfare. . . . Improvement of command decision-making will
enable artificial intelligence simulation systems to mimic the
commanding officers' mental activities and be extensively used in
command activities in the near future."
- Fixed positions will become obsolete. They may be moved to
sea, such as the U.S. Marine Corps has proposed for amphibious
maneuver operations with defensive facilities at sea for mobile
protection.

In conclusion, General Wu suggests that peacetime military
innovation will proceed to "shift from the traditional formula of
'technology pushing' tactics to that of 'doctrine pushing.'" This means
that "the progress of military technology and development of weapons
will be guided by thingking about future operations."

Stealth Weapons with Chinese Characteristics
Cao Benyi writes in "Future Trends in Stealth Weapons" that "the great importance of stealth weaponry in modern warfare has gradually been realized by China's scientific and military experts." Therefore, "It is necessary for China to make every effort to develop stealth technology." Cao states that great progress has already been achieved since the 1980s and that tests have by now "been completed in the case of a number of entire aircraft and a large number of components. . . . For example, the Research Institute of the Beijing Iron and Steel Complex has developed a coating material of superfine metallic particles with radar wave absorptions properties." Cao advocates six steps:

- "Expand the stealth wave band"
- Design external contours to eliminate angular reflections and mirror reflections
- Use the most modern radar wave absorption materials
- Limit heat radiation from propulsion systems
- Use electronic counter measures, increase the outer impedance load, send false targets
- Use radar testing to develop radar under wide-band conditions.

Cao emphasizes that "the appearance of such new technologies as sandwich-intertwined wave-absorbing materials and self-programming materials have opened up new roads for the development and manufacture of radar-indiscernible materials." But for China, "Costs of stealth weaponry must be reduced and production must be made economically more acceptable." Cao believes that China must "import from abroad advanced technologies and equipment, and establish as quickly as possible a research organization," but at the same time "research must also be undertaken in anti stealth technology." He says the U.S. Defense Department ranks stealth technology second among its seventeen technology projects of the highest importance, so he concludes that "this makes it very obvious that in future warfare stealth technology as well as antistealth technology will both be indispensable."

Mi Zhenyu on Weapons Development for the 21st Century
Many observers believe that Chinese concern with future warfare dates only from the Gulf War in 1991. However, one of China's most important studies of future warfare was published as early as 1988 by

a team under the leadership of General Mi Zhenyu, a Vice President of the Academy of Military Science—*China's National Defense Development Concepts*, which suggests:

- China is in long-term competition with other major powers.
- The "gap between the weapons and equipment we now possess compared to those of advanced countries is 20 to 25 years."
- "If our objective for the year 2000 is merely to shrink this discrepancy to ten to fifteen years, then from the point of view of effectiveness, it would seem to be high, but from the point of view of competitive effectiveness, it would only be an impractical increase in quality, perhaps even a decrease."
- "When we compare the discrepancy of one or a half generation of weaponry in the year 2000 with the two to three generation discrepancies today, the difference in competitive effectiveness could prove even greater."
- "If we do not start today to plan to be better, to be ahead of everyone, how can we possibly make use of the opportunities, and become latecomers who surpass the old-timers?"

In a long discussion of technology, General Mi points out:

- Electronic technology is making possible "automatic searches, identification and attack, and ten-fold the precision of these weapon systems to the point of near-perfect accuracy."
- Stealth technology has raised the survivability of weapons for surprise attacks.
- High-energy laser weapons for antiaircraft defense, tactical laser weapons, high-power microwave, and plasma technology are providing the foundation for the creation of directed energy weapons.
- Technology increases the importance of preemptive strikes or first strikes.
- Not only will "space forces" be created and expanded but even a "robot force" will have to be deployed using multipurpose robots in future warfare.

General Mi warns, "To rank within the world's family of nations, to live and survive in the 'global village' in this universe, each nation must come up with ideas for a 'grand strategy.'"

Tactical Experiments

In "Tactical Studies," Yang Wei observes that "the PLA enjoys a good reputation in the world after overcoming very strong enemies on several occasions," but he warns against "being intoxicated by the glories of the past." He offers an approach such as "in 1929 when the German military did not have any tanks [but] a young officer, Heinz Guderian, broke though the bondage of traditional thinking" and invented the *blitzkrieg*.

Six New Combat Concepts

The COSTIND journal *Contemporary Military Affairs* published an article in February 1996 by Ch'en Huan on "The Third Military Revolution" which Ch'en calls "the rapid development of information technology, stealth technology, and long-range precision strike technology." Ch'en predicts new operational concepts will appear in future wars.

- **Long-range Combat:** "There will be three main forms of long-range strikes in the future: the first form is the one in which the air arm independently carries out long-range strikes; the second form is one in which the long-range strike combines with the long-range rapid movement of troops transported by land and sea with the vertical airdrops of airborne forces; and the third form is five-dimensional—air, land, sea, space, and electro-magnetic—long-range combat."

- **Outer Space Combat:** "The following new-concept weapons will come forth in a continuous stream—all of these weapons will make outer space the fifth dimension operational space following land, sea, air, and electromagnetism: Laser weapons, ultra-high frequency weapons, ultrasonic wave weapons, stealth weapons, mirror-beam weapons, electromagnetic guns, plasma weapons, ecological weapons, smart weapons, logic weapons, and sonic weapons.

"Because the efficacy of these new-concept weapons depends on the hard-shell support of a space platform, once the space platform is lost their efficacy will be weakened and they will even become powerless. In this way the two sides in a war will focus on offensive and defensive operations conducted from space platforms in outer space, and these operations will certainly become a new form in future wars. In the U.S. Armed Forces a new service—the

Space Force—is being discussed, showing that the idea of outer space combat is close to moving from theory to actual combat."

- **Paralysis Combat:** By striking at the "vital point" of the enemy's information and support systems one can at one blow paralyze the enemy and collapse his morale.
- **Computer Combat:** "Relevant data show that, before the outbreak of the Gulf War, American intelligence organizations put a virus into Iraq's air defense system which led to the destruction of 86 percent of the Iraqi forces' strategic targets in the first one or two days of the war." Ch'en proposes that "with the aid of electromagnetic waves, a virus can be injected from a long distance into the enemy's command and communication systems and into the computers on his aircraft, tanks, and other weapons, causing 'nonlethal destruction.'"
- **Radiation Combat:** "In the wars of the past, the power to inflict casualties mainly depended on the effects of kinetic energy and thermal energy, but the weapon systems produced by the third military revolution mainly use sound, electromagnetism, radiation, and other destructive mechanisms. . . .The main radiation weapons are laser weapons, microwave weapons, particle beam weapons, and subsonic wave weapons; they possess enormous military potential."
- **Robot Combat:** "The main type of military robot on active service or about to be put on active service in the armed forces of various countries of the world are vehicle emergency robots, mine-laying robots, minesweeping robots, reconnaissance robots, transportation robots, electronic robots, and driver robots. Later there will appear engineer robots, chemical defense robots, patrol robots, and even unmanned intelligent tanks, unmanned intelligent aircraft, and other 'robot soldiers'."

Magic Weapons, Optical Parallax, No Consensus Yet

In his article, "Military Conflicts in the New Era," Zheng Qinsheng points out that the well-known scientist Qian Xuesen "laid bare the essence of the military revolution" to be information technology. Zheng, like Chang Mengxiong, advocates new measures of effectiveness. He writes, "Information and knowledge have changed the past practice by which military capacities were simply measured by numbers of armored divisions, wings of the air force, and aircraft carrier combat groups."

Today, Zheng writes, "We also need to count invisible strengths, including calculation capability, volume of telecommunications, reliability of information, and real-time reconnaissance ability."

In a rare remark that apparently criticizes Local War theorists, Zheng asks "Where shall we place the nucleus of high-tech development? Where shall we put the main emphasis of local high-tech wars?" Zheng reveals that "a consensus on these issues has yet to be reached throughout the army. People still tend to place greater emphasis on hardware instead of software, and on the present instead of the future. Such a transitional 'optical parallax' is hindering us from gaining a correct grasp of major contradictions."

Zheng concludes by recommending "a conscientious study of" the military revolution, new ideas on military development, and "'magic weapons' that can really serve our purpose."

A People's Information War?

In "Information War: A New Form of People's War," Wei Jincheng suggests "the concept of people's war of the old days is bound to continue to be enriched" and proposes that it would be carried out "by hundreds of millions of people using open-type modern information systems." Wei sees the possiblity that "the enemy country can receive a paralyzing blow through the Internet."

Nanotechnology Weapons

Major General Sun Bailin's paper, "Nanotechnology Weapons on Future Battlefields," describes American and Japanese efforts in this field and concludes that "a variety of indications show that nanotechnological weapons could well bring about fundamental changes in many aspects of future military affairs. Nanotechnology will certainly become a crucial military technology in the 21st century!"

l

PART ONE:
The Strategic Thought
of Deng Xiaoping

Senior Colonel Peng Guangqian, Strategy Department of the Academy of Military Science, was an Atlantic Council Senior Fellow in 1995. Here he is seated in the cockpit of a U.S. F-15E.

The editor, Michael Pillsbury, in the Great Hall of the People, being greeted by Deng Xiaoping, in 1983.

DENG XIAOPING'S STRATEGIC THOUGHT

Senior Colonel Peng Guangqian

Deng Xiaoping's strategic thought constitutes a scientific system with rich content. As opposed to philosophical thinkers, Deng Xiaoping's strategic thoughts were not the result of study; rather, they grew out of practical necessity in the course of leading and planning the unprecedented socialist modernization of the huge Asian country with a quarter of the world's population. They are characterized by the times and practicality. On this point, Deng Xiaoping's strategic thoughts are innately consistent with Mao Zedong's strategic thoughts. However, comparatively speaking, the main ideas of Mao Zedong's strategic thoughts matured during the revolutionary war years. His most brilliant thought was that which guided the millions of Chinese people to engage in the magnificent people's war. In this sense, we can say that the main body of Mao Zedong's strategic thoughts was composed of military strategic thoughts that guided the war, whose objective was to seize power through military struggle and to strive for our national independence and liberation.

This paper first appeared in China Military Science *(Spring 1994). Senior Colonel Peng Guangqian works in the Strategy Department at the Academy of Military Science, Beijing.*

Deng Xiaoping's strategic thoughts were formed and developed under the new historic conditions after the proletariat had gained power. They are based on the practice of Chinese socialist modernization as well as peaceful development in the world. Therefore we can say that Deng Xiaoping's strategic thoughts have modern China and the world as the framework, with their main goal as the peaceful development of China and the world at large. They can be epitomized in three major parts: international strategic thoughts, national development strategic thoughts, and national security strategic thoughts.

Seeking Peace and Development

Deng Xiaoping always thinks with a view on the general trend of mankind's development and has the international strategic environment as the backdrop. That is an important characteristic of Deng Xiaoping's strategic thoughts. He believes that the development of China can not be separated from the world. Deng Xiaoping's international strategic thoughts contain the following main points:

- Through comprehensive analysis of the current situation, the new features of the basic contradictions in the world, and the new changes in the international political and economic structures, he has developed a traditional understanding of war and revolution. He has drawn the important conclusion that peace and development have become two big strategic issues in the world today, thus pointing out the theme and the essence of our age.
- When assessing the strategic environment, he carefully studied the changes in the forces of war and peace in the world today, and changed the long-held viewpoint that world war was imminent. He made the new strategic judgment that a new world war could be postponed or avoided if we did a good job.
- After the disintegration of the old world strategic structure, and with the new growing trend toward multipolarity, he was the first to propose building a new international political and economic order based on the five principles of peaceful coexistence, and made plans for new structures and gave new input on the reorganization of the international order in the new era.
- On the principles of handling international relations, he went beyond the limitations of the cold war strategic thinking and bloc

strategic thinking, to propose that the highest criterion governing state-to-state relationships is the national interest, and that we should unswervingly pursue an independent foreign policy, opposing hegemonism and power politics. He insisted that we should place our national sovereignty and security first, and genuinely take our country's fate in our own hands.

• On the question of solving disputes in the world, he took safeguarding peace and promoting economic development as the starting point. Seizing the historical opportunity when the world forces for peace had surpassed the force for war, he creatively put forward new ideas like "one country, two systems" and "joint development" in order to solve disputes peacefully in the world.

Socialist Modernization Drive

Development strategy is the core of Deng Xiaoping's strategic thought. Taking into consideration the characteristics of our times, the international challenges and opportunities that we face, the socialist development stage that we are in, as well as the purpose of the Chinese Communist Party and its goals in managing the country, Deng Xiaoping made a comprehensive analysis of the fundamental tasks, strategic objectives, steps, and focal points that we face at the initial stage of socialism. He put forward a whole set of ideas on creating socialism with vitality and revitalizing the Chinese nation.

Having studied the actual conditions in our country, and with great courage and realistic spirit, he drew the important inference that we are still at the initial stage of socialism, and set the strategic tasks for building a socialist market economy, thus he cast away the radical ideology that we had long been perplexed with. The theories of socialism at the initial stage and of the socialist market economy are the cornerstones of Deng Xiaoping's national development strategy. They have made important contributions to Marxism and laid the theoretical foundation for the speedy and healthy development of China's socialist modernization in the new era.

On the strategic goals of development, Deng Xiaoping issued calls to further liberate and develop production forces, to increase the comprehensive power of our socialist state and to increase our people's living standard continuously. He pointed out that the ultimate aim of the Chinese people is to turn our country into a prosperous, strong, democratic, and civilized socialist modern state.

With regard to the strategic steps for development, he linked long-term goals with arrangements for each step of development and set a realistic "three steps" development strategy. First, from 1981 to 1990, we should double our gross national product and basically solve the problem of food and clothing. So far we have already realized the first objective. Then, by the end of this century, our goal is to have our GNP reach $1 trillion, with a per capita income of $800 to $1,000. In other words, our goal is to reach a level of comparative prosperity. Within the ensuing 50 years, we shall strive to approach the level of developed countries and basically realize our goal of modernization.

Deng Xiaoping also had the strategic idea of "one central task and two basic points." That is to say, we should take the socialist modernization construction as the central task, while adhering to the policy of reform and opening up and upholding the four basic principles. This should be our Party's basic line in the new era. It has been proved by history to be the only correct line and is the lifeblood of our Party and people of all nationalities. We shall never have any doubt about this line.

On the strategic focal points of development, he made it clear that we should pay attention to economic development at all times, and wholeheartedly work on the four modernizations. He emphasized that the focal points are agriculture, energy, transportation, science, and education. For the first time, he put forward a thesis about science and technology being the main production force, and Chinese intellectuals being a part of the working class. He formulated a series of important policies on "respecting knowledge, respecting talents," and on holding a position in the area of high technology.

On the strategic requirements of development, he stressed that we should face up to the serious challenges of international competition in the current global economy as well as in the area of science and technology, and seize upon the historical opportunity. At a time when the international strategic structure is undergoing profound changes, and the socialist movement is temporarily at a low ebb, we should calmly observe and cope with the situation, be good at keeping a low profile, and try our best to do our work well in China.

On the strategic means of development, he stressed that we should take Marxism as our guiding ideology, and use practice as the only criterion of truth. We should not see books as dogmas, and not blindly copy foreign models. Rather, we should liberate our minds, seek truth from facts, go our own way, and build socialism with Chinese characteristics.

Creating a Stable Environment at Home and Abroad

The development of our country is closely linked with its security. The gist of Deng Xiaoping's strategic thoughts on national security is about creating a peaceful and stable strategic environment and a favorable situation, and providing strong security protection for the nation's development. Their main points include the following.

On the starting point of national security, Deng Xiaoping emphasized the idea of mutual security as well as security for the whole. He stressed the security interests of our own country as well as the security interests of relevant countries. He closely linked our national security with the security of our neighbors, our region, and even the world at large, so as to build up a genuine and reliable security environment.

On the building of national security strength, he dismissed the old idea of merely seeking military power, and instead suggested that we develop the comprehensive power of the country. National security lies in the overall development of the country, and national security strength should be thoroughly strengthened.

With regard to the function of national security strategy, he pointed out that we should first of all strive to prevent the breakout of war and have crisis situations under control. The maintenance of peace will ensure that our national economic development and the smooth continuation of the four modernizations not be affected by the chaos of war. At a time when reform and opening up and socialist modernization are increasingly being carried out, Deng Xiaoping specially emphasized that we should uphold our independence and sovereignty, defend our socialist cause, and guard the policies and lines formulated since 1978. We should make sure that our country enjoys a long period of peace and stability.

On the relationship between national defense development and economic development, he stressed that defense development must be subordinated to and serve the needs of national economic development. Defense development is only a part of national economic development, and should be planned and developed in coordination with national economic development. The armed forces should actively support and participate in economic development, and the rich defense industry resources should be put into use in national economic development. We should greatly develop our civilian industry and try in every possible way to develop our national economy. When the overall situation is improved, and the national power greatly strengthened, it will be easier for our national defense development.

With regard to the guiding ideology for armed forces development, he stressed that we should have the combination of a small but highly trained standing army with strong large reserves. We should reduce the number of people in the armed forces, but improve the quality of our army, including overall qualifications of our officers and soldiers. The level of defense equipment should be raised, and an appropriate force structure should be established. We should strive to improve the fighting capability of our armed forces, so that they will meet the requirements of modern warfare.

On the strategy for military action, he insisted that we should have a policy of active defense, and practice people's warfare under modern conditions. We should be good at learning the new characteristics and new patterns of limited warfare under modern high-technological conditions. We should give full play to our strong points while striking the enemy at its weak points. We shall adopt flexible tactics to win future wars against aggressors.

The close interconnection between the above three parts constitutes the complete entity of Deng Xiaoping's strategic thoughts. The national development strategy is the core of Deng Xiaoping's strategic thoughts. The problem of development is not only a global strategic problem in the world today, but the main challenge and historical task that modern China is facing. Only when the problem of development is solved, our national comprehensive power is strengthened, and our people's living standards greatly increased, can our nation's ambition be realized and can we really stand up among the nations of the world. We could then effectively raise the level of the material and spiritual civilization of socialism and have genuine national security and international standing. The strategic thoughts on national development have all along occupied a leading position in Deng Xiaoping's strategic thought system. Other strategic thoughts are based on and conditioned by it. However, Deng Xiaoping's strategic thought on national development does not stand out in isolation, but is closely related to strategic thoughts on national security and international strategy. The development of modern China can not be separated from the outside world, especially at a time when the world is growing smaller each day. In the information age of closer relationships, practicing isolationism is suicidal. At the same time, the development of the country is not possible without necessary security protection. Because hegemonism and power politics still exist, we should definitely not give up our sacred right of self defense. Therefore, Deng Xiaoping has always considered China's development in the context of the overall world strategic situation and has adopted an active posture in international society, in order to acquire more energy for development through international exchanges. When he thinks of the problem of development, he thinks of opposing hegemonism and power politics and safeguarding world peace. He strives to have a stable security environment and a favorable international strategic situation to facilitate development. In Deng Xiaoping's strategic thoughts, international strategy and national security strategy must be subordinated to and serve the national development strategy. They are the precondition and basic guarantee for the realization of the national development strategy and are integral parts of Deng Xiaoping's overall strategic thought.

In summary, the focal point of Deng Xiaoping's strategic thought is about peace, development, stability, security, and national revitalization. It is the basic line in the development of Deng Xiaoping's strategic thought, and is the essence of his strategic thought.

DENG XIAOPING'S THEORY OF DEFENSE MODERNIZATION

General Zhao Nanqi

National defense has always been a high priority in Deng Xiaoping's strategic thinking. As the chief engineer of the Chinese modernization drive, Deng Xiaoping has always seen the modernization of national defense as an important component part of the four modernizations. Viewed from the strategic angle of global trends, and taking the fundamental national interests as the starting point, he has given comprehensive answers to a series of important theoretical questions on the building of China's socialist national defense in a period of relative peace.

The Guiding Ideology for National Defense Construction

The guiding ideology for national defense construction is the theoretical foundation for making general policies for national defense construction. Having a correct understanding of the problems of war and peace in modern times, and recognizing the need to change the focal point of domestic work, Deng Xiaoping changed the guiding ideology for national defense construction in a timely fashion. On the question of war and peace, he rejected the viewpoint that world war was unavoidable, and made the judgment that world war could be

General Zhao Nanqi , President of the Academy of Military Science, Beijing, from 1993-1996, wrote this article for China Military Science *(Spring 1994).*

avoided. On the trend of our times, he pointed out that the new trend is peace and development. On the focal point of domestic work, he replaced class struggle with economic construction as the central task. The three conclusions were drawn at different times, but were related and affected each other. Because of these conclusions, we are required by history to have strategic changes in the guiding ideology of national defense construction.

Since the founding of new China, it had been the viewpoint of our Party for a fairly long period of time that war was unavoidable, or even imminent. It was objective and reasonable at the time, but it put our national defense construction in a constant state of having to cope with the imminence of war. It affected our national economic construction and restricted the development of national defense and armed forces building. Deng Xiaoping began to consider this problem in the mid 1970s. In 1975, he said that there would be no world war in 5 years time. Since the Third Plenary Session of the Eleventh CCP Central Committee, the focal point of our Party's work shifted from class struggle to economic construction. But still many comrades both within and without the Party were concerned about the danger of war. Deng Xiaoping paid closer attention to the changes in the international situation. Each year he would say that war would not break out in 5 to 10 years. On October 10, 1984, he was more explicit in pointing out that our views had changed somewhat on the issue of the dangers of war. He said the breakout of war was still a possibility, but the factors for checking the outbreak of war were increasing. On March 4, 1985, he further pointed out that there had been pleasing development of the forces for checking the outbreak of war. On June 4, 1985, he finally made a clear statement at an enlarged conference of the Central Military Committee. He said that we had changed our original viewpoint on the imminence of war after analyzing the international situation. He believed it possible that world war would not break out for a fairly long period of time, and the maintenance of world peace was promising. On September 14, 1985, he further pointed out that war could be avoided if we did a good job.

On the basis of the new understanding of the issue of war and peace, Deng Xiaoping has made new judgment on the trend of the times. He believes that peace and development are the two major issues in the world today. His viewpoint has improved our understanding of the current international situation and is a prerequisite for making a correct strategy. Our understanding of the world today has changed from the point of view of war and revolution into one of peace and development. The change requires not only scientific analysis and judgment, but strategic courage as well.

After the Third Plenary Session of the Eleventh CCP Central Committee, we changed our viewpoint of the international situation and we changed our policy. First, we changed our views on war and peace, and we believed that there would be no world war in a relatively long period of time. Secondly, there was an important change in our foreign policy. We changed our strategic policy on a united front to fight against Soviet hegemonism, and we adopted a foreign policy of independence. After that we set our minds on economic construction. The essence of the change was to make full use of the period of relative peace without major wars and to pay close attention to making plans for our modernization drive. Additionally, in accord with the national economic construction, we should constantly increase our national defense strength, and improve our capability of self defense under the conditions of modern warfare.

Focusing on Economic Construction, Readjusting Defense Strategy

Having had a correct guiding ideology for national defense construction, we should work out a scientific development strategy for national defense, so as to make national defense construction most cost effective. As the development of national defense depends on the overall economic development of our country, the development strategy of national defense should first solve the problem of correctly handling the relationship between economic and defense construction.

Mao Zedong, in his article "On Ten Relationships," clearly explained the correct way to handle the relationship between economic and defense construction in times of relative peace. However, owing to various reasons, this was not well practiced in reality. Deng Xiaoping paid close attention to this strategic problem. In 1977, he pointed out that the modernization of national defense would be possible only after the development of the country's industry and agriculture. In 1980, he said that if the budget for the military was too large, it would not be conducive to economic construction. If the armed forces had too many servicemen, it would affect its modernization. It is our policy to reduce the number of people in the armed forces, so as to save money for the renewal of equipment. It would be even better if we could save more money for economic construction. In 1984, he further pointed out that we were in a time when the whole country should wholeheartedly support the national economic construction. The army should in no way hinder the overall situation of economic development, and must be subordinated to it. Moreover, Deng Xiaoping put forward specific suggestions for action—e.g. the air force could vacate some airports either for joint military and civilian use, or simply for civilian use, to support the nation's aviation business. The navy's ports could also be jointly used or turned over to civilian control, so as to increase our nation's shipping capability. In order to put the idea into effect, Deng Xiaoping especially emphasized at an enlarged conference of the Central Military Committee in 1985 that we must do well in our economic work, that to do so is our main objective, and everything else should make way for it.

Subsequently, he put forward a development strategy for national defense that suited China's conditions. He asked the armed forces to exercise forbearance in this century, and resolutely made the important decision to cut the military by one million servicemen. He also established new means for the building of defense science and technology, the defense industry, and the reserve force for national defense.

In light of the realities of the new era, Deng Xiaoping raised the goal of military development and proposed to have a revolutionary, modern, and regular military. To meet the requirement of modern warfare, and taking into consideration the conditions of our military, Deng Xiaoping pointed out that the key issue for our military was to enhance its ability to fight a modern war. The command system should gradually be modernized. We should have a strong air force, as control of the air is a must in modern warfare. Navy construction must pay attention to real fighting capability. We must rely on science, and only by doing so will we have a future. He paid special attention to regularization. Speaking during a military exercise in northern China in September 1981, he personally added "regular" to the goal of building a strong revolutionary, modern military. Among the three goals, modernization is the central task and the criterion is improvement of fighting capability. Regularization means systematization and rule by law, because in that way it would be effective and more reliable. Revolutionization is the guarantee of modernization and regularization. The military must be true to the character, that is to say that, it is the armed forces of the Party, of the people, and of the country.

Functions and Tasks of National Defense

The functions and tasks of national defense require the whole country to carry them out. The military is the main body of the national defense force, and shoulders the main tasks. The functions and tasks of our military are clearly stipulated in the constitution. Article 29 of the constitution says, the tasks of the national armed forces are to strengthen national defense, resist aggression, defend the country, and defend the people working in peace. In light of the domestic and international situation that we faced in the new era, Deng Xiaoping gave further clear definition to the function and tasks of our army. At the enlarged conference of the Central Military Committee on November 12, 1989, Deng Xiaoping pointed out that the army forces should make further contribution to the safeguarding of our national independence and sovereignty, the safeguarding of our nation's socialist cause, and the safeguarding of the lines and policies formulated since the Third Plenary Session of the Eleventh CCP Central Committee.

On the development of the military and the national defense, Deng Xiaoping stressed this from the angle of the antiaggression and emphasized putting the military and national defense in the overall context of safeguarding national interests. He clearly pointed out in 1979 that it's inconceivable that our regular army, the public security organizations, the courts, and prisons should wither away. In his speech at the military exercises in northern China in 1981, he said that our army is the pillar of the dictatorship of people's democracy and should be the model in carrying out the lines and policies of the Party. After the political turmoil in 1989, he further stressed the importance of stability in the military. Our military should always be under the leadership of our Party. It should always be the guardian of the country, of socialism, and of our people's interests.

After the adjustments in our national security strategy and in our development strategy, and along with the speedy development of our national economy, the content of our national interests has been continuously enlarged. In light of the needs of our national security in the new era, Deng Xiaoping pointed out that the fundamental task for our army is to make further contributions to the safeguarding of our Party's basic line.

The most important thing that the army should do to safeguard the basic line is to provide a security guarantee for the central task of economic construction. Deng Xiaoping said on many occasions that the two prerequisites for our modernization drive are a peaceful international environment and a stable domestic situation. Therefore, what we most hope for are peace and stability. So far as the international environment is concerned, the bipolar world has ended, and world war is now avoidable. However, the world is undergoing complicated and profound changes. There are many uncertainties, and the dangers of war still exist. Our army should maintain sharp vigilance, shoulder the sacred duty of defending our country, and be prepared to fight against aggression. Domestically speaking, we are still in the initial stage of socialism, and we do not have a solid economic foundation. There is no enemy class, but hostile elements do exist. At the same time, we still face the problem of reunification of the motherland, and will soon resume the exercise of sovereignty over Hong Kong and Macao. Furthermore, we are accelerating the speed of reform and opening up and will come across many new problems and contradictions in the course of setting up a socialist market economy system. We need a stable domestic situation, and the military is duty-bound to fight against aggression and to safeguard the domestic stability.

New Ways To Use the National Defense Force

Utilizing Comprehensive National Power

Deng Xiaoping believed that strong comprehensive national power is the effective guarantee for safeguarding the national security as well as world peace. In other words, comprehensive national power is the decisive factor in determining the strength of the national defense force. Deng Xiaoping once pointed out in 1980 that the successes we had in our economic construction would determine the role we would play in international affairs. When our country is developed and more prosperous, we shall have a bigger role to play in the world. The reunification of the motherland likewise depends on the success of our economic construction. Deng Xiaoping also pointed out that a stronger China means that there would be a more reliable peace in the world, for a more developed China would greatly strengthen the force for peace to restrain the breakout of war.

Strive for the Settlement of Disputes Through Peaceful Means

Under the new conditions of our times, safeguarding peace is in accord with the fundamental interests of our country. History has shown that mankind can not solve every dispute by going to war. Based on years of observation and study of the international situation of social struggle, Deng Xiaoping creatively put forward new ideas on international dispute solving through peaceful means. He has said that we need to have new ways to solve the various disputes in the world today. New problems need to find new ways. He pointed out that we should use peaceful means and not war to solve problems. It would be most proper to solve international disputes through peaceful means. For example, on the question of Nansha islands, we have proposed that on the condition of their recognizing Chinese sovereignty, we could have joint development with relevant countries. With regard to the political and economic problems in the world, we propose that a new international political and economic order be established. Creating new ways to solve problems—which normally are pursued but not necessarily solved through war—by using nonviolent means is, in Deng Xiaoping's words, quite unconventional and requires one to have strategic courage to make the suggestions.

People's Warfare, and the Strategy of Active Defense

We do not want war, but we should be prepared to fight to defend our national interests. What kind of guiding ideology and strategy should we adopt if and when war is forced on us? Deng Xiaoping believes that under modern conditions, people's warfare is still the magic weapon for defeating the enemy. He has pointed out that should the enemy come now, practice has shown that so long as we uphold people's warfare, we will be able to win the war in the end with the weapons we have available. We have always had the experience of being able to defeat a superior enemy force with our inferior weaponry, because we have been fighting just and people's wars. As people's warfare is different now than in the past (those wars were fought with different equipment, by different means and in different forms), we need to remember Mao Zedong's thoughts on military affairs and study people's warfare under modern conditions. By doing so, we will be in an invincible position.

In light of the changes both at home and abroad, and based on the ideas of people's warfare, Deng Xiaoping has reestablished the strategic policy of active defense. The nature of the strategy is defensive, but it is active in substance at the same time. In the event of war, we should adopt vigorous measures to fight. Our point of departure should be to defeat the enemy's superior force with our inferior equipment. Deng Xiaoping has also put forward a series of ideas on the question of future warfare, e.g., strategic thought on the navy's offshore defense and the air force's control of the air. He asks the whole armed forces to strengthen the study of people's warfare under modern conditions and to develop military science for our country.

Practice has shown that Deng Xiaoping's theory on national defense construction is in accord with the theme of our time and suits the needs of modern warfare. It reflects the needs of our national security in peacetime and serves as the guiding principle for military development and for the development of our national defense in the new era.

DENG XIAOPING'S THEORY OF WAR AND PEACE

Colonel Hong Baoxiu

In order to correctly formulate policies, it is important to have a scientific analysis of the international situation and an accurate assessment of the trends of war and peace. After the Third Plenary Session of the Eleventh CCP Central Committee, Deng Xiaoping put forward a series of new points of view and judgments on the issue of war and peace, thus enriching the theory of war and peace.

Trend of the Times: Peace and Development

As early as October 31, 1984, Deng Xiaoping said, "There are two outstanding problems internationally, one is the problem of peace, and the other is the north-south problem." In March 1985, he said again, "The real major issues of the world today, issues of global strategic proportion, are the problem of peace and the economic problem or the problem of development. The problem of peace is the east-west problem, and the problem of development is the north-south problem. In summary, there are the issues of east, west, north and south." Deng Xiaoping vividly summarized the complicated current international issues into four words, and brought to light the major contradictions in the world today, expounding that the theme of our times has changed from war and revolution to peace and development.

Colonel Hong Baoxiu is a researcher in the Department of Scientific Research, National Defense University, Beijing. His paper is from China Military Science *(Spring 1994).*

Based on the understanding of the theme of the world today, Deng Xiaoping put forward guiding principles for domestic and foreign policies that conform to peace and development.

With regard to our foreign policy, Deng Xiaoping pointed out, "We adopt a foreign policy of opposing hegemonism and safeguarding world peace." He stressed, "China is a force for the maintenance of world peace and stability, and is not a force of destruction. The stronger China becomes, the more reliable world peace will be. In the past, there were people in the world who believed that China was 'warlike'. I and other Chinese leaders, including late Chairman Mao Zedong and Premier Zhou Enlai, have stated on many occasions that China hopes for peace most. . . . It is important for us to set up an image of force for peace, and for restraining war. That should be the actual role we shall play in the world." Under the guidance of this policy, we have improved our relations with the United States and the former Soviet Union, strengthened our cooperation with Third World countries, and energetically developed our relations with Europe and Japan. Deng Xiaoping has all along adhered to the foreign policy of safeguarding world peace. In the late 1980s and early 1990s, with drastic and profound changes taking place in the world, Deng Xiaoping asked us to calmly observe and cope with the situation and hold our ground. He pointed out, "We should persist in having exchanges with all countries, and should strengthen our exchanges with the United States and the Soviet Union. No matter what happens in the Soviet Union, we should calmly develop our relations with it on the basis of the five principles of peaceful coexistence. That should include our political relationship and we should not hold any debate on ideology."

With regard to our domestic policies, Deng Xiaoping emphasized that we should take full advantage of the historical opportunity of international relaxation and speed up our own development. He said that there would be a relatively long period of peace in the world, a world without the outbreak of a third world war. We should firmly grasp the central task of economic construction, taking advantage of the opportunity. Now is the best time for reform. During his inspection tour of southern China in 1992, Deng Xiaoping said, "I worry about missing the opportunity. . . . If we do not develop, or if we develop too slowly, there will be problems when people make a comparison. . . . Troubles occur in some countries in the world.

Essentially speaking, the reasons for these are the bad performance of their economy, people don't have enough to eat and wear, the increase in wages is eaten up by inflation, and there is a decline in the standard of living." With a strong sense of urgency and responsibility, Deng Xiaoping has repeatedly stressed the need to speed up our development. He pointed out, "Whether we can withstand the pressure of hegemonism and power politics, and uphold socialism, will depend on whether we can have a speedy development and realize our development strategy. . . . So long as we can accomplish this, we will be as stable as Mount Taishan."

New Predictions for War and Peace

On the issue of war and peace, the traditional point of view holds that so long as there is imperialism, wars are unavoidable. After the Third Plenary Session of the Eleventh CCP Central Committee, Deng Xiaoping made new predictions and judgments on the developing trends of war and peace of our times. In his speech at the enlarged conference of the Central Military Committee on June 4, 1985, he said that our viewpoint has always been that war is unavoidable and imminent. After careful observation of the situation in recent years, we now believe that "it is a possibility that world war on a large scale will not break out for a relatively long period of time. The maintenance of world peace is promising." Deng Xiaoping's new judgments on world war are correct conclusions based on the scientific analysis of the international situation.

Wth the rivalry and confrontation between the two large groups of east and west and between two superpowers ended, the major factors that could lead to world war no longer exist. "Only the two superpowers have the capability to fight a world war, others do not have such a capability." The old situation of U.S.-Soviet confrontation changed after the disintegration of the Soviet Union. The danger of a U.S.-Russian collision leading to a world war has greatly lessened. Different forces in the world are disintegrating and realigning, and new antagonistic military groups that are capable of fighting great wars will not be formed for quite a while.

As arms race among world powers has receded to second place, and development in economics, science, and technology has become the focal point of competition. Deng Xiaoping pointed out, "The new scientific and technological revolution is fast developing in the world. Economics, science, and technology are increasingly taking on prominent roles in the global competition. The United States, the Soviet Union, developed and developing countries are all facing the situation seriously." For some time that the major military powers of the world have been cutting down the number of their armaments, and the arms race has been cooling down. Major powers are carrying out economic reforms and adjustments, and vigorously developing new high technology, in order to have economic and technological superiority and gain the initiative strategically.

The world economy is developing in the direction of regionalization, globalization, and groupings, resulting in interdependence and integration, and has become an important factor restraining the outbreak of world war. After World War II, the economic activities of the world became more and more globalized. We have seen surges in the development of multinational corporations, international merges, joint ventures, and the internationalization of share holders. Currently, there are 37,000 multinational corporations in the world, and their products account for 40 percent of the world's total. As economic life becomes more internationalized, the features of regionalization and groupings become more prominent. As the world economy becomes more integrated, it creates situations of interdependence. Under such circumstances, should one side launch a war, it not only strikes the other side but damages its own interests as well.

The terror of nuclear weapons is also an important factor restraining the outbreak of war. Deng Xiaoping once said, "Both the United States and the Soviet Union have a lot of nuclear as well as conventional weapons. Each is capable of destroying the other, and neither dares to strike first." After the disintegration of the Soviet Union, the United States and Russia quickened their pace of nuclear disarmament. The presidents of the two countries made statements that they no longer see each other as targets of their strategic nuclear weapons—but they still own over 95 percent of world's nuclear weapons. According to their disarmament agreements, the two sides will still maintain a stockpile of 20,000 nuclear weapons. Therefore, nuclear terror remains an important factor restraining the outbreak of war.

As the world's multipolar process speeds up, the forces for peace outweigh the elements of war, effectively checking world war. The end of the old structure has seen the quickening of the trend of multipolarity. Though the United States has become the only superpower, it lacks the economic power to dominate the world. Germany and Japan have increased their economic power and political influence, but their military strength is still constrained by various domestic and international factors. The Soviet Union has disintegrated, but Russia is still a strong military power, particularly it is a nuclear power that should not be overlooked. Though Third World countries are in a relatively difficult situation, they are a force to be reckoned with in international politics. With its political and social stability, and with its independent foreign policy of peace, China has become an important force behind the preservation of world peace and stability. In a word, acceleration of the world's multipolar process has created a situation whereby various forces are increasingly balancing each other. This shall be advantageous to world peace.

World war can be avoided, but it does not mean that there will be no wars in the world. As Deng Xiaoping believes, "World war can be postponed, but accidental incidents and local circumstances are not entirely predictable." After the end of the Cold War, there was an imbalance of international forces. New factors of instability are on the rise in some regions, and there has been an increase of local wars and military conflicts. Many countries have changed their armed forces' central task to countering regional threats and being prepared to win local wars.

Hegemonism, the Root Cause of the Modern War

It was the viewpoint of Marx and Engels that private ownership and the existence of classes were the root cause of war. Lenin raised the point that "modern wars grow out of imperialism." On the basis of analysis of the post-World War international situation, Deng Xiaoping pointed out, "The contention for hegemony is the cause of the current world's intranquillity. . . . war is closely associated with hegemonism." He expounded on the Marxist theory of the root cause of war and brought to light the root cause of modern wars.

Deng Xiaoping once said, "There is global hegemonism as well as regional hegemonism in the world." Since World War II, global hegemonism has constituted a menace to world peace, while regional hegemonism has been an important factor causing local wars and military conflicts. Relying on their relative strong power in the region, some countries have been pursuing expansionist policies and constantly creating disturbances. They have provoked military conflicts or local wars with their neighboring countries. This has been a major cause for modern wars.

Because hegemonism is the chief menace to world peace, we must oppose hegemonism in order to safeguard world peace. Deng Xiaoping said, "The Chinese foreign policy can be basically summed up in two sentences. One is that we oppose hegemonism and safeguard world peace. The other is that China will always belong to the Third World." He also stressed, "Whoever practices hegemonism, we will fight against him, and whoever commits aggression, we will fight against him."

New Analysis of Forces for Safeguarding World Peace

Lenin believed that the proletariat was the key to peace. Stalin proposed that the prevention of world war and the safeguarding of world peace in large measure depended on the unity and strength of the socialist camp. Based on Mao Zedong's theory of three worlds, and in accord with the changes in the international situation in the 1980s, Deng Xiaoping made a new assessment of the forces for safeguarding world peace.

First, the Third World is the mainstay of the forces for peace. Deng Xiaoping believes, "The growth of forces for world peace has outpaced the growth of forces for war. The forces for peace consists, above all, of the third world." The population of the Third World accounts for about three-fourths of the world's total. Third World countries have long suffered from aggression and domination by foreign countries. They have had too much suffering because of backwardness and aggression. They eagerly desire a peaceful international environment in order to devote major efforts to the development their economies.

Second, China belongs to the Third World and is an important force for safeguarding world peace. Deng Xiaoping said, "China will always belong to the Third World. . . . As the most populous nation among the Third World countries, China is an important factor for the development of the forces for world peace." Since the founding of new

China, it has played an important role in the fight against war and in safeguarding peace. In the 1950s, China put forward the five principles of peaceful coexistence and won the approval of peaceful forces in the world. In the 1970s, a triangular relationship evolved under the exceptional international environment. China played a restraining role in the contention for hegemony between the United States and the Soviet Union. As our modernization construction continuously forges ahead, our international standing will rise.

Third, the second world of developed countries are also an important force checking war. In one of his meetings with foreign guests, Deng Xiaoping said, "Europe is the crucial region for determining the question of war or peace. Western Europe and Eastern Europe are both forces for the safeguarding of peace. They both want development. The more they are developed, the greater the forces for peace will be." He also said, "The people of the United States and the Soviet Union do not support war either. The world is big and complicated, but if you look at it closely, there aren't many people who are really for war. The people want peace and are opposed to war."

By assessing the forces for world peace, Deng Xiaoping has changed our old way of analyzing according to class, ideology, or social system. He has told us that, not only the proletariat and socialist countries are forces for peace, the capitalist countries can also become forces for peace. Not only the people in the capitalist countries can become forces for peace, their governments can also be forces for peace in a given period of time.

New Ways to Solve International Disputes

In the past, classical Marxists emphasized that the safeguarding of world peace should be accomplished through war and revolution. How do we solve international disputes and safeguard world peace in the age of peace and development? Deng Xiaoping has said, "there are a lot of disputes in the world, and we need to find a solution to the problem. I have been thinking for many years as how to use peaceful means and not war to solve the problem. . . . We Chinese stand for peace, and hope to solve disputes by peaceful means." In accordance with the above view, he creatively put forward new ideas on safeguarding world peace and solving international disputes mainly by peaceful means:

- Adopt a forward-looking attitude. Let bygones be bygones, and open up the way to the future.
- Try to find common ground, while reserving differences. This principle can be applied to handle specific contradictions and conflicts between countries, and can also be seen as a general principle on understanding and dealing with international relations in our age of world peace and development.
- Adhere to the principle of "one country, two systems." We shall adhere to the principle of "one country, two systems," and resume the exercise of sovereignty over Hong Kong in 1997, and over Macao in 1999. The successful handling of the question of Hong Kong and Macao will be of great significance for the great cause of the reunification of the motherland, the revitalization of the Chinese nation, and the maintenance of peace in Asia and in the world. It will also provide new experiences for solving problems between states left over by history.
- With regard to territorial disputes in the world, we can shelve disputes and have joint development first. Take the Diaoyu Island and Nansha Islands for example. We could shelve the disputes on sovereignty and have joint development. Joint development simply means the opening up of oilfields under the seabed near those islands, either by joint venture or operation, and with interests enjoyed jointly. There is no need to fight and no need for many rounds of negotiation. This was yet another new way proposed by Deng Xiaoping to develop our good neighbor relations and to stabilize the international situation.
- Peace talks. Deng Xiaoping has always advocated the settlement of international disputes through bilateral and multilateral talks. Our goal is the stability of the international situation and the maintenance of world peace.

DENG XIAOPING'S PERSPECTIVE ON NATIONAL INTEREST

Colonel Hong Bin

The views on national interests are the views that concern those fundamental questions like the survival of the nation and development requirements. Deng Xiaoping's views on national interests form the essential basis by which he conducts state affairs and makes important strategic decisions. To learn Deng Xiaoping's views on national interests is the starting point to understanding the logic of his strategic thoughts and strategic decisions.

Our National Interests Are the Common Interests of All the Chinese People

National interests are closely linked with the main requirements of the states, classes, nationalities, and other social groups. Different social groups have different values and requirements, so their views on national interests and on the nature of the national interests would not be the same.

Whenever Deng Xiaoping speaks on the issues of national interests like sovereignty, national reunification and national development, he often associates these with our people's requirements, wishes and emotions. In September 1982, Deng Xiaoping talked with British Prime Minister Thatcher on the question of Hong

Colonel Hong Bin is a member of the Strategy Department at the Academy of Military Science, Beijing. This article is from China Military Science *(Spring 1994).*

Kong. He said, "If China does not recover Hong Kong in 1997, that is, 48 years after the founding of the People's Republic of China, no Chinese leader or government would be able to explain this to the Chinese people. People would have no reason to have confidence in us." When speaking with an Indian delegation on the Sino-Indian border issue, Deng Xiaoping said, "This is a problem left over by history. You have your people's emotions, and we have ours. The two sides would only be able to persuade our own people by taking a package plan." When commenting on the reunification of the mainland and Taiwan, he said we should take the method of "one country, two systems. . . . By doing so, we would be able to give an explanation to the people." When commenting on the policies safeguarding the national interests, he said, "I want to tell you today that our policies will not change. No one will be able to change these policies, as they are effective and correct, and have the support of the people. Since they have the support of the people, whoever wants to change them will be opposed by the people." These comments have shown that the national interests that Deng Xiaoping talked about are inseparable from the requirements and wishes of the broad masses of the people. Our national interests are the common interests of all the Chinese people. The nature of our national interests is its affinity to the people.

We may understand the nature of our national interests from these aspects:

- The nature of our national interests is determined by the nature of our socialist state. In socialist countries, the broad masses of people, including all nationalities, people of all social strata, have become masters of their countries.
- The essential substances of our national interests are exactly the things that our people need most and are most concerned about. Deng Xiaoping emphasized, "Our people's living standard has indeed improved. Our country has become more prosperous. Our international standing is on the rise. These are major issues." These are exactly the essential substances of the national interests. The national survival interest is connected to the improving living standards. The prosperity of the nation accords with the national development interest. The rising international standing points to the interest that the nation has in international status and in its international relations.

● The value of our national interests hinges on the requirements and wishes of our people. The country consists of different social groups. These social groups do have common interests, but have some differences as well. When making important policy decisions on matters of national interests, we shall always do so in accordance with the general and the most ardent requirements and wishes of the people. Deng Xiaoping often reminds us to ask more questions, such as, "What do the people need. . . . would people agree to this. . . . would we be able to explain this to the people." We should give consideration to the people's wishes and make decisions accordingly. By so doing, our national interests will always be consistent with our people's common interests.

National Interest As the Ultimate Criterion

In his meeting with U.S. President Nixon, Deng Xiaoping said, "When considering relations between states, we should mainly proceed from our national strategic interests. . . . We should not raise a great fuss about historical grievances, or about differences in social systems and ideology." Instead, "We should take our national interests as the highest criterion when conducting talks and dealing with problems." Deng Xiaoping used the word "highest criterion" in the meeting and clearly showed the exceptional importance the national interests hold in strategic policy decisions on conducting state affairs:

● National interest fundamentally reflects the common requirements of all the people and concerns the most important issues cared about by the people. They are the matters that have an important bearing on the security, well-being, and honor of the whole country.
● Our national interests are the common interests of all the Chinese people. Our national interests embody and outweigh the interests of classes, nationalities and other social groups.
● When dealing with state to state relations, the differences in social systems and ideologies should be subordinated to the national interests. We should maintain friendly exchanges with other countries regardless of their social systems or ideologies. On the other hand, we should uphold the national interests as the

highest criterion when dealing with state to state relations. Under no circumstances should the national interests be sacrificed.

• "As a big country we should have our own dignity and our own principle to abide by." We should rely on ourselves to safeguard our national interests and never rely on alliances or depend on a foreign country to pursue our national interests. As national interest is the highest criterion in handling state-to-state relations, we should do things according to our national interests and not depend other countries' wishes.

National interest is the criterion that we use to set our strategic goals. Our strategic goal is to realize development interest and safeguard national security. We want to have a prosperous economy, stronger comprehensive national power and higher international standing. We should develop further detailed considerations in the fields of economics, politics, military affairs, and foreign affairs to pursue our national interests. National interest is the criterion that we use to determine our relations with other countries. Ours is a peace-loving country. We would like to have friendly relations with all the countries in the world based on the five principles of peaceful coexistence. But no country should infringe upon China's interests, and "should not expect that China would swallow such a bitter pill." National interest is also the criterion that we use to judge the rights and wrongs of the strategic decisions. In international relations, nations normally judge the rights and wrongs of their strategic decisions according to their national interests. Deng Xiaoping pointed out, "The Chinese people have their own national dignity and sense of pride. It is their great honor to love their country and devote all their energy to the socialist construction. It is their great shame to see the interests, dignity and honor of their socialist country being infringed upon." To judge the rights and wrongs of a domestic or foreign strategic decision, we should first of all make sure it has not damaged the national interest. For instance, when commenting on the soundness of our Hong Kong policy, he said, "The maintenance of prosperity and stability in Hong Kong is in keeping with the vital interests of China." When commenting on the question of reunification of China, he said, as a special administrative region, Taiwan will be able to enjoy special policies, but "on the condition that it should not infringe upon the interests of the unified country."

Safeguarding the Interests of the Country is Safeguarding the Interests of the Nation

Deng Xiaoping places special emphasis on the identity of safeguarding the interests of our country with safeguarding the interests of the Chinese nation. When speaking on questions relating to national interest, he often mentions the "unity of the Chinese nation," or "the descendants of the Chinese nation." In using the word nation, he refers not simply to the Han nationality or minority nationalities, but to the entire Chinese nation, to include all nationalities. The nation is the main body representing the interests of the whole people and has the same meaning as the word country does. Deng Xiaoping often uses the concept of "Chinese nation" and "country" alternately. He links patriotism with safeguarding the national interest, and sees any activity that places the national interest first as patriotic conduct safeguarding the national interest.

The Chinese nation is the largest nation in the world, comprising over one-fifth of the world's population. The Chinese people have the same language and culture and a unique way of being identified with their country. Deng Xiaoping has said that we should strive for the great unity of the whole Chinese nation. Every Chinese, no matter what clothes he or she wears, and no matter what position he or she takes, should have the sense of the pride of the Chinese nation. He has made repeated statements that the cause we are undertaking is the cause of national revitalization. Safeguarding the national interest by our Party is safeguarding the interests of the whole Chinese nation. All Chinese people should unite under the banner of national interest. The unity of the Chinese nation means the unity of one-fifth of the world's population and is a tremendous force. The unity of the Chinese nation itself reflects the national interest of our country.

The reunification of China lies in the interest of our country as well as in the interest of the Chinese people. As Deng Xiaoping said, "The realization of the reunification of the country is the aspiration of the whole nation. If we could not accomplish it in one hundred years, we should do it in one thousand years." It has been a big problem long under consideration by Deng Xiaoping to work out solutions to the Hong Kong and Taiwan questions and for reunification of the country. To this end, he has proposed the strategic idea of "one country, two systems," which is based on the fact that the Mainland, Hong Kong,

Taiwan, and overseas Chinese have all identified themselves with the country and with the Chinese nation.

Deng Xiaoping's comments on the identity of safeguarding the interests of our country with safeguarding the interests of the Chinese nation are comments centered on the unity of the nation, safeguarding the sovereignty and the reunification of the country, as well as the goals of promoting the prosperity of the country. His aim is to safeguard the fundamental interests of the country and for the peace and progress of the world. This kind of national unity is wholly just and fundamentally different from the "narrow nationalism."

National Interests with a Global View

When dealing with questions that involve interests of other countries, or state-to-state relations, Deng Xiaoping often takes into consideration both our national interests and the national interests of the other countries. When commenting on the Sino-U.S. relationship, Deng Xiaoping said to the U.S. special envoy Mr. Scowcroft, "To get along with each other, we should respect each other and show consideration for the other side. We'll then be able to resolve the disputes. It won't do to show consideration for just one side. When both sides yield a bit, we should be able to find acceptable and good ways." He has also reminded people, "From the global point of view, the development of China is conducive to the world peace and to the economic development in the world." Deng Xiaoping has raised an important principle and a new way in the safeguarding of national interest. That is to say, we must widen our outlook and consider questions of national interest in light of the relationship between the countries concerned and with a world view. This is an important strategic thought of ours in safeguarding the national interest.

In international relations, national interests of various countries are obviously interrelated. The change in one's national interests might touch upon the national interests of the other countries. In handling state-to-state relations, we should follow the principle of harmonizing the common interests of the people of the world with our own national interests. That is to say, on the premise of safeguarding the fundamental interests of our country we should integrate the national interests of our own with the interests of the people of the world, as well as with the national interests of the countries that we are dealing with. We should fully recognize that our national interests and the common interests of the people of the world coincide and actively seek new ways and new methods to solve disputes in order to have peaceful coexistence with all the countries in the world.

Deng Xiaoping once said to some American friends, "China is of special significance in the world, and it has a bearing on the stability and security of the international situation. Should there be turmoil in China, it would create a big problem, and would certainly affect the world. It would neither be a good fortune for China, nor for the United States." He often reminds heads of states from abroad to notice the big market advantage of China, "hoping that international businessmen would consider cooperation with China from a global perspective. History would show that those who have helped us would gain benefits greater than their assistance." It would not only be beneficial to the construction and development of our country, but would exert profound influence on the promotion of peace and development in the world.

Sovereignty and Security Come First

The national interests are reflected in the fields like national sovereignty, security, economic development, international standing and dignity and are put in the order of priorities.

As Deng Xiaoping has clearly pointed out, "The sovereignty and security of the country should always come first." The sovereignty of exercising independence is the essential symbol of a nation being an independent entity in international relations, while security is the precondition of the survival and development of a nation. Therefore, sovereignty and security should be placed ahead of all other national interests. The above statement shows that national sovereignty and security are highly placed in the structure of our national interests and indicates the resolute stand and clear attitude we hold in safeguarding these interests.

Deng Xiaoping's view of national interest emphasizes the importance of national sovereignty and security and has a high practical relevance. First, on the question of national sovereignty and security, there is no room for maneuver. On the question of Hong Kong returning to the motherland, Deng Xiaoping said to Mrs. Thatcher, "On the question of sovereignty, there is no room for maneuver for China. Frankly speaking, the question of sovereignty is not a question that can be negotiated with." This clearly shows that, at no time and under no circumstances, should we barter away national sovereignty and security interests.

Second, resist the talk about "the idea of sovereignty is obsolete," and resolutely safeguard national sovereignty and security. Currently, some people in the west have tossed out ideas like "a civil war is not domestic affair," "human rights are above sovereignty," etc. As Deng Xiaoping has refuted,

> Some countries have used as pretense the stuff like human rights and saying socialist system is not rational and illegitimate. But actually, they want to infringe upon our national sovereignty. Those countries who practice power politics have absolutely no right to talk about human rights. They have harmed too many human rights in the world! Starting from the Opium War of aggression against China, they have harmed too many human rights in China! . . . The Chinese people will never accept any action that violates the norms governing the international relations, and will not yield to pressure. . . . China will never let other people to interfere in its internal affairs.

Long-term Interests of the Country

Deng Xiaoping has repeatedly pointed out that, when considering and making decisions on questions of national interests, we should focus on the long-term interests of our country. Our long-term interests are those that concern our "national capability" and important interests that reflect the "symbol of prosperity and development stage" of our nation. "National capability" means the full strength of a nation in conquering nature and not being conquered by other nations. It also means the comprehensive power of a nation. This capability is mainly reflected in a nation's level of development in the field of science and technology, and in it's economic power.

In safeguarding national interests, long-term national interests should always be placed first. When there is a conflict between long-term national interests and immediate partial interests, we should put the interests of long-term development first and should not be concerned with just the present. When our long-term national interests require us to sacrifice some immediate partial interests, we should be willing to pay the price and suffer some losses. We should have the courage to sacrifice some immediate partial interests in exchange for long-term important interests. Deng Xiaoping once reminded us on the question of opening up, "We should hold high the banner of further opening up and be courageous. It is certain that we will suffer some losses for the present. But we should not be afraid of that, so long as it is beneficial in the long run."

Deng Xiaoping believes that the above principle and ways of safeguarding long-term national interests are not only applicable to our country, but to other countries as well. He often talked to foreign leaders about the necessity of avoiding quibbling over some past and immediate interests. Instead, each state should focus on the long-term interests of its own, and try to solve disputes by seeking common ground while preserving differences. In his meeting with Mr. Gorbachev, he said, "The purpose of our meeting is to put an end to the past, and open up the way to the future. Putting an end to the past means that we do not need to talk about the past. The emphasis should be put on the matters of opening up the way to the future." When commenting on the Sino-U.S. relations with Mr. Nixon, he stressed that the two sides "should each focus on its own long-term strategic interests. At the same time, the two sides should respect each other's interests and do not make a fuss about past grievances." In his talk with former Japanese Prime Minister Nakasone, he especially emphasized the need to "be far-sighted to develop Sino-Japanese relationship." It's in the interests of both sides.

Stability Is the Highest Priority

Deng Xiaoping has stated on many occasions that the main purpose of our political reform is to have a stable environment: "Stability is the highest priority of interests for China. . . . It is the key to China's effort to shake off poverty, and to realize the four modernizations. . . . The essential condition for China to reach its goal of development is to have a stable domestic and peaceful international environment." The reason that Deng Xiaoping called stability the highest priority of interests is because it is an overall reflection of national interests like national sovereignty, security, and economic development at the present stage.

Only by maintaining social stability can our economic reform measures be carried out, a fine investment environment be set up, and the talents of the Chinese people be focused on the four modernizations drive. In this sense, stability is currently the highest priority of interests that we must maintain.

ADHERE TO ACTIVE DEFENSE AND MODERN PEOPLE'S WAR

Senior Colonel Wang Naiming

In the new era, though world war might be postponed or avoided, local wars and regional conflicts are far from over. We eagerly hope for peace, but peace is achievable through struggle. We are devoted to development, but development needs defense which is achieved through readiness to fight. In the new situation of tremendous change in strategic environment and rapid development of military technology, the question is how to seize and maintain strategic initiative and to win victory in the future anti-aggression war. As the leader of our party and the top military leader, Deng Xiaoping has established for us to practice active defense policy and people's warfare under modern conditions. This is the fundamental guiding policy for our national defense construction and army building.

The strategic thinking of active defense was created by revolutionaries like Mao Zedong during the Chinese revolutionary war, with Marxism as guidance, raised the general principle of active defense to a strategic level, and was applied in the Chinese revolutionary war as a strategic guidance. It emphasizes that the nature of our military strategy is defensive, but also active in requirements. It requires the organic integration of offense and defense, and achieving the strategic goal of defense by active offense; when the condition is ripe, the strategic defense should be led to counter attack and offense.

Senior Colonel Wang Naiming is a member of the Strategy Department, Academy of Military Science, Beijing.

In the revolutionary war times, revolutionaries represented by Mao Zedong resolutely opposed the wrong line of passive defense, and adhered to the strategic policy of active defense, and led the revolutionary war from victory to victory. After the founding of new China, the strategic policy of active defense again played an important guiding role in the war to resist the United States and assist Korea, in the self-defense fight on the border, as well as in the national defense construction, opposing hegemonism and in the struggle to maintain world peace.

In the new historical period, we should still adhere to the strategic policy of active defense, and this is because the policy reflects the objective law of war, and is the most vital essence of Marxist military theory and Mao Zedong's military thought, and it still plays a positive role of guidance in real life military struggle.

Peace and Self-reliance

The strategic policy of active defense is a component part of the national security strategy and must be subordinated to and serve the overall strategy of the country. Deng Xiaoping has said, "China's policy is never to seek hegemony. Our foreign policy goal is to strive for world peace. On the premise of that, we should concentrate on the modernization drive, develop our country, and build socialism with Chinese characteristics." The socialist China has shown the world that China is opposed to hegemonism and power politics and is the staunch force for the maintenance of world peace. The military strategy of China is defensive and not offensive, is self-defensive in nature and not expansionist, and is consistent with the socialist nature of our country and with our peaceful foreign policy.

A Scientific and Stable Defense

"The most effective defense is still achieved by offense" (*Military Works of Marx and Engels*, volume 4, 327). Mao Zedong once explicitly pointed out that, "Only the active defense is the real defense, and is the defense for the counter attack and offense." Deng Xiaoping has also said, the active defense is not just simple defense, it has offense in it. The integration of defense and offense reflects the developing law of war itself.

The Inferior Force Confronts a Superior Enemy Force

We are still in the initial stage of socialism. The 15 years of reform and opening has increased our GNP many folds, and strengthened our national power, but has not fundamentally changed the relative backwardness of our economy and culture. For a relatively long time, our country will not have a large amount of funds for the modernization of our army. The speed of our army's modernization will still be lower than those of the developed countries and regions. The weaponry of our armed forces will still be in an inferior condition, and this situation will probably continue for several decades. Under the circumstances, our armed forces must adhere to the strategic thought of winning against a strong force with a weak one, and winning against a superior force with an inferior one. Even when our country is developed in the future, we should still adhere to the strategic policy of active defense.

World Peace and Development

The current world has witnessed the end of cold war, and the international structure is developing in the direction of multipolarity. Major powers of the world are focusing on strengthening their comprehensive national power and adjusting strategies; they have reduced their armed forces and improved quality, in order to gain initiative in the 21st-century world arena. We are also developing our productive forces to increase our comprehensive national power. This has been the trend in the world. The strategic policy of active defense emphasizes the principle of self-defense, and aims at peace and stability. It is not only conducive to the national construction in China, but also conducive to world peace and development.

Requirements of the Modern War of Technology

The local wars of today have changed from using conventional weapons to using high-tech weapons. The high-tech local wars have caused drastic changes in the forms of war and methods of combat. It requires that the armed forces be of high quality, the combat plan to anticipate for all eventualities, war material structure and arrangement be reasonable, battlefield construction be prepared in advance, fast reaction capability of the army be improved, and the command and control method be steady. The strategic thinking of active defense stresses that strategic guidance should be in a planned way, have the initiative, and be flexible, and it stresses active and not passive military action, and this fully meets the requirements of modern warfare.

As compared with the past, the strategic policy of active defense in the new period contains many new contents.

- The national interest is the highest criterion in handling the question of military strategy.

  —The safeguarding of national sovereignty and national security should always come first. National sovereignty and national security are the highest manifestation of national interests, as well as the interests of the Party and the people. The safeguarding of national sovereignty and national security should be the highest criterion for our army's strategic action.

  —We should resolutely safeguard the socialist system and the basic line of our Party. Chinese history tells us that apart from the socialist road we have no other choices. Once the Chinese Socialism is forsaken, China is bound to return to the semicolonial and semifeudal status. There will be no one relatively well off; even basic food and clothing will not be ensured. So the army and the state political power should all safeguard the socialist road, the system, and the policies.

  —We should resolutely safeguard the social and political situation of national stability and unity. The development of the national economy and the further reform and opening up all require a stable social and political environment, otherwise, it would not be possible to carry on the economic construction and reform and opening up, and the success achieved so far would also be lost. In China, the first priority is the requirement of stability. All those factors that affect the stability should be properly handled, there should be no concessions or accommodation, and turmoil is not allowed in China. Reform is the motive force, development is the goal, while stability is the precondition. The three should be organically integrated. Our armed forces are the strong pillar for the people's democratic dictatorship, and it is our honored mission entrusted by the active defense strategy to safeguard the peaceful and stable environment for the economic development and reform and opening up.

- We should win the war, but should also be able to contain the war. In the new historical period, our central task is to carry on the socialist modernization construction and greatly develop the productive forces. The highest goal of our military strategy is to create a strategic environment of long-term peace and stability to ensure the smooth construction of the country. For this goal, the focus of our attention should be to win the war, but at the same time, we should also strive to contain the breakout of the war. In practice, we should handle well the relationship between winning the war and containing the war, and we should have the capability to win the war. Without the capability to win the war, we simply can talk about the question of winning the war and containing the war.

- Strive to improve the ability to fight the local wars of modern technology, and especially high technology. The recent Gulf War has shown that high-tech weapons have played the main role in certain phases, areas, regions or even the whole process of the war. We can expect that in the future anti-aggression war, both sides of the combat will use the then available high-tech weaponry. So it is entirely necessary to stress the importance of improving the ability to fight the local wars of modern technology, and especially high technology.

To be suited to the local wars of modern technology and especially high technology, we should follow the basic active defense strategy and strategic guidance formulated by Deng Xiaoping, actively study the characteristics and regular patterns of high-tech local wars, and seek appropriate measures to deal with it. For example, how to fight the people's warfare well under modern conditions? How to gain control of the air and command of the sea at crucial moment at certain areas, and gain initiative and avoid being in a passive position? How to deal with enemy's strike from afar, and how to deal with surgical strike? How to carry out rapid mobilization in certain localities? How to protect the important strategic direction and resist the enemy's strategic air strike? How to do a good job in combat material storage, and structural adjustment to ensure the winning of the local war? How to work out the modernization of the command system of the armed forces, and ensure a steady, timely, confidential and continuous command? How to work out a good integration of fight and deterrence, offense and defense, and use forces flexibly and in a timely fashion? How to take the initiative in our hands, and contain the escalation of the war, and be reasonable, advantageous and appropriate? And how to establish a theoretical system for the high-tech local wars, etc.? We should pay attention to the study of these questions.

● In the strategic guidance, we should be resolute as well as flexible. Commanders of war in their strategic guidance, should analyze the situation scientifically, make commitment cautiously, foresee risks, make careful planning, face difficulties squarely, and prepare for all kinds of eventuality. At the same time, in their combat guidance, they should use force flexibly, in a timely fashion, and in accordance with the actual situation in the battle they should pay attention to the method of fighting and halt fight in time. In the future high-tech local war, we must not only consider the question of winning the war, but also the question of the risks involved. We should consider the war on the land, but consider more the war in the air and on the sea. We should not only consider the existing high-tech weaponry, but also the high-tech weaponry in development. We should not only consider fighting with a single enemy, but also the participation of more than one powerful enemy. We should not only consider fighting a fast war, but also a protracted war. We should not only consider winning with a superior force, but also winning with an inferior force, and our standing point should be placed on the latter. Only then can we be both resolute and flexible in our strategic guidance.

The most important thing in carrying out the strategic policy of active defense is to practice people's warfare under modern conditions. The current people's warfare is different from the people's warfare of the past, the equipment and means are different now. When conditions change, the forms that people's warfare take will be different.

The people's warfare should be suited to the development of modern conditions. We must be clearly aware that the rapid development in modern productive force and science and technology and their wide application in the military area surely will have an important effect on the people's warfare under modern conditions.

Since the end of the Second World War, there has been no new world wars, but local wars have occurred one after another and have become the basic norms of war; the means of war have been changed from conventional to high-tech weapons, and forms and methods of war have also changed. This new situation requires us to carefully study the people's warfare under modern conditions, in order to meet the challenges of the future military struggle.

Under modern conditions, the practice of the people's warfare means the direct preparedness against war, but it also means the enduring construction of national defense. It involves the Party, the government, the military and the civilian, and involves political, economic, scientific and technological, military, diplomatic, educational and cultural and other areas. The strength of a nation's defense is not simply determined by its armed forces, but is determined by the comprehensive national power that is the foundation for supporting the armed forces and preparedness against war. So the mobilization of the whole nation to be concerned about the national defense, to link our work with the revitalization of the nation, and with the national security and development is an important manifestation of the practice and development of the idea of people's warfare under modern conditions.

For the people's warfare under modern conditions, we should pay attention to improving weapons and military skills, and focus on the research and making weapons suited to the people's warfare under modern conditions, including the minimizing of high tech weaponry and reducing the carrying weight for the single soldier. As weapons are imported, we should at the same time train modern military talents and improve the quality of the personnel. Then we will be able to improve our equipment and make the people's warfare more forceful.

The people's army is the backbone force for the people's warfare under modern conditions. Since the Third Plenary Session of the Eleventh Party Central Committee, Deng Xiaoping has led the army in carrying out a series of important reforms. He stressed that army building should be subordinated to and serve the overall situation of national economic construction, the goals of army building in the new era should be realized in steps and phases. He led the reform of the structures of the army and reduced one million servicemen, and formed the combined army corps. Our army has taken a big step on the road to better troops and high efficiency.

The integration of field army, local army, and militia will be the basic organization form for the people's warfare under modern conditions. To improve the structure of the armed forces for the people's warfare under modern conditions, Deng Xiaoping made reforms and adjustments in the national defense reserve force. He reinstated the reserve system. The building of the militia has carried out the policy of limiting numbers, improving quality, focusing on the key units, and laying a good foundation, and has entered a new phase of development.

The integration of defense and commerical industry during both war and peacetime in the construction of national defense is an important item of practicing the idea of people's warfare in the new era. According to the instruction by Deng Xiaoping that the defense industry should be incorporated into the state plan, an important decision was made in July 1986 that the defense industry be incorporated into the national economic system, and the defense industry and defense science and technology should be converted to commercial production after meeting the requirements of the military. The defense projects and people's air defense projects throughout the country have started to serve the national economic construction, and these are beneficial to the country and to the people, and have created fine conditions for the people's warfare under modern conditions.

We should carry out long and lasting national defense education among the whole nation to lay a solid social foundation for the people's warfare under modern conditions. The strength of the people's warfare lies in the millions of the masses of people. Only with the people's concern, support and participation, can the idea of people's war be realized. During the peace time when our central task is focused on economic construction, it is important to carry out long and lasting national defense education among the whole nation, so as to arouse people's high political enthusiasm, inspire national spirit, and increase the cohesiveness of the nation.

DEFENSE POLICY IN THE NEW ERA

Colonel Fang Ning

We have formed a national defense policy of maintaining peace and self-defense by the whole nation in the new historical era. I believe that the essential substance of our national defense policy in the new period can be summed up as follows.

Defending Sovereignty and Ocean Rights and Safeguarding National Security

Part of the essential substance of the national defense policy is to clearly define the basic aims of the national defense. As a socialist country, we have consistently opposed aggression and expansion. The aim of our national defense is to defend our national territorial sovereignty and ocean rights, and safeguard our national security and development. The territory of a country is a natural material condition for the survival and development of a country. It includes territorial land, air space, and waters, as well as all living things, treasures, and resources underground and in the ocean, and they brook no intruding and violation by foreign forces. Sovereignty is the fundamental symbol of a country, and is the ultimate power a country wields to independently handle its domestic and foreign affairs. Sovereignty

Colonel Fang Ning works in the Department of Military Systems, Academy of Military Science, Beijing. This article first appeared in China Military Science *(Winter 1994).*

includes domestic and foreign aspects, and the two are interdependent and can not be separated. Without sovereignty, there would be no independence and honor of the country, and there would be no political system and social criterion to speak of. Looking at the relationship between the territory and sovereignty, we see unity in defending the national sovereignty and defending the national territory. Only when a nation is able to exercise sovereignty over the territory, can it call the space its territory. The integrity and unification of a nation's territory are also symbols of independence and dignity of sovereignty. When one's territory is invaded, it means the loss of sovereignty. When one's sovereignty is intruded, its territorial integrity is also difficult to ensure. Therefore, the safeguarding of national territory means the safeguarding of national sovereignty at the same time.

The exercise of national sovereignty is not limited to the territory. For example, national ocean rights are not limited to territorial waters. According to "The Territorial Waters and Adjacent Areas Law of the People's Republic of China," we not only have sovereignty over territorial waters, but also exercise control rights over the adjacent areas. The law stipulates, "The areas immediately adjacent to the territorial waters are the adjacent areas of the People's Republic China. The width of the adjacent area is twelve nautical miles. . . . In order to prevent and punish those acts that violate the security, customs, financial, health or entry and exit laws and regulations on the territorial land, inland waters or territorial waters, the People's Republic of China is entitled to exercise control rights over the adjacent areas." At the same time, according the "United Nations Law of the Sea Convention" of April 1982, we have 200 nautical miles of special economic zone, as well as two million square kilometers of offshore continental shelf. We have corresponding rights over these sea areas. These rights exceed the scope of the territorial waters, but according to the international law of the sea, they still belong to the just rights of a country. Therefore, they are within the scope of national defense.

The purpose of national defense is not restricted just to the defending of the national territorial sovereignty and ocean rights. The highest criterion of national defense activities is the safeguarding of national interests as a whole. The essential components of national interests are security interests and development interests:

- National security interests are the essential condition for a nation's survival and development, and it is first of all determined by the integrity of the territory and the independence of sovereignty. National security interests also include the consolidation of the political power and the stability of the society. For the purpose of safeguarding the political interests of the ruling class, the defense forces of any country will prevent and fight against schemes of subversion by domestic and foreign opposing forces. The national defense forces are therefore responsible for the all round safeguarding of national security.

- There are many aspects of development, but economic development is doubtlessly the central task. The economy is the foundation of a nation. The national defense should safeguard not only the national security interest, but also the national development interests, and especially the national economic development interests, including interests in domestic economic construction, development of land resources, overseas investment, international trade, etc. In peace time, the safeguarding of national development interests by national defense forces is mainly to ensure a good and peaceful development environment for the nation.

Realization of a Modern National Defense

The aim of our national defense construction involves those areas related to the national defense, like the military, politics, economy, science and technology, education, and law. The aim of national defense is an important component part of the general aim of our national construction, and should be subordinated to the general aim of national construction.

Our constitution stipulates, "We should gradually realize the modernizations for the industry, agriculture, national defense and science and technology." In order to safeguard the national security and development, China must have a modernized national defense. At present, the chief contradiction that our defense construction faces is between the objective requirements of modern warfare and the relative low level of modernization of our national defense. Resolving this contradiction will be the central task for our national defense construction. The modernization of national defense is a developing and comprehensive concept; it has different meanings at different periods of time, and has different standards. Currently, it has the following features:

- Its purpose is entirely for the self-defense, for safeguarding results of the socialist construction, and for safeguarding national security and development.
- The construction relies on the joint efforts of the whole nation. In our country, the interests of the people are consistent with the interests of the country, and the construction of national defense is everybody's responsibility.
- It is based on independence and self-reliance.
- It attaches importance to the development of defense science and technology, and the development of military high technology in particular.
- It gives full play to the human factor, and pays attention to raising the quality of the personnel, especially the scientific and technical and military quality.

The modernization of our national defense can not be separated from the central task of economic development but should be gradually realized on the basis of the continuous development of the national economy. The economic construction is the central task, and the army is required to give active support for the national economic construction, and to take moves under the overall situation of economic construction. At the same time, the modernization of national defense is incorporated into the national modernization drive, and the Party, the Government, and people of all walks of life should be concerned about and support the modernization of our national defense.

A Highly Trained Standing Army with a Large and Strong Reserve Force

The armed forces are the backbone of the national defense, and the structure of the armed forces is the key to the construction of a national defense. A standing army is an active military unit a sovereign country must maintain in peacetime, and it can carry out combat mission at any time. It is an important component part of the political power and is the main body and backbone of the armed forces. Strengthening standing army building is an important guarantee for strengthening national defense forces, and for containing and winning war. It is a necessary requirement for safeguarding national interests and is also a strong pillar for the maintenance of domestic stability. But the size of the army should be properly controlled in peacetime. We should build a small but highly trained standing army; our national strength would not be able to support a large standing army, and it is not necessary anyway.

The building of a small but highly trained standing army must include the following points: First, the direction for the development of the standing army construction should be correctly set. On the condition that safeguarding national interests and national security is ensured, the size of the standing army should be appropriate. Second, we should improve the structure of establishment for army units, and this becomes even more important when our weaponry is relatively backward compared to that of developed countries. Through scientific arrangement and combination, we should put the manpower and weaponry into better and closer formation, and combine the different armed services. The capability of coordinated action of our armed forces should be improved. Third, according to the conditions in our country and the requirements of future warfare, we should renew our weaponry and at the same time pay attention to developing our own advanced products, making a few effective weapons. We should attach importance to the comprehensive make up of the weaponry, as well as the fighting capability of weaponry in all fields and full process. We should adhere to the policy of doing more research, but producing less. The army should gradually be equipped with relatively advanced weaponry, but old and new weaponry should both have a place in the army. Fourth, the requirements of the modern warfare should be taken as the departure point, and there should be continuous reform in the training. The training should have focus, and the degree of intensity and difficulty should be maintained at a high level. We should try to have training in conditions similar to actual combat situations. At the same time, we should pay special attention to the education and training by military academies and schools, and special talents of different kinds should be trained to meet the requirements of modern warfare.

While building a small but highly trained standing army, we should also greatly strengthen the construction of a reserve force. This will be a necessary condition for winning future wars and is also an important measure to strengthen the national armed forces. The reserve forces are mainly composed of militiamen and various reserve services and are the basis for the expansion of the army during war time. They will have great significance in the process and results of the war. A country with only a standing army but without a strong reserve force, cannot be said to have a complete national defense, or a strong national defense. Therefore, we must attach great importance to the role played by the reserve forces. While strengthening the building of the standing army, we should build a high-quality, quickly mobilizing, strong reserve force with a sufficient number of people. The standing army and the reserve force should be planned in coordination. The leading organization, personnel arrangement, weapons and equipment, education and training, and supporting supplies should be scientifically arranged, so that the two are both properly provided for and can assist and complement each other, and can develop according to the requirements.

Self-Reliance and Independence

Independence and self-reliance were the weapons we used to win the revolutionary war and are the essential experiences we have in our socialist construction. They reflect the fundamental interests of the Chinese people, our unremitting efforts to improve ourselves, and our desire to stand among the nations of the world.

Through independence and taking the initiative in our own hands we mean to make decisions on the goals, focal points, steps, and measures of national defense construction according to the actual conditions of our country and to strive to achieve the goals of defense modernization based on the reality. We will not rely on any big power, or group of powers, nor will we form any alliances with any big powers or submit to pressure from any big power. Through self-reliance we mean to base our national modernization drive on our own strength and seek development and modernization mainly through our own efforts.

Ours is a large country with long borders and coastlines, vast seas and air space, and complicated geographic conditions. We need to build a strong defense system that can effectively maintain our national security. This would not be possible by relying on a third country, or through spending a lot of money. Developed countries do not really want to see us with a strong national defense and will restrict and block us on the advanced military technology and equipment. At the same time, to put national defense in other's hands would harm our national sovereignty and would in a sense reduce or even lose the meaning of national defense.

It is of great significance to insist on independence and self-reliance in the process of national defense modernization. First, we will be able to take the initiative in our own hands in the construction of national defense, and avoid being controlled by others. Second, we can increase the cost effectiveness in the construction of national defense and do more work with less money. Third, we shall facilitate the development of our national economy and science and technology, and that will be conducive to enhancing comprehensive national power. Fourth, it will enhance our sense of national pride and confidence. But, self-reliance and independence does not mean adopting a closed-door policy and working on our modernization construction with our door closed to outside world. While we adhere to the policy of independence, we must also stick to the opening policy and actively introduce advanced foreign technology and ideas. We should draw successful experiences from abroad with goals, focuses, and in a planned way. In the area of defense related science and technology, we shall seek appropriate foreign assistance in the light of our needs and possibilities, importing some advanced technology and equipment to make up our deficiencies. By doing so, we will raise the starting point of our national defense construction, avoid some detours and shorten the process of our national defense modernization.

Linking Defense with Commercial Industry

When we say that we shall link defense with commercial industry, during war and peacetime, we mean that during our normal time of national construction we should have a long-term point of view. We should take into consideration future requirements of warfare, and make appropriate arrangements. Military requirements and civilian needs, during war and peace, should be considered and planned in coordination. Our defense construction should be combined with our national construction as a whole.

Defense requirements during war are quite different from peacetime needs. Normally we need to maintain a certain level of defense production, but we must not overproduce military products. This will require an appropriate transfer of defense production into the commercial sector during peacetime. Meanwhile, to solve the contradiction between the defense construction and national economic construction, and to solve the problem of an inadequate defense budget, our national economic construction should also take into consideration our national defense needs. In terms of efficiency, this will bring about better defense cost effectiveness with less spending. Judging from the actual situation, it seems feasible to carry out the policy of linking the military with the civilian and linking the normal time with the war time. The convertibility of science and technology for both defense and commercial use has laid the foundation for linking the two. Other developed countries also stress this linkage. They may have different models, but they all try to combine the defense industry with economic construction, and in doing so, they promote the development of defense construction and push the national economy at the same time.

With regard to the leadership structure of the national defense, it is preferable as much as possible to put as much as possible defense leadership within the leadership structure of government departments, different regions, different professions, and every front of endeavor during peacetime. By doing so, it will be good for management of defense construction in peacetime and help us cope with emergencies and limited wars.

On the point of scientific research and production of national defense, the defense industry should actively join in the national economic construction, and give appropriate consideration to the development of commercial products. Defense science and technology should be given full play, thereby bringing along commercial technology. On the other hand, those defense industries that have been converted to commercial production should reserve the capability to produce military products. The overall distribution of the national industry should also take into consideration the requirement of war, and appropriate measures should be taken, so that in the event of need there will be timely changes. With concern for both the defense and commercial industry, which must support each other, the army is embodied in the people, and both military and economic efficiency is achieved.

The reserve force, which has as its base militiamen and reserve personnel dispersed in every field of economic construction, is the backbone of the production force and should receive full consideration as a vital force. At the same time, the leadership should be strengthened and organized perfectly, and the military and political qualities of the reserve force improved, so as to meet the requirements of the modern warfare.

On the point of military economy work, the military economy should be incorporated into the national economy as much as possible. We should fully utilize the military supply capability of the national economy. Special military materials are mainly supplied according to the national plan, while general materials for both defense and commercial use should rely on market supply, and daily necessities and services should rely on society. The idea that the army is a self-contained society should gradually be changed.

The training of personnel, the export of military products, transportation preparedness, etc. are all important aspects of the policy of linking defense and commercial industry. It should be specially emphasized that we should through national legislation and planning and control, try to combine defense construction with the infrastructure construction in the economy as much as possible. In our infrastructure construction of railways, highways, airports, port facilities, and communication facilities, we should take national defense requirements into consideration.

The Strategy of Active Defense

The strategic thought of active defense is an important part of Mao Zedong's military thought and is the summation of the experience of our Party and our army's long-time struggle.

The adoption of the strategy of active defense is determined by the nature of our country and by our basic national policy. The purpose of our national defense is to resist foreign aggression and is self-defensive in nature. Therefore, we should adopt such a strategy.

In the new historical era, we are facing a lot of new situations and problems when adopting the military strategy of active defense. First of all, the purpose of war has been changed. Our army fought to seize political power before the founding of new China, but after that, we fought to defend political power. We will be required to defend cities and more places in future anti-aggression wars. Second, combat conditions have changed. As there is progress in science and technology, and development in weaponry, combat conditions are daily becoming more complicated. The fighting space is not only expanded on the ground, but also expanded in the air and space and on and under water. Third, combat is taking different forms. In the past, our army was used to changes and a combination of mobile warfare, positional warfare, and guerrilla warfare. In future wars, we shall choose main combat forms with flexibility and in accordance with new situations. We shall continue to use ingenious combinations of different forms of combat.

Under the new historical conditions, in order to carry out the military strategy of active defense, we need to make accurate judgments on the threat of war. We should be concerned about any realistic threat against our national territorial integrity, but should not overlook any long-term threat against our national security. We should be prepared for defensive wars, in light of the characteristics and requirements of local wars of high technology. We should adhere to the principle of gaining mastery by striking only after the enemy has struck. We should not provoke a war and should not resort to force rashly. When we are forced to use force, we should be good at seizing the opportunity to fight and controlling the fighting scale as well as the scope, trying not to let the war escalate. Our strategy of active defense emphasizes the use of various combat forms and methods flexibly to achieve our strategic goal. In future wars, as there will be more diversified combat targets, combat scales, and means and forms; also, future wars will be more sudden, faster, and more intense, and we should be able to respond quickly and effectively in light of the differences in timing, space, opponents, and challenges.

Adhere to People's Warfare under Modern Conditions

People's warfare is mobilized and carried out by the broad masses of people in order to seek the liberation of the broad masses of people and to resist foreign aggression. People's warfare is the weapon that we have used to fight against domestic and foreign enemies, and to win the war.

Because of the rapid development of science and technology, and especially of high technology and its wide application militarily, there have been many new changes and new characteristics in modern wars. But these changes and characteristics have in no way reduced the role and function of people's warfare in future anti-aggression wars. At the same time, the future people's warfare must also adapt to the characteristics of modern wars, which have the following main features:

- Resolutely rely on the masses of people. Our national defense struggle is for safeguarding our country, our people working in peace, and of our people's fundamental interests. This is the basic condition on which we can have people's warfare. Future anti-aggression wars will mainly be fought on the Chinese territory, either locally or in large areas. The great consumption of war will need the great masses of people to produce and supply the war materials, or even to directly take part in the fight. Therefore, we must fully rely on, mobilize, and organize the broad masses of people to fight the war. We must also organize a broad united front, trying to win the great majority of people internationally, including people of our enemy state over to the anti-aggression side.

- Build a people's army that can meet requirements of modern war. The people's army will be the backbone in a people's war. This army must be under absolute leadership of the Chinese Communist Party and have strong revolutionary political work and continuously strengthen the revolutionization. At the same time, we should greatly strengthen the modernization and regularization of the people's army in the light of requirements of a modern war.

- The armed struggle will be the main form, but will also need the cooperation of other forms of struggle. We shall persist in the armed struggle, and at the same time do not give up other forms of struggle, and fight an all round and complete people's war. Under modern conditions, we shall still adhere to and carry on the fine traditions of revolutionary war years. We shall organize the broad masses of people to take part in the political, economic, cultural,

and medical work, and to actively support the army and the front. Hence the people's war is fully and completely carried out on the political, economic, military, diplomatic, cultural and every front.
• Stress cooperation of the field army, the local armed forces, and the militia, and this will be the organizational guarantee for the winning of the people's war. The field army and the local armed forces will perform combat duties separately, the militia will be the reserve force and will basically assist the regular army to fight in a certain area. The three will have a division of labor, and have different combat missions, but their objective is the same. It would not be possible to defeat the enemy without the correct form of organization and a clear division of labor.

Safeguard Peace and Oppose Hegemonism

China pursues a foreign policy of peace and has all along adhered to developing relations with other countries on the basis of the five principles of peaceful coexistence. We do not seek a sphere of influence in any place in the world, and we do not want an inch of land from another country. In the future, when our economy is developed, our country has become strong, and our national defense force strengthened, we shall still resolutely not practice hegemonism and power politics. At the same time, we shall oppose anyone who practices hegemonism, including regional hegemonism. China has always maintained that all countries in the world, no matter whether they are large or small, rich or poor, strong or weak, should be equal in international affairs. We are firmly opposed to the big bullying the small, the rich oppressing the poor, and the strong humiliating the weak.

In the new era, our national defense will continue to regard safeguarding peace as an obligation. We are opposed to the arms race and the expansion of the arms race into the outer space. We stand for the nuclear disarmament, for reducing conventional arms, and the destruction of chemical weapons. We are opposed to the spreading of nuclear weapons to nonnuclear countries. In order to safeguard peace, we have been working hard to use peaceful means to solve international disputes that involves our country, and are against resorting to force rashly.

But, safeguarding peace must have a strong national defense force to back it. The national defense will only be able to prevent aggression when it has the capability to resist aggression. Through the analysis of our national defense policy, we may summarize it as follows: safeguarding national interests, maintaining peace, following the idea of people's warfare, practicing the military strategy of active defense, adhering to the road of independence and self-reliance, carrying out the policy of linking defense and commerical industry during war and peace, and gradually realizing the modernization of national defense.

PART TWO:
Future Security Trends

Top: *Atlantic Council Directors Stan Resor and former Ambassador Chas Freeman with General Li Jijun, Vice President of the Academy of Military Science, and General Yu Qifen, Director of the Strategy Department, Academy of Military Science*

Bottom: *General Xu Huizi, Deputy Chief of the General Staff, Chinese People's Liberation Army (left) greets General John Shalikashvili, Chairman of the Joint Chiefs of Staff, August 24, 1994*

U.S.-CHINA MILITARY TIES

General Chi Haotian

For many years, despite the ups and downs in China-U.S. relations, the two National Defense Universities have managed to maintain communications, which has contributed positively to closer understanding between the two military forces and the improvement and growth of military-to-military ties. This is indeed very reassuring.

I am here at an important moment in our relationship. Not long ago, President Jiang Zemin and President Clinton held a successful meeting in Manila. That meeting was of great significance, for it was a meeting of reviewing the past and looking into the future and laid a good foundation for the establishment of a 21st-century-oriented relationship between China and the United States. At present, there exist favorable opportunities for our two countries and two militaries to improve and develop their relations. My current visit is aimed precisely at working with Secretary Perry to reactivate the process which we two set in motion when he visited China in October 1994. My visit also signifies a new beginning in the relations between our two militaries. I am convinced that, so long as we make concerted efforts in the spirit of equality and consultations our military-to-military ties will continue to move forward and give positive impetus to the improvement and growth of relations between the two countries.

Your university is the top military academy in the U.S. and the cradle for generals. As a veteran soldier, I wish to take this opportunity to exchange views with you on issues of mutual interest.

General Chi Haotian, Vice Chairman of the Central Military Commission of the People's Republic of China, made this speech at the U.S. National Defense University on December 10, 1996.

To begin with, I would like to share with you some of my observations on the current world situation. With only three years to go before the 20th century ends, mankind is about to cross the threshold of another millennium, bringing what we accomplished in the past into the future. At this turn of the century, we can see a world that is caught in profound and complex changes; profound because such changes touch upon the fundamental question of "where the world is headed," and complex because they involve the readjustment of interrelations between various forces in the world. This is a time of difficulties and challenges on the one hand and opportunities and hopes on the other. At present, the international situation as a whole is moving towards relaxation and the trend towards a multipolar world is accelerating. To maintain world peace and promote economic development has become the shared desire of all people. However, the world is no tranquil haven, but a place fraught with deep-rooted clashes of interests, with some regions reeling in conflicts and chaos. Facts have proved that peace and development remain the two major themes of the present-day world, yet both fall short of being satisfactorily addressed. Although mankind aspires to peace, the time of peace remains elusive. Although economic development has become a universal desire, development around the world still comes under interference. In my view, a lasting peace and brisk development in the world still calls for close attention and unremitting efforts by statesmen and people of all countries.

Both China and the U.S. are major powers in the Asia-Pacific and have a keen interest in what happens in this region. At present, when international relations are undergoing tremendous changes, the Asia-Pacific region as a whole has maintained stability. However destabilizing factors, both immediate and potential, still exist and should not be overlooked. The Chinese Government and people are fully aware that China's economic growth and political stability are important factors for a prosperous and stable Asia-Pacific, which, in turn, creates a favorable external environment for China's economic development. The Chinese Government and people have made and will continue to make positive efforts to promote peace, stability and development in the Asia-Pacific region.

Now, I want to discuss in greater detail China's defense policy. I know this is also a question of interest to you. If I could summarize the topic in one sentence, it would be: China is a developing socialist country; the nature of its social system and its national security interests determine that it follows a defensive defense policy. This defense policy includes mainly the following:

• First, the basic goals of China's defense policy are to consolidate national defense; resist foreign aggression; safeguard state sovereignty over territorial land, air and waters, as well as maritime rights and interests; and maintain national unity and security. It is also a principal mandate bestowed on the People's Liberation Army (PLA) by China's current Constitution which was promulgated in 1982. The PLA follows a strategy of "active defense". That means, a principle of defense, self-defense and striking only after being attacked is followed at the strategic level. Yet this defense is an active one, not a passive one that would often land the forces in a disadvantageous position.

• Second, a basic principle for China's defense construction is to subordinate it to, and serve the country's overall economic program. China has persisted in incorporating defense construction in the overall economic planning of the nation, so that they will meet the needs of both peace time and war time, both civilian use and military use and both immediate and long-term interests. To subordinate to and serve economic development, China has for years maintained a tight control on its defense expenditure. Since the beginning of the 1980s, though the absolute size of defense appropriations has somewhat increased over the years, its share in both the GNP and state budget has actually shrunk. In 1996, China's defense budget was 70.227 billion RMB yuan, or the equivalent of about 8 billion U.S. dollars. Considering the fact that China has the largest population and the third largest territory in the world and that it has a land boundary of over 20,000 kilometers and a coastline of 18,000 kilometers to defend, it is fair to say that its military expenditure is indeed very modest and for defensive purposes only.

• Third, the focus of the military work in China is to build a better force with Chinese characteristics. The PLA is required to be a force with a high political standard, high military capability, a fine style of work, strict discipline and strong logistic support. Since 1975, the Chinese military has gone through several rounds of streamlining reorganization and restructuring, downsizing its troops from over 6 million to less than 3 million today. As for weapon and equipment development, we have, in actively implementing our military strategy of active defense, relied mainly on ourselves in research and development, supplemented by appropriate imports. The modernization level of the weaponry and equipment of the Chinese military is still very low. Constrained by limited national strength, we can only improve gradually as our national economy becomes stronger.

● Fourth, an important component of China's defense policy is to commit to world peace and human progress. Pursuing an independent foreign policy of peace, China does not enter into alliances with any country or group of countries, nor does it participate in any military blocs. It is opposed to any form of hegemonism, power politics, and acts of aggression and expansion. It stands for the peaceful settlement of differences and disputes between countries through consultations and is against the use or threat of force. China has all along stood for effective disarmament and arms control on a fair, reasonable, comprehensive and balanced basis. It has actively participated in relevant international disarmament and arms control talks and earnestly fulfilled its obligations under the treaties it has signed. To date, China is the only nuclear power that has undertaken not to be the first to use nuclear weapons under any circumstances and unconditionally not to use or threaten to use nuclear weapons against non-nuclear weapon states. China has also actively participated in U.N. peace keeping operations, making a positive contribution to world peace and stability.

China pursues a defense policy that is defensive in nature. This is out of the need for safeguarding state sovereignty and territorial integrity and maintaining lasting peace and stability for the country. China has never invaded any country nor has it stationed a single soldier abroad. However, there are still some people around the world who keep spreading the fallacy of the "China threat", arguing that a stronger China will threaten others and become a destabilizing factor in the Asia-Pacific region. I believe these people have ulterior motives. They are not happy to see China in development and progress. As is known to all, China's modern history is one that saw its territories ceded and its people subjected to foreign aggression, plunder and enslavement. In more than one century from the Opium War in 1840 to the founding of the People's Republic of China in 1949, imperialist powers, on several occasions, invaded China or turned it into their own battleground, nibbling away and seizing millions of square kilometers of Chinese territory. Even today, China's Hong Kong and Macao still await to be recovered. Taiwan, for reasons known to all, remains in a state of separation from the rest of the country after its return to China. As an old soldier who went through the winds of war in the first half of this century, I am keenly aware of the deep scars that agonizing chapter has left on the hearts and minds of our people. It teaches us that to live a peaceful tranquil and dignified life, our people must have the capability to defend themselves. It teaches us that the miseries the Chinese people went through in recent past must not be repeated either in China or in any other part of the world. Peace should be enjoyed by people of all countries. Even if China becomes stronger in the fixture, it will never embark on external aggression and expansion.

China has always attached importance to China-U.S. relations, believing that a stable and sound China-U.S. relationship not only serves the fundamental interests of the two peoples but also contributes to world peace and stability. Our bilateral relations have zigzagged in recent years. It is not surprising for us to have some disagreements, given our differences in economic development levels, social and political systems, cultural traditions and value judgments. Practice has proved that as long as our two sides bear in mind the fundamental interests of the two countries and adopt a correct attitude of consultations on equal footing and mutual respect, then in the spirit of "enhancing confidence, reducing trouble, developing cooperation and avoiding confrontation," we will be able to gradually iron out the specific problems in our bilateral relations.

Here, I feel compelled to mention the Taiwan question, an issue that is the key to and at the heart of whether China-U.S. relations can be stable and grow stronger. Settling the Taiwan question is China's internal affair. The position of the Chinese Government in this regard can be summed up as "peaceful reunification based on one country, two systems." We hope to see a peaceful settlement yet refuse to renounce the use of force. This policy is a result of careful consideration. The marked improvement in the relations between the two sides of the Taiwan Straits in recent years accords with the common interests of the people on both sides. It also contributes to peace and stability in the Asia-Pacific and serves the interests of the United States as well. However, the Taiwan authorities have, in disregard of the overall interests of the Chinese nation, gone farther and farther down the road of conniving at and participating in activities aimed at splitting the motherland, which has caused tension in cross-Straits relations. I would like to point out here, that if those elements on the Island who are eager to see China dismembered and themselves becoming more important with foreign support should cling to their wrong course and slip further astray, the Chinese Government and people will not sit idly by. The entire Chinese history shows that whoever splits the motherland will end up condemned by history. Neither history nor the people will forgive him. The international relations in the Asia-Pacific, since the end of World War II, have also proved that the sole correct approach to avoiding tension in the region is to firmly oppose the separatist tendency and foreign meddling in the Taiwan question.

Frankly speaking, the Taiwan question should not have been a problem in today's China-U.S. relations. After the end of World War II, in accordance with the principle established by the Cairo Declaration and reaffirmed by the Potsdam Proclamation, Taiwan was restored to China. However, for reasons known to all, Taiwan has since been separated from the rest of China. In 1972, China and the United States issued the Shanghai Communique, which was followed by the Communique on the Establishment of Diplomatic Relations and the August 17 Communique. In all these three Communiques, which constitute the foundation of China-U.S. relations, the U.S. Government recognized in clear terms that there is but one China and Taiwan is a part of China; that the Government of the People's Republic of China is the sole legal government of China and within this context the U.S. will only maintain unofficial relations with Taiwan; and that the U.S. will not seek to pursue a long-term policy of arms sales to Taiwan and its sale of arms will be gradually reduced and eventually stop. The U.S. Government has also on many occasions made it clear that it is up to the Chinese on both sides of the Straits to settle the Taiwan question. We hope that the U.S. Government can keep its promise. Facts over the years have repeatedly shown that when the Taiwan question is handled properly, China-U.S. relations will fare well; conversely, if not handled properly the relations will fare rather badly with endless troubles. To put an end to the state of separation across the Taiwan Straits and fulfill the grand cause of national reunification is the unshakable will of all Chinese people, the people in Taiwan included. This is an important issue of principle that bears on China's sovereignty and territorial integrity and directly touches the national sentiments of the Chinese people. I am confident that the American people, having experienced a Civil War themselves, should and will understand the resolve and determination of the Chinese people to safeguard state unity and oppose national separation.

As an old Chinese saying goes, one may extend his vision by standing on high ground. That is, the higher one stands, the farther he can see. It is our sincere hope that the U.S. Government may stand on a higher plane and get a broader view on the issue of Taiwan. The high ground here is to maintain and develop the friendship between the Chinese and American peoples by respecting the feelings of the Chinese people. The high ground here is also to maintain and develop China-U.S. cooperation and promote stability in the Asia-Pacific region by strictly observing the principles of the three China-U.S. Joint Communiques. In fact, we have never made any undue demands on the U.S. on the Taiwan question. Just as Mr. Deng Xiaoping put it during his visit to your country in 1979, there is nothing we want the U.S. to do, but something we want the U.S. not to do.

Before I left for my current visit I received a book entitled "Pearl Harbor in Pictures" from Admiral Preher. A famous epigram is inscribed in the book: Remember Pearl Harbor. Precisely 4 days ago was the 55th anniversary of the bombing of Pearl Harbor. World War II bound China and the United States together in an earnest cooperation against their common enemy. I hope China-U.S. relations today can still reflect the spirit of that sound and positive cooperation. I hope in particular that the armed forces of the two countries will make a major contribution to the steady growth of China-U.S. relations.

THE INTERNATIONAL MILITARY SITUATION IN THE 1990s

Major General Yu Qifen

The developments and changes in the international structure determine the world military environment. Ever since the late 1980s, when Gorbachev pursued a new ideology, the conflict between the Soviet Union and the United States has decreased, while cooperation increased. By the beginning of the 1990s, the two countries had reached an agreement on reducing strategic nuclear weapons by 30 percent, destroying chemical weapons, ending military support for Afghanistan, and reducing tactical nuclear weapons. They also pushed for the reopening of bilateral peace talks between Arabs and Israelis in Oslo. All these actions benefitted peace in the world. The radical changes in Eastern Europe, the reunification of the two Germanys, the disintegration of the Soviet Union, the collapse of the Warsaw-Treaty Organization, and the end of the bipolar structure have ended the political and military rivalry between the East and the West represented by the two super-powers, the Soviet Union and United States, which had lasted the 40 years since the end of World War II.

The 1990s have seen an era of peace and development. It has become common that conversation replaces conflict. Economic growth is now the key strategic target of many countries' concerns and efforts.

Major General Yu Qifen is the Director of the Strategy Department at the Academy of Military Science, Beijing. This article is from China Military Science *(Spring 1995).*

This more peaceful world affects the international strategic pattern, while military trends affect the international strategic pattern. Military struggle is subordinated to political and economic interests, and politics is the sum and substance of economics. The disintegration of the Soviet Union has weakened political, economic, and military power in the regions of the former Soviet Union. In Russia, the internal economic depression, together with the unstable political situation, will not be a dominant factor affecting the international security and tranquility. At present, the United States is still the number one superpower politically, economically, and militarily; however, it is not as strong as it used to be. It can no longer control the whole world. Japan and Germany grow stronger and stronger with the "peace dividend." The economic development of the European Community and the Western European Union, and the economic growth in China, India, ASEAN countries, and Brazil have enabled more and more countries to become influential in international security. As a result, this has led to the rapid development of multipolarity.

In order to be more powerful in the future, the great political and economic powers and regional alliances have all made full use of the relative peace to strengthen and develop their economies and have made improvements in their comprehensive national power, their main strategic aim. In his inauguration speech in January 1993, President Clinton said that the national security of the United States was mainly economic security; that the American people, having experienced over 40 years of sacrifice and after spending hundreds of billions dollars, had won the peace dividend, which they could use to invest into their future. This shows that the U.S. Government is determined to develop its economy, which has been given first priority. In fiscal year of 1991, the U.S. economy fell by -1.2 percent. In fiscal year 1992, it recovered, with an increase of 2.1 percent, and in fiscal year 1994, it rose to between 3.5 and 3.6 percent. Many developing countries as well as countries in the West have identified economic development as their main goal in order to strengthen their comprehensive national power.

In general, the world situation is moving in the direction of relaxation, and there is the possibility of no world war for a relatively long period. With the ending of the bipolar structure between the East and West, many countries had talks in order to build a peaceful order. However, there still exist many conflicts and problems resulting from the Cold War. Furthermore, some major powers are vying for the leading role in the transition to a multipolar structure and continue to practice hegemonism and power politics. This has led to regional wars and armed conflicts in some hot-spot areas. Quite a few Third World countries are still in the difficult situations of turmoil and economic difficulties. This shows that upheavals exist in the relaxed world order and unstable factors hide in stability. The situation is complex and changeable. It should not be ignored.

With the 1990s came a series of inevitable and profound changes in the international military situation. On one hand, many countries have made their first priority the development of their national economy. They have made appropriate changes in their military strategy that it is subordinated to and serve political and economic development. On the other hand, the objective reality, including a reduction in the risk of a U.S.-Russian war or a world war, has enabled countries all over the world, especially in the West, to change their military strategies. The great changes in the international military environment have thoroughly disturbed the old order and have given rise to some new features, new problems and new trends in a new era.

Adjusting Military Strategy

Every country, especially the major Western nations, has made great efforts to change military strategy in accordance with the relaxed international situation and to improve its economy. The United States has changed its strategy of "containing the expansion of communism" into "expanding global democratization" and changed its military strategy accordingly. The key change is from "preventing the Soviet Union from launching a widescale war" to "dealing with the regional conflicts in the Third World" and preventing the rise of "new global opponents." Early in 1989, the United States started to change its military strategy because of the easing of tensions between it and the Soviet Union. The two nations were having talks and cooperation instead of conflicts. In August 1990, President Bush put forward the "new strategy for defense." In February 1992, U.S. Secretary of Defense Cheney formally listed it in the 1993 DOD Annual Report as the "Strategy for Regional Defense." Derived from President Bush's proposal of a new strategy for defense and Mr. Cheney's own idea mentioned in the 1991 DOD Annual Report, it said that the United States should make it a first priority to deal with regional conflicts rather than dealing with the Soviet Union's global challenges. The strategy requires the following conditions:

- In military arrangement, the "forward deployment" needs to be changed to "forward present plus reinforcement."
- For combat doctrine, the key lies in the speedy deployment to deal with contingencies.
- Regarding combat targets, it would be the regional military powers that threaten the United States strategic interests, instead of the Soviet Union.
- For war preparation, the United States should get ready to deal with regional conflicts and not world war, and switch its target from Europe to broad areas in the Third World.
- In its force structure, the United States should stress the ability to reorganize.
- In army formation, it should implement the "policy of crack troops." In developing military equipment, it should stress weapons of high technology. Since he became the President, President Clinton, proposed the "win - win" strategy, clearly pointing out that he would win battles in both the Persian Gulf area and in North-East Asia. He demanded that U.S. Armed Forces, in order to adapt to the strategic requirements, stress improving four combat capabilities: rapid deployment logistics, battlefield information, precision strike, and flexibility.

The collapse of the Soviet Union and the disintegration of the "Warsaw Treaty" group made the military security of the NATO nations, especially those countries in Western Europe, move eastward hundreds, or even thousands of miles. The strategic warning time has increased from a few days to a few weeks or a few months. The United States and the Western countries have won "strategic depth" in time and space, which has laid the objective foundation for strategic changes. Owing to Russia's and other Warsaw Treaty nations' partnerships with the United States and other western countries, the NATO nations have determined to change their "tactical reaction" policy to "crisis management" policy, and their combat focus from "battlefront defense" to "all position defense." NATO countries clearly want to improve their ability to avoid conflicts and to get well prepared for any military action within their region.

Russia and Ukraine within the CIS have also put forward new theories on military and security ideas. The first important target of military strategy is border disputes. They stress that military forces should be able eliminate regional wars and armed conflicts within a short period of time.

The United States and NATO nations, for the sake of their own security, have one after another changed their military strategy to strengthen their ability to control and interfer in Third World countries. Thus, it has pushed Third World countries, for their own interest and national security, to change their military strategy in order to strengthen their national defense forces and their ability to prevent regional wars.

Reducing Expenditures, Improving Quality

In order to meet the needs of their new military strategies, the United States and Western countries have, on a big scale, reduced military expenditures, reduced the number of military personnel, changed the system structure, reformed military exercises, improved the quality of life for service personnel, developed military technology, and improved quality. Many Third World countries have, based on their own countries' situation and military strategy, reduced the number of armed forces to improve the quality and strengthen their defense capability.

Reducing Defense Spending in Developed Countries

Since coming to office, President Clinton has emphasized cutting defense spending. In the 1990s, apart from defense spending for the Persian Gulf War in 1991, all military expenses, including their ratio to government expenses and the gross national product, have decreased. Defense spending for each fiscal year was as follows: in 1990, $291.4 billion; in 1992, $273.8 billion; in 1993, $277.9 billion—all of which, respectively, were, as a percentage of government expenses and gross national product, 26.98 and 5.33, 19.6 and 4.7, and 19.2, and 4.3 percent. The Clinton administration planned to reduce defense spending by $100 billion from fiscal year 1993 to 1997, and maintain the defense budget at $210.0 billion in fiscal 1997, which would account for 3 percent of the gross national product, the lowest since 1939. Apparently, the Clinton administration was criticized by the military and political circles for its wide-scale reduction in defense spending. Secretary of Defense Cheney assumed that reducing defense spending and the promise of expanding security were contradictory to each other and would weaken the U.S. Armed Forces. Recently, due to pressure from the Republicans who won the mid-term election in Congress, Mr. Clinton could do nothing but promise to increase the defense budget by $26.0 billion in the next 6 years.

Since 1991, Western countries have taken measures to reduce defense spending; in Britain, the defense budget was 24.0 billion pounds ($40 billion) in 1992. If the inflation rate was deducted, actual defense spending decreased by 2 percent, when compared to 1991. In 1993, spending decreased from 4 percent to 3.4 percent of the GDP, while in 1995, it decreased to 3 percent. In France, the defense budget in 1992 was 195.0 billion francs ($37 billion). It took up, respectively, 14.8 and 3.26 percent of government expenses and the gross national product. Actual defense costs decreased 2.3 percent, compared to 1991, taking into account the inflation rate. In Germany, the defense budget in fiscal 1992 was DM52.1 billion ($32.5 billion), which took up 12.3 percent of the federal government budget and represented a 0.8 percent decrease from the previous fiscal year. Beginning in 1993, Germany cut DM1.5 billion every year, a decrease of 3 percent. In Italy, the 1992 defense budget was L26,560.2 billion ($22 billion), which, when taking into account the inflation rate, was in fact a reduction in actual spending. In Japan, defense spending remains the same, 1 percent of the gross national product.

Contrary to defense budget trends in the United States and Western countries, some Third World countries have increased defense spending with the development of their economies, in order to strengthen their national defense. For example, South Korea established the strategy of "Self Defense." In 1990, it spent about $9 billion for defense, which took up 5 percent of its gross national product. In 1991, it spent $10.1 billion, an increase of 9 percent over fiscal year 1990. Between 1990 and 1995, South Korea planned to spend $240.3 billion for research on weapons and equipment. In the early 1990s, the increasing rate of defense spending in ASEAN countries was between 5 and 10 percent. For instance, in Indonesia, compared to the previous fiscal year, defense spending in fiscal year 1991 increased by 10 percent; in Malaysia, 15 percent; in Singapore, 29 percent; in Thailand, 20 percent. These countries made efforts to modernize weapons and equipment to strengthen their navies and air forces. There is also a trend of increased defense budgets in Middle-East and Persian Gulf countries. In Saudi Arabia, the defense budget increased $800 million over the previous fiscal year. Kuwait planned to spend as much as $5 billion to purchase weapons and equipment. In 1992, the defense budgets of Iran, Syria, and Turkey increased, respectively, by 17, 16, and 8 percent over the previous fiscal year. Israel increased its defense budget by $300 million, regardless of the economic depression and the reduction of government financial expenses.

Improving Quality, Reducing Armed Force Quantity

In order to meet the needs of new military strategy changes, the United States and Western countries have all done research and developed guidelines and programs to strengthen military quality. The United States has worked out "The Concept for the Development of Three Services by 2000" and "The Plan for Developing National Defense by 2000." In its 1993 Department of Defense Annual Report, the United States declared that its armed forces will be of high quality and well-trained, have multiple capabilities in fighting, and be able to be sent worldwide quickly and defeat all opponents, quickly reacting to all kinds of critical situations. In order to meet these requirements, the U.S. Army, Navy and Air Force all have developed strategic guidelines. The U.S. Army put forward a new concept to build a new 21st-century army that can be dispatched quickly all over the world; the U.S. Navy proposed to carry out the strategic idea of "from the sea to the ground" to guide the Navy buildup; and the U.S. Air Force voiced its strategic theory on "global flexibility for global combat" as part of its plan for air force construction.

In January 1993, after his inauguration, President Clinton decided to further U.S. Armed Forces simplification. The plan requires reducing the current armed forces from 2,100,000 in 1990 to 1,400,000 in 1997; the commanding headquarters from 10 to 8; Army forces from 18 divisions to 10; navy warships from 547 to 340; aircraft carriers from 14 to 10; the Marine Corps from 194,000 to 159,000 troops; and air force wings from 24 to 10. As for strategic nuclear power, the United States has reduced international ballistic missiles from 1,000 to 500, strategic bombers from 295 to 176, and strategic missile submarines from 33 to 18. By the beginning of the 21st century, it is predicted that the United States will have reduced strategic nuclear warheads from 120,000 to 3,500.

The Western countries and some developing countries, according to their own needs for military strategy, have reduced their armed forces, built rapid response armies, and strengthened the quality of their armed forces. The "British Defense in the 90s" indicates clearly the importance of improving the quality of the armed forces and made it the first priority of their armed forces restructuring. By the mid-1990s, the British Armed Forces will be reduced from 308,000 (in 1992) to 246,000. Meanwhile, Britain will expand its rapid response force and improve its rapid response ability, and plans to create one tank division, one division with light equipment, and one combined mobile air force division to form a main force for NATO. France has put forth "Plans for the Army in 2000" and "Military Equipment Plan for 1990-1993," under which strengthening combat capability is a priority of army restructuring and a rapid response army consisting of five special divisions (47,000 troops) has been created. The German "White Paper on National Defense," Japan's "Developing Plan for Defense Force in Mid 1991-1995," and the Netherlands's "1993 National Defense White Paper" have all indicated clearly the principles and the scope for reducing troops and promote rapid response forces. Many developing countries, too, have emphasized reducing quantity but improving quality.

Improving Weapons and Equipment

The Americans believe that the key to a deterrent force lies in technological advantage during peacetime. While reducing troop numbers and defense spending, U.S. Armed Forces emphasized improving military personnel living standards and developing technology for weapons and equipment. In order to retain the advantage in military technology in the next century, the U.S. Defense Department put forward in 1990 the program on key technology exploration. It includes the following seven fields: global reconnaissance and telecommunication, accurate strike, air superiority and defense, marine control and submarine superiority, advanced combat vehicles on the ground, computers and electronic equipment, software engineering, etc. Meanwhile, the United States used a large portion of its military budget to expand the exploration of military technology. In fiscal year 1993, with the reduction of military expenditure by a big margin, the United States still spent $33.8 billion on the research of technical equipment for modern weapons, which was $1.8 billion more than the previous fiscal year. By the end of this century, the U.S. Armed Forces will have spent $2 billion for the development of information technology. From 1992 to 1993, the British Government's military budget was £245.4 ($46 billion), of which 37 percent was dedicated to weapons and equipment.

Some Third World countries have imported advanced weapons and equipment, especially for the navy and air force, in order to hasten modernization of weapons and equipment. Countries such as India, ASEAN nations, and some Middle East countries have spent several hundred billion dollars to purchase modern weapons and equipment.

Reforming Military Training

In its summary report on the 1991 Persian Gulf War, the United States claimed that the abstract system for high technical weapons and equipment was useless. Only well-trained troops will be able to grasp the system of high technology for arms and equipment and will keep on winning wars. Many countries assume that military training is a key measure to guarantee a high level of competence among the armed forces and is the "realization of a modern army." Therefore, they have taken the following measures:

• They stress that officers and soldiers all should have a higher level of knowledge in science and technology. In Britain, 25 percent officers and soldiers graduate from college or university. A quarter of soldiers in French troops graduate from senior high school. Germany, requires 8 months of training at the Hamburg Academy for commanders above brigade level, in addition to the standard courses of the 21-month training session.
• They require a combination of training and exercises. The French Army has made it clear that troops under the regiment level must do training in divided teams. They must spend 100 days in field training, while the regiment tactic training days must take up 45 to 60 days. In Britain and Italy, all brigades every year take part in combined services exercises. The Western European countries widely believe that the "true military academy" relies on military maneuvers. It is an all-round test of training for soldiers

in military, political, educational, psychological and physical ability.

● They stress full use of training centers and modern training equipment. In recent years, the U.S. Army has reinstituted the annual "Louisiana Maneuvers" and has set up six combat labs to develop low-cost experimental sample training systems of high efficiency in order to improve troop quality and competence. In Britain, there are three big military training centers for special battle training. In France, there are as many as 13 big training centers, where every year each regiment is able to do three military training sessions. In Denmark, there are three training centers for battalions, regiments, and artillery to have practice with live ammunition. The air force and military academies also do training there.

Disarmament and Arms Control

During the Cold War, disarmament and arms control became a mere formality. After the Cold War, there was a big improvement in disarmament and arms control. However, while troops were reduced and defense spending was cut, the threat of proliferation of weapons of mass destruction, such as nuclear, biological, and chemical weapons, appeared. While the international community was trying to control these destructive weapons, there emerged the tendency to compete in the research, development, and purchase of high-technology conventional weapons. Furthermore, the United States and other Western countries practiced a double standard for arms control, which led to a complex situation in disarmament and arms control.

The United States and the former Soviet Union were the two superpowers and also the main targets for disarmament and arms control. In 1991, the two countries reached an agreement to reduce by 30 percent their strategic nuclear weapons and to destroy their chemical weapons. In January 1993, the United States and Russia signed the U.S.-Russia SALT Two Treaty. According to the treaty requirement, by 2003, Russia and the United States would keep, respectively, 3,000 and 3,500 nuclear warheads, but they could further improve their quality, thus there still is a great threat to world peace and security. This means that although they have reduced the number of strategic nuclear weapons, Russia and the United States still have enough to threaten world peace and security. The two nations are still in a position of nuclear hegemonism.

Although these two nuclear powers have begun to reduce nuclear weapons, there still exists the crisis of proliferation of weapons of mass destruction. It is estimated that, by the end of the 1990s, there could be about nine developing countries that have nuclear weapons, over 30 countries with chemical weapons, 10 countries with biological weapons, and 20 countries with long-range missiles. If terrorists ever possessed these weapons, international order and security would become even more complicated. Thus, it has become a common goal in the world to prevent and control the proliferation of weapons of mass destruction. U.S. Secretary of Defense Aspin once claimed that the global expansion of ballistic missile technology and massive destructive arms has become the most critical and risky threat to America's safety after the Cold War. The Clinton administration has listed it as the key problem of U.S. defense strategy to be solved as soon as possible and has demanded active measures in the political, diplomatic, and military spheres to cope with the threat of proliferation of weapons of mass destruction such as nuclear, biological, and chemical weapons. Nevertheless, one must be aware that the United States and other Western countries have adopted double standards in the prevention and curbing of proliferation of weapons of mass destruction. On one hand, they have targeted their opponents, the Third World countries, with pressure and threats. On the other, they were indulgent to a few countries that favored the West.

While the United States, together with other Western countries, is trying to stop the expansion of weapons of mass destruction, they are at the same time doing their best to develop high-tech conventional weapons and have sold a large quantity of modern arms and equipment to Third World countries. In its 1995-1999 national defense plan, the United States decided to develop F-22 invisible combat aircraft, "Patriot" modern anti-aircraft missiles, ammunition for accurate guided missiles, and weapons of high technology like electronics warfare systems. Japan, working together with the United States, will carry out the plan for tactical missiles, import the E-2C air warning devices and command aircraft, and speed up the research on FSX fighter. Russia plans to equip the MG 29B fighter, the C-300 antiaircraft missile, and modern warships with electronics warfare systems and other weapons of high technology. At the same time, some

Middle East countries have, since the Persian Gulf War, imported from the United States and other Western countries weapons and equipment at an expense of over $30 billion. By 1995, it could be as much as $54.6 billion, and if spending on training and maintenance is added, it could be $127.4 billion. The ASEAN countries also have spent a lot to purchase modern combat aircraft and warships. Statistics have shown that in 1991, the United States alone signed contracts with over 50 countries to export weapons, making a profit of as much as $9 billion; in 1992 it exceeded $10 billion, and in 1993, it reached $15.7 billion. This shows that disarmament and arms control remain a key and complicated international issue.

Developing a Regional Security Systems

Regional systems are emrging as the global strategies structure moves toward greater multipolarity. In Europe, the disintegration of the Warsaw Treaty organization put an end to the conflicts between the two big military groups. Some former Warsaw Treaty nations in Central and Eastern Europe requested membership in NATO. The United States and some Western countries tried to expand NATO to these countries. However, Russia strongly opposed it, believing that NATO would extend the strategic front toward Russian border regions, which would not be tolerable. At a recent European Security Conference, President Clinton and President Yeltsin had a tit-for-tat argument. President Clinton insisted NATO should expand eastward, while President Yeltsin asserted that it would be absolutely impossible for the United States to dominate Europe and the whole world. New internal problems have constantly emerged in the United States and Western countries. First, the West European Union (WEU) went from a "military forum" to an actual European defense organization. In December 1991, at the conference held in Maastricht, the European Economic Community declared that the West European Alliance was part of the European political alliance, and was a liaison institution between the European Community and NATO. On November 1, 1993, the European Community started to carry out the "European Alliance Treaty." According to the regulations of the treaty, the European Community would work out a common strategy on security, foreign affairs and defense. Meanwhile, France, Germany, and Belgium have organized both European regiment headquarters and European troops to be commanded by the West European Alliance. The European Security Council, which was involved in security talks among Western countries, the former Soviet Union, and Eastern European countries, became an institution for mutual trust and security, disarmament negotiation, cooperation, and conflict adjustment. In Europe, there is a security structure consisting of NATO, EC, WEA, and CSCE (which has changed its name to European Security and Cooperation Organization). The conflict for domination between the United States and European countries is getting more and more tense. Germany has dared to say "No" to America. France and Britain are strongly dissatisfied with America's lifting of the arms embargo in Bosnia. Italy refused to cooperate with America's armed interference in Somalia. At a conference of CSCE, French President Mitterrand was clearly against America's proposal of NATO's expansion towards Eastern Europe. On November 18, 1994, the leaders of France and Britain met in Paris, making a decision to set up the "French-British Air Force" and the "United Council for French-British Air Force." The two nations reached an agreement on future European defense, bilateral military cooperation, and resolving the conflicts in Bosnia.

At the same time, the Asia-Pacific region also plans to set up new a system for security and has put it on the agenda. According to the new situation of stability and economic development in the Asia Pacific region, some countries in the Asia-Pacific region have proposed new proposals for a bilateral or multilateral security system. During his visit to South Korea in 1992, President Yeltsin suggested building a "multilateral negotiation system" and a "Reconciliation Center for Conflicts," for the purpose of coordinating security and cooperation in the Asia Pacific region. In July 1993, the Clinton administration proposed the founding of a "New Asia Pacific Community." Yet, based on the current security system, Japan insisted on developing a multilateral security system and taking a "double track." The ASEAN countries, according to the "ASEAN Regional Security Forum," advocated expanding the development of a security system so that Asia Pacific countries could participate. In October 1994, the ASEAN countries held the second summit conference in Bogor, Indonesia, and issued the "Bogor Declaration." They had talks and consultations on economic cooperation and security in the Asian-Pacific region. Some countries in the Asian-Pacific region criticized and resisted the so-called American democracy and human rights. No doubt, this is a challenge to America's attempt to retain a dominant position by setting up a new political and economic system in the Asian-Pacific region.

In addition, great changes have taken place in regions of the Middle East, Africa, and the Americas, in the   political economic cooperation organizations, and in the systems of security cooperation and dialogue. For example, the North American Free Trade Zone was founded on January 1, 1994, followed by the Summit Conference of American States. This will certainly push forward the political and economic development and the social stability in the regions and countries in the Americas.

Regional Wars and Armed Conflicts

After the end of the bipolar system, the countries and people in some regions of the world, which used to be under the control of the two superpowers and suffered a lot in the wars of the passed decades, had a strong desire to put an end to the conflicts and tensions. With the support of the United Nations and the international community, there has been a tendency by means of peaceful negotiations to end domestic fights and resolve the disputes among countries, with some successful results. South Africa ended its racial government and realized national reconciliation; in the 1994 election, Mr. Mandela was elected president. In Namibia, Mozambique, and Angola, cease- fires were achieved one after another, and national elections or negotiations were held. In the Middle East, Arab nations and Israel reopened peaceful negotiations in Oslo, Norway, in 1991; in 1993, Palestine and Israel reached an agreement that the Palestinians could have autonomy in the Gaza and Jericho regions; in 1994, Palestine and Israel signed a formal autonomy communique in Cairo. Afterward, Jordan and Israel issued the "Washington Declaration" to normalize the two countries' relations, endingd the 46-year-old confrontation. The great improvements in the Middle East peace process will definitely push forward the peace progress between Syria and Israel, and between Lebanon and Israel. In Asia, the Soviet Union withdrew from Afghanistan, Vietnam withdrew from Cambodia, and all the conflicting parties in Cambodia held elections on time to build up their homeland. Historical experiences show that the disputes among nations should be resolved by means of peaceful negotiations, which is the only and best way to solve problems.

On the other hand, with the collapse of the Soviet Union, the balance of power was lost. In the past, there was a big confrontation between the two superpowers, the two giant military groups, and the two kinds of social ideology. Some national and ethnic conflicts, factional disputes and territory issues did not break out. But with the loss of the balance of power, the confrontations became more and more tense. In the end, a series of internal wars and conflicts broke out among countries. In Europe, in the once-peaceful Balkan region, war broke out in Yugoslavia and Bosnia. In some independent countries and regions, wars and conflicts happened frequently. In the Persian Gulf region, Iraq invaded Kuwait, which aroused the indignation of peace-loving people of the world and led to the Persian Gulf War, a joint effort of allied countries headed by the United States. This was the most massive and costly regional war since WWII and used a large quantity of high-tech arms and equipment. In Africa and America, some regional wars and conflicts also occurred. According to rough statistics, in 1993 there were 32 regional wars and conflicts in the world, of which 12 were continuations from 1992. Of these wars and conflicts, 10 were in the former Soviet Union, 3 in the Balkans, 3 in the Middle East, 7 in Africa, 1 in Latin America and 1 in Asia. This shows that past conflict regions were in Asia, Africa, and Latin America. Today, Europe and the former Soviet Union have become battle fields where wars and conflicts occur frequently. In 1994, there were 39 regional wars and armed conflicts in the world (a little more than that in 1993), among which 26 were extended from 1993 and 13 were new ones. At present, 24 have ended and 15 are still going on.

More U.N. Peacekeeping Activities and Interference by the West

After the end of Cold War, the United Nations played an important role in peacekeeping. This has greatly pushed conflicting sides to cease military activity for peaceful negotiation. Figures showed that in the past four decades, from the founding of the United Nations to 1988, the United Nations had participated in peacekeeping activities 16 times; however, from 1989 to 1994, the United Nations directed peacekeeping activities 18 times. The areas covered Asia, Africa, Middle-East and Europe. For 17 activities, over 70 countries were involved; there were over 2,000 military observers, and Blue Helmet troops numbered over 73,000. It cost dearly; in 1994, $3.6 billion was spent.

U.N. peacekeeping activities benefit the conflicting sides by promoting more talks and fewer conflicts. But at the same time, it means new interference from the Unites States and other Western countries. Some of their doings have the tint of hegemonism and power politics. They have advocated the theory that "Domestic wars are not internal politics, human rights are above sovereignty." They interfere in other countries' internal affairs in the name of "democracy, reform" and "human rights." They have imposed their "human rights" concept on people in other countries, and sent out troops at will under the name of "defending peace," to overthrow governments, to set up no-fly zones and "safe areas," and to arrest the leaders of opponent forces. All these activities have caused uneasiness among Third World countries.

FUTURE MILITARY TRENDS

Gao Heng

After the end of the Cold War, the focus of the major countries in the world turned from military confrontation using nuclear weapons to power confrontation of allied countries. However, the constant increase in military forces remains a constant historical trend. Thus, people are studying seriously the many new characteristics in the world military situation.

Troop Building

World war became less possible after the Cold War ended. Though frequent regional wars occur, the world's major countries do not get involved in them. They seek better quality in military equipment rather than quantity in defense spending. America has further cut its military spending and reduced troops. For instance, in 1990, its defense spending was $301.6 billion; in 1991, it was $297.2 billion; in 1992, it was $295 billion; in 1993, it was $293.5 billion; in 1994, it was $263.4 billion. It is expected to be even less in 1995. From 1993 to 1998, the Americans will reduce military spending abroad by $60 billion. Russia has done the same; it has been reducing its troops

Gao Heng is a Research Fellow at the Institute of World Economics and Politics, Academy of Social Science, Beijing. This article is from World Economics and Politics, *no. 2 (1995).*

and military spending for years and will further cut its military expense. For example, in 1994, military orders were reduced by 70 percent, and programs for military scientific research were reduced by 40 percent. From 1988 to 1992, Russia reduced military troops by 40 percent. From 1992 to 1993, it reduced navy warships from 548 to 460; by 2000 warships are expected to number only 300. In 1994, Russia's military expenditure was $29 billion. Between 1993 and 1994, Russian troops were cut by 600,000, down to a total of 2,200,000; by 1996 they will be 1,900,000. In comparison to the United States and Russia, Britain, France, and Japan have made fewer reductions. In Japan, since 1990 defense spending increased from 0.9 to 6.11 percent. Owing to personnel expense, which took up 42 percent of military spending, and the high cost of consumer items, there has not been much reduction in the defense budget.

Troop cuts and reduced defense spending do not reflect the whole situation regarding the troop structure of a country. In fact, these reductions emphasize concentration on "quality in force development." For example, under the new conditions, the Americans have put more effort into equipping troops with high technology and stressing tactics to deal with regional wars. Regarding missiles, they pay more attention to building regional defense. In general, the United States cares much more about rapid response ability. Awakened by the Persian Gulf War, some small countries (i.e., ASEAN members) have actively followed examples of the world's major countries by stressing "quality in force development."

Preparing for War in Depth

"Preparing for war in depth" is the basis of the "Grand Strategy" system. After the Cold War ended, the world's major countries took this principle more seriously than ever. What they have done specifically is to develop troops, arms, and high-tech equipment. The United States and other Western countries have formally put off (or given up) the strategic programs planned during the Cold War for a strategic defense initiative and space stations. They have worked out a strategic program for the "information highway." No doubt, this is a great part of preparing for war in depth. It is a major revolution in military affairs regardless of its speed. Facts will show that the whole globe could become a unified battle field. Traditional arms and equipment (intercontinental missiles, planes, warships and tanks) will become information weapons. There will be no border between armed forces and people; war's effects will be more focused. Thus, the major countries in the world have put every effort into carrying out the plan. We can say that almost every field related to comprehensive national power is linked closely to "preparing for war in depth."

Regional Wars

After the Cold War, there was less possibility of wars among the world's great powers and they stressed a unified defense and the curbing of regional wars. The Persian Gulf war was an example. In recent years, U.S. strategy has been to fight two regional wars at the same time. It worked with Japan and other countries to plan a "regional missile defense system." In Western Europe, the Americans tried to reform NATO to help deal with Bosnia. It also cooperated with ASEAN countries in order to better handle future wars in the South China Sea. These countries would do their best to make their actions legal, behind the front of the Security Council. The United States and other major countries would then gain the authorization of the Security Council (e.g., setting up no-fly zones in Iraq). It is a fact that at present, Western countries have won great strategic power by acting behind the front of "peacekeeping activities."

Regional Wars

After the end of the Cold War, the conflicts once constrained by the U.S.-Soviet standoff were exposed. The cause of the regional wars lies in historical grievances, national conflicts, factional and territorial disputes, power seeking, outside penetration, resources scrambling, economic friction, and arms expansion. In recent years, regional wars took place frequently and the number of wars increased. Potential hot-spots became actual hot-spots. The areas of regional wars shifted. Before and immediately after the end of the Cold War, the Middle Eastern, African, and Asian-Pacific areas were conflict sites. In recent years, however, there has been great improvement in the Middle East peace process. Bilateral relations improved greatly between Palestine and Israel, between Jordan and Israel and between Syria and Israel. The Iraq-Kuwait conflict was resolved on a political track (Iraq has officially recognized Kuwait's sovereignty and the Iraq-Kuwait border line). Wars still exist in Africa (Rwanda and Somali), yet the number of wars has been reduced. In Asian-Pacific areas, regional wars (internal wars in India-Pakistan and Cambodia) are under control. To compare with the above mentioned areas, Bosnia and southern Caucasus have become sites of conflict. This shift shows that conflicts have intensified, and penetration from outside has strengthened. This has become a trend requiring special attention.

High-Tech Regional Wars

When the Cold War ended, high-tech regional wars became an important phenomenon. In recent years, the technology used in regional wars has increased. The military strategy focus of the great powers is on long-range deployment and unified systems of "air, ground, and navy forces." To realize the goal, the armed forces must turn their "mechanization" into "information." The United States has, in order to realize this great goal, reduced its troop size and defense budget. It has concentrated on high technology in regional wars, on building "digital troops," "digital battle fields," and "digital war," which has become the key goal of the U.S. military. "To make full use of experimental technology" has become a keynote in American force development.

Crisis Management

With the end of the Cold War, the major powers entered the period of domestic economic, political, and military adjustments. They adopted a policy of indirect involvement to handle regional conflicts and wars, except the Persian Gulf War. If it was an emerging situation, they used "crisis management policies." In Haiti, Korea, Iraq (in 1994), and Bosnia, the United States and related countries used this policy to win without using armed force. This means that a big country like the United States would have to maintain its joint forces to avoid lagging behind other forces, putting itself in an unfavorable position. It also means that military force serves as a "deterrent force" and supporting force in diplomacy.

Developments in Nuclear Expansion and the Arms Trade

After the Cold War, some major powers, for their own benefit, reduced troop size and defense spending. Controlling defense spending has become a trend in big countries. In recent years, Japan and ASEAN countries have pushed other countries (including China) to join the U.N. registration system for military equipment as early as possible, in order to improve transparency. Meanwhile, Japan and ASEAN countries have greatly increased their military budgets and replaced standard military equipment with high-technology equipment. According to Japanese calculations, the Japanese military budget has reached $45.9 billion (second after the United States). Western statistics show that Southeast Asian regions in recent years have become the second biggest arms market (after the Middle East). What's more, smuggling nuclear material has been one of the important components in nuclear proliferation. According to news from the West, Russia and Germany are key sources and transmission stations for nuclear proliferation. Some medium-size and small countries have obtained nuclear materials and technology via these sources. Facts proved that there exists simultaneously the phenomena of major powers reducing defense spending while some medium-size and small countries cause more instability and unpredictable problems in the world.

U.S.-Russia Military Relations

Since the end of the Cold War, the United States and Russia have established a "strategic partnership." In the past couple of years, because of changes in Russia, more complicated problems emerged in U.S.-Russian relations:

● Conflicts occurred between the United States and Russia because of Middle Eastern and European countries' membership in NATO. The Russian Government worried about the security in the western part of its country being threatened. In fact, the United States and Russia were in a hostile situation over the issue of the former Yugoslavia. In February 1994, the Russian Government sent peacekeeping troops.

- The United States and Russia had tense disputes on the issue of peacekeeping in former Soviet Union regions. The Russian Government claimed that it would turn the independent parts into a unified economy of high technology and a politically cooperative regional organization within a short time. The Russian Government also requested recognition by the West of its special responsibility for peacekeeping in the east part of the former Soviet Union. However, the United States and the West worried that it would bring danger to the security of American strategic regions and the West if Russia becomes a Russian Empire. U.S. officials once declared, "The U.S. Government will use every means for the prevention of the worst situation happening in Russia."

- The United States and Russia have never stopped their power seeking in the Middle East. In the past 2 years, Russia not only restored its weapon supplies to Syria, but ignored Iraq's arms smuggling. In October 1994, Russia openly criticized American military action of deploying forces. In addition, the United States and Russia have had both open strife and veiled struggle. American officials have said that there still exists danger from Russia and aggressive nationalism will inevitably appear. In November 1994, President Yeltsin pointed out that the United States would be tough toward Russia in its foreign affairs strategy and military affairs, and that it is possible for both to get involved in military conflicts.

Owing to all kinds of problems in the world, the major powers will continue their changes of strategy at home and abroad. There will be great change in military strategy, too. The following trends will emerge in world military strategy:

- *The Situation of "No Big Wars, Constant Small Wars" Will Continue.* After the Cold War, the world situation became that of "one superpower is getting stronger and stronger." However, the United States will fail to dominate the world. Its power to control and support world affairs will weaken. Especially under the circumstances of tense competition among the allied countries, the chances of using military means is greatly reduced. This means that it is impossible for the United States to launch a major war. With the collapse of the Soviet Union, in the next 10 to 15 years, there will not be another superpower hostile toward the United States.

Even if Russia becomes stronger, it will not be as powerful as the former Soviet Union, because a multipolarized pattern will control U.S.-Russia military options.

It is different for small wars; these will occur frequently. Especially in the Balkans, Caucasus, and Africa, small wars will not cease. In the coming years, small wars will increasingly occur. It is estimated that in the mid-1990s, small wars will break out from time to time. By 2000, the number of small wars may decrease. In Central and South Asia, which surround China, small wars will never stop. In some regions, hostilities will be reopen. Of course, it is possible that some potential hotspots (e.g., the South China Sea) could become real hotspots. In areas like Central and Latin America, small wars will exist constantly.

● *The Major Powers Will Keep on Exporting Military Arms.* After the Cold War, the major powers followed the strategy of "Quality in Building Armies." Thus, in order to save money and replace military equipment, they exported military equipment and arms. The United States, taking advantage of the Persian Gulf War, sold large quantities of arms to Middle Eastern and Southeast Asian countries. The Russians have increased arms exports to relieve economic difficulties. After his return from visiting India, President Yeltsin sped up arms and military technology exports to India and Pakistan. Britain, France, Germany, and Italy, not wanting to fall behind, followed the same course. The reasoning behind this strategy is, to build quality arms, compensation must come from arms exportation. Controlling Third World wars and turbulence requires arms. To develop their economies, they need to accumulate money by means of exporting arms. To develop their own high technology they must export arms. In terms of arms market growth, the Middle East market is shrinking, the Southeast Asia arms market is getting saturated, and the Balkan market is expanding.

● *The Cry for Strengthening the U.N. "Peacekeeping System."* After the Cold War, there were frequent regional wars and conflicts in the world. In order to stabilize the situation, a secure system was needed. During the Cold War, the world situation was controlled mainly by the United States and the Soviet Union, but afterward a different system needed to be worked out. Owing to the development of the world multipolarized pattern, the United

Nations took the historical responsibility. In fact, the United Nations was playing such a role already. U.N. peacekeeping troops were active in Cambodia, the Persian Gulf, the Caucasus, Somali, Rwanda, and Bosnia. However, such peacekeeping usually runs against the disposition of the U.N. Security Council and has had negative effects. In order to change this, some countries have proposed to set up U.N. regular rapid response troops. Surely this will cause more conflict and friction, but it is fair to organize such forces under the United Nations, which would be easily accepted by most countries. Thus, in the future, there will be a rising cry to strengthen U.N. peacekeeping missions, which will produce more historical chances for establishing international order.

• *A More Complicated Situation in U.S.-Russian Nuclear Disarmament.* After the Cold War, the United States and Russia reached agreements on nuclear arms control. Facts have shown that both sides have done a lot of preparatory work. However, new problems emerged because of big changes in Russia's foreign strategy. Here is what the Russians have done: Russia wants to use its nuclear arms to regain its position as a superpower, and Russian officials requested a review of the U.S.-Russian agreements on nuclear weapons. In May 1994, the Russian Ministry of Foreign Affairs admitted that Russian foreign policy has turned away from unilaterally favoring the West. Instead, Russia proposes to carry out a flexible policy of balance among different power centers to form a balance of power beneficial to Russia. On the U.S. side, the Republicans won a dominant position in both the House and Senate in the mid-term elections. The Americans suggested a "tougher policy" toward the Russians. This will make a more complicated situation in U.S.-Russian military relations. No doubt, it also includes the issue of whether the agreement of both sides on nuclear reductions will be completely fulfilled.

• *There Will be Indirect "Military Conflict" Between Russia and the United States over Middle and Eastern Europe.* After the end of the Cold War, Middle and Eastern Europe became places where Russia and the CIS were fighting for power. America did not weaken NATO because of the disintegration of the Soviet Union and the Warsaw Treaty; on the contrary, it wants to extend NATO's reach. In June 1994, during his visit to Europe, President Clinton claimed that NATO would, should, and will be expanded next year. There are two phases to this: First, NATO's range of operations would expand to the Middle East, and second, the countries in Middle and Eastern Europe would join NATO. Based on this, Russian officials claimed that because of the change in the military balance of the Warsaw Treaty, much attention should be paid to Russia's ideas. Extension of NATO is anti-Russian hysteria. In Russia's view, the three countries of the Baltic Sea were beyond its control. However, it wants to control the former Soviet republics. It requested that the West offer it "special power" so as to carry out peacekeeping policy in the former Soviet Union and Eastern Europe, saying that it is a trial for NATO. Because of this, Russia slowed its military withdrawal from Eastern Europe and its nuclear reductions. But it hastened the military unification in the former Soviet republics. This means that Russia will not give in on military issues, but will start to build a new "defense line" that will be in a position of "military confrontation" with the Americans. Yet, such a confrontation would be limited and indirect and would not be the same as during the Cold War. Nevertheless, the confrontation will not easily change.

- *Japan Will Complete Its "Preparation" for Becoming a Military Superpower.* After the Cold War, Japan was in an international security situation that had been greatly changed. Under such circumstances, Japan was not satisfied with the situation of being a "big economic country, small political country, and tiny military country." But, because of pressure from home and abroad, Japan dared not to voice publicly its goal of becoming a "military superpower." It wants to be an "international superpower," i.e., a political superpower. In recent years, Japan requested to become a permanent member state of U.N. Security Council, in order to play the role of a political superpower. A review of Japan's activities in the past decades needs serious investigation and forecasting. According to Japanese officials, the following points were assured:

-Japan possesses nuclear fuels and technology to produce 1,000 to 2,000 atom bombs. Recently, Japan imported a large quantity of nuclear materials.

-Japan can make intercontinental missiles (it successfully launched the H2 rocket).

-The Japanese Navy is on the top of the list for its capability in East Asia, and it is developing its sea-battle ability.

-The Japanese Government has in fact given up its "three nonnuclear principles" (to allow the presence of American nuclear forces) and the policy of "defense on its own land."

-Japan has trampled on its Peace Constitution and passed a new law authorizing a Japanese military role in peacekeeping operations.

-Japan is second in defense spending, after the United States.

-The Japanese Government advocates "new nationalism" and is preparing to become a military superpower. In general, Japan could within a few months be a nuclear superpower if the Japanese Government made the political decision. Surely, Japan more completely carry out its "preparations."

● *There Will Be a Big Gap in the Military Capability Between China and Other Relevant Countries, and China Will Face a Big Challenge.* After the Cold War, China faced a less severe military threat from the major powers. But, in the future, the gap between China and other major powers will be wider. This is because:

-China's military expenditure per capita is extremely low, and it is sharply different from that of major powers and would not be able to be solved within a short period of time.

-China's high-tech military equipment is still in the embryonic stage and will not support military forces.

-Chinese soldiers' educational level cannot meet the needs of modern war; this cannot be resolved quickly. According to a report from the West, in terms of "quality" in nuclear weapons and regular weapons, India, ASEAN countries, Taiwan, Japan, Russia, and the United States are superior to China. Such a "quality gap" is expanding rapidly. Thus, China is facing a severe strategic issue that needs to be dealt with seriously.

FUTURE SECURITY TRENDS IN THE ASIAN-PACIFIC REGION

Senior Colonel Yao Youzhi
Colonel Liu Hongsong

The Asian-Pacific region is an important area in international society. After the collapse of the polarized patterns and the Cold War, its strategic position rose greatly. Compared to other regions in the world, the current security situation in the Asia-Pacific region is relatively stable. During the Cold War, most of the countries in the Asian-Pacific region did not deeply get involved in the conflicts between the two blocs of the East and West. Thus, after the Cold War, the relative strength was kept in balance in the Asian-Pacific region. Most of the countries carry out the policies of peace, neutrality, and nonalignment. In the past decades, these countries have concentrated on economic development and followed the policy that economic development promotes political stability, and that political stability protects economic development. However, because of many unresolved historical problems in the Asian-Pacific region, there are a lot of crisscross contradictions and various potential crises. The unbalance and diversity in politics, economics, military, and culture have caused uncertainty in security development and have led to a complex situation in Asian-Pacific security.

Senior Col. Yao Youzhi and Colonel Liu Hongsong work in the Strategy Department of the Academy of Military Science, Beijing. Their essay comes from China Military Science *(Spring 1994).*

Self-Reliance to Deal with Outside Threats

Owing to historical reasons, there exist internal contradictions and conflicts in many Asian-Pacific countries. In order to maintain the countries' unification and social stability, some Asian-Pacific countries' security policy has long been focused on the management of the internal security environment. With the collapse of the polarized blocs, military adjustments by America and Russia, the rapid development of the economies in the Asian-Pacific region, as well as increased modernization, these Asian-Pacific countries have turned their focus from internal security to external defense. They will mainly rely on self-defense and an allied defense to maintain the countries' security and regional peace and stability. During the Cold War, the ASEAN countries relied on America for protection, while the Indochina countries, headed by Vietnam, were aided by the former Soviet Union in defense and economics. Now, after the Cold War, these countries will rely on self-defense and maintain security themselves. As a result, some countries have focused on self-reliance to maintain security and to cope with outside threats. In the 1970s, the military defense in ASEAN countries was mainly used to deal with guerrilla forces that fought against the governments. For a while, guerrilla activities lessened or were suppressed. Then there were changes in international and regional situations, which caused the ASEAN countries to concentrate on outside threats and modern wars instead of internal rebellions.

A Focus on Security and Development

During the Cold War, the confrontation between the two political and military blocs, America and the Soviet Union, was caused by differing ideological and political systems. After the Cold War, the two blocs' ideological conflicts were eliminated.

At present, in view of the development of the new world political situation, the Western countries no longer concentrate on resisting socialism, because the socialist movement is at low ebb and not a threat to the West.

The change in the ideological disputes among the countries led to the change in international patterns from regional politics to regional economics. During the Cold War, regional economic groups were divided based on each countries' social and political system. The economic and trading relations among countries of different social systems were controlled by political relations. Many regional economic groups have the characteristic of common security. ASEAN was set up during the Cold War to meet the needs of politics and security. With the elimination of the confrontation between East and West, regional economic groups started to be gradually indifferent to ideology. Many Asian-Pacific countries, in order to deal with the new international situation, gave up the fight over ideology and made adjustments in their internal and external policies, focusing on their own peace and development. Some countries have even reformed their political system.

The development of regional economic groups, however, has caused conflicts based on security and development. In the competition of fundamental interests, Japan is the number one opponent of the United States. The contradictions between America and Japan will be more serious in the future.

Security Benefits in Politics, Economics, and the Military is Becoming More and More Obvious

After the Cold War, international relations focused on economics although the remnants of the Cold War still existed. Time passed, but the former institutions of the Cold War remained. The huge nuclear weapons warehouses and military industries still exist. It will take time to eliminate the result of widescale competition in military equipment, while regional competition in military equipment grows. America is rebuilding the patterns of Asian-Pacific defense and has fanned its military forces, which means it takes the United States as the axle, and the U.S.-Japan, U.S.-Korean, U.S.-Philippines, U.S.-Thailand, and U.S.-Australia bilateral military alliances as fan-shaped spokes that radiate U.S. military force to the whole Asian-Pacific region. Some conceptual ways of thinking and defense ideology formed during the Cold War will continue to have influence.

Nevertheless, new views on economic security have gradually become the mainstream. With the formation of the new world pattern, a new era of competition for comprehensive national power focused on economics is approaching.

During the Cold War, the range of power and the fight for interests were mainly retained by military means. Military force marked a country's international position. The phenomenon of "military giant but economic dwarf" and "economic giant but military dwarf" was the then-contradictory outcome of military and economic forces in international relations. Such a phenomenon would not exist in a time when economics dominate. Economic influence is getting more and more important for politics. In the international market, a country's strong economy will not only expand its influence, increase its profits, strengthen its internal currency and balance its international income and expense, but also will greatly improve its reputation and political position in the world. Economic competition is playing an important role, replacing the military as the dominant force in foreign relations.

Rapid developments in science and technology and the wide application of high technology in production have caused developed countries to concentrate more on internal development while they expand their capital accumulation. In turn, this pushes them to shift their competition from military and political strength to comprehensive national power and particularly economic strength. Economic factors have become important marks in judging a country's international position. In a country's general strategy, economic development plays a more important role; in regional and international relations, the regional economy plays a more important role in politics. The regional blocs have focused on economic cooperation instead of political and military cooperation, and they also stress unified security viewpoints of politics, economics, and defense rather than only those of military security.

Resistance to Western Values

Serious ethnic disputes have long existed because of historical hatreds and unbalance in politics and economics caused by colonialists. The same nation could be split into two regions or multiregions. Pushed by general support for national unification, it is possible to realize reunification. However, countries with many nationalities are having trouble with ethnic coflicts, which are very hard to settle while simultaneously maintaining unification. With the development of unbalanced politics and economics as well as outside interference, the national separatist trend will be more and more serious. The combination of nationalism, national egoism, and some countries' local chauvinism will form a trend against the general trend of world peace and prosperity.

Religious issues have become an important factor in Asian-Pacific security and conflicts. The Asian-Pacific region is one of the three big birthplaces for religion in the world, as well as the meeting place for all kinds of cultures. There exist big differences in religions and religious parties and contradictions and conflicts are hard to reconcile. In recent years, two points regarding religion aroused the world's attention: the religious unification of nations and regions, and religion's clear political intent that directly attacks the country's political power. Social upheaval caused by religious forces, interference, and conflicts is a big issue. Usually, the religious disputes mix with ethnic conflicts, which complicate and intensify the contradictions and disputes.

Yet, there are many common points in culture, especially in values and ideas, in the Asian-Pacific region. Indeed, common culture has provided prerequisite conditions for promoting regional stability and cooperation.

At the same time that Asian-Pacific countries are resisting Western values, the Oriental culture, or modern Confucian culture, has had an immense influence in promoting the unification and development of Asian-Pacific countries. The East Asian cultures, in which Chinese culture is considered the mother culture and which once experienced an ancient glorious development period, have had great influence on civilization. Today it has great appeal to modern society. In the past decade, the Singapore Government has advocated Confucian culture, for the purpose of correcting excessive egoism, utilitarianism, and hedonism and to help people overcome spiritual void. The key ideas of the oriental culture are self-reliance, trust, helping each other, harmony, honesty, and thinking of others. People believe that the rapid economic development in the Asia-Pacific region is closely related to the great influence of the Oriental culture.

Bilateral and Multilateral Understanding and Cooperation

It is a trend in international political, economic, and security development to have talks on understanding and cooperation. After the end of the global Cold War, there has been a move to set up a multilateral security system in the Asian-Pacific region. Since the

Washington Conference, held after the First World War, the Asian-Pacific countries have gone through five different historical periods during their efforts to form a collective or multilateral security system. The first period was the Japanese-American competition in the Asian-Pacific region during the first half of the 20th century. The second occurred when the two superpowers were in competion with each other. The third was when the former Soviet Union advocated the Asian Security System. The fourth was during the formation of the economic cooperation system in the Asian-Pacific region and before the Soviet Union made its strategic adjustments. The fifth is the new period, since the 1990s, when each Asian-Pacific country has wanted to create a security system. The informal talks in the Asian-Pacific Economic Cooperation Organization marked the opening of discussions on Asian-Pacific multilateral security.

The Asian-Pacific countries are seeking establishment of multilateral understanding and cooperation, which shows their comprehension of historical development; their predictions of the world's future; their eagerness for mutual economic compensation; and their desire for internal benefits. In general, a country has four reasons for wanting to create such a system:

- To make clear its own position in the security of the Asian-Pacific region in order to maintain the country's security environment
- Through collective talks and consultation on security, to realize a balance of power in the regions
- To attain rights for its own security in order to weaken multinational coordination and power patterns that are not favorable to itself
- To use multilateral forces to prevent the risk of one country or a group of countries dominating the Asian-Pacific region.

However, because of each country's interests and strategic goals in the Asia-Pacific region, complex struggles will definitely occur during the process of each country seeking multilateral understanding and cooperation in the Asian-Pacific region.

The Broad Goal for Maintaining Security

While each country is seeking economic interests and security, they are excluding and fighting each other. At the same time, they constrain each other, cooperate, reconcile, and even merge together. The contradictions that emerge during a security struggle also reflect its crisscross character (e.g., you know me well and I know you inside out).

Such circumstances make Asian-Pacific countries a unity of opposites. Many countries focus on their own benefits, actively resolve problems and conflicts, strengthen collective cooperation, and promote development of economic centralization, and regionalization. They focus more on issues about human existence and development. In national security and defense, these countries have mixed feelings about potential threats with no obvious target. Some countries have purchased weapons and equipment to expand their defense system, but they do not have a clear idea of who the enemy is. This complicated security situation is becoming more and more obvious with international economic centralization and regionalization, and the development of cooperation and political talks.

Medium-Size and Small Countries' Participation in Regional Security

At the end of the 1990s and at the beginning of the 21st century, the United States, Japan, China, and Russia will become the leading forces determining Asian-Pacific regional security. Of these countries, the Unites States is still the main player making decisions about Asian-Pacific regional security. The Clinton administration proposed an expanded strategy to change the former security policy that dealt with the Soviet global threat to one focused on regional conflicts that threaten global benefits. In its Asia-Pacific policy, the United States reemphasizes the concept of a power balance, which means maintaining military forces in the Asian-Pacific region and keeping the regional balance of power. It also re-established treaty alliance relations between the United States and Japan, Korea, Australia, Thailand, and Philippines. America considers the U.S.-Japanese alliance as the "center of stability."

The Japanese Government considers it to be a major "contribution" to security to seek political talks actively with each country in the Asian-Pacific region and to help the United States to push democracy in the Asia-Pacific region. Russia started to adjust its policy of sliding too much toward the West in late 1992 and has adopted a policy of even treatment of Europe and the Asian-Pacific region. Meanwhile, they are trying to improve relations with each Asian-Pacific country. China expands its range in foreign affairs and develops its relations with neighboring countries on the basis of the Five Principles of Peaceful Coexistence. In general, the security policy of these Asian-Pacific countries will decide the future security pattern and situation in the Asian-Pacific region.

At the same time, the medium-size and small countries in the Asian-Pacific region have also taken an active part in security affairs and have sought the right to speak on Asian-Pacific security matters. The ASEAN countries started to take a positive attitude toward dealing with regional security issues. They not only have many internal discussions on the subject but also have held talks with related countries that do not belong to ASEAN in order to improve its reputation in the region and thoroughout the world.

A Flexible Regional Security System

In the long run, difficulties and disputes will exist in the Asia-Pacific region. The ethnic confrontations and territorial disputes that are related to a country's fundamental interests will not be easily reconciled. Sharp struggles over religious, social systems, unification, and separation will remain. Nevertheless, the goal of maintaining stability in the Asia-Pacific region meets the needs of the majority of countries' interests. So the Asian-Pacific countries will unite as one to work out a flexible regional security system that will assure that countries will help each other and cooperate, but will lack an internal focus. Such a system consists of not only military security but economic security. In view of the security developments in the Asian-Pacific region, there will be a mixed, pluralized security system in this area. All kinds of security systems will be put into action, such as bilateral and multilateral, area and regional, formal and informal, etc. Compared with conflicts between the two blocs during the Cold War, the security cooperation in the Asian-Pacific region will be characterized by proaction and prediction, not simply taking action after a crisis has occurred; it will stress the overall situation, mutual relations, and future influence, especially the potential impact on human's existence, and it will be based on self-reliance, in order to maintain each country's security.

Peacefully Resolve Disputes

The development of commodity and market economies was late in many countries in the Asian-Pacific region. In recent years, the market economy has developed rapidly. The development of commodity and market economies makes Asian-Pacific countries rely on each other, which strengthens their consistency and mutual control of interests. This will be beneficial for preventing war and maintaining peace. When the commodity economy was backward, invaders gained much from war by means of violence. However, in modern times, the price of war will be much greater than anything gained from war. In such circumstances, economic development will lessen the chance of a war for economy interests. Especially in the nuclear era, the saturation of nuclear weapons becomes a threat to human existence. The disaster and terror of war force people to recognize the concept of "mutual security." As a result, with the development of international economy and market unification and expansion of each country's openness on security policy, peaceful resolution of disputes will be the first choice.

China and Security Developmentsin the Asian-Pacific Region

China occupies a very important strategic position in the Asian-Pacific region. Because of China's rapid economic development, stable political environment, flexible open-policy, and successful foreign activities, China's international reputation is getting stronger and has attracted attention from other countries in the world.

The world cannot exist without China, let alone the Asian-Pacific countries. China's economic development relies on the world. With the daily growth of the economy and expansion of the open-door policy, China, with a population of 1.2 billion, is a giant market. In addition to trade relations, China is also a very attractive market for investment. All countries, both in the West and in the Asian-Pacific region, have a chance to enter China's market. In security cooperation,

China plays an important role in diversion, self-control, and balance among the Asian-Pacific countries.

After the collapse of the Soviet Union, the triangle relation among the Unites States, the Soviet Union, and China no longer existed. In a certain sense, China's strategic position in the world was lowered. On the other hand, the disintegration of the Soviet Union made China's position in the Asian-Pacific region comparatively more important than before. This is because China's role and influence became obvious both in resolving the hot issues in the Asian-Pacific region and in economic cooperation with neighboring countries. China is a key force in maintaining the balance of power, stability, and development in the region.

Generally speaking, the security situation in the Asian-Pacific region, like international patterns, is in a transitional period. Both pre-Cold War and post-Cold War characteristics exist, but with a gradual shift toward the latter. There will be the tendency of development and reform, which reflects the transition from internal management to external defense, from unilateral defense to bilateral or multilateral defense, from sole target to wide-range target, from big countries' domination in defense to big countries' leading role and medium-size and small countries' self defense, and from hostile defense to hostility combined with talks.

The Asian-Pacific region's security is very important to world peace. In the future, through economic development, the Asian-Pacific regional security situation will be kept in balance and move in the direction of security and stability. The countries will be tolerant under a prerequisite of insisting on principles, and reach more common viewpoints and agreements. However, there is the possibility of conflicts in certain areas because of multiple and unbalanced contradictions in the Asian-Pacific region.

MANAGING CHINA'S
FUTURE SECURITY CRISES

Captain Zheng Jian

National Defense Security Crisis (NDSC) is a kind of tense political-military situation caused by external or combined internal and external hostile actions, which can endanger the national security and can even potentially lead to war. It is a special form of conflict among countries. NDSC control is a very important strategic stage in the struggle for national defense security. It is a kind of management and control mechanism for solving defense crises. Its aim has two aspects: one is to prevent a crisis from occurring, the other is to control a crisis's horizontal and vertical escalation, making every effort to limit its destructiveness and other negative influences and to end the crisis at the lowest cost and prevent the outbreak of war. Seen at a macroscopic level, NDSC control is actually a kind of strategic guidance aiming at avoiding war. With the disintegration of the Soviet Union and the end of the bipolar structure, it is possible that the threat of all-out invasion to China has been eliminated. Our security environment today is one of the best since the founding of our country. But in today's world, hegemonism and power politics still remain. There are also many historical and practical contradictions and conflicts of interests in the areas of politics, economics, military, nationality, religion, and culture between our country and some of our neighbors. In the future, some of these contradictions and interest

---

Zheng Jian is a research analyst in the Strategy Department, Academy of Military Science, Beijing. This article is excerpted from his AMS thesis.

conflicts may have the potential to cause a NDSC endangering our defense security. If an NDSC occurs in the future, there may be some of the following circumstances:

- Pluralized opponents with stronger or weaker powers than ours.
- External offensives may take place, seizing the opportunity of our internal disturbances.
- Chain reactions from many directions.
- We will face the opponents' comprehensive threats.
- Indirectly concerned countries or international organizations may manage to intervene.
- Local crisis, generally not endangering our country's overall security.
- Hard struggles may reoccur over a long period of time.

Links in Strategic Guidance

- Forecast crisis situations scientifically. This is the first important task to avoid crises. To forecast crises, we should start from our national interests, analyzing the strategic environment of the world and environment around our country; analyzing accurately the conflicts of interests in politics, economics, military, nationality, religion, and culture among our neighbors, especially the current conflicts in economics, nationality, and religion; track and analyze related countries' internal and external policies and their comprehensive powers (especially development of military power, social situations, etc.); and assess whether or not they have the ability and potential to provoke conflict. When analyzing a crisis, we should pay special attention to the analysis of potential contradictions and conflicts of interest, observing the changes in the related country's internal political situations and external policies and judging the possibility of sudden changes, so that we can take measures as soon as possible. To forecast crisis situations scientifically we need to combinr both historical and logical methods, and traditional scientific and modern scientific methods. At the present time, modern scientific methods should be emphasized. Forecasting also needs good intelligence support. The intelligence support and forecasting of an NDSC should take into account political, economical, diplomatie, and other related state security and intelligence systems. Permanent organizations are needed to forecast crisis situations.

● Stop potential internal disturbances in time to prevent opponents from utilizing them. The symptoms of disturbance must be found and stopped as soon as possible. In case disturbances break out, we should gather a dominant power to suppress them rapidly. And if they are difficult to suppress, we must contain their sphere of influence.

● Develop interdependent relationship mechanisms to contain confrontation and promote cooperation. This means to establish interdependent relations with possible opponents, or establish them to a certain degree because of the requirements of common interests in one or more areas (political, economic, military, scientific, cultural, national, and religious). Interdependent relations mean that neither of the two sides can move without the other. If this happens, the interdependent countries' interests regarding existence and development will be harmed and sometimes, this harm can even be fatal to one or all sides.

The concrete measures we can choose in developing interdependent mechanisms are as follows:

-Politically, participate selectively in the process of world and regional political integration.

-Economically, participate selectively in the process of world and regional economi integration.

-Militarily and securitywise, participate selectively in international and regional security mechanisms. Reject military alliances directed against our country. Cooperate with countries, including some potential opponents in order to cope with the common security threat.

-Scientifically and culturally, exchange science and technology developments.

-Develop multilateral security relations and maintain the balance of world strategic powers in order to restrict possible opponents.

● Relax relations and soften contradictions in order to establish the confident international mechanisms:

-Enhance links and exchanges with possible opponents. The key principle behind these actions is to promote confidence, understanding, and good will and eliminate misunderstanding. Especially with information sent to the other side, it must have a certain degree of believability. Possible concrete measures include setting up a "hot line" with possible opponents, finding stable mechanisms of exchange and consultation with the possible opponent, and raising the transparency of sensitive problems concerning national defense.

-Keep effective control over military elements. Almost all theories of crisis control emphasize this point. The military elements here mean mainly the construction, movement, and deployment of the army, the significant actions of the army, the introduction of important thoughts and views, and military actions concerning foreign affairs.

-Handle disputes with possible opponents with principle and flexibility and strive for a peaceful solution. When handling disputes, we should take a longer and wider view. Regarding problems that are of significant concern to our national interest, such as sovereignty, we must make no concessions; this is a principle that cannot be forsaken. But in the handling of concrete problems, we can have some flexibility. The basic train of thought is to analyze the disputes layer by layer, avoiding the differences on the principle layer, to find common interests. Then, making this the base, both sides should make necessary concessions to change the conflict into cooperation and settle disputes at least temporarily and maybe even forever. In this way, the contradictions between possible opponents and us may be relaxed, and confidence and understanding may be promoted, avoiding a crisis. There are three points to be made. The first one is to avoid a policy of appeasement. The second is to avoid increasing passivity and for us to solve disputes in the future. The last is that we should consider the theory that handling disputes with principle and flexibility is not only a temporary way to increase confidence and avoid crisis, but is also a way to solve disputes permanently. We must strive for this without hesitation.

• Give play to the role of military deterrence. In order to deter a possible crisis, we must:

-Develop diversified and multigradational deterrent abilities.

-Both give play to our traditional advantages and lay stress on the new military technologies and theories as well.

-Attach importance to the survivability of our military abilities.

-Determine the developmental intensity of the deterrent power according to the national security situation.

● In the operation of deterrent power, we must:

-Coordinate closely with the nation's political and diplomatic actions.

-Deploy it correctly, deterring the opponents with our advantageous posture.

-Make clear to the possible opponents our determination of self-defense.

● Adopt a prudent policy toward the intervention in foreign affairs, especially the unusual ones of our neighbors.

● Be fully prepared to cope with crises. At first warning we should strive to resolve a crisis. We should have preparatory plans to cope with all possible crises. The command systems needed to cope with crises should have preparatory plans set up; these should be exercised regularly according to the plans. The ones that have been set up or are part of organizations should also be tested regularly. The power, mainly military power that can be deployed in peacetime to cope with crises, should be deployed according to internal and external environments. Other forces should also maintain a certain degree of emergency status for crises.

Links in Strategic Guidance

United Direction and Rapid Reaction

These are the demands of a period of a crisis. Especially during the short time before a crisis breaks out, we must do our best to identify crisis signals. Once the signs are discovered, we should ascertain the problem quickly, striving to determine the opponent's interest as soon as possible. When we know that an opponent is attempting to provoke a crisis, the power to deal with it should go as quickly as possible to the highest command organization of the state.

Internal Conditions for Coping with External Crises

If an NDSC occurs, causing internal disturbances, we must suppress them rapidly. We must also determine if there are other potential internal disturbances. If an NDSC occurs without internal disturbances, still we need to prevent them while we are coping with the crisis.

Peaceful Support

We should give play to the power of the United Front, opening up the second line actively to unite international peaceful strength.

Solving Crises Through Peace Talks

Peace talks include informational links and diplomatic negotiations between two sides. Smooth informational links play an important role in relaxing tense situations and, further, in stopping a crisis. Informational links during a crisis tell an opponent of our peaceful aspirations. The links must be continuous and timely and also confident and mutual. The manner can be varied. At the center of the talks necessary to cope with a crisis are diplomatic negotiations. These can be either open or secret, formal or informal. During a crisis, if an opponent asks us to negotiate actively, we can participate according to the situation. If the opponent does not have this intention at that time, if necessary, we must manage to force him enter negotiations. We can repeatedly appeal to the opponent for negotiation; draw support from other countries' mediation, intervention, and other diplomatic actions; tell an opponent of our aspirations for peace and our sincerity; and strive to gain an opponent's cooperation "with tacit understanding." To insure the success of the negotiations during an NDSC, we should adhere to the following principles:

- Keep tight control over military elements. It is not only an important principle to avoid a crisis, but also a absolutely necessary principle to cope with a crisis.
- Maintain continuous informational links. There is one point here should be specially emphasized: when negotiations are suspended for some reason, information links must not be broken.
- Handle concrete affairs concerning the negotiations flexibly. The aim we take in negotiations should not be extreme; it is the conflict of interest, not the pure moral principles, that we should focus on. Flexibility of action and appropriate restrictions should

be maintained. We should also consider the problems the an opponent's position.

- Combine struggle with negotiation. During a crisis, only by daring to struggle can peace be won. Even if an opponent is more powerful than us, we should also dare to struggle. Struggling may mean peace. This is the dialectics of crisis control.
- Control the rhythm of the action properly. To cooperate in negotiations, the rhythm of our actions should be controlled according to the stage of the crisis. The aim in doing so is to give an opponent enough time to exchange information with us, judge the state of affairs, take actions to contribute to easing the situation, and react to our suggestions, in order for the negotiations to go more smoothly.

Means to Defeat an Opponent's Escalation

When the opponent has the intention of escalation deterrence but hasn't practiced it, we should strive to contain it ahead of time. When these measures won't do and the opponent starts to practice escalating deterrence, there are two basic theories on how to defeat it.

- Handle rigidity with flexibility, secure our position without being provoked, and bear the pressure of the opponent's escalating deterrence within a certain range, neither escalation with the opponent nor surrendering to him, to prevent the opponent's expectations from coming true. This may end the crisis.
- Withstand, even break, the opponent's escalating deterrence with equal escalation tit-for-tat, and contain further escalation in order to defeat it. In the concrete operative patterns of the opponent's escalation deterrence, those most dangerous are parawar actions. To cope we must strive to avoid them. If these measures don't work, on the one hand, we should use related countermeasures, strategies, and principles to cope with the crisis. On the other hand, there are some basic ways to defeat an opponent:

-Ruin the opponent with temporary avoiding actions.

-Warn the opponent with limited actions.

-Withstand the opponent's deterrent military actions, reduce or eliminate the deterrent effect, etc.

Chain Reactions of Crises

All the countermeasures to avoid crises discussed in this thesis can be used according to the circumstances. But with regard to a crisis having already taken place, the following points must be stressed:

- Closely watch the strategic trends of the possible opponents.
- Attach importance to the different interests of potential and real opponents. When we are coping with real opponents, we must try our best to avoid damage to potential opponents' interests.
- Clarify the gains and losses and make clear our strong determination to defend our national interest to possible opponents, especially the ones who want to provoke crises, to contain their purposes.
- If it is possible, strive to lead possible opponents toward forming a united front with us against common enemies.

In case the situation of chain reactions of crisis occurs, we should unify planning with due consideration for all concerned and hold the focal point.

Preparing Against War

The problems of preparing against war is beyond this thesis, but there is one point that must be stressed: Only when we are ready meet any surprise attack can we effectively prevent a crisis from happening. Meanwhile, all the actions for preparation against war should be coordinated with crisis control.

PART THREE:
Modernizing for Local War

Clockwise, from top left: General Zi Wuzheng, PLA General Staff Artillery Department Director; a guided missile destroyer; China's intermediate-range ballistic missile; and China's F-7 fighter.

DEFENSE MODERNIZATION IN HISTORICAL PERSPECTIVE

General Liu Huaqing

This year is the 100th anniversary of the Sino-Japanese War (1894-1895). It is of great significance for the China Military Science Association and Military Academic Research Committee of the Chinese Navy to organize this academic seminar jointly to mark the commemoration day.

The Sino-Japanese War, which broke out in 1894 and was a great event in Chinese modern history, was an aggressive war launched by Japanese imperialists. It ended with the complete collapse of the Chinese northern naval force and total defeat on land in the eastern part of Liaoning Province; several hundred thousand Qing servicemen were knocked down at one blow. After being defeated, the government of the Qing Dynasty was forced to sign the "Sino-Japanese Treaty of Shimonoseki" and cede territory and pay indemnities which humiliated the nation and forfeited its sovereignty. After the war, several imperialist powers started a new surge in the carving up of Chinese territory, speeding up the process of Chinese semicolonization. China faced an unprecedented crisis.

However, this war greatly stirred the Chinese nation. Since the beginning of modern times, China, a great nation in the East, had been not only repeatedly defeated by Western powers but also by Japan, its eastern neighbor, which rose rapidly after the Meiji Restoration.

General Liu Huaqing is Vice Chairman of the Central Military Commission. This paper is from China Military Science *(Winter 1994).*

Now, Chinese citizens with high ideas were aroused by this harsh reality and developed an entirely new view of the world. Rising with force and spirit to save the nation from subjugation and ensure its survival, they went in search of plans to save the nation and its people from impending danger. This resulted in the Reform Movement of 1898 and the Chinese bourgeois democratic revolution of 1911. Under the leadership of the Communist Party of China, the Chinese people fought wars bravely, one after another, for several decades, finally winning victory in the new democratic revolution and ending the humiliating history of being helplessly trampled by others for more than a century since the Opium War. The Chinese people attained national independence, unification of China and people's democracy, thus initiating a new epoch of socialism in China.

The Chinese nation is a great one, striving unceasingly with unflinching courage. Instead of sinking into degradation after being enslaved by the big powers, China made great historical advances out of tremendous historical disasters. Our great motherland again stands like a giant in the Eastern world. Today, the situation in the world and China have changed tremendously and stand at the threshold of a new century. The world structure is speeding up its development toward a multipolar world. Peace and economic development are the two major goals for which people throughout the world strive. The Chinese people are advancing along the socialist road, with Chinese characteristics pointed out by Comrade Deng Xiaoping, and have achieved much. They stride forward toward the next century full of confidence. We are now commemorating the Sino-Japanese War so we never forget our national humiliation and can be enlightened by this historical lesson. The war affords us a useful reference in carrying forward the socialist modernization of our country. Chairman Jiang Zemin repeatedly proposed that everyone should have some knowledge of Chinese modern history, to understand the past deeply, grasp the present correctly, and advance toward the future even better through the study of our history.

An important reminder of the Sino-Japanese War is that we must modernize our national defense. A strong national defense is the fundamental guarantee of the sovereignty and security of a country. The final result of the Sino-Japanese War had a major influence on the course of Chinese history—it emphasized that security is the precondition of the development of a country. The government of the

Qing Dynasty was defeated because China at that time was economically backward and militarily and politically corrupt and degenerate. Backwardness meant China took a beating. Before the war, the Qing Dynasty was complacent and conservative about its military strength and turned a blind eye to the danger of the Sino-Japanese War, and even went so far as to build up the Summer Palace with the military funds for the Navy. Lessons learned from the past will be the guide for the future. Now, the world is in a period of relative peace, yet quite unstable. Hegemonism and power politics still exist, and the major states of the world are building up their national defense despite the end of the Cold War. They are all revising their military strategy and continuously renewing their weapons. Great changes have taken place in warfare, because of rapid developments in science and technology. We should notice that the level of weapons modernization in our army still has far to go. So, we must pay close attention to building a high-quality army and modernizing our self-defense capacity in response to world military situations.

Along with building a modern national defense, the Chinese people should demonstrate patriotism. During the Sino-Japanese War, which was a large-scale war against aggression in Chinese modern history, the great patriotism of the Chinese people was prominently displayed. The patriotic officers and men, with Deng Shichang, captain of the *Zhi Yuan* warship, fought dauntlessly, facing death with no regrets and daring to perish heroically at the hands of the Japanese invaders. This lofty national integrity and heroic spirit of defying brutal suppression are good examples for us to follow and worth our eternal admiration. Patriotism is a great banner and a mighty strength of spirit. In today's China of hastened reform, open-door policy, and socialist modernization, we should continuously promote the spirit of patriotism, carry on the education of patriotism, and instill a sense of national defense among the Chinese people, thus further enhancing the cohesion of our nation. Further more, the Chinese Liberation Army must think of danger in time of peace, adhering to the concept of all-time preparedness and constantly maintaining a high vigilance in order to fulfil our army's sacred duty. We must safeguard the sovereignty of our territorial land, air, and sea, our maritime rights and interests, and the unity of our motherland, and do our utmost to provide a firm and powerful guarantee of safety for our socialist modernization. Devoting ourselves to the building of our army and the cause of national defense should become a lofty aspiration for every one of our servicemen.

In a review of Chinese history it becomes clear that it is quite necessary to concentrate our efforts on the issue of how to enhance the construction of our country's coastal defense. History tells us that whether one has maritime sense and can pay attention to the building of our coast defense is supremely important to the rise or decline and the honor or disgrace of a nation.

Since the beginning of the 1970s, the strategic importance of the oceans has increased day by day. Exploitation of the ocean has turned into an important condition for coastal countries in developing their economy and overall strength of national power. It is certain that the ocean will be more and more significant to the long-term development of a country. We must understand the ocean from a strategic level and its importance to the whole nation. We should safeguard our maritime rights and interests and security at sea and build a powerful coastal defense. Comrades in our army must have an even deeper understanding of the importance of enhancing our coastal defense.

In modern times, Chinese people suffered from imperialist invasions. Since the founding of the People's Republic, China has consistently pursued a peaceful foreign policy and opposed hegemonism in any form. China will never seek hegemony and never invade other countries and is an important force in safeguarding world peace. The only purpose for which we augment our navy's strength is to uphold and defend the sovereignty of our territory. Through the efforts of several generations, our navy has greatly improved its military equipment, personnel, and training, but it still does not meet the needs of the present situation. It should be foreseen that potential local war at sea in the future will possibly be a high-tech confrontation. We must keep these lessons of history in mind and arouse our vigilance with a strong sense of duty.

As early as the beginning of the 1950s, Chairman Mao pointed out that China should build a powerful navy. Comrade Deng Xiaoping demanded in the 1970s that our navy forces "must serve our national goals." On this occasion of 100th anniversary of the Sino-Japanese War, we should build our people's navy even better and make a greater contribution to modernizing our national defense.

FUTURE LOGISTICS MODERNIZATION

General Fu Quanyou

Deng Xiaoping attaches great importance to the logistics modernization of our armed forces, considering the question of logistics construction in the context of the overall strategic situation. He has made many important statements on logistics in accordance with the new requirements of modern warfare and the new situation that our logistics construction faces in the new era. He has emphasized the importance of the modern logistics to the modern army and modern war. He asks us be subordinate to the overall situation of national economic construction, making full use of the limited defense budget. We should race against time and prepare for anti-aggression war. We should pay special attention to the study of the new situation and the new problems facing our logistics. We should improve the standard of management in our logistics, and learn to do more work with less spending. Things should be straightened out in our logistics, and the good tradition of hard and honest work should be carried on. His instructions have become important parts of the theories on defense building in the new era, and have given guidance to the revolutionizing modernization, and regularization of our logistics.

General Fu Quanyou is Director of the General Staff Department and former Director of the General Logistics Department, People's Liberation Army. This essay was translated from China Military Science *(Spring 1994).*

A Clear Understanding of Logistics

As the modernization of the armed forces progresses, the role and function of logistics become more important. The fourth Middle East war in the 1970s, the war over Malvinas in the 1980s, and the Gulf War in the early 1990s have all attested to this. In the early days of our Republic, Mao Zedong pointed out, "To the modern army, it is of extreme great importance to organize good logistics in the rear area." Deng Xiaoping said in 1978, "As military science and technology develops, and our military equipment gradually improves, we have to come up with new situations in our logistics. In the past, ours was an army of millet and rifles, and our dependence on logistics was not great. Now that the situation has changed, our military supplies, arms and ammunition, and military equipment are all dependent on the supply from a strong rear." President Jiang Zemin also pointed out, "There would be no high combat effectiveness without a strong logistics supply. Fighting under the condition of modern technology, there is the problem of a big consumption of materials, the complexity of the technical aspect, and the demands of time requirements. The dependance on logistics and technology is much greater. We should fully recognize the role and function of logistics supply, and continuously strengthen our logistics construction."

Faced with this new situation, we should not only make sure that the army is well prepared for military struggle, but also make sure that the army maintains a good standard of living, that army cohesiveness is strengthened, and that combat effectiveness is improved. Our logistics department staff should clearly understand the responsibilities they bear and be firmly committed to servicing the army. Catering to the needs of the grass-roots units and servicing the army wholeheartedly should be the point of departure for our logistics. We should strive to ensure good service and efficient supply; our motto should be "we serve." We should make sure that our logistics serve the army, our department offices serve the grass-roots units, and higher levels of authority serve the lower levels. Warehouses, hospitals, recreation centers, supply stations, and army service stations are windows on the spirit of logistics. We should improve the quality of our service through promoting good service activities, and create good images. Good service for the armed forces in the remote and hardship areas should be our priority. The investment of expenditures and materials should favor the grass-roots units and the remote and hardship areas. We should continuously improve the level of logistics service to facilitate overall army modernization.

Modernize Logistics Within National Economic Construction

Military modernization being subordinated to the overall situation of economic construction is a scientific policy that will ensure a prosperous country and a strong army. Military power in the final analysis is based on economic power. The scale, speed, and quality of army building are all conditioned by the country's economy. On a weak economic foundation, military maintenance is constrained by economic conditions; thus it is difficult to develop and strengthen the military. Only when the economy is developed and the economic power strengthened will it be possible to build a strong and solid national defense. Deng Xiaoping has therefore emphasized, "The four modernizations can be summed up as economic construction. There would not be the modernization of national defense without the necessary economic foundation. . . . The modernization of national defense can only be based on the development of the whole sector of industry as well as agriculture." Therefore, we must exercise restraint and adhere to the central task of economic construction.

We should strive to develop our national economy, because without the development of our national economy there will be no military modernization. Stressing military reconstruction but ignoring the national economic construction will certainly affect the speed of economic development and fundamentally constrain the speed of military modernization. To gain the initiative in the next century, many countries in the world now choose the road of giving priority to the development of the economy, science, and technology. Deng Xiaoping's idea that military modernization be subordinated to the overall goal of national economic construction is suitable for the conditions of our country and of our military and is absolutely correct.

An important principle of logistics in the new period is to serve and be subordinated to the overall situation of national economic construction. We should attach importance to the overall situation, starting out from the overall interests of the nation and the military. We should give up individual or local interests for the sake of the whole, and immediate interests for the sake of long-term interests. We should firmly establish the concept of the overall situation, and overcome and prevent selfish departmentalism and decentralism. We should conscientiously put the interests of our unit or department under the interests of our nation and the military. Just as military modernization is subordinated to the overall situation of economic construction, logistics construction should be subordinated to overall military modernization.

The fact that we show consideration for the overall situation does not mean that we are passively exercising restraint, attempting nothing and accomplishing nothing. We should be eager to make progress in the context of "subordination and restraint." We should liberate our minds, renew ideas, and use our brains to find our way toward reform. New ideas and new ways should be tried in our efforts to strive for the continuous development of logistics modernization.

Improve Logistics Supply Capability

In the field of logistics, doing an excellent job for combat readiness is an important aspect of being prepared for an anti-aggression war. Modern wars, especially high-tech local wars, have raised new and higher requirements for combat readiness in the field of logistics. We should carefully study and seek new ways to deal with the question of combat readiness in the field of logistics. We should closely follow military strategic policy in this new era, to ensure that the entire armed forces are well prepared for military struggle, and at the same time greatly improve the combat readiness of the logistics itself. We should pay close attention to the building of emergency support forces for logistics, and make serious adjustments in the structure of combat material stockpiling. The portion of high-technology materials should be increased. Materials stockpiling should be combined with that of production capability, and stockpiling by the military should be combined with that of civilians. The logistics mobilization structure should be improved and we should study and formulate rules and regulations concerning mobilization during wartime. The building of a logistics reserve force should be strengthened, and preparation work for logistics mobilization should be carried out. In light of the characteristics of a high-tech war, we should stress the study of theories, principles, and methods of wartime supply.

Equipment for logistics is an important component part of military equipment and an important factor in fighting capability. Acceleration of the modernization of logistics is a key way to improve the capabilities of logistics supply. In future wars, without an advanced logistics supply, costs will increase and the time it takes to win a war will be prolonged. We should have a sense of urgency about updating our logistics. There should be a unified plan for overall logistics and for combat equipment, as well as a coordinated development between the two. Priority goals should be set with an obvious focal point. Currently, we should first of all increase the mobility of logistics supply and improve the capability of emergency supply.

Human beings are the decisive factor in war, including the area of logistics supply. It would be impossible to improve wartime capability of logistics supply without high-quality personnel suited to high-technology war. Therefore, the training and education in the field of logistics should be strengthened and be seen as a basic project in the improvement of logistics supply capability. In order to strengthen training and education in the field of logistics, training and education reforms should be implemented. We are in a time of rapid development in science and technology. High-technology arms have come into the combat field, with many features of modern warfare. Training in and education of logistics should incorporate the realities of modern war, quickly changing from coping with general warfare to dealing with the problems of logistics supply on a high-technology battlefield. We should pay attention to the needs of supply under high-technology conditions. The intensity and degree of difficulty of training should be raised, and the contents and methods be reformed. We should try to find different ways to train various logistics forces. Training on new equipment, with new technology, to gain new knowledge, should be increased. Training in the areas of mobility, supply, rescue operation, repair work, and protection under different conditions should be stressed. Real combat situation training should be increased. Methods of training in the field for night warfare and for expedient materiel supply should be studied. Training and real combat situations should be closely related.

Modern science and technology are the most important factors of logistics capability. Research in logistics will generate great cost effectiveness not only for the military but for the economy as well. Therefore, strengthening research in logistics will be of great significance to logistics modernization and improvement of logistics supply capability. In order to do this, our leaders at various levels should strengthen their awareness of science and technology. The idea of building a strong army by relying on science and technology and improving logistics through science and technology should be genuinely fostered. Scientific research work should be put on the agenda, and an atmosphere should be created so that the entire logistics forces attach importance to science and technology. Scientific research should focus on logistics modernization and on logistics supply under high- technology conditions. President Jiang Zemin stated, "In the field of defense science and technology, we should focus on researching and developing some key technologies," and we should concentrate our manpower, material, and budget on a number of high-technology items that influence overall logistics work. We should give full play to our scientific research department's skills and knowledge and tap their potential. On the basis of high-quality research and achievements, we should promote popularizing and utilizing the results of scientific research by organizing the transfer of research results, offering technical service and consultation, and signing technical contracts. Our logistics department has a lot of intellectuals and technical professionals and is a department with a high concentration of skills and knowledge. We should uphold Deng Xiaoping's policy of "respect knowledge, respect talents," and create an environment in which people's talents will emerge and be fully utilized. We should give full play to our scientific research workers' talents and creativity.

Reform the Logistics Field

As the country has set up its socialist market economy system, the environment of military logistics reconstruction has seen great changes. For a long time, logistics reconstruction was been carried out under the planned economy system. The various aspects of the logistics construction are all suited to the planned economy system. As the economic system changes, logistics construction faces new situations. We should keep in mind Deng Xiaoping's instruction: "Pay attention to the study of the new situations and new problems of logistics work under new historical conditions." We should raise our reform consciousness, follow the development of the situation, and make sure that the guiding ideology, our goals, supply system and logistics

124

methods in this new era are in step with the establishment of the socialist market economy system. Logistics reconstruction should be pushed to a new phase.

In the defense industry we should adhere to the method of "linking peacetime and wartime production, and having compatible utility for both the military and civilians." In the last few years, we have made some progress and had some pleasing results. The defense industry has been connected with the civilian industry. After ensuring that the military has all of its needed supplies, the defense industry has entered the market place, and reform has been carried out in all production areas. We have organized the transfer of defense industry technology to commercial use. The portion of commercial products made by the defense industry has increased year by year, thus creating wealth for the country and greatly invigorating the industry itself. Furthermore, logistics department units have made improvements in the long-time problem of single-product and low-efficiency manufacturing, by tapping potential markets and expanding plant functions. On the basis of accomplishing various logistics tasks, they have provided services to society, which both facilitated their own development and also brought about greater economic and social cost effectiveness. Social forces to improve logistics supply have also greatly promoted military logistics reconstruction. We have trained a great many people, providing them with skills suitable for defense and commercial sectors, thus providing a source of talents for both military reconstruction and civilian economic development. Practice has shown that, under the conditions of a socialist market economy, it is correct and practical that the logistics industry adhere to the principle of linking peacetime and wartime production that has both defense and commercial applications.

According to the principle of linking unified supply with separate supply, it will be a long-term task to carry out adjustmenta and reform in the logistics supply system. Currently, the materials and services that various military forces use should be procured accoding to the principle of proximity and convenience, and we shall further improve the supply system by allocating supplies, medical services, and repair work according to region. This will meet the needs of the army to strengthen combined forces and raise efficiency and will also be in accord with the market economy trend of to strengthening cross sectorial ties and raising efficiency. The essential criterion is to improve the capability of logistics supply and to improve the combat effectiveness of the armed forces. We should deepen the reform of the logistics supply system and gradually establish a centralized, unified, flexible and highly efficient logistics supply system suited both to the military strategic policy of the new period as well as to the development of the socialist market economy.

We should actively carry out reform in a way that will allow us to raise money, stockpile and provide supplies. At present, the logistics department should work with the main channels of government. We should take the initiative in reporting to the relevant government departments our military supply needs and gaining support of the country. We should work through legislation to ensure there is a large stockpile of necessary military materials for the armed forces. In addition, we should study new channels, methods, and measures for increasing military materials and stockpiles, by actively exploring the market. With regard to stockpiling military materials, Deng Xiaoping pointed out that the army "should not store too much, otherwise there will be waste. . . . What is the use of storing too much. We should not store too much because the service life of materials is limited, and things become useless after storing them for too long."

In the future, apart from storing combat-use materials according to regulations, materials and equipment that have both defense and commercial applications should be ordered by contract according to market conditions. We should use specially designated civilian enterprises to supply the set amount of materials at agreed upon times, and let society shoulder more responsibility. We should have various and useful ties with the large and medium-size commercial enterprises and establish stable channels of supply. Army supply stations should be connected, exchange and redistribution of supplies should be strengthened, and unified supply should be organized. When logistics has really adapted to the new track of the market economy, when it can better use the market mechanisms and work according to market prices, we will be able to closely follow the steps of the national economic reform, and the reform of logistics will continuously progress.

Strengthen Logistics Management

The shortage of defense funds has always been a bottleneck constraining the modernization of our military, and the tension between supply and demand is not likely to ease. Under the conditions of scarce funds and big demands of reforms, we should strengthen logistics management and use the limited amount of funds efficiently. We shall use less money, accomplish more, and do a better job, for this is the only option for us in the strengthening of our army's logistics construction in the new era.

To strengthen logistics management, we should above all manage according to rules and regulations. Deng Xiaoping pointed out, "In the past, we did not have much property. But we have more things now. It is a new problem for us to manage the logistics work well. We need to have a whole series of rules and regulations that are suited to the new situation and can solve the problems. We should fight against those who have no regard for the financial rules and regulations, and oppose extravagance and waste." Rules and regulations governing logistics work should be perfected and be strictly followedin order to regulate the various activities of logistics work. We should prevent willful use of funds, materials, and equipment, and conduct technical operations. Logistics work should gradually become systematized, standardized, and regularized. All those actions that violate financial regulations should be seriously dealt with, and the maintenance of a system of standards and financial disciplines should be taken seriously.

Financial administration is the key to strengthening of logistics management. Military logistics is, in a certain sense, financial administration. On the premise that the defense budget cannot increase much, the rate of defense modernization is, to a large degree, determined by the management of logistics and especially the management of the defense budget. Deng Xiaoping said, "Those who do the logistics work should learn how to manage things well, and should learn to use less money and do more chores. . . .The defense budget as a portion of the government budget can not be increased now, and it is the job of the army to use the money effectively. It takes a lot of knowledge to know how best to spend money, and we need to study carefully . . . strict budgeting. The policy should be correct, and the method right." We should examine the annual budget and its implementation, to make sure the money is correctly spent and the amount is appropriate. Because the defense budget is tight, we should concentrate our financial resources and focus on key projects. Taking into consideration the need to continually improve the living standard of the troops, the military expenditure should be tilted toward equipment, key forces, and key direction. That is to say, to ensure stability of the armed forces, we must modernize the armed forces. At the same time, we should closely follow and assess the results of the actual spending after the funds have been distributed. Auditing and supervision by the broad masses should be perfected, in order to meet the requirement put forward by Deng Xiaoping that "the money should be put to better, rational use, and should be used genuinely to improve combat effectiveness."

The foundation of logistics management lies at the grass- roots level, and when the performance of logistics management at the grass-roots unit is good, the whole logistics management system will be excellent. Therefore, leaders at different levels should attach importance to logistics management at the grass-roots level. "Regulations on Logistics Management at the Grass-roots Level," issued by the Central Military Committee, lists important regulations for grass-roots level reconstruction of the whole military. These are regulations for the standardized management of logistics at the grass-roots level. Each level should work according to headquarters requirements and consider the implementation of the regulations to be part of its day-to-day management. Emphasis should be laid on improving the quality of the managers and raising the standard of management. The self-managing capability at the grass-roots level should also be strengthened. We should rely on the masses to do a good job in logistics management at the grass-roots level in order to ensure that everyone cares about management, everyone takes part in it, and everyone encourages its development.

Logistics management is a scientific matter, and the strength of the members of the logistics department determines the results of the management. Deng Xiaoping has repeatedly emphasized the importance of training logistics personnel. We must use various ways and means to strengthen the training of logistics personnel to increase the number of good managers. Better software for logistics management is the essential solution to the improvement of the logistics management.

Strengthen Improvement of the Logistics Department

Logistics personnel, especially the leaders, should set good examples, and not take advantage of being in a favored position. They should be honest in performing official duties and be good managers.

According to the plan of the Party and Central Military Commission, we should further carry out our anticorruption policy and advocate honesty. Army logistics is in charge of money and materials and is vulnerable to the corrupting influences of pleasure seeking, money worshiping, and extreme individualism that exist in a developing socialist market economy. To carry on the excellent tradition of hard work and thrift in the new era, anticorruption and pro-honesty activities should be seriously carried out and not conducted perfunctorily or superficially.

We should reform our production and management, and maintain the distinctive character of the people's army. The army is basically dependent on public revenue, but it is necessary to undertake some production in order to make up for the deficiency of public funds. But the army should not attempt to completely support itself. It would be extremely dangerous to put all its energy into business and making money. All combat units below the level of corps must not engage in business activities, but instead engage in agricultural and side-line production. Production and business activities should be grouped together and be under the unified management of a larger unit. The financial affairs of production and business activities should be strictly managed and earnings from production should be distributed in a unified way. It should be stressed that illegal acts will not be tolerated in production and business activities. This is an important policy for the military in the new era, and should be resolutely, earnestly, and fully implemented. We should fully understand the significance of rectification and reform in our production and management. Through rectification and reform, we can carry on the fine tradition of hard work and thrift, strengthen the development of honest administration and Communist Party style in the army, and better perform the essential duties and functions of our army.

CHINA'S STRATEGIC
NUCLEAR WEAPONS

Major General Yang Huan

China's Second Artillery Corps, a strategic missile troop of the People's Liberation Army, mainly has the task of strategic nuclear counterattack. The research as well as the development of strategic nuclear weaponry are the foundation for constructing and developing the Second Artillery Corps.

China's strategic nuclear weapons were developed because of the belief that hegemonic power will continue to use nuclear threats and nuclear blackmail. From the day of establishment, the People's Republic of China faced a major economic and technology blockade from hostile powers. Further, it also faced serious nuclear threats from hegemonism. To oppose nuclear war, smash nuclear blackmail, safeguard national security and sovereignty, and keep peace throughout the world, China needed a powerful national defense and its own strategic nuclear weapons. At that time, the Central Committee of the Party, Mao Zedong and Zhou Enlai made a wise decision—to make China's strategic nuclear weapons independently. This decisive and timely step paved the way for developing our strategic nuclear weapons.

Major General Yang Huan was Deputy Commander, Second Artillery (Strategic Rocket Forces), PLA. His paper is excerpted from Defense Industry of China, 1949-1989 *(Beijing: National Defense Industry Press, 1989).*

As early as 1956, Mao Zedong pointed out, "We also need the atom bomb. If our nation does not want to be intimidated, we have to have this thing." In June 1958, he stated, "To make atom bombs, hydrogen bombs, and intercontinental missiles, from my point of view, is perfectly possible in ten years." Later on, he further instructed us that development of strategic nuclear weapons should "have some achievement, and be fewer but better." What Mao Zedong said gave us a clear guidance on our effort to research and manufacture our strategic nuclear weapons. It is not hard to imagine how difficult it was during those days in China to develop advanced weapons with a weak economy and a backward scientific and technological community. But under the leadership of the Central Committee of the Party and its specialized committee, all Chinese people gave strenuous support to the cadres, the experts, the technicians, and the PLA officers and men who shouldered the responsibility of developing our advanced weapons. These people exerted themselves to carry out a determined struggle for the final victory. They lived plainly, they worked hard, they devoted themselves selflessly to the projects, they relied on their own efforts in research and manufacturing, and after an extremely hard struggle they surmounted the difficulties at last.

On October 16, 1964, our first atom bomb exploded successfully; on October 27, 1966, we succeeded on our nuclear missile trial test; on June 17, 1967, our first hydrogen bomb was exploded. These tests allowed made us step into a new period, that of mastering the development of nuclear missile weapons. China's achievements within such a short period of time evoked a strong response all over the world. The Chinese Government has declared again and again, "China is compelled to conduct nuclear tests and develop nuclear weapons in order to break the nuclear monopoly; China's nuclear weapons will be used definitely for self-defense; the Chinese Government has always advocated an all-round prohibition and a complete destruction of nuclear weapons in the world." This is the fundamental stand China maintains on possessing nuclear weapons.

In 1958 we built up the special Artillery Corps, then on July 1, 1966, the Second Artillery Corps was officially established with approval of the Central Military Committee. In the last 20 years, the Corps has gradually been developed and strengthened and equipped with different kinds of nuclear missile weapons it made by itself. The Second Artillery Corps trained in the use of weapons, coordinated training, battle simulation and tactical exercises, and successfully launched different types of missiles and improved both its ability to master strategic weaponry and fighting capability. At the same time, it strengthened its research work on the formation of weapons systems, weapons use in battle, and development of such systems, and improved weapon quality. It has also done a great amount of work on command systems, battlefield construction, weapons testing, and maintenance and repair. The Second Artillery Corps has become a well-trained strategic missile corps with a certain level of nuclear counterattack capability.

For over 30 years, we developed our strategic nuclear weapons from short-range to medium-range to long-range and intercontinental missiles, and provided our army with a number and variety of missiles and nuclear weapons. Our armed forces are now capable of striking back with nuclear weapons, which greatly strengthens our national defense and our international status. Additionally, it helps to weaken the nuclear monopoly of the superpowers, contain nuclear war, and safeguard world peace.

Since the 1980s, the international situation has relaxed somewhat, but the role of military force in national security policy has not decreased. The number of strategic weapons owned by the big nuclear powers has already surpassed the saturation level, and weapon technology has reached a very high level, constituting a serious threat to world peace and security. At the same time, the problem of nuclear proliferation and especially the concern of nuclear weapons falling into the wrong hands have become more and more serious, and there is no end to the regional arms race. We should have a clear mind and maintain vigilance when facing such a situation, and should also follow the development of the high technology in the world, maintaining our strategic nuclear weapons in accordance with the actual conditions of our country.

The research and development of our first generation of strategic nuclear weapons were a great success, but we must understand that there is still a great distance between the world's advanced level of technology and our own. Our historical experience has shown that for the sake of our national security interests, and for world peace and stability, we must develop strategic nuclear weapons and keep pace with the advanced world level. Ours is a developing country that is engaged in economic construction. Our Party Central Committee and the Central Military Committee have, according to scientific analysis of the international situation and in consideration of the actual conditions of our country, made decisions to change the strategic thinking that guides our military development. Under the current situation, the development of our strategic nuclear weapons should focus on long-term goals. We should develop advanced weapons that suit our national defense strategy, and at the same time we should improve current weapons to raise the quality and the comprehensive fighting capability. Science and technology should be our guideposts, and we should aim for advanced levels of 21st century technology, strengthening the study of single-item high technology weapons. We should work hard on the survival, fast reaction, accuracy, and break-through and high-command technologies for weapons systems. These should be the direction for the development of our strategic nuclear weapons. We should conduct research in the following aspects:

- Improve the survivability of the strategic nuclear weapons. Survivability is an important factor in waging a nuclear counter strike. We should strengthen research on small, solid fuel and highly automated mobile missiles and on the technology of invisibility, for reinforcing defense work against nuclear or nonnuclear strike; and improve the survivability of missiles before launch and in flight.
- Improve the striking ability of strategic nuclear weapons. Accuracy and power are chief factors used to judge weapon striking power. To increase the credibility of limited nuclear deterrence, we should work to improve accuracy, and our new generation of strategic weaponry should be of higher precision.
- Improve the penetration technology of strategic weapons. Strategic weapons can be used in actual fighting only when they can penetrate enemy defenses and reach and strike the target—a necessary condition to protect itself and destroy a target. In an era when space technology is developing rapidly and a defense system with many methods and many layers is appearing, we should pay special attention to the study of break-through technology.

To sum up, we conclude that the development of strategic nuclear weapons is one main aspect in strengthening national defense and is an important symbol of modernization for our military. In future development, the advanced qualities of strategic weapons will rely to a large degree on the development of the high technology and reflect the comprehensive power of a country. To safeguard more effectively our national security and territorial integrity and sovereignty, plus the socialist modernization construction, we must have a modernized army and improve and develop our strategic nuclear weapons. We should, in accordance with the actual conditions of our country, develop a limited number of high quality strategic nuclear weapons that could be used effectively to strike back against an enemy using nuclear weapons to attack us. We should strive to build a small in number but effective strategic missile corps with Chinese characteristics, and make further contributions to the safeguarding of our country, world peace, and the progress of mankind.

NUCLEAR SHADOWS ON HIGH-TECH WARFARE

Major General Wu Jianguo

The development of weaponry has undergone a long historical process. Nuclear weapons came into being in the middle of this century, creating a place for themselves in the history of weapons development and on the war arena. Along with the rapid development of modern science and new technology, high-tech weaponry has played an enormous role in some of the recent local wars and demonstrated a broad range of development. We are now entering an era in which high-tech weaponry is used in combat operations. In such an era, are nuclear weapons still useful? Will nuclear warfare break out? Is nuclear deterrence still effective? These are issues for debate about future high-tech warfare that cannot be avoided. This article expresses my humble opinions about them.

The Development of Nuclear Weapons Will Continue

The dropping of atomic bombs on Hiroshima and Nagasaki in August 1945 by U.S. troops proclaimed the advent of a nuclear era. With their unprecedented tremendous power, it shocked people's hearts,

Major General Wu Jianguo is a former Associate Professor and Dean of the Antichemical Warfare Academy. This paper was published in China Military Science, *no. 4 (Winter 1995).*

became a significant bargaining chip of military strength, and cast a nuclear shadow over warfare. Between the 1960s and 1970s, the role of nuclear weapons was inappropriately exaggerated. The prolonged situation of the Cold War and particularly the emergence of high-tech weapons and high-tech warfare have made people understand more clearly the limitations of nuclear weapons. However, we must note that the existence of a large number of nuclear weapons and the continuous development of nuclear technology are facts that brook no argument. We cannot simplistically think that the emergence of high-tech weaponry has replaced the position and role of nuclear weapons, neither can we believe that because of their extremely gigantic destructive power, nuclear weapons have totally negated their own prospects for use.

For several decades after World War II, various military powers vied with one another in the research and development of nuclear weapons. At present, countries possessing nuclear weapons include the United States, Russia, Britain, France, and China, and the total number of nuclear warheads currently throughout the world exceeds 20,000. Of this total, 95 percent are in the hands of the United States and Russia, who have the power to destroy the world many times. A series of treaties and agreements on nuclear disarmament has been concluded in recent years. However, even after they have been completely implemented, in the year 2003, the United States will still possess 3,500 strategic nuclear warheads, with a total equivalent weight of approximately 900 million tons, and 999 carrier vehicles; Russia will still possess 3,000 strategic nuclear warheads, with a total equivalent weight of more than 700 million tons, and 975 carrier vehicles. If we compare the above two sets of figures with the amount of bombs dropped by the U.S. troops during their 3-year war of aggression in Korea and the 8-year war in Vietnam, which totaled 680,000 tons and 1.5 million tons, respectively, it is not difficult to imagine that the force of the "remnant" nuclear weapons is still extremely formidable.

Since the Cold War ended, the danger of a world war has been growing smaller and smaller, but local military conflicts have never ceased. In light of the issues cropping up in various local wars, especially in the Gulf War, and to meet the requirements of the new pattern of military strife, some military powers stepped up their research and production of new-type nuclear weapons with very small TNT equivalents. Such small-sized nuclear weapons have a degree of destructive power, yet the possibility of using them will not be negated because their equivalent weights are not too big and the destruction they cause is not too disastrous.

As disclosed in the autumn 1992 issue of *Strategic Review,* some people proposed that three kinds of nuclear weapons with small TNT equivalents should be developed:

- One is a small-size, ground-penetrating nuclear weapon with an equivalent of 10 tons. It explodes at 10 to 15 meters beneath ground surface, and its pressure will reach 25 meters deep, with a capability to destroy heavily fortified command posts and all underground defense works except bunkers. The shock waves produced by the nuclear explosion cause only slight damage to the building facilities within about 100 meters, and the danger of radiation is also controlled within a relatively small range. This kind of nuclear weapon can also effectively wreck enemy airports and other important military facilities. During *Desert Storm*, the multinational troops repeatedly bombed Iraqi airports, but that did not produce a satisfactory result because the craters blasted by the bombs were rapidly filled in. However, a ground-penetrating nuclear warhead is capable of creating a strong radioactive crater with a radius of 15 meters and a dimension of 3,000 cubic meters, which is very hard to repair. Hence, it can disable the functions of an airport.
- The second is a small-size, anti missile nuclear weapon with an equivalent of 100 tons. If an antimissile missile is equipped with a nuclear warhead with a small equivalent, it will not only accurately intercept the attacking missile in the sky, but also disable the nuclear, biological, and chemical warheads of the attacking missile.
- The third proposed nuclear weapon is a small-size, ground-to-ground or air-to-ground nuclear weapon with an equivalent of 1,000 tons. According to the article, "the appropriate scale of U.S. nuclear weapons could prevent the recurrence of the tragic retreat in Dunkirk. When the U.S. emergency troops arriving at the war zone were unable to hold back the enemy's attack, a display of a small-sized nuclear weapons with an equivalent of 1,000 tons would probably have made the enemy submit obediently."

Certainly, the future development of nuclear weaponry is far beyond the issue of size; indeed, the focus is on other aspects, including the individualized antipersonnel and destructive effect, the method of lead-in explosion, the technology of adjustable equivalent (with plug-in component), and the enhanced ability to penetrate defense lines and survivability, all of which are well along in development. All this has added to the flexibility of nuclear use in actual operations. As a matter of fact, both the United States and Russia clearly understand that the existence and continued development of nuclear weapons is an objective reality in the present world. Because so many of nuclear weapons still exist and their functions are further improving, then there is a material foundation for using them. In this regard, nuclear weaponry is still the sword of Damocles hanging over the people of the world.

A Nuclear Environment in Future Battlefields

Today, the world is in a historical period of drastic changes, the pattern of multipolar forces is taking shape, the international situation is moving toward relaxation, and peace and development have become the theme of the present world. Therefore, we can anticipate that a new world war will not break out and nuclear warfare is avoidable. However, the world today is not trouble free, hegemony and power politics still have not withdrawn from the historical arena, the international situation is still very complicated, and the flames of war arising from local conflicts have never died out. Owing to multifarious factors, the nuclear shadow still cannot be cast away from future battlefields.

Warfare is violent action. More than 100 years ago, the capitalist strategist Clausewitz pointed out, "The use of violence knows no bounds. Therefore, a belligerent will oblige its opponent to use force as it will itself, thus producing a kind of interaction. As viewed from this conception, such interaction will inevitably lead to extreme." Warfare is the continuation of politics, and a kind of bloody politics at that. Nuclear warfare and high-tech warfare are both instruments subordinate to the purposes and requirements of wars. When countries possessing nuclear weapons and high-tech conventional weapons are involved in a war in which the conflict is intensifying, the possible use of nuclear weapons cannot be ruled out. Nuclear weapons, therefore, are still a trump card in the hands of nuclear nations.

Thomas F. Ramos, science adviser to the senior officer responsible for nuclear weapons in the U.S. Department of Defense said: "No reasonable evidence indicates that conventional weapons will be reliable shelters to cope with enemies possessing and intending to use nuclear weapons." His remarks express the consensus of some military strategists studying the Gulf War.

As estimated by some Western specialits/analysts, there are at least 12 countries which claim to have ballistic missiles and at least 25 countries that have probably developed or are developing nuclear, biological, and chemical weapons. Using this estimation, some Western publications maintain that "the world has ushered in an age of nuclear proliferation." In 1974, India carried out its first nuclear blast, which kicked off the nuclear emulation in South Asia. In 1988, India successfully developed the PRITHVI medium-range ground-to-ground missile with a range of 2,000 meters, and the capability of carrying nuclear warheads. On March 24, 1993, South African President De Klerk addressed a special session of the National Assembly, saying that South Africa worked out a limited nuclear deterrent program in 1974 and had produced six atomic bombs by the end of 1989, and that all the said nuclear weapons had been dismantled and destroyed in early 1990. It was also revealed by the South African media that if the expansion of nuclear powers shown an intimidating color, South Africa will install warheads into its missiles and will probably develop and deploy neutron weapons. Israel is one of the countries that had nuclear weapons in its possession relatively earlier. Moreover, it was prepared to use them during the fourth Middle-East war.

Other data also stated that countries like Argentina and Brazil will also be able to manufacture nuclear weapons. With the rapid development of science and technology, the technology of making nuclear weapons has almost become an open secret. The disintegration of the former Soviet Union not only resulted in a brain drain of a vast number of scientists engaged in nuclear weapon development, but also threw the supervision of nuclear materials into chaos, considerably enlarging the scope of nuclear proliferation. A terrorist organization or a maniac could, some day, claim possession of an atomic bomb and use it as a tool of intimidation and blackmail, and no one would think that this was a tale from the Arabian Nights.

What merits our attention is that in a high-tech conventional war, a nuclear environment may still emerge even if nuclear weapons are not used. The more society advances, the greater the demands for energy will be. In order to satisfy the demands for energy, nuclear power stations were built. According to the data released by the International Atomic Energy Agency in March 1994, at the end of 1993 there were 430 nuclear power plants with a total installed capacity of approximately 345 million kw operating in various places throughout the world; these accounted for more than 17 percent of the world's gross power generation. It is predicted that by 2001, there will be 558 nuclear power generating units with a total installed capacity of approximately 460 million kw all worldwide, which will account for 24 percent of the world's gross power generation. The peaceful utilization of nuclear energy is a piece of joyous news to mankind. Meanwhile, the extensive use of nuclear energy also constitutes a latent threat to peace and the existence of human beings. The accident at the Chernobyl Nuclear Power Plant that occurred in April 1986 inflicted air pollution on 16 Russian oblasts and victimized 250,000 people. In Ukraine, 370,000 people suffered injuries in varying degrees as land covering 40,000 square meters was polluted, and more than 2,000 residential areas were evacuated. In future high-tech warfare, if an enemy intentionally or unintentionally attacks nuclear power plants or other facilities using nuclear energy with high-tech conventional weapons, the secondary nuclear radiation produced and the nuclear environment brought about would likewise do harm. In June 1981, Israel dispatched four aircraft to launch a sudden attack on an Iraqi nuclear reactor southeast of the capital Baghdad, dropping 16 tons of bombs in two minutes and hitting all the targets. Fortunately, the reactor was not yet operational; otherwise the attack would have resulted in very serious consequences.

Nuclear Deterrence Will Be Used in Local Wars

The local wars that broke out after World War II were mostly carried out under the conditions of nuclear deterrence if the Western powers were involved in them. During the Korean War, U.S. Commander-in-Chief MacArthur once threatened a sudden attack of atomic bombs on China's northeast and coastal strategic targets. After Eisenhower came to power, he again ordered the Pentagon to formulate a nuclear program aimed at China. During its war of aggression in Vietnam, the United States also made nuclear threats and was prepared to resolve the issue with nuclear weapons. After the armed conflicts on Zhenbao Island between China and the Soviet Union in 1969, Brezhnev considered initiating a nuclear attack on China in an attempt to ruin China's nuclear facilities. In the Malvinas Islands War, Britain carried tactical nuclear weapons on its huge fleet and was prepared to use them if its conventional operations failed. In particular, the multinational coalition troops headed by the United States used extremely advanced high-tech weapons in the Gulf War, and although they held the trump card, they still deployed 800 to 850 tactical nuclear weapons on three sides of Iraq. What is more, U.S. troops considered using radio flash bombs but, because of political considerations, they were not approved by U.S. President Bush. In response to Saddam's repeated threats to use chemical weapons, the British Government warned again and again that its troops would retaliate by using tactical nuclear weapons should Iraq resort to using chemical weapons. Bush also hinted that he would give field commanders freedom when necessary. These countries threatened to use nuclear weapons in conventional wars because they believed that with nuclear weapons in hand, psychologically they would be able to hold a dominant position, which would enhance troop morale and frighten the enemy on the one hand, and restrict the enemy's use of some conventional means on the other, thus changing the direction of the war. These past events should not be forgotten.

At present, nuclear deterrence is still a strategic pillar of military power. U.S. President Clinton thinks that the United States must build up military muscle that suits the new age, and this military muscle must have the capacity of nuclear deterrence. Nuclear deterrent force is an effective form of security. The 1993 defense report submitted by the U.S. Defense Department to Congress proposed that an all directional global defense system of strategic nuclear deterrence to prevent limited nuclear attacks should be set up, under which the former nuclear deterrent strategy chiefly aimed at the Soviet Union should be readjusted to an all-direction and multilevel nuclear deterrent strategy aimed at both the former Soviet Union and other regions.

On September 25, 1995, President Clinton ordered the Energy Department to maintain the three major nuclear weapon laboratories to ensure that U.S. nuclear deterrent capacity remains effective. Russia set up a defense ministry in March 1992, then founded its nuclear strategic forces and made the development of strategic nuclear weapons a top priority in the future development of eight technical weapons. President Yeltsin said that a strategic nuclear force was the foundation of Russia's military strength. In November 1993, giving sanction to the new Russian military theory, he officially abandoned the Kremlin's 11-year-old commitment that in a conflict it would not be the first to use nuclear weapons. In its 1992 defense report, France claimed that it merely wanted to have the "most rudimentary" nuclear deterrent for as a way to cope with various kinds of unexpected events and check possible encroachments on its interests by potential enemies.

In the meantime, France announced that it is continuing to focus on the development of a submarine-launched strategic nuclear missile system to ensure the reliability of its nuclear deterrent strategy. At his first news conference after assuming office as president on June 13, 1995, Chirac declared that France would resume its nuclear tests in the South Pacific. The French Defense Minister maintained that President Chirac had made a "very serious decision." British Prime Minister Major said, "As far as Britain is concerned, laying down the nuclear shield in whatever manner is an indiscreet move. Britain holds on to its views that as long as the CIS countries are still in possession of nuclear weapons, Britain should retain its own. The number of British nuclear weapons will not be determined by that of other countries, but by whether or not they are sufficient to make potential enemies feel incapable of sustaining their losses."

Deterrence and actual combat are complementary and closely interrelated. Generally speaking, the military strategy of all countries has a dual character of deterrence and actual combat. Before a war breaks out, a country will, by way of military deterrence, try to make the opposite side refrain from launching an attack rashly, so as to provide a powerful backing for its own political, economic, and diplomatic activities. Once military deterrence does not work, it will strive to win a victory through actual combat, so as to remove obstacles to its political, economic, and diplomatic activities. Militarily, the immense effect of nuclear weaponry is that it can serve as a deterrent force and, at the same time, as a means of actual combat. Some countries, even those of the Third World, also consider possession of limited nuclear strength to be a significant way to contend against the deterrence of big powers or to deter one another in order to make up for the deficiency of their conventional forces.

Military history after World War II has principally centered on the two superpowers that applied nuclear deterrence to each other and contended with each other for nuclear hegemony. After one of the superpowers disintegrated, a "crowd of heroes" rose up. As a result, conflicts that were in the past covered up by the Cold War surfaced with each passing day, and the collision and coalition of various political forces intensified simultaneously. Some regional powers were not weakened by the superpowers' relaxed control over them. On the contrary, they will, perhaps, go their own way even more willfully on the issues of possessing and using nuclear weapons. Both the United States and Russia believe that future nuclear threats will primarily stem from small nuclear nations in certain regions. Hence, the world situation of nuclear deterrence will be transformed from the previous global nuclear deterrence and confrontation between the United States and the Soviet Union to multiple and regional nuclear deterrence and confrontation. In future high-tech local wars, the struggle between nuclear deterrence and counter nuclear deterrence will be even more complex.

We are materialists, so when we study an issue, we must proceed from the objective reality rather than from a subjective wish and, through investigation and study of objective reality, we derive our principles, policies, and measures. The study of issues concerning warfare can be conducted in the same way. Comrade Mao Zedong said a long time ago:

> Investigation and study are very important. When we see someone hold something in his hand, we should look into the matter. What is he holding in his hand? It is a knife. What is the use of a knife? It can kill a person. Whom will he kill with the knife? He will kill the people. After probing into these matters, we should further the investigation: The Chinese people also have hands, and they can hold knives too. They can forge one if they have none. . . .

We love peace. China's development and possession of a small number of nuclear weapons is entirely for self-defense. Since the very first day when China had nuclear weapons in 1964, it solemnly proclaimed that it would never be the first to use nuclear weapons at any time and under any circumstances. China also made the commitment that it would never use or threaten to use nuclear weapons toward nuclear-free countries or regions. At the same time, we clearly understand that only by relying on the arduous work of the people all over the world can the objective of genuinely eliminating nuclear wars and genuinely obtaining world peace be realized: "It is a universal truth since ancient times that proficiency in warfare is not tantamount to bellicosity." The stronger our national defense muscle and the more sufficient our preparations for high-tech warfare under the condition of nuclear deterrence, the smaller the possibility of the outbreak of nuclear war.

We wish that the day will come when the nuclear shadow will disappear from the blue sky and the people the world over will live under the sunshine of genuine peace. To hail the early arrival of this day, we should work with greater stamina and diligence.

RESEARCH AND DEVELOPMENT OF ARMOR

Major General Chen Benchan

The manufacture of tanks and armored vehicles, which started from zero in China, initially began with imitations but now has been replaced with our own designs and manufacturing. As early as the end of 1945, the PLA set up its first tank corps using tanks captured from its enemies during battles. By 1949, when the People's Republic of China was founded, the PLA already had two armored divisions and two armored regiments, and equipped these corps with 410 American or Japanese tanks and 367 armored vehicles, all captured equipment. On the basis of this we started constructing and developing our own armored weaponry.

On September 1, 1950, our Armored Corps was officially established. To meet the needs of the tanks corps we bought over 400 tanks and mobile guns from the Soviet Union. Immediately after that, the tank corps made use of the equipment during the war to Resist U.S. Aggression and Aid Korea, and forcefully backed the infantry's operations. In 1956, we began to set up the tank industry. Until 1959, we copied designs to make medium-sized tanks (model 59) for our troops. Then, starting from the latter half of 1958, a magnificent stage in the history of the developing of our tanks began, a time when we designed and made our own tanks. After a hard struggle of

Major General Chen Benchan was Director, Armor Department of the General Staff, PLA. His essay originally appeared in Defense Industry of China 1949-1989 *(Beijing: National Defense Industry Press, 1989).*

4 to 5 years, as we manufactured model 62 light tanks, we finalized the designs of model 63 amphibious tanks and model 63 armored vehicles. Then four major series were gradually formed according to the requirements of our operations and capacities that would adjust to specific terrains and climates. They were medium-size, light, amphibious, and armored carrier tanks. Step by step, they became the mainstay of our armored weaponry.

During the Cultural Revolution, the research and production of tanks were seriously damaged. Though the scientists, technicians, officers and men in our defense industry worked hard to achieve some progress, and the design of the medium-sized model 69 tank was finalized along with a number of accessory automobiles during this time, on the whole, the level of technology and the quality of the equipment was not much improved, and the distance between the most advanced technology and ours grew.

Since the Third Plenary Session of the 11th Party Committee, the policy of reform and opening to the outside world has brought opportunities for the rapid development of science and technology in our national defense. In the wake of a strategic transformation in the guiding concept on the construction of our army, we have strengthened the strategic research about how to develop weapons and developed an overall plan of development. The plan and the policies we put into practice in developing weapons were constructive and reliable, so the research and development of tanks and armored vehicles embarked on a steady and healthy road and achieved much progress. During this period, we did much research and finally manufactured over 10 new types of weapons, including the main battle tanks, caterpillar infantry battle vehicles, armored carriers, mobile antiaircraft guns, antitank missile launchers, armored command vehicles, tank bridge-making vehicles, tank rescue haulers, and tank transporters. Using advanced foreign technology, we actively improved our existing weapons, improving fighting capability and increasing the amount of equipment and weapons in every unit of the armed forces. Our armored weaponry has played an important role in training and preparing to prevent war, as well as in self defense.

We have achieved great progress in the development of armored weaponry after a tortuous experience. The many successes and failures have made us understand better the characteristics and rules of development:

- Strengthen research on developing weapons, and base macro decisionmaking on science. In the past, weapons development was much affected by political movements, the organizational system, and factors like personnel changes. We did not work according to scientific rules. In recent years we have, through wide discussion, decided upon an active and cautious policy for weapons development. We have formulated development principles with Chinese characteristics for the tanks and armored vehicles and made long- and medium-term development strategy and plans. Therefore our weapons construction is done through long-term planning, good coordination, and priority development. The democratic and scientific method we adopt in our models and decisionmaking process is the important foundation for the constant and steady development of our weaponry.

- In weapons development, we should consult with the department that uses them. The armed forces are the direct users of weapons. In the making of set models, they should pay attention to the testing of these models. In recent years, we have verified our weapons models in actual battle and paid attention to the integration of tactics and technology as well. We have strictly carried out model testing according to testing standards, regional adaptation testing, and special testing under nuclear and chemical conditions. We have asked representatives from the armed forces to take part in the management of scientific research. This is of extreme importance for meeting the battle requirements of the armed forces and ensuring weapons quality. As reform of defense science and technology progresses, we should actively carry out contract systems under the guidance of the defense industry, respecting the decision of the chief engineer in matters of technology, and encouraging the initiative and creativity of the broad mass of scientists and technicians.

- We must uphold the policy of taking the initiative and actively importing technology, which is a shortcut for the development of weapons. Independence and self reliance comprise our basic national policy; this is also the policy we must follow in weapons development. But in the development of technology, we should try to create anew and be good at learning and inheriting—these two are complementary. In the early days of our new Republic, we learned from the advanced experience and technology of the Soviet

Union, jumping over the traditional technical development stage. This way the research and manufacturing of tanks were quickly on the track, and we were able to shift from copying to designing and manufacturing our own tanks. At the end of the 1970s, through importing advanced technology, we were able to facilitate the quick development of our tanks and armored vehicles and shorten the distance between the advanced-level and our own. Today we take the initiative with imported technology, stressing utilization and development and gradually form weapons systems that have our own characteristics.

• We need to step up innovation and expand the accumulation of technology, key factors in weapons development progress. The research of weaponry in the past followed the traditional way, that is, a model led the research work or even the production of accessories. This resulted in a lack of accumulation of technology, passive and insufficient research on models, a long research period, and many unnecessary repetitions. It should be a profound lesson for us. In recent years, we supported and directed innovation that correlates to the background of the models. We adhere to a principle that the component parts take priority over sets of equipment. In addition, we imitated the good points of advanced scientific and technological results from abroad and make use of them in some projects. We broke through the line of demarcation between the departments and the industries and encouraged competition. All the efforts produced a remarkable effect.

• The development of tanks and armored vehicles must follow a process in which the vehicles are classified and grouped and put in a standardized series. If the army wants to enhance the overall operation capability of the armored corps, there will be a variety of requirements for weaponry. Since the 1960s we have believed that all kinds of accessory vehicles should be derived from a basic model design that can be flexibly changed. In weapons research and manufacture, besides carrying out the principle of standardization from beginning to end, we tried every possible means to enhance the universality of the component parts. This universal concept is useful not only to help crate standardized products but also to lower the costs of contract work, simplify the training of our army, and ensure logistics supplies.

- The development of weaponry needs a stable troop of scientists and technicians. In the early 1960s, along with the modernization construction of the armored corps, we founded the Scientific and Technical Research Institute of the Armored Corps and the Institute of Engineers for the Armored Corps. We gradually had a team of scientists and technicians that combined theory with practice. They worked together with the national defense industry department and made contributions to our first generation of tanks. Because of the advent of the cultural revolution, the teaching system and research institute of the armored corps suffered great damage and much talent was lost. Both the positive and negative experiences have made us realize that in order to develop weapons it is important to have a team of scientists and technicians rich in practical experience and full of creativity. Under the current new situation, we should take strong measures to ensure the stability of the team, and create favorable conditions for the upgrading of knowledge and the growth of talents.

- The organization that uses weapons should create a favorable technical system and environment for the development of new weapons. "Without technology there would be no armored corps," these were the famous words that former Commander of the Armored Corps General Xu Guangda used to say about the construction of the armored corps. At the founding of our armored corps, we established the department of technology and laid the organizational foundation for weapons development. When the first generation of new weapons was decided upon, documents for the use, repair, testing, and technology were edited, weapons were tested and their fighting capability, ease of use, and reliabilty were constantly improved. We created favorable conditions for the development of new types of weapons. Tradition and experience in this area should be upheld and carried forward.

We are facing new opportunities and challenges at a time when modernization is our central task and there is a new technological revolution going on. We should grasp the opportunity and gradually establish a weapons system that has Chinese characteristics and that meets the requirements of future anti-aggression war.

The development of armored weaponry should proceed from reality and in accordance with the actual conditions of our country and our army. We should go our own way and not follow the footsteps of the others. The future development of tanks and armored vehicles should follow these principles:

- Pay attention to fire power, improve overall quality, and increase survival capability.
- Reform current weaponry in a planned way and strengthen combat capability.
- Take into account terrain and weather conditions and improve adaptability.
- Form modular sets with fewer basic models but higher standardization.
- Strive for advanced, reliable, economical, and easier-to-operate weapons.

These principles were established after summing up the experiences of developing armored weaponry. In our future development work, we should put them into practice, strengthen test methods to ensure a weapon's long life, gradually certify, research, manufacture and equip for a complete set and arrange for advanced research, manufacture, production and improvement. At the same time. we should speed up the training of personnel and technical research so as to maintain good development momentum.

Motorization and armoring our troops are the developing trends for the modernization of our army. Fast-reaction and quick-strike capabilities will be important factors for our armored corps in winning future anti-aggression wars. Weapons for our armored corps in the year 2000 must meet the requirements of future warfare. Our armored corps should improve the ability to strike deep, react fast, and coordinate well with the air force. The overall efficiency and adaptability should be improved, and weapons systems with appropriate combinations of different levels of quality should be formed. At present, we should give priority to the development of new types of main battle tanks, infantry fighting vehicles, automatic battle command complexes, and anti-aircraft vehicles. At the same time, we should selectively improve our current weapons and improve their reliability and fighting capability.

We are confident that under the correct leadership of the Central Committee of our Party and the Central Military Committee, and with the great efforts of all people in the defense industry and armored corps, the working capacity of our armored weaponry will be greatly improved, and the capacity of combined-operations will reach a new level. It is a difficult and heavy task, however, as long as we persist in our efforts, we will definitely achieve our aim.

REFORMING DEFENSE SCIENCE, TECHNOLOGY, AND INDUSTRY

General Ding Henggao

The development and reform of defense science, technology, and industry are now in a key stage. A new situation and some arduous tasks lie ahead of us. This is mainly reflected in the following:

- Owing to the needs of modern technology, especially in a high-tech regional war, we have to speed up research and development of new weapons and develop our national defense science and technology in order to reach the advanced world level.
- The second strategic goal of socialist modernization is for us to continue to carry out a policy of linking the army and civilians and to accelerate this step of strategic transition so as to release more power into the main battle field of national economic construction.
- The basic object and whole plan of national economic system reform call for further liberating and developing military productive forces to form a new system suited for socialist market economy that would combine with the practices and special features of the national defense industry. The necessary prerequisites to complete these tasks are to uphold a practical and realistic style of work, emancipate the mind, and under the guidance of Deng Xiaoping's thoughts on building a socialist

General Ding Henggao serves as Chairman, Commission on Science, Technology and National Defense Industry (COSTIND). This article originally appeared in China Military Science *(Summer 1994).*

society with Chinese characteristics, to research and approach the major problems, to enhance our sense of principle, orderliness, predictiveness and creativity.

Position and Effect in National Strategy

Faced with new conditions and wanting to speed up the reform and development of defense science and technology, we must first of all fully understand its vital importance. President Jiang Zemin pays great attention to this. He asserts that the key to developing defense science and technology is to heighten its level. This is not only the requirement of the new military strategy but also that of the whole modernization drive. We can deepen our understanding of these points from the following three aspects:

- Defense science, technology, and industry are the major material bases on which we can realize our army modernization. The use of modern weapons is a sign of a modernized army, and is also one of the factors for improving the combat effectiveness of an army. The biggest problem we have in the construction of a modern army is the lack of up-to-date weapons. With the deployment of high technology in the military domain, the precision of weaponry has improved, the intensity of the battle has greatly increased, and other characteristics of war like swiftness, abruptness, three dimensions, mobility etc. have become more conspicuous. As the Gulf War clearly showed, the one who possesses high-tech superiority will have the upper hand on the battlefield. To fundamentally change the backwardness of our army's weapons, and strengthen the material base we count on to deal with local wars of modern technology, especially those under high-tech conditions, we must speed up the research of new and high-tech weapons , and raise the level of modernization of our weaponry. Weapons modernization is, in the final analysis, determined by the modernization of our defense science, technology, and industry. Therefore, we must seize the opportunity and speed up the development of our defense science, technology and industry, to ensure the realization of the modernization of defense.

- Defense science, technology, and industry are important symbols of our comprehensive national power. At a time of peace and development, world competition is essentially about comprehensive national power, and the key is the competition in science and technology. National defense science, technology, and industry represent a nation's economic and technological power and are important pillars of the comprehensive national power. They are also essential for the raising of the nation's status. China is a developing country with a low per capita income. One of the reasons that we are not looked down upon in the world is that we have built a relatively complete defense industry, and we have been able to research and manufacture various types of conventional and strategic nuclear weapons independently. Deng Xiaoping said, "If China did not have atom bombs and hydrogen bombs, and had not launched satellites since the '60s, China would not be called an important, influential country and would not enjoy the international status that it does today." Such things reflect the ability of a nation, and also symbolize the prosperity and development of a nation. In the last few years, we have achieved a series of breakthroughs in defense science, technology and industry. Both the new developments in the research of weaponry and the successful launching of satellites for foreign countries further promote the strengthening of comprehensive national power and raise our international status.

- Defense science and technology are the leading forces for the development of our national high-tech industries. Nowadays, more and more countries attach great importance to science and technology and are developing their high-tech industries as if they were in a race. It has become a strategic focal point and a common practice. Deng Xiaoping once said, "Whether it was in the past, at present, or in the future, China is determined to develop its own high technology and to occupy a position in the domain of high technology in the world." On the whole, defense science, technology, and industry belong to high-tech industry, and they can stimulate high-tech industry and cause great advances in it, especially in three aspects:

    —To go through the processes of research, experimentation, and production in the defense industry, we need a lot of new materials, new technologies, experiments with new methods, and efficient facilities for production. This is bound to make strict demands on basic industry and result in a series of industrial breakthroughs and improvements.

—Then, some new high technologies, such as nuclear technology, telemetry and remote sensing technology, automatic control, electronics and computer science, precision machinery, meticulous chemical, etc. were originally and successfully used in the defense industry and have gradually formed some new competitive industries through their application in the civilian sector.

—Finally, the military departments and enterprises make full use of their superiority in equipment, technology, and talented personnel directly to develop new high technology products, which, to a certain degree, have filled in the gaps in the fields of science and technology and raised the overall level of the national economy.

Contradictions in the Development of Defense Science and Technology

With changes in international affairs and hot competition in the high-tech world, all countries are readjusting their national strategy and defense strategy and pursuing the development of modern technology, especially high technology, as the key measures to strengthen comprehensive national power and defense strength, and thus gain the strategic initiative. Historical experience has proven that all starting points and guiding ideology in our work should alter with changing situations. Analyzing the distinguishing features of modern technology, especially high technology, and taking into consideration our national and military conditions, we need to seize the opportunity to speed up the development of defense science and technology. We also need to correctly understand and handle some important relationships:

- The relationship between the part and the whole. Defense science and technology are parts of a complicated system involving a wide range of areas. Some of them are urgent in the short view but not so from the longer view. Therefore, we must pay special attention to the overall balance, clearly defining our priorities and tilting toward the major projects. When we form development strategy or policy on technology, we should start from the overall development of defense science and weapons research and manufacturing. We should focus on raising overall efficiency and properly handling the relationship between the part and the whole. The relationship between requirements and possibility. For a considerably long time, the gap between available funds and the large investment needed for developing high-tech weapons will be a restriction on development. For this reason we must make great efforts to balance production with rational disposition of funds in all projects. Additionally, we should get rid of and guard against extravagance for instant benefit, repeatedly spending money for quick results followed by a quick reversal, and so on.

• The relationship between making the focal points stand out and coordinating the different branches of development. It would be best if we choose projects that will play both an important role in strengthening the fighting capacity and the deterrent power of our armed forces, and a vanguard role in raising the level of defense science or the level of the whole nation's science and technology. For the major projects, we should concentrate manpower, material resources, and financial resources to ensure their implementation. Meanwhile, we need to coordinate the overall development of all weapons with science and technology.

• The relationship between the requirements of demand and the push of technology. To program weapons development we have to adhere to the principle of linking demand requirements with the push of technology. On the one hand we should make thorough studies of the requirements of local war under the circumstances of modern technology, especially high-technology. On the other hand, we should lay stress on discoveries in the development of new and high technology, which will raise the effectiveness of weaponry. A new concept and a new system of weaponry should be formed and the structure of weaponry renewed and optimized constantly.

• The relationship between long-term and short-term interests. Proceeding from the requirements of high-tech war, we ought to manage to do research on some weapons with a higher starting point in accord with the plan and the focal point, and utilize results in scientific research to improve existing weaponry and military equipment. To obtain staying power, we should also do research in advance, reserve more technical capacities and keep up with the advanced world technology, so as to raise the overall level of defense science and technology.

• The relationship between the efficiency of the whole and the efficiency of a single unit. A local war under the circumstances of modern high technology is a confrontation between two systems within a given battleground. We need to study both operational policy and weapons development from the standpoint of systematic operations to raise the efficiency of the whole and hence the quality of our weapons system. If we do not examine the quality of our weapons system as a whole, even if we have numerical superiority or an advanced single weapon, we can not make the most of these weapons as a whole.

• The relationship between the offensive and defensive. In a future anti-aggression war, our country will uphold the concept of active defense. It means that active defense is not just defensive, it is offensive as well. Our air-defense weapons system and even the whole weapons system should have two capabilities. It could greatly help overall quality and effectiveness if we possess one or two effective weapons that can assume the offensive.

• The relationship between defense and commercial use. With the development of modern science and technology, defense and commercial products become more and more compatible. While we emphasize the conversion of defense technology into commercial use, we must study defense-commercial dual purpose technology and possible transfers from commercial technology to defense use. Development of defense products should actively use commercial technology, so that it will have a solid foundation for development.

Optimum Disposition and Proper Use of Resources

A problem that restricts or affects the development of the defense industry is the improper defense industrial structure. For this reason, our fundamental goal for modernizing the structure is the optimum disposition and full liberation of the military productive force. As the international situation changes and new technology steadily develops, many developed and developing countries find a flexible military industrial structure to be an important strategic measure in restructuring their national defense industry. Currently, we have made good progress in defense industry adaptation, but the situation is still short of what is expected—for example, problems such as activities too large in scale, overextended battle lines, low-level production, inefficiency and so on still exist. In the future, any defense industry should follow and serve the needs of the military strategy in the new era and be suited to the building of the country's socialist market economy system. Additionally, we should pay attention to the following points in our guiding ideology:

- Speed up modernization by relying on progress in science and technology. Science and technology are the number one factors in the productive force. With the rapid development in science and technology, economic competition in the world has more and more become the competition of a product's level of technology. Modern warfare is also, to a degree, the competition of high technologies. Adjustment in the structure of the defense industry and improvements in its of research and manufacturing capabilities should be conducive not only to the rapid development of national defense science and technology but also to research and manufacturing of high-tech weapons, and to the integration of research and production. We should pay attention to the development of mature technological products and useful foreign products to improve our existing equipment, and to raise its technological level. We should also be aware of the requirements of a high-tech local war and focus on the research and manufacturing of high-tech weaponry. To raise the level of technology, and to have rapid development, we should put advanced research in a strategic position and concentrate our resources on breakthroughs in key technologies. At the same time, we should pay close attention to the improvement and renewal of technology and the coordinated development of technology, equipment, and materials. Additionally, we should conduct our research and production of military supplies by relying on science and technology and by improving the quality of our workers.
- Adhere to the principle of contracting the front and stressing the main point. At the present time, the units that are responsible for research and manufacturing of military products do not have that many projects or funds. In addition, some shortcomings like scattered resources and repeated projects still exist, causing a longer period of research or manufacturing and a lower productive

level. In future modernization, we should cut down those projects that are outdated and make allowances for those that are really advanced. We will mainly derive our plan from the tasks, and take the investment as the foundation, concentrating the research and production in some major enterprises and academies or scientific institutes. Moreover, we should concentrate them in a number of workshops or laboratories within an enterprise or an institute. As a number of scientific bases and major production bases are formed, we will concentrate resources and try to fulfill the task of manufacturing military products on time, guaranteeing quality and quantity.

• Apply economic methods to promote modernization. In the past, we adjusted the defense industry structure depending on the plan and administrative method. Under the overall situation of building a market economy system, we should apply more economic methods, particularly insisting upon the role of the market and giving full play to the function of our market system. For instance, the start or the abandonment of our scientific projects, or the increase or decrease of production power, should be decided according to the requirements of the domestic and international markets. The market will play a fundamental role under the macro adjustments and be controlled by the state.

The Transition from Military Industry to Market Economy System

The Fourteenth Party Congress made it clear that the goal of our economic system reforms is to build up and improve the socialist market economy system. The third plenary session of the Fourteenth Party Congress further confirmed the framework of our socialist market economy system and put forward requirements for the initial buildup of the socialist market economy system at the end of this century. How to speed up the reform of the military industry, and build a new system that meets the requirements of the market economy are important issues to study and answer.

The military industry is an component part of the whole economic system of the country. Its production, circulation, distribution, and exchange activities cannot be separated from the national economy. Therefore, it must be subordinated to the need to set up a new economic system in the country, and speed up the transition to the socialist market economy. The transition from a highly centralized, command and planned economic system to a market economic system is a great change of strategic significance for the military industry. The key to what is actually a profound revolution is the proper handling of the relationship between the plan and the market. Deng Xiaoping has emphasized on many occasions that both the plan and the market are tools of economics. President Jiang Zemin pointed out, "The scope, degree, and forms of integration of the planned and market economicscan be different at different times, in different areas and regions." According to the realities and characteristics of the military industry, we should pay attention to the following three points for the present time:

- National security is the foremost reason for the research and production of military products. Its funding mainly relies on investment by the state, and the state is the monopoly buyer of the products. There should be strict planning and management of the research and production of military products by the state. The state should purchase these products, and production should not be regulated by the market. Concerning the allocation of resources, the state plan should still play the leading role and be the main control point.
- Reform of the research and production of military products should be directed toward designing a contract system. Through economic contracts, there should be clear relations of interests between the supply and the demand sides, and there should be unity of responsibility, rights, and interests. The essence of a purchaser/contract system is to shift to the market economy, changing administrative management to management by economic means.
- As an economic activity, the research and production of military products should follow the law of value, and adapt to the changes in supply and demand, making full use of the role of the market. At the same time, control by the state should not be weakened or negated. During a shortage of resources, or an imperfect market, the strengthening of state control would be conducive to giving full play to the advantage of socialism in

concentrating resources on big projects, and achieving better results and efficiency from limited resources.

The resolution of the third plenary session of the Fourteenth Central Committee of our Party pointed out that the building of the socialist market economic system is to use the market system as the principle means to allocate resources under the authority of the state. Through several years of experiment and practice we have found that in order to have the market play a role in the defense industry, we need to recognize the importance of using price as a lever and introducing competition to gain efficiency in the allocation of resources, to motivate enterprises. Currently, there is a strong desire to reform the pricing of defense products. But the budget for the armed forces is very tight, and because there have been big increases in the prices of raw materials, it would be very difficult to carry out such reform. Further, a reform would involve big adjustment of interests in supply and demand, and is closely related to financial and monetary system reform, as well as enterprise reform. Therefore, to have military products appropriately priced, and to have a new pricing system, we need to ask the government to have an overall plan to solve the problem. To conduct the reform in the pricing of defense products, with a smooth transition, we should price military products on the basis of actual value and not the market-bearing price, as with civilian products. In principle, we should use both adjustment and the role of the market, with emphasis on adjustment. The government may apply the laws of value and supply and demand, taking into consideration the ability of different sides to cope with the reform and adjusting unreasonable pricing of major military products at an appropriate time. With regard to generally low-priced military products and their accessories, apply a price based on supply and demand, and gradually adjust prices to reflect the market price.

Another outstanding problem is the introduction of competition into defense industry reform. Competition is necessary to encourage creativity and to raise efficiency. In the early 1980s Deng Xiaoping said that there can be competition in weapons production. Some weapons can be produced by more than one department, and the army can choose to buy the better products. But in recent years, because of the unsmooth structure, the unclear division of government and enterprise, interference by the administration, and the weak concept of market, the competition mechanism has not been given full play in the research and production of military products. According to the experiences of the developed countries, and in light of the actual conditions in our country, we should actively introduce competition in the research and production of military products. But the scope, items, and forms of competition should be chosen according to actual situations. For example, in terms of scope, competition can be carried out in the same trade, in the defense industry system or in the whole country in certain cases. In terms of weapons systems, there can be competition in subsystem or in single unit equipment. In terms of items, we can start out in small and medium projects, and when we have more experience, we can then gradually press forward. In terms of forms, we can have competition among units and even within the same unit.

Opening to the World

The current world is an open world. We must notice that the general trend of development in the world economy and in science and technology is increased mutual infiltration, interdependence, and integration. Any country that wants to speed up development has to carry out an open policy. Deng Xiaoping said, "Opening to the outside world is of great significance. It is impossible for any country to have development in isolation and with its door closed, neither would it be possible without the strengthening of international exchanges, and importation of advanced experiences, science and technology, and funds from the developed countries." In fact, even in the confidential and sensitive military sphere, the countries of the world are not closed to each other. Many countries not only import advanced technology and equipment from abroad, but also carry out broad cooperation in the area of military high technology, and have joint research and production of new types of weapons. There is still a gap between the level of our national defense science, technology, and weaponry and that of developed countries. To make quick advances, we need to be self-reliant, but at the same time we should open wider to the outside world. There are two key points in the opening of national defense science, technology and industry:

- Increase exports. To satisfy domestic needs, the defense industry should try to develop products for export and expand exports. This will then open a source of income and accumulate funds to be used for imports. It will facilitate links with the international market, and through competing in the international market, the quality and character of our products will improve. Domestic and international needs can be considered as a whole, and scientific research and production will increase. It will also help to break the international monopoly and raise our international status. We must be aware that our products for export are not very competitive or cost effective. To achieve some breakthroughs in the international market, we need to dare to compete and carefully plan for long-term benefits. We should formulate a correct export strategy and adopt effective measures. For instance, we should try to open new markets, and concentrate on large and new projects. In response to market needs, we should promote the research and development of new types of products for export, raising the technological level of our export products so as to increase our competitiveness. Management of enterprises engaging in foreign trade should be further changed. We should increase the motivation for developing new products, improving quality, lowering cost, and increasing foreign exchange. We should constantly strengthen our competitiveness in the international market and open new venues for our foreign trade.
- Import technology. Deng Xiaoping pays special attention to the importation of technology. He has clearly pointed out, "Science and technology are the common treasures of mankind. Every nation, every country should learn from the strong points of other nations and countries, and learn from the advanced science and technology of others." In the process of our opening to the world, we should seize every favorable opportunity to import advanced technology from abroad, especially new and high technology. We should expand our technology cooperation and exchange with foreign countries. We should be good at linking imports with our own creations. Imported technology should be well digested and widely applied and used. The starting point of our research should be raised, and our ability to be self-reliant should be strengthened. While doing a good job in importing technology, we should create favorable conditions and adopt flexible measures to attract

talented people from abroad. This will be beneficial to the acceleration of the development of national defense science and technology, as well as the training of talented people for national science and technology.

Training Defense Scientists and Technological Experts

Scientists and technology experts are the creators of science and technology. Science and technology experts in the defense industry play a special role in the development of national defense science and technology and weaponry, and to a large degree determine the development progress of new high-technology weapons, and even the successful realization of the goals of modernization for national defense and army building. Under the overall situation of reform and opening up, and the development of a market economy, the conditions for the existence and development of national defense science and technology personnel have undergone great changes. We need to use new thinking to select and train talent. Deng Xiaoping once said, "We need to open up a way, so that talented people will grow to maturity quickly. We should not block talent. The constant emergence of talents means the success of our cause." Under the new situation, the building of the national defense corps of science and technology experts should pay special attention to the following three points:

- Liberate our minds and change our way of thinking. We should not simply rely on the state to supply us with experts. A new way is to attract and train science and technology experts through competition and promotion. The building of a high-level national defense corps of science and technology experts would not be possible without the support of the state and the improvement of the overall situation. But the national defense departments and units of science and technology should realize that reform and opening up have provided opportunities for them to attract more talent. They should focus on strengthening vitality and competitiveness and creating fine conditions to attract talent. They should be good at discovering, uniting, and making use of talent and maintaining a degree of superiority in the competition for talent.

• Change the environment for talent. What Deng Xiaoping once said is significant and worth pondering:

The most important point, which I am most concerned with in the reform of the economic system is talent. In the reform of the scientific and technological system, what I am most concerned with is also talent. . . . We should create an environment, in which talents showing themselves could appear. The reforms should create such an environment.

Under the traditional planned economy system and personnel system, national defense science and technology experts were normally assigned through state planning and administrative means. As the development of the market economy and the reform of personnel system moves forward, we should, under the guidance of the state, pay attention to exploring the opportunities for recruiting and selection through labor markets and facilitate the appropriate promotion of talent, to create a balance of supply and demand. We should also gradually set up a system of training, evaluation, examination, recruiting, promotion, and awards for talented people.

• Take a long-term point of view and train talent for the next century. In the competition for talent in the world today, competition for young and middle-aged talent is very intense. Many developed countries believe that the greatest challenge facing national defense science and technology is attracting and retaining needed talent, especially for key technologies. To strengthen the building of our national defense corps of science and technology, we should face up to modernization, the world, and the future, and focus on selecting and training a group of young and middle-aged leaders in science and technology who will advance to the forefront of global science and technology in the next century. Senior scientists and technological experts should make the historical responsibility of training young people their first priority. At the same time, concerned departments and units should not stick to a certain pattern but select talent, especially young talent, and boldly make use of them, letting them shoulder heavy responsibility in making technological breakthroughs, accumulate experience, and grow to maturity quickly.

A Scientific, Authoritative and Effective Overall System

National defense science, technology, and industry are very important strategically and have a unique pattern of development. Only by strengthening overall control can we take into consideration national and military strategic requirements and make timely decisions and arrangements in light of national economic, scientific, and technological realities based on collective wisdom and scientific proof. According to historical experiences and future trends of development, we should pay attention to the following if we want to raise the authoritativeness and effectiveness of the overall control system:

- Strengthen the centralized and unified leadership of the Party and the state. During the 1950s and 1960s, we lacked economic power and qualified technical personnel, and we faced a very serious international situation. We made atom bombs, hydrogen bombs, and satellites, and we made major breakthroughs in other fields of high technology. The most important reasons for these successes were the wise decisions of Chairman Mao and the Party Central Committee, and the high prestige enjoyed by the central government headed by Premier Zhou Enlai. Judging from the experiences of foreign countries, the development of high technology, especially military high technology, is strictly regulated and controlled by the state. Under our current system, the strengthening of centralized and unified leadership is mainly the strengthening of decisionmaking, at high levels on the development of the defense industry, major projects, and important issues like the integration of defense and commercial industries. Under centralized and unified leadership, the different levels of administration should be responsible for their own management work.
- Decisionmaking on the major issues should be scientific and democratic. One important lesson we learned from both positive and negative experiences in the past is to ensure correctness in decisionmaking and efficiency and effectiveness in execution. The key to both of these is that decisionmaking should be scientific and democratic. Along with the steady development of new-tech revolution, modern weaponry is increasingly associated with high technology, and its cost has more than doubled. In addition to the

changeable and unstable international situation, various intricate problems place higher demands on decisionmaking. Those important decisions related to development strategy, planning, goals, and focal points of the defense industry and weapons development are related to complicated systems engineering, and they should be suited to the changes in the international situation and rely on possible national power. The modernization of our army places demands on national defense research and production and science and technology; it is especially high technology that provides a great push in the development of weapons and equipment. These two points should be emphasized. Only through an all-around assessment and a comprehensive balance of strategy, tactics, economics, and technologies can we ensure that any decisionmaking is correct and its execution effective. To make fewer false starts and avoid mistakes, we should adhere to a strict decisionmaking process while making decisions. The decisionmaking system should be improved, and we should give full play to the consulting departments' role in the making of decisions, especially paying attention to the advice by experts. We should also pool the wisdom of the masses, and the basis for the decisionmaking should be scientific and democratic.

• State planning should be based on scientific methods and earnestly carried out. The state command plan for the research and production of military products has the effect of law and should not be changed by any one or any unit without authorization. Of course, under the overall situation of a market economy, the command plan should also strictly follow the law of value, reflect the changes in supply and demand and give play to the economic lever. On the premise that energy supply, main materials supply, and transportation are provided by the state, all departments and enterprises should give priority to fulfilling the research and production tasks for military products, and strictly carry out contracts according to the law. Those who have violated the state plan or can not fulfill the plan, should be seriously dealt with.

• Set up a fairly complete law system. We could say that a market economy is a legal economy. In order to carry on the research and the production of military products in a systematic fashion and achieve standardization, regularization, and legalization, we should continue improving the existing laws and regulations, emphasizing development of the basic law of research and production in the defense industry. Moreover, we need to make and issue new administrative decrees in accordance with the new problems or new situations we might be facing in research and production. We should have strict management procedures, work according to objective laws, and ensure the sustained, rapid, and healthy development of the national defense industry.

CHINA'S ARTILLERY DEVELOPMENT

Major General Zi Wuzheng

Firepower is the basic element of combat strength and artillery troops are the main firepower of the army. These are the chief forces for launching a ground offensive with firepower and the main forces for air defense in the combat. In peacetime, artillery troops are important components of the conventional deterrent forces for containing war. The degree of modernization of artillery troops directly affects the coordinated fighting ability of the armed forces and affects the modernization process of national defense.

The people's artillery troops were born and rapidly grew and became stronger during the revolutionary war era. Since the founding of new China, and under the direct leadership of the Party Central Committee, the State Council, the Central Military Committee, and the Headquarters, it was through nearly 40 years of hard work by various industrial departments that our artillery weapons development has made important achievements and greatly improved our fighting capability. But owing to the disturbances of the Cultural Revolution, the limits of our national financial resources, and problems with structure and in our work, our artillery weapons at present are quite backward. Compared with the advanced level of foreign artillery, we are facing serious challenges. When looking to the

Major General Zi Wuzheng is Director, Artillery Department of the General Staff. This article is from Defense Industry of China, 1949-1989 *(Beijing: National Defense Industry Press, 1989).*

future, we need to sum up the experiences of 40 years of equipment development, grasp favorable opportunities, and facilitate the development of equipment in order to strengthen the power of the "god of war."

The Historical Turning Point

Since the founding of new China, artillery weapons have experienced important changes. In the early days of the People's Republic, artillery weapons were mostly guns, vehicles, and optical instruments captured in war and made in other countries. During the period of resisting the United States and assisting Korea, we bought a number of weapons from the Soviet Union. Starting in 1953, we began to manufacture Soviet-style artillery and instruments and formed a weapons system based on Soviet artillery. Under the guidance of the policy of independence and self-reliance, in 1958 we began to design and manufacture artillery weaponry by ourselves. Over 30 years we have successfully made a large number of weapons, instruments, and vehicles, gradually replacing the Soviet equipment. At the same time, we trained a production force of dedicated scientists and technology experts in comprehensive fields of specialty. We have built up the material and technical bases for design, research, testing, production, and maintenance, are capable of manufacturing different kinds of weapons, and have entered a new stage of research and manufacturing artillery weapons on our own.

Our artillery weapons are no longer composed of mismatched types of guns and vehicles. Today we use sophisticated ammunition, and our artillery reconnaissance and firing calculation instruments are no longer operated by hand. We have developed a cohesive system of artillery and ammunition, accompanied by accessories; reconnaissance, command, communication, survey, and meteorology instruments; and vehicles. A series of different types of artillery has been formed, and part of the artillery, instruments, and automobiles has been or is being upgraded. Since the 1970s, we have gradually been equipped with antitank and antiaircraft missiles, and new types of missiles are in the development. Different kinds of reconnaissance radar, air reconnaissance systems, laser-range finders, night vision instruments, and fire command systems are in various stages of research, production, and operation. With the development of this equipment, the fighting capability of our artillery troops has been continuously improved. In the various combats we have been involved in since the founding of new China, our artillery troops have played its special role and made important contributions.

Arduous Tasks

In the new historical period, we are faced with the serious challenge of modernizing the design of our artillery weapons. We are still lacking in certain types of new weapons and we have not been able to form a complete set of equipment. For instance, we still have not met the demand for various missile systems, new types of ammunition, motorized artillery, and advanced electronic and optical reconnaissance instruments, as well as fire command systems. The whole artillery weaponry system is too old. Because of the new technology revolution, artillery weapons of advanced countries are high-tech and high quality, and the distance between the advanced countries and ourselves might be enlarged if we do not do a good job. We are relatively slow in upgrading the equipment of our troops. The antitank, antiaircraft, and neutralizing fire power still cannot meet the basic requirements of modern warfare, especially for antitank and antiaircraft warfare. Further, there is the need to develop different kinds and types of weapons. The technology is getting more and more complicated and more expensive. On the other hand, our level of science and technology is relatively low, our budget very limited, and the contradiction between the need and the possibility is very pronounced.

But at the same time, we must realize that though there are many difficulties, opportunities and favorable conditions do exist. The relaxation of the international situation, the change from the imminence of war to a period of peace has provided us with a favorable environment and valuable time for the modernization of our artillery weapons. Our Party's policy of reform and opening up has provided the opportunity to import advanced technology from abroad, utilize the results of the new technology revolution, reform our system of scientific research and equipment management, improve efficiency in investment, and accelerate development. Our science and technology, especially the development of high technology and its application in the research and production of artillery weapons, as well as our 40 years' experience and technological foundation, have provided the conditions for the development of advanced artillery weapons.

In short, modernization of artillery weapons faces serious situations and arduous tasks, and it will be through a long period of hard work that we will gradually realize modernization. If we have favorable timing and opportunity, and adopt correct policies and strategies, we will be able to succeed and make steady progress. We should start from reality and look toward the future, make an overall plan, and strive to realize the goal of artillery weaponry modernization in a planned and systematic way. Before the end of this century, we should pay attention to the research and manufacturing of key new weapons and equipment, improve and upgrade in a planned way the current weapons and equipment we are using, raise the overall fighting capability of our artillery troops, and lay a good foundation for the realization of all-round modernization in the next century.

Development with Chinese Characteristics

In the last 40 years, the development of artillery weapons has gone down a tortuous road. When reviewing our work, the most important lesson is that the modernization of artillery weapons should take into consideration the actual conditions of our nation and our army, and we should pursue development with Chinese characteristics:

- Persist in and develop the fine tradition of self-reliance and hard work, and make coordinated efforts to overcome difficulties. In the early 1960s, we faced the serious situation of a total foreign technological blockade, Soviet withdrawal of experts, and economic difficulties at home. Our scientists and technicians worked on artillery weapons. There was close coordination between the industrial departments and units that used the equipment, and between the research units and the production units, and we were able to achieve important results in a relatively short period of time. For example, the 63 model of the 107mm rocket gun and the 63 model of 130mm rocket gun took only 5 years to research and manufacture and were quickly used to equip the armed forces. In the new historical period, we should uphold and develop this fine tradition and further raise the quality and level of our scientific and technical troops so as to achieve better results.

• Strengthen model development and testing in development and practice decisionmaking scientifically. The construction of artillery weaponry is complicated, and only through a scientific decisionmaking process can we avoid making serious mistakes. Therefore, we should strengthen testing. We should use scientific methods to predict both requirements for artillery weapons in future anti-aggression wars and our national economic and technical capabilities. On the basis of systematic analysis, we should choose the correct development direction and goals and systems and series, and form practical plans, policies, and measures. Around 1970, under the direct leadership of the Central Military Committee and Marshall Ye Jianying, antitank weapon were made top priority for development. The antitank weapons system and requirements under the division level were clearly defined and intensely researched, and results were soon achieved. In fewer than 10 years, there were breakthroughs in the development of rocket launchers, recoilless guns, antitank guns, and antitank missiles. On the other hand, because there was no clear direction and mistakes were made in the decisionmaking, we took detours in the development of antiaircraft guns and howitzers, and progress was slow. Past experience has shown that artillery troops should make equipment research work a priority, developing test models to determine development direction, equipment systems, tactical technology requirements according to our strategic thinking, and battlefield situation and tactical principles, thus providing choices and possibilities for scientific decisionmaking.

• Shorten the battle line, pay attention to the focal point, have advanced planning for every stage and make advanced artillery weaponry. It has been proven that the results of seeking big and complete projects at an unrealistic speed are often "a lot of research but little equipment." At present, weapons development should be subordinated to the overall national economic construction, and we should be more careful in planning, stressing the key projects. I believe that in the development of artillery weapons that it is preferable to have fewer but better products. We should, based on scientific testing, carefully select key projects, concentrate our energy on developing basic models, and produce in appropriate quantity, to equip our forces for fighting capability. At the same time, we should strengthen advanced research, emphasize technological development, and choose a leaping-forward development model in order to shorten the distance between the advanced countries and ourselves. Before the year 2000, we should research and manufacture a number of advanced weapons.

• Face the world, improve technology through importation, digestion, development, and creation. Our artillery weapons were developed by importing and copying. Now that we are facing the challenge of a new technological revolution, we should further open up to the world and utilize the favorable conditions of opening up and actively to import advanced, appropriate technical equipment and a scientific way of management. In the 1950s, our weapons were based on Soviet artillery weapons. We achieved some progress, but at same time there were some far-reaching negative results. Our artillery weapons should eliminate Soviet-model features but not blindly copy Western models. Our military thinking, strategic policy, and combat principles should be our guides, and we should proceed from the actual conditions of our economy and science and technology levels, to gradually form our own technical style and weapons system. We should take the road of developing weapons research and manufacturing with Chinese characteristics.

LOGISTICS SUPPORT FOR REGIONAL WARFARE

Major General Yang Chengyu

This article focuses its attention on the characteristics of regional wars using modern technology, especially high technology, and studies how to improve the logistic support of our army. The author believes that the logistics of our army should try hard to improve the mobility of contingency operations in order to meet the requirements of rapid mobile operations, the three-dimensional multisupport capability in order to meet the requirements of joint operations of various services, the sustained and unceasing support ability in order to meet the requirements of continuous attack operation, and the defense and survival ability of logistics in order to meet the requirements of defense operations or rear services. The author also points out that training qualified personnel for logistics in our army and constructing logistical equipment based on science and technology are also strategic criteria for "powerful support."

Modern technology, especially high technology, is widely applied in the military field, which gives regional wars special characteristics. These mainly include the high flexibility of operations, close combination of all forces, extreme continuity of operations, and extraordinary fierceness of the rear defense struggle, among others.

Major General Yang Chengyu serves at Headquarters, General Logistics Department, PLA, Beijing. His paper is from China Military Science *(Summer 1995).*

Under modern technology, the new characteristics of regional wars create even more requirements for logistic support of our army, centering on the general aim of "powerful support."

Mobile Capability of Contingent Operations

Speed is precious in war. Under high-tech conditions, war breaks out suddenly and operations are mainly maneuvers. Many nations have set up their rapid-reaction units to deal with regional war. Rapid-reaction troops will be able to play their full role depending on logistics. A commander of rapid-reaction troops of a western country said, "Whether the rapid-reaction troops are able to achieve success depends eighty percent on logistic work." To deal with high-tech regional wars in the future, the first troops to be affected or to be used will be the rapid-reaction troops in charge of operational missions. To enable quick reaction to unexpected incidents, mobile logistic contingency support capability will be greatly needed, working jointly. Only thus can we ensure victory in every battle by acting quickly against a quick enemy to deal with emerging situations. Logistic support should be based on the principles of combining peace with war, unity between construction and management, stressing the main points and improving step by step. It must put into effect everything in organization, equipment, materials supply, training, and systems, so as to form a reliable contingency supporting capability. Forces should be developed with special training in supply, rescue, repair, and transport, flexibly composing themselves to form modern-style combinations so that they can do multipurpose support tasks jointly or single support tasks separately.

Transportation is key to support combat forces so that they can quickly and flexibly conduct operations. Recently, some regional wars showed that the battlefield supply line was shortened while the strategic supply line was relatively extended. In the Gulf War, U.S. troops quickly threw 550 thousand troops into war and transported 770 thousand tons of goods and materials, relying on their powerful mobile contingency support capability, especially strategic transportation capability, although the U.S. homeland is separated from Iraq by vast oceans. What the U.S. Army transported in the first month in the Gulf War altogether exceeded what it did in one year in the Korean War. So the U.S. Army's new edition of "operation program" lays great stress on improving the capability of getting troops in. The capability of global rapid deployment of troops for operations has become the cornerstone of the U.S. Army's strategic threat. Our country is able to conduct war in self-defense, relying on its home land, but it covers a vast expanse of land, and our communications and transport are rather poor, so it is worth considering and studying how to ensure deployment of mobile troops quickly and flexibly to the site of an incident. Our communications and transport development will be increasingly strengthened and expanded with the vigorous development of our national economy. From a long-term point of view, means of transporting troops will also be improved. The capability of deploying military forces and delivering materials will be increased step by step. Taking the present conditions into account, we should, in advance, place a certain amount of logistic strength and war material in areas of possible conflicts so forces may obtain support immediately. That is the way that we, relying on our own territory to conduct war, can make good use of space to gain sufficient time and, remaining where we are, control delivery and action.

Three-Dimensional Multisupport Capability

The U.S. Army's new edition of "Basic Operations" has outline a new combat concept of conducting joint battles in air, on land, by sea, and in outer space, instead of what was mentioned before: conducting combined air and land battles. They think, "Any battle the ground forces take part in is bound to be a joint one. . . . In the whole combat zone the special-type joint battle operations will be conducted by air and sea, and what is more, they will be supported from outer space."

Future high-tech regional war will concentrate the army, navy, air force, and outer space forces of various services on the same battlefield to conduct joint operations and support one another. To meet the requirements of joint operations, it is necessary to establish a multipositional and multilevel logistic support system and improve three-dimensional logistic support.

From the horizontal standpoint, it is necessary to establish a joint logistics system of various services and arms. It is a developing trend in many countries to carry out logistics jointly among all three armed services. In the Gulf War, the logistics organization stipulated that, with regard to support, the U.S. Army's central command on the home land was under the charge of the logistics department of the Joint Chiefs of Staff. At theater level, a Central Command logistics department was controlled and coordinated by the logistics officers.

The Chinese People's Liberation Army's joint logistics system of three armed forces must be based on actual conditions and possess its own characteristics. It will take some time for us to realize the joint logistics plan of three armed services in the best sense of the term, but we must try hard to make progress in this field. In recent years we have tried putting into effect a network-type support system according to separate regions. We obtained better results and necessary experience. Besides what has already been achieved, we should create favorable conditions in all fields and gradually increase and expand the supply of component parts. The requirement is to unify the supply of commonly used materials for all three armed services, the repair of equipment in common use, medical care for common wounds, and arrangements for communications and transport. Meanwhile, various services and arms must keep their specific character in addition to those in common. Only in this way can logistics capability be improved comprehensively.

From the vertical standpoint, it is necessary to establish a three-level supply system with strategy, campaign, tactics, and logistic work connected together. Marshal Liu Bocheng said, an army's rear area is like a huge tree, the strategic area like a tree trunk which stands motionless, and each campaign's rear is like a branch, only half moving, but the tactical rear is like leaves, entirely moving. A perfect, highly effective logistical support system must be a whole body with motion combined with stillness, the first joined to the last, a comparatively stable strategic rear base to rely on, a half-moving campaign rear working as a link and a full-moving logistic service attached to the troops. Under high-tech regional war conditions, we still want to lay stress on the construction of the strategic rear bases, devoting major efforts to strengthening campaign support so as to form both the supporting point and overall support capability. Thus, no matter what enemy you conduct operations against, or which direction you go toward, you still can rely on stability to cope with changing factors in order to provide strategic or campaign multipositional support.

From the vertical standpoint, it is necessary to link together ground forces, navy, air force, and outer space force and a multilevel logistics support system. Like forces in many other countries, the Chinese People's Liberation Army logistics department needs to alter the old support mode in which ground forces took the main support and support was provided on an interim basis to other forces. To develop support by air and sea is the key link of building multilevel logistics support. It is also worth our attention to perfect ground-force support for field operations. At the same time, great attention must be paid also to the comprehensive use of railways, highways, underground tunnels and artificial facilities, and useful natural conditions. Only when the support system combines army, navy and air force mutual supply and joint transportation by train, boat, air and tunnel will it become possible to give effective complete logistics support to all services and arms in wartime.

Sustainment Capability for Continuous Attack Operations

In future high-tech regional wars, both fighting sides will concentrate crack troops and modern weapons, perhaps continuously applying these means: maneuver against maneuver, air strike against air strike, assault against assault, jamming against jamming, not allowing each other any breathing spell. This sort of intensive, quick, and fierce conflict may inevitably expend a large amount of materials, damage equipment and facilities, and cause heavy casualties. If the logistics department is not prepared very well before operations and can't keep the supplies coming, then we are bound to lose the battle.

In the Gulf War, two strange phenomena appeared: two "long" and two "short." That is, it took a long time to get ready for operations, but a short time to conduct actual combat; a long time to make an air-attack, but a short time to engage in ground battle. Many factors explain these phenomena. The most important is a high-technology regional war's high intensity and consumption rate can influence and decide the course and the outcome of war. In this sense, the multinational forces won the battle in the Gulf War at a high financial cost. In 6 months, U.S. troops spent a total of $61 billion and used over 30 million tons of various materials. Four times more materials were consumed each day per single fighting man than in the Vietnam War. The ammunition consumption each day was 20 times more than that of the Korean War each day. Logistics support on such a large scale benefitted mostly from an effective mobilization system that developed a continuous transport capability. So in the U.S. army's new edition of "Operation Program," they lay stress on continuous military operations and stress military actions before, in the middle of, and after war. In order to ensure the continuation of military action and be able to withstand losses and consumption caused by intensive, quick and fierce conflict, it is necessary for a logistic department to get fully prepared before war and give strong and continuous logistic support.

Our country is large and still undeveloped. With our supply and demand problems not well solved, how can we strengthen logistics development for preparedness against war and improve contiguous support capability for war time? First of all we must firmly have a comprehensive concept, accepting national economic development and submitting to self-sacrifice as the first consideration. Only when our national economy has been developed can the national defense development rest on a solid material base. Then logistics support can be provided continuously from the rear of the country. Of course, the defense budget is strained at present, but we can't remain inactive, accomplishing nothing. Logistics personnel must use the concept of seeking results from management and from self-restraint. When it comes to how to manage and make good use of funds, there is a lot that can be done. According to the requirements of force development and future defense operations, it is very important to make scientific use of funds in a reasonable way and in an appropriate amount. For example, it is necessary to give priority to building key troops, supporting the preparation of battlefields in the directions and areas where the operations will occur, and the development of new equipment for war. Storing and acquiring materials for war must be nationally coherent with structural improvements concentrated at the main positions. Only by concentrating our limited financial and material resources effectively can we strengthen logistical war preparations and give reliable continuous support to some key troops, in the vector toward which operations will go when war breaks out.

We must firmly foster the idea of overall rear service for a People's War, making soldiers compatible with civilians, and connecting peacetime with war, so as to give full play to the system of powerful support by both soldiers and civilians as a whole. In this new historical period, we need to improve gradually the logistic mobilization system and establish the law of logistic mobilization, making it lawful and conforming it to the standards for conscripting reserve personnel, stockpiling, and preparing war materials, collecting means of transport, and mobilizing technical personnel. Thus, we can transfer latent support capability into actual support strength immediately when war breaks out. It is necessary to frequently consult with state and local governments. When deciding on economic development projects, we should consider not only the needs of the people, but also the military's requirements, and obtain results that are beneficial both for preparing against war as well as for the economy and society. Now our country is studying and developing "National Defense Law," which will afford us a legal basis for starting national defense mobilization work and establishing a logistic support system of soldiers compatible with civilians.

Improve the Defense and Survival Ability of Rear Services

The targets of attack in modern wars have expanded to battlefield in full depth. One of modern war's main characteristics is to attach great importance to operations in the enemy's rear. It tends to threaten and weaken the enemy's key point if you attack its support system, thereby exerting a great influence over all its operations. It is a very important aspect of operations to destroy the enemy's support system. In the Gulf War the multinational troops headed by the U.S. forces struck heavy blows mainly at Iraqi forces' logistic bases and transport lines, thereby making their supply capability drop 90 percent and leaving Iraq's troops on the south line without ammunition and provisions. Iraq's troops were thus utterly routed at the first encounter. In future high-tech regional wars, the rear base and communications lines will tend to be the first target of sudden attack by enemy, so the guiding principle of sudden attack and counterattack around the rear area will run through the whole operation course. Whether or not to effectively to carry out the rear defense struggle plays a very important part in the logistic survival. Without powerful rear defense capability, the safety of the logistic personnel and the facilities cannot be ensured, nor can the powerful logistic supplying support be organized and carried out. In accordance with the characteristics and special requirements of the rear-defense operation in future regional wars, when waging a rear-defense struggle, we must put into effect the policy of "defense combined with attack," and "taking the defense as the dominant means" so as to carry out the whole defense. It is still necessary to build a strong protection and transportation system, running through in length and breadth, with conveyance, attack, and repair connected and employing various camouflage techniques. Making logistic troops conduct operations and reach the indomitable and skillful level like or almost like that of combat troops is a new problem worth paying close attention to. "Ferocious and violent as the devil is, the magic means to vanquish him is more powerful." In all previous revolutionary wars and the Korean War (1950-1953), we successfully created rear-supply and defense methods with Chinese characteristics. In a rear-defense struggle under modern high-tech conditions we can still find effective ways to improve the logistics capability.

Because rear services ensure not only front support but also rear defense operations, it seems to be more important and conspicuous to improve logistical organization and commanding capability. In future wars it should be carefully studied how to organize command in a concentrated and united way as well as by acting promptly at one's own discretion. It involves several factors: qualified personnel and equipment, whether to improve mobile support capability and sustainment; unceasing supporting capability; or strengthen the rear-defense and command-organizing capability. Therefore, we must pay attention to and do a good job in training the logistic personnel contingent, improving logistics and scientific and technical equipment as strategic measures to provide strong support. Qualified personnel and top-quality equipment, closely combined with scientific and reasonable arrangement and establishment, can ensure and also serve as a firm foundation for winning a possible high-tech regional war and improve logistics supporting capability all around.

REFORM OF CHINA'S DEFENSE INDUSTRY

Shun Zhenhuan

Structure and Main Problems

China's defense industry system after 1949 was basically modeled on the plan in the former Soviet Union. It has been a highly centralized system since the first 5-year plan. Under the circumstances of a weak economic base, then, this system played an important role in concentrating abilities on those priority projects in the defense industry and rapidly improving the levels of weapon development and production. However, along with national reform, opening up, and the policy of developing the national economy, this kind defense industry system is not suited to the new situations.

A highly centralist planned economy can not meet the needs of the tremendous changes in military supplies. Those state-owned enterprises of the war industry command vast reserves of qualified scientists and technicians, high-level technology, well-equipped facilities and great potential. During peacetime there are fewer military production quotas, therefore many productive forces are left unused. But during wartime military supplies increase sharply and are urgently needed. In the face of today's unceasing changes in military strategy and operational modes as well as the continual improvement in weapons, modern war requirements for weapons and equipment have grown considerably.

Shun Zhenhuan is Senior Researcher at the State Planning Commission.

The special military enterprises could hardly satisfy the needs for supplies expended in warfare, even in a regional war. As a result, we should try to reform our present system in accordance with the objective requirements.

Because the military enterprises represent a small group, we can not hope such a closed system will encourage civil industry development. The Soviet Union proved this argument. The Soviet Union adopted a plan of highly centralized but separate military and commercial industries. Although there was remarkable success in the production of munitions, the price that was paid was the sacrifice of other civil industries that should have grown. Like the Soviet Union, China devoted major efforts to developing the A-bomb, the H-bomb, satellites, and nuclear-powered submarines with limited funds and an inadequate technical force. While some areas in the defense industry came up to advanced world standards, much of our general mode of production lagged. Shortcomings such as high consumption, high cost, inefficiency, and low quality were present everywhere, and some advanced defense technologies were set aside for years. Obviously this is harmful to the national economy.

The system has not solved these long-standing problems; for example, defense and commercial industries are separate, enterprises are isolated from each other, manufactures and imports are duplicated, and factories, whether large or small, are unnecessarily affected.

Management and administration followed conventional supply systems. The state issued projects, allocated materials of production, bought products, and assumed sole responsibility for profits and losses; consequently, enterprises were dependent on the state, and workers dependent on the enterprises. The military product price was fixed (cost and 5 percent of profit). One factory, one price, no matter the volume; the more cost, the more profit, and vice versa.

A poor variety of products made it difficult for military enterprises to be productive. Because most of the enterprises, over a long period of time, were preparing for war and targeted only military products, it was not until 1979 that the output value of commercial products in four war-industry departments finally accounted for 8.1 percent of the total output value.

The state had total control over military enterprises so that they could not develop their own designs. Lacking power and function, and with responsibility being divorced from profit, the enterprises were not at all vigorous.

From the 1960s to the mid-1970s, the movement called the construction of the third defense line was fully under way. Almost all the enterprises, were committed to large projects, pursued high production targets and were eager to succeed. They practiced the tactics of "mountain," "dispersion," "cave," "village," and so on. This finally resulted in a far-flung front that was too large in scale.

Success and Experience in Defense Industry Reform

After the CCP's Third Plenary Session of the Thirteenth Central Committee, China's defense industry was steadily reformed, as restructuring of the state economic system was implemented. During the past decade, the State Council and Military Commission of the Central Committee passed a series of resolutions: the State Council governed directly the six departments formerly run by the State Defense Science and Industry Commission but headed by both the State Council and Central Military Commission. According to their special needs, every military department, restructured themselves, from the governing body to administrative setup to product structure to internal organization to work patterns and distribution. The variety of changes propelled the defense industry forward. The success and experiences laid a good foundation for further reform.

New Merits of Military Production

The whole defense industry entered a new strategic stage of history after the reform. Scientific research for military products is carrying out a policy that emphasizes small scale and advanced levels. By putting stress on the foundation, strengthening key science and technology, and keeping in step with high technology, we are amking progress and are renewing our military production.

There are some new achievements in the nuclear industry. New nuclear weapons designs have given our strategic missile force the ability to counterattack, which is one of the important factors that helps establish our nation's international status. A new generation of research has also made considerable headway. The completed high-flux engineering test reactor provides a significant medium for development in the nuclear industry.

In the last decade, aviation industry factories have manufactured the most modern aircraft in history. Of the more than 20 types of aircraft on our assembly lines, 75 percent are new types that were put into production this decade. A new lot of fighters, attack planes, bombers, helicopters and unmanned planes have been furnished to the army to replace old ones. The fact that more advanced warplanes have been designed and finalized marks our capability to make aviation product designs of our own.

The ordnance industry is quickening its pace of renewing heavy weapons. The industry has been fruitful in manufacturing modern tanks, armored carriers, infantry fight vehicles, heavy-caliber guns, and antitank missiles.

Numbers of special ships—oceangoing comprehensive monitoring ships, oceangoing survey ships, oceangoing supply ships, landing ships, and minesweepers—are proof of the development of the ship-building industry. These ships successfully completed many trials. According to statistics, within the China Shipping Industrial Company, the output value of new-style products accounted for 60 percent of the gross value of industrial output, and of those products, 38.6 percent came up to the advanced world standards of the 1980s, including 47.7 percent of necessary ship-building industry accessories.

The successes in the space industry have attracted worldwide attention, especially the results in strategic missiles, space technology, and tactical missiles. In May 1980 we successfully launched a long-range carrier rocket to the Pacific for the first time. In October 1982 a rocket launched underwater from a submarine showed a qualitative leap in our strategic missile technology. The manifold tactical missile weapon systems finalized one after another are increasing the modern combat effectiveness of the troops. Today, our space technology reflects the advanced world standards:

- *The satellite retrieving technique.* Only the United States, the former Soviet Union, and China have mastered the technique, and China has successfully retrieved 11 satellites in succession
- *The multisatellite technique.* Following the former Soviet Union, the United States, and the European Space Bureau, China was the fourth country that launched several satellites at once with one carrier rocket.

- *Space measurement and control technique.* We have built more than 10 ground-observing stations containing complex monitoring and telecommunication centers, as well as oceangoing and tracking monitor ships, which together form a network that has world-class level measuring precision.
- *High-energy, low-temperature fuel rocket technique.* This represents a modern level of rocket science that is the same as that of the United States and France.
- *Earth stand satellite launching technique.* China is one of five countries that can launch such a satellite.

Great Advances in Commercial Products

Since the Third Plenary Session of the Thirteenth Central Committee, civilian production of the defense industry has made great strides. The proportion of commercial product output value in the industry has risen from 8.1 percent in 1979 to 62 percent in 1990.

Concerning the military enterprises located in 'three-line', from 1980 to 1987, the output value of their commercial products increased at an average rate of 40 percent a year, and in 1987 reached around 50 percent of the value of all military enterprises in the whole nation. According to preliminary estimates, departments in the defense industry have completed more than 400 main commercial product assembly lines, developed over 300 kinds of key products, and sent over 7,000 commercial products to market. For the last 10 years, they have supplied, to domestic and foreign markets, large quantities of products and technical equipment for energy, traffic, light textile, and other trades, and have technically transformed assortments of spare parts for import equipment to improve food machinery, packing machinery, and medical instruments. Isotopes (and their outcomes) have been used into agriculture, industry and medical services. Commercial aircraft is one good scene of prosperity: over 500 passenger transport planes are flying for over 70 airlines, and 13 main line passenger planes made cooperatively with Mydao Co. have been delivered to the General Administration of Civil Aviation of China. Three military factories, in Chongqing, Baotou, and Taiyuan, have the capacity to produce 5,000 open freight cars in 1 year but the investment is only 40 percent of what is needed to build these same items.

During the sixth 5-year plan, 193 kinds of commercial products made in defense industry departments won national gold, silver, or national invention prizes.

Through 10 years of experience and practice in developing commercial products, military enterprises created a set of rules for product development, administration, management and restructuring, organization, sales, and service:

- Develop production and subsistence, centering on production.
- Combine close-technology with multispecialized products, stressing technology products.
- Develop high-value, high-technology products and low-value, labor-intensive products, stressing the former.
- Develop key support products with side products, stressing key support products.
- Develop their own products and do those recommended by competent authorities, stressing their own developing.
- Use available military industry techniques combined with foreign advanced techniques, and take available military industry technology as the dominant factor.
- Introduce key-technique and equipment combined with assembly lines, stressing key techniques and equipment.
- Combine specialized assembly lines with mixed-assembly lines, stressing serialized assembly lines.
- Readjust structure, bring potential into full play, and reform production, combining all with building new assembly lines.
- Do both cooperative production and independent production, stressing cooperative production.
- Factories raise funds by themselves using every channel, and apply for state loans, stressing the former.
- Combine the plan with the market, relying mainly on the plan.
- Purchase raw materials and necessary accessories by themselves, supplemented by state allotments, stressing factory purchases.
- Sell not only according to competent authorities but also by enterprise-operated sales departments, stressing sales through the enterprises' own channels.
- Combine quality and credit with benefits, stressing quality and credit.

The Export of Commercial Productions

For a period of considerable time our defense industry basically did not export because until the reform and the opening up we did not want to be munitions merchants. In the Third Plenary Session of the Thirteenth Central Committee, we did away with that idea. Several departments in the defense industry have set up foreign-trade companies, featuring defense/commercial, industry-commerce, and technique-commerce enterprises. Trade contacts with more than 50 countries or areas exist. By the end of 1987, 65 military factories or enterprises were assigned to be the bases for exporting commercial mechanical and electronic products or to be independent enterprises with the right to conduct foreign trade on their own.

Commercial nuclear fuel has entered into the overseas market with the government's approval. The metal calcium made by the nuclear industry also occupies a certain status in international market.

Aircraft made in China were on display at the International Aviation Fair. Six Y-12s, a light multiuse plane of our own design and manufacture, was sold to overseas buyers. Another new medium-range transport plane carrier-8 was also exported. The British General Administration of Civil Aviation, recognized as a worldwide authority in aviation, issued a certificate of quality to our carrier-12 in 1990; this signifies that the carrier-12 has reached a world-class level and increases the plane's export channels. Besides the eight already sold, we have also signed contracts for 14 other carrier-12s. Our aviation industry system as a whole has exported several hundred aircraft to about 10 countries, and has also exported aircraft engines, carrier equipment, parachutes, and aircraft spare parts. We manufactured aircraft parts and engine parts for a dozen foreign factories or companies, thus earning foreign exchange totalling 12 million.

Ordnance industry manufactured and sold their motorbikes, bicycles, and others to the United States and other countries or areas. During just the first sixth of the 5-year plan, the exports and projected contracts of the whole ordnance industry were 80 percent of the total business of the preceding 30 years.

Our space technology started servicing the international market. The Long-March-2, Long-March-3, and Long-March-4 carrier rockets were put on the international market one after another. In 1987 and 1989, we provided carrier service to the former West Germany and France using our retrieval satellites. Our new Long-March-2E and

Long-March-3 carrier rockets will launch satellites for Australia and an Asian satellite company. This is a indication that China is entering the international space technology international market and is catching up with the advanced world.

The shipbuilding industry was unwilling to lag behind in their export business. In the latter half of 1981, the world's shipbuilding output was less than half its actual production capacity, and many shipyards went bankrupt. But China's shipbuilding output rose uninterrupted, doubling from 1986 to 1987. And during the first seventh of the 5-year-plan, ship exports were 1.53 million tons, twice as much as that during the first sixth of the 5-year-plan. The volume of export was 40 percent of the general volume of ship-building. The trade volume of export business reached $2.3 billion, three times as much as during the first sixth of the 5-year plan.

Military Technology Shifts to Commercial Use

- *Initial Trial Sale of New Developed Products.* This means to sell products of the partner's own manufacture, which are not brought into line with the civilian production plan but have a higher technology level.
- *Technology Cooperation.* Both sides make full use of their own favorable conditions and technological superiority to share work and cooperate with each other according to the rules of their contracts.
- *Contracting Projects.* These are contracts for surveying and designing industrial and commercial projects.
- *Technology Shareholder.* Actions when one exchanges his technology as a price for buying shares and cooperates with another who introduces the technology. Both sides constitute an economic stake.

The conversion of military technology to commercial uses has many objectives. It may be domestic or external. Domestically, it can be geared to big enterprise or small township factories and even used in the agricultural sector.

The transfer of military technology to commercial technology may occur in various ways and forms. Through mediums such as technical interchange and the technology market, both sides can strike bargain, or by means of direct talks they make agreements. The following ummary of our practices in carrying out technology transfers amke clear the five areas in which we find it important to engage jointly:

- Joint efforts in the research and development of the state's major items of technological innovation.
- Utilizing the state or district's major capital construction and technology to rebuild items.
- Joint programs to carry out each city or district's economic development.
- Combine efforts to import advanced foreign technology and equipment, and to evaluate, digest, assimilate, and redesign the state's needs.
- Give full play to the technical forces in the Ministry of Machine-building and the Ministry of Electronics Industry.

Joint Defense/Commercial General and Special Policies

Although this is not easy, it is a good beginning and lays a foundation for building military/commercial joint efforts. There are five general policies on the conversion from defense to military/commercial joint enterprises:

- With regard to service, the military enterprises change from formerly serving only the defense industry to serving the military sector prior to others and managing in an all-around way to serve both the defense industry and commercial industry for national economic construction.
- About product structure, the national defense industry has been changing step by step from one production method to various types of production and administration. Now the variety of products made by the industry show that the industry has the ability to make not only war products but also commercial products.
- Concerning enterprise structure, the industry should adopt a style of cross union in order to cooperate with other industries in economics and technology.
- For product development, the focus should be transferred from general products to high-quality, high-tech, intensive-tech products for both the domestic and export markets

- On management, military enterprises should expand from production alone to the development of new products, technical training, market forecasting, and repair services.

Taking Further Steps to Restructure the National Defense Industry

The ultimate aim of restructuring our defense industry is to build a integrated system of defense/commercial production viable for both war and peace times. In addition, we should build a multi-administrative policy body we can centralize or decentralize. The system must guarantee that the State Council and Central Military Commission are able to keep national defense under their macro control, which includes control of the direction, scale, speed, layout and structure of national defense development. Moreover, it will help national economic actions to keep its vitality, separate organization from production and streamline administration.

Suggestions about how to make various military enterprises more efficient include further reduction of scale, adjustment of structure, strengthening macrocontrol, increasing necessary investment, and making serious efforts to develop commercial products. To realize defense/commercial production unity, the national defense industry should serve the Four Modernizations, meaning take on a double task:

- One, they should center their intelligent and capable power on research and developing new weapons, track foreign high technology, lay a good technological foundation, heighten technical levels, and provide service for strengthening the combat effectiveness of our army.
- Two, in their commitment to support national economic construction, they should energetically support the transfers from defense to commercial technology.

From now on, to reform our national defense industry, we must concentrate on eight aspects:

- To *develop an appropriate scale for military production, institute a system of so-called small military production but great mobilization.* Appropriate scale of military production is the basis of national defense industry and its modernization. In peacetime, too much volume of military products might be unfavorable to national economic development, whereas too little could be unfavorable to national defense construction and might shrink it. So the scale depends on military needs but is restricted by China's economic limitations. Compared to some other countries conditions, the national defense sector has abilities to design and produce, much more than in peacetime. If our national defense industry wants to be good at meeting emergencies, to be able to produce not only in peacetime but also in wartime, a system of so-called small military production and great mobilization, should be considered as a way to restructure the existing national defense system. The new system keeps the appropriate productive scale in peacetime by managing the whole business according two different factors, standing ability and mobilizing ability. Standing ability means not only meeting the orders of military equipment every year, but also taking on the tasks of replacing the old with the new, researching and developing new weapons, trading military products, and following a policy of "more research and development, less production; higher level, small batch; more technology reserve, less product reserve." Mobilizing ability means, based on the core of standing ability, make full use of existing surplus energy, and then design a mobilizing plan, finally working out mobilization rules and perfecting its regulations, depending on the district economy and industry. It will help to strengthen industry administration and cooperation, thus building gradually a mobilization system of rational distribution, perfect regulation, and quick-action that is efficient and qualified and that pursues joint defense/commercial production in both war and peacetime.

● *To restructure the existing administrative system and enhance the enterprises' vitality.* There are six rules we have to follow in restructuring our national defense industry:

1. National defense economic and administrative systems need to get onto the right path of the socialist market economy.

2. The reforms must accord with economic construction, upholding the four cardinal principles as well as continuing the reform and opening up.

3. The national defense construction is the strategic development principle.

4. The reform should suit the needs of the system and the operation of the socialist market economy.

5. A policy of joint defense/commercial production in war and peacetime is the policy that must be implemented from beginning to end.

6. Every plan must consistently adhere to combining national safety with national economic benefit.

The national defense system will adjust its industrial and productive structure, according to the principles of planning, rational division of labor, mutually complementary advantage, and coordinated development. The department responsible for military enterprises will send the plans for adjustment of research and production of military products one by one, down to their enterprises as soon as possible. This will further restructure these enterprises by making them more self-governing so that they have the rights and duties that average state enterprises have. It will help most of them to become socialist commercial firms, and manufacturers that are able to run a business by themselves and assume sole responsibility for their profits or losses. In addition to fulfilling military orders, it will intensify the reform of the administrative system by pursuing and perfecting production, and by rewarding the hardworking but punishing inferior quality and indolence, it willencourage military enterprises and their workers.

Military enterprises need to heighten their commodity consciousness, market sense, and competitive ideas and keep aware of market information isre always changing, the factories should constantly develop new products on the basis of market requirements. They also must foster the three kinds of motivation forces that modern factories have: inventing or finding new technology, applying new technology to production, and promoting products to domestic and external markets.

The military sector should introduce competition through separate cost accounting for defense and commercial products, which would solve the problems that arise from sharing equally regardless of ability or contribution. A small accounting unit exists within every factory. Under certain conditions, a branch or workshop of a factory will run relatively independently, whereas the group of enterprises that possesses economic strength will properly retain the power of decisionmaking over investment.

After talking with departments and districts concerned, the factories, which must have approval not to undertake military production, can according to their technical specialty and equipment situation, decide to whom they are subordinate. They can also not change subordinate relationships and just incorporate each kind of products into commercial departments or districts, taking responsibility for production plans and product types.

We encourage interindustry, interdepartmental, and interregional relationships. The factories can arrange their production on the basis of voluntarism, mutual benefit, specialized cooperation, and responsibility, and can develop new products by way of economic or technical cooperation with each other.

We will give energetic support to export commodities and urge enterprises to be familiar with the concept of two resources and two abilities. They should open up their own path to international markets through widespread cooperation and strengthen their competitive power through high-quality, low-priced products.

The enterprises located in the third defense line could, if possible, open a "window" in coastal cities or special to develop commercial products. The experiences of the last few years have showed that there are some principles we have to follow:

1. Focus on exports, combine production with trade, technology with commerce, and recognize that specialization is important but promote a diversified economy.
2. Actively depend on the backbone of the enterprises, uphold import but cooperate with internal; take products as the key factors to give full play to the "window."
3. Have both exports and imports to keep the foreign exchange balance and to win more foreign exchange; to bring economic benefits, stress advanced technology that could improve the quality of products, increase the variety, speed up the replacement of the old with the new, and lower the consumption of resources and materials.
4. Putting the stress on the key products that are intensive science and technology, take the above-mentioned road of import, digestion, creation, and development.

5. Boldly attract the investment of foreign capital, raise funds in every way, and actively use them.

6. Give full play to the enterprises and enhance competitive power through union with others.

7. Make full use of favorable conditions, create special districts or open cities as bridges to trade with Hong Kong, Taiwan, and surrounding countries, and then expand to other countries and areas.

8. Enable special districts to become centers for training managers, engineers, and other qualified personnel.

9. Strengthen the enterprises by adjusting both the plan for military production and the quantity of important civil production and by removing factories from the third line; formulate specific policies for reorganization, merger, and cooperation of the enterprises; and implement a rational organized system for each enterprise and form competent groups of enterprises in the spirit of voluntary participation and mutual benefit.

• *Macroguidance and coordination.* While arranging production, research, and construction, the State Planning Commission and all departments and districts concerned will, according products and the division of administration, merge commercial and defense production in line with state, industry, or district plans. This needs overall consideration, all-round arrangement, rational distribution, plus looking ahead and behind and proceeding from the interests of the state. There will be support of any item or product in the aforesaid plans. The above-mentioned governing groups will treat defense or commercial production equally and arrange investments, loans, and materials for both without discrimination according to the principle that although defense production is the same it has priority in the near future.

If military sectors are able to research or manufacture some product and are able to ensure its long-term supply, the commercial sector will no longer produce this kind product.

To protect national industry and avoid unnecessary equipment imports or technology re-introduction, the military sector should utilize existing abilities as fully as possible to produce things that can supply the market over a long period of time and to guarantee the products' quality and quantity.

When, in commercial industries, products are needed to expand production or some items require a large research basis, the military enterprises' surplus abilities, technical superiority and facilities should first taken into account. For any items needing technological reconfiguration, we should choose the better one between a defense or a commercial enterprise.

The nation will broadly guide the defense sector to cooperate with the commercial sector to developcommercial products. This will depend on market requirements and on enterprise's expertise. The aim is coordination rather than unchecked independence.

Defense and commercial units may have mutual concerns and need to exchange information, solutions, and motivations. The industries, departments, and districts will set up mediation netowrks and go between them to solve related problems.

We will link the military development plan with each regional economic development program.

● *Parts of products will be directionally developed for a long time.* The experience in that last decade shows these are the rules we have to follow:

1. To avoid harming the interests of the whole, arrange production and technical reconfiguration, in accordance with state industrial policies and macroscopic guidance as well as the requirements of domestic or foreign markets, and not based on just what enterprise wants.

2. In transferring military technology to commercial uses, choose products similar in structure and close in technology, use existing workshops and facilities, and strive for little investment but high production.

3. Devote major efforts to technology-intensive equipment that is difficult for commercial enterprises to manufacture, as well as to famous, excellent, new, and special products; fill the gap and eliminate shortages in technology.

4. Develop substitutes for import products or analyze foreign technology and master imported products as much as possible for reproduction and imitation.

5. Proceed from the actual situations of each factory or each product in deciding the technology methods for mass production, sticking to coordination on specialties.

The state economic complex and related department or district will stipulate that some enterprises will have a long-term commitment to manufacture and develop certain productsaccording to the above rules. The military sector can turn production tasks over to the commerical sector. In peacetime, this division of tasks would not be altered, and the commercial sector will not generally invest in expanding the productive capacity of the products. If disputes arise regarding significant commercial items, we may settle them through public bidding. The military production will proceed in a planned way, avoiding blind competition and duplicate construction and research.

• *Further apply military technology to the national economy.* Our defense industry has mastered more advanced technologies through backbreaking research and the manufacture of weapons. It will take effective measures to transfer these technologies to commercial uses, making them productive forces for the whole society, and pushing commercial technology forward, helping it master foreign techniques of production and scientific knowledge.

• *Military enterprises also need necessary technological renewal.* Among the military enterprises, not a small number have to face the problem of obsolete equipment. A national industrial census indicates that advanced equipment makes up only 3 percent of all equipment in the military sector, whereas it is 12.9 percent in commercial sector. About 40 percent of equipment used in some old military factories is over 20 years old, and some of it dates to World War Two. If not replaced, the existing assembly lines could not meet the needs of the renewed military or commercial production, especially under mass production.

• *Raise special funds for developing commercial products only.* Nowadays the urgent issue is to provide much-needed funds to transfer military technology to national economic construction. Each military department raises funds in every possible way and rationally cuts down expenses, but the state should provide financial support in the coming few years.

• *Lay down national defense production rules.* As part of modernizing the defense industry, we ought to draw up a set of regulations. It will be used to produce, research, reform, and renew military products. Also, it must involve the policies on remuneration and welfare, as well as on training workers, engineers, and managerial personnel in military enterprises. In addition, it should stipulate policies on raw material supplies, labor force disposition, productive coordination, peacetime preparation, and wartime mobilization within military sector.

CATEGORIES OF MILITARY SCIENCE

Lieutenant General Zheng Wenhan

Military science is a system of knowledge about war, laws for guiding wars and principles of war preparations and combat operations. Military science plays an important role in guiding force development and provides theoretical methods of fighting and winning a war. The objects of the study of military science are wars and other activities of military practice.

War and Laws for Guiding Wars

The most important task of military science is to study the causes of wars, the nature of wars, the relation between war and politics, economics, science, geography, etc., and to explore the law of emergence of wars and development, so as to lay the foundations for guiding wars correctly.

According to the characteristics of the moves of contradictions, any war has its generality and individuality, universality and particularity. The common law of war moves and war development is defined to be the general law of wars, and the general law exists in the special law of wars as the universality and generality exist in the particularity

---

Lt. General Zheng Wenhan is a former President of the Academy of Military Science, Beijing. This paper is from Zheng, ed., An Outline of Military Science *(Beijing: Academy of Military Science Press, 1994).*

and individuality. In order to guide a war correctly, it is necessary for us to have a good grasp of not only the general law of wars but the special law of wars. The law of wars is an objective reality, which always acts in wars and affects them spontaneously and mandatorily, no matter whether you have thought about it or have not. Thus, we say that laws for guiding wars are concrete and lively expressions of the dynamic theory of knowledge as reflected in the reality in wars.

Theory and Method of Operational Command

The theory and method of operational command are relative to forms and means of military activities that depend upon the main task of the army, the object of operation, weaponry and equipment, operational capacity, and the enemy's strength and intention, all of which contain the theory, method, and means to conduct war, campaign, and combat. With the rapid development of science, technology, and the expansion of war scale, the difficulties and complications in operational command increase daily. The military academia has paid much attention to doing research on how operational command could meet the requirements of the development of military technology. Consequently, strategies, operational science, tactics and army command science are created. Operational method is not unchangeable but develop with material production, scientific progress, and enrichment of war knowledge. An important task of military science is to study, explore, and create new operational theories, principles, and methods based on production development and scientific and technical progress, so that we can keep a fail-proof position in future wars.

The Theory of Armed Force Construction

Armed force construction and its development strategy are another important research area, which mainly includes the theories of armed force organization, construction and system of leadership; its structure and quantity; weapons and equipment; education and training; and administration, politics, and logistics support. Accompanying the studies on these theories and their applied principles is the development of the military system science, military education and training science, military administration science, military politics, and military logistics.

The armed forces, as a part of the state machine, have been developing continuously with the development of productive forces and war. In order to maintain national security interests, countries have always paid special attention to all aspects of the construction of armed forces such as military constitutions, education and training, weapons and equipment, reserves force construction, logistics support, and so on.

Weapons and Technical Equipment

Weapons and technical equipment are the material foundation for an army's combat effectiveness. Since war first emerged in society, weapons and technical equipment have been the essential materials for an army and have become the vital material means to fight and win wars. Military applications are almost always given priority major inventions or improvements are always given priority to apply to the military. In the history of war, the development of weapons and equipment can be divided into several stages, namely cold weapons, hot weapons, nuclear weapons, and high-tech weapons. The magnificent development of weapons and technical equipment and their applications to the army promote the development and change of military organization, war patterns, and operational ways and methods. Anyone who looks down on the great role of weapons and technical equipment or has no necessary weaponry and technical equipment would pay the price of blood in a war. On the one hand, the development of weapons and technical equipment has been exerting a tremendous influence on the development of armed forces, the final result of war, and the evolution of military arts. On the other hand, the needs of war and the evolution of military theory conversely ask weapons and technology to meet their requirements and promote the innovation and development of weapons and technical equipment.

With studies on the trial manufacturing, production, and use and maintenance of weapons and technical equipment, people created weaponry, ammunition science, shooting science, ballistics, military engineering, navy technology, air force technology, armored force technology, nuclear physics, military electronics, military chemistry, and astronautics.

Military History

Military history is one of the earliest subjects of military science. Military history records the events of war and facts of military activities which reflect the operational ways and methods and operation principles applied by opposing sides in the war. There were numerous books about military history in ancient Greek, Rome and China. In order to win a victory, ancient military scientists paid tremendous attention to the study of war history and the exploration of strategy and principle for directing wars. In the study of the development of military thought, operational method, and armed forces buildup, in order to sum up the experience and lessons of war, people created various subjects and sciences such as war history, military history, history of military science, military historical material science, compiling historical literature science etc.

Military Geography

Geographic environment and natural conditions have had important influence not only upon war, but also on national army construction and military thought. War and military activities have always been conducted in a certain space. If you want to control wars, you should research geographic conditions and their influence on military actions. You should research natural geography conditions, understand which condition is favorable to military operations and which is not, and know how to give full play to the strong points and avoid weak points. The main task for military geographic studies should be having a clear understanding about an enemy state's strategic pivot, the hub of communications, the center for politics, economics and culture, and strategic military, political, and economic areas and objects.

The Others

With the progress of modern science and technology, it is a developing trend for science to be increasingly split and synthesized. The scope of military science studies is continuously widening. A lot of new subjects, such as military operational analysis, war mobilization science, military future science, the science of military law, and so on are emerging.

In conclusion, the seven fields mentioned above form the various subjects related to military science. These are the sciences of military thought, military art, theory of armed force construction, military technology, military history, and military geography. All are interdependent, influence each other, promote each other, are closely tied together, and constitute the integrated theory system of military science.

Classification by China

In 1948, Mao Zedong said that military science mainly included strategy, tactics, economics, politics, and military culture.

In 1959, the President of the Academy of Military Science Marshall Ye Jianying said military science could be divided into three parts, namely military thought, military art, and military technology. In February 1960, he put forward a new set of classifications, as follows:

MILITARY SCIENCE
I. Science of Theory
  A. Military Thought
    1. Strategies
    2. Operations
    3. Tactics
  B. Military Art
    1. Military System Science
    2. Military Mobilization
    3. Military Training
    4. Military History
    5. Military Geography
II. Science of Technology
  A. Military Technology

We think that the theoretic system of military science should include military thought, military art, theory of armed force construction, military technology, military history, military geography and other frontier science:

MILITARY SCIENCE
A. Military Thought
    1. Military Dialectics
    2. Ancient Military Thought
    3. Bourgeois Military Thought
    4. Proletarian Military Thought
B. Military Art
    1. Strategies
    2. Operational Science
    3. Tactics
    4. Army Command Science
C. Theory of Armed Force Construction
    1. Military System
    2. Military Education and Training
    3. Military Management
    4. Army Politics
    5. Military Logistics
D. Military History
    1. War History
    2. Military History
    3. History of Military Science
    4. Science of Compiling Military Literature
E. Military Geography
    1. Military Geography
    2. Military Meteorology
F. Military Technology
    1. Weaponry
    2. Science of Shooting
    3. Ammunition Science
    4. Ballistics
    5. Navy Technology
    6. Air Force Technology
    7. Armored Force Technology
    8. Military Engineering
    9. Ballistics Missile Science
  10. Nuclear Physics
  11. Astronautics
  12. Military Electronics

13. Military Chemistry
G. Frontier Science
  1. Science of Military Law
  2. Science of Military Future

Military science takes war, a special social phenomenon, as its object of study. It is a kind of comprehensive science, which has close relations with social science, natural science, and philosophy.

The Relationship Between Military Science and Philosophy

Almost all military scientists, in modern or ancient times, in China or elsewhere, attach importance to analyzing and demonstrating war, the objective law of war, and the law of directing war from the angle of philosophy. The earliest military thought was contained in philosophic works. Since the development of military science, military theory gradually separated from philosophy and developed independently. Mao Zedong integrated military theory with philosophic theory, advancing a new concept of military dialectics to form a new subject in military science.

The Relationship Between Military Science and Social Science

Social science takes social phenomena as its object of study, while military science takes war activities, a special social phenomenon, as its object of study. War is a part of society as a whole. It is not only the main task for military science, but also an important task for social science to research the origin, the cause, the nature, and the development of war. The difference between them is just a different angle, a different emphasis of study. There is a famous sentence asserted by Clausewitz that states, "War is the continuation of politics by other means." By this he meant to stress that all strategy, all military activity, must be subordinated to clear political motivation and goals. Politics is pregnant with war, and war is its highest and the most violent form. It is imperative to have not only wide basic knowledge of military science but also a rich knowledge of politics, economics, and history from the social sciences for military science studies.

The Relationship Between Military Science and Natural Science
War activity has always been affected and restricted by the conditions of topography, climate, and hydrology. There is no exception to this in modern or ancient times, in China or elsewhere. Furthermore, the weapons and equipment that are the important elements of an army's fighting capacity, are restricted by not only economic capacity but also science and technology. Technology determines tactics while tactics in turn promote technology. Parts of military science is closely related with the physics, chemistry, geography, meteorology, astronomy, geology, and hydrology branches of the natural sciences. The combination of military science and these subjects has created relevant frontier science and intersecting science. Finally, many new and developing subjects in social science and natural science such as system engineering, theory of information, theory of control, theory of probability, future science, and electronic computer technology have been applied in the military field one after another. Thus, a lot of new military subjects have been created such as military system engineering, theory of military information, theory of military control, and theory of military system, which have enriched and developed the field of military science.

DIALECTICS OF DEFEATING THE SUPERIOR WITH THE INFERIOR

Senior Colonel Shen Kuiguan

Although instances of defeating a powerful opponent with a weak force can be cited from the early period of Chinese history, the establishment of a topic related to this concept has gone through a long process.

The concept of defeating a powerful opponent with a weak force, or defeating the enemy even when outnumbered has continually been put forward by people from the Yin, Zhou, Ming, and Qing Dynasties. Using historical materials, and on the basis of scientific conclusions about the development of war, Mao Zedong creatively and comprehensively explained the issue of defeating the superior with the inferior. He pointed out that war is a competition to win superior subjective initiatives between the commanders of two forces backed by financial capacity and military strength. The correctness or incorrectness of the subjective factor will turn the inferior into the superior, or passivity into initiative, or vice versa. We can conclude from Mao that the key to defeating the powerful with a weak force is making the most of subjective initiative. The weak force can change its unfavorable position and defeat a relatively powerful enemy.

There are some basic points about the definition of defeating a powerful enemy with a weak force:

Shen Kuiguan is a Professor at the Air Force Command Institute, Beijing; his paper originally appeared in China Military Science *(Winter 1994).*

First, the concept of superiority and inferiority covers a great deal. It is the manifestation of the overall balance of many factors between both belligerents.

Second, defeating the superior with the inferior is the result of integrating material and spiritual conditions. Without the first, it will be spiritual omnipotence; without the second, will be mechanical materialism. To stick to the dialectical unity of the two conditions is the correct dialectical materialist point of view.

Third, defeating the superior with the inferior must go through a certain course, that is, there are three periods: resisting the superior with the inferior, turning the inferior into the superior, and defeating the superior with the inferior.

Fourth, defeating the superior with the inferior, and defeating the inferior with the superior are dialectically related. They are related as ends and means, or whole and part. Defeating the superior with the inferior ends in campaigns and major battles. Overall this must be assured by first defeating the superior with the inferior *piecemeal*. They are mutually complementary

Modern high-tech war is a fierce competition using high-tech weaponry under nuclear deterrent or conventional conditions. In such a war, it will be difficult for the side that is at a disadvantage in technology and military strength to defeat the opponent, because the high-quality combat capacity of high-tech weaponry widens the disparities between the two sides. Although it is extremely difficult for the weaker side to defeat the powerful in a high-tech war, it is still possible.

The law of conversion from superiority to inferiority or vice versa is an important principle of military dialectics. It reveals the inexorable trend that the changes of balance between the two belligerents that is caused by the mutual functioning of many factors determines the mutual conversion of superiority and inferiority. As the conversion determines the ending of a war, it is a general principle dominating war development. Chairman Mao Zedong said, first, superiority and inferiority are a pair of important categories restricting victory or failure in a war. What we mean by superiority is the advantageous position in military strength and combat posture. It is composed of superior political conditions, powerful military forces, abundant material base, full war preparations, correct operational direction, advantageous natural conditions, favorable mass opinion, and international support, among which some factors occupy a dominant position. Inferiority refers to the disadvantageous position in military strength and combat posture. It contains political backwardness, weak military strength, insecure economic base, insufficient war preparations, poor leadership, disadvantageous natural conditions, unfavorable mass opinion and lack of international support, some of which play a leading role. Superiority and inferiority exist in all kinds of wars, they influence and determine the combat strategies, mode of operations, operational preparations and combat course, and finally, the victory or failure of the war. Second, superiority and inferiority are dialectically related:

- They are differentiated, antagonistic and mutually exclusive.
- They are interrelated, mutually inclusive and infiltrated.
- Under certain circumstances, they are mutually converted. That is to say, superiority can be turned into inferiority and inferiority into superiority under certain conditions.

Comrade Mao Zedong once said, "The advantageous position of the enemy can be weakened through our efforts and its disadvantages can also be intensified through our efforts. The same is true with our side. Through our efforts, our superiority can be consolidated and our shortcomings can be overcome, which will lead to our final victory and the defeat of the enemy."

Altering the overall balance of combat factors between two belligerents is the practical foundation of defeating the superior with the inferior. As Sun Tzu, world-famous ancient Chinese strategist, pointed out,

The victory or failure of a war is determined by Five Factors and Seven Aspects. The Five Factors are justice, weather, geography, command and regulations. Only when the commander has a thorough knowledge of these five, will he be able to defeat the enemy. Which side has justice? Which commander is more capable? Which possesses more favorable natural conditions? Which side enforces the law more strictly? Soldiers of which side are more assiduous in military training? Which side is more strict and fair in meting out rewards and punishments? By comparing the seven aspects, I can judge which side will win at last.

Later, some renowned strategists proved it from different angles and levels. Based on his understanding of the law of wars from the long history of China, Comrade Mao Zedong clearly stated, "Doubtlessly, victory or defeat in a war is determined by the conditions of both sides in the areas of military forces, the political situation, the economic conditions and the natural surroundings. But more than that, it is also determined by the capacity of subjective direction."

In other words, victory or failure in a war is not determined by a single factor or certain factors, but by changing the overall balance of all factors between two belligerents. One may be backward in weaponry or economics, but he may also be in a far more advantageous position than his enemy in political and geographical conditions, and subjective direction. As long as one makes the most of his strong points and takes advantage of the enemy's shortcomings, he can turn the enemy's advantage into disadvantage, his own disadvantage into advantage, and even with his inferior weaponry, he can defeat the enemy's superior weaponry.

Evidence of defeating the superior with the inferior has occurred in modern wars. In air force actions, examples are too numerous to mention individually. We have the earlier ones of the Battle of Britain, the Battle of Moscow, and the Battle of Stalingrad, and the recent ones of the air force actions in the Korean War and the Middle East War. The Vietnam War can be cited as a typical example of defeating the superior with the inferior in modern wars. It proved the fact that, with correct strategic principles, proper strategies, flexible tactics, and high operational efficiency, inferior forces will be able to defeat the superior enemy.

During the Gulf War, the victory of the United States and the defeat of Iraq can be explained by the great role of high-tech weapons. But the real cause for the victory of one side and the defeat of the other does not lie only in technical factors but also in the comprehensive superiority founded on many war factors, particularly the political nature and the subjective direction of the war. From the moment of its invasion of Kuwait, Iraq found itself in a completely isolated position in international opinion. Additionally, its economic dependence, inflexible strategies and passive defense tactics added to its inferiority, which consequently caused its inevitable defeat. A comprehensive understanding and analysis of the Gulf War are needed in order to avoid the erroneous conclusion that it is impossible for a weak force to defeat a powerful opponent in a high-tech war.

The basic way to defeat a powerful opponent with a weak force in a high-tech war is to bring the overall function of its operational system into full play, to persevere in defeating the superior with the inferior in crucial battles, and, through the integration of the above two aspects, attain the goal of turning the inferior into the superior and finally defeat the enemy. Bringing the overall function of its operational system into full play just means to strengthen the capacity and efficiency of the whole operational system that is composed of all the war factors. By perseverance in defeating the superior with the inferior in every crucial battle, we mean to muster superior forces and weapons, bring about favorable combat posture, and destroy the enemy. Bringing the overall function of the operational system into full play is a prerequisite for defeating the superior with the inferior in every crucial battle, and in turn, the victories of these battles will strengthen the overall function of the operational system. They are interrelated, organically integrated, and mutually supplemented.

The theory that bringing the overall function of the operational system into full play and persevering in defeating the superior with the inferior in every crucial battle is essential to defeating the superior with the inferior is based upon the following two points.

- The above-mentioned theory is the necessary embodiment of the law of the victory of the superior. War is the contention of the overall strength of the two belligerents. The law of victory of the superior is an objective law free of man's will. In modern wars, great changes have taken place in the means, forms, process, and scope of operations, but the law of the victory of the superior remains unchanged. In order to defeat a powerful enemy, the weak force must strengthen itself in the overall function of the operational system, which, of course, cannot be accomplished in a day. It must go through the process from quantitative change to qualitative change, during which, by means of mustering the superior forces and weaponry on the major battlefield, the weak force will be able to obtain a partial superior position and win in a small theater of war. Should continual victories be gained, the partial superiority will be turned into overall superiority and the final victory of the war can be won.

• The above-mentioned theory is the method of subduing the superior with the inferior in modern war. In high-tech war, it is impossible for the inferior side to obtain the overall superiority in a short time, but it is possible to muster its superior forces and weapons to a point. Usually, certain internal structures, certain parts or links of the superior side may be comparatively weak, and with the inferior side, there may also be some aspect or links which it has an advantage that is missing in the other side. To attack the weak part of the enemy with our strong force will undoubtedly result in victory.

With the help of military dialectics, we can not only get to know the ways and methods to defeat a powerful opponent with a weak force in a high-tech war, but we can also further understand and master the ways and methods of how to defeat the superior with the inferior. They can be summarized as the following:

• Defeating the enemy by making *key elements* superior. It requires the improvement of advantageous operational elements so as to maintain and developsuperiority. Modern wars are the entire confrontation between two belligerents in the overall function of operational systems including their many levels and factors. The promotion of each level and each factor is an important basis for bringing the overall function of the war system into full play. With one's overall function inferior to the enemy's, one must try to promote the major levels and factors; meanwhile, try to weaken some levels and factors of the war system of the opposing side. As a result, the inferior will become the superior and defeat the powerful enemy.

• Defeating the enemy by making *structure* superior. This refers to maximizing the overall function of our own system to defeat the superior enemy. Structure determines function and function affects structure. It is the basic requirement of the system for structure and function to be united on the basis of practical need. People's war has always been the major weapon used by our army to defeat the enemy, and it is crucial to the promotion of our combat structure. In a high-tech war, one should still depend on the principles of the people's war to defeat the superior enemy, for people's war can maximumly promote our combat superiority and degrade the enemy's superiority. In a high-tech war, as long as we persist in allying various armed forces, combining various combat forms and integrating armed operations with non-armed operations, we can employ the great role of people's war and isolate the enemy.

• Defeating the enemy by making *strategy* superior. Strategy is essential to the directions of the army. Without it, one can hardly succeed. In a high-tech war, superior strategy is significant to defeating the powerful opponent with a weak force. In the Third Middle East War, Israel was obviously at a disadvantage in the prewar period, but its successful use of superior strategies led to Egypt's erroneous judgement in operational orientation. With Egypt's focus turned to the Gulf, Israel launched a surprise attack on Egypt and destroyed most of its air force.

• Defeating the enemy by making *operational methods* superior. Better operational method has constantly been the most direct and effective measure to subdue the enemy. In a high-tech war, the abruptness, speedy rhythm, variations of mode, and high efficiency of an operation have made the operational method extremely important. In the Gulf War, Iraq mechanically used the regular operational method under the technical conditions of a high-tech war, adopted the linear defense method, and lost good combat opportunities, while the multination forces, headed by U. S. troops, adopted the nonlinear combat method and launched surprise attacks and won the war.

In addition, there are the methods of "defeating the enemy by making *the dynamic state* superior" which means changing the combat postures of both sides, and "defeating the enemy by making *time-space* superior" which means making correct choices and seizing opportunities.

In conclusion, high-tech war is a relative concept, which reveals different characteristics in different periods of time, but the law of mutual conversion of the superior and the inferior is a permanent concept. No matter what new techniques or weapons are used, there is the possibility of a weaker force defeating the powerful opponent. So long as we stick to the combat principles of defeating the superior with the inferior and actively create the conditions, we will be able to win victory in future high-tech wars.

NOTES ON MILITARY THEORY AND MILITARY STRATEGY

Lieutenant General Li Jijun

Maturity of War Comes Earlier than Maturity of Peace

In the 20th century, the scale, forms, and means of war as well as the corresponding military theories have reached a level hitherto unknown. This century has seen great progress in science, technology, and social development, but has also suffered from the unprecedented catastrophes of two world wars. The 20th century holds unusual significance for the Chinese people. At the beginning of the century, the united army of eight countries invaded Beijing, and the powers carved up China. One hundred years later, and at the end of this century, China will be a comparatively well-off socialist society, and Hong Kong and Macao will return to the motherland. It can be said that the Chinese people were in a state of misery and suffering at the beginning of the century, but enjoy stability and well-being at the end of the century. The change was achieved through the hard struggle, blood and sacrifice of lives by countless martyrs, and fine sons and daughters of the Chinese nation. When they examine their conscience at the end of this century, the Chinese people will feel no qualms for the century or for mankind.

Lieutenant General Li Jijun is Vice-President of the Academy of Military Science, Beijing. This article is from his book, Military Theory and Conflict *(Beijing: Academy of Military Science Press, 1994).*

We can expect that in the next century the possibility of the breakout of world war will be minimal, but the peace is far from reaching maturity. As a multipolar world structure gradually comes into being, there will be contradictions of economic interests among multiple centers, and complex ethical and cultural conflicts make the occurrence of local war and military conflict unavoidable. While the global economy moves towards integration, regional economic interests affect many countries, so some local wars or military conflicts may see the formation of coalitions. The participation of big powers and the purchase of modern military weapons and equipment by smaller nations or regional groups make it possible that local wars or military conflicts could also be high-tech. At the turn of the century, the problems and requirements that world military theory and strategy will face are as follows:

- How long will it take for the world to develop from a system of one super power and multiple centers to a new world strategic structure of multipolar balance? Every country without exception will consider its own strategic problems with this as the large backdrop. It took about 40 years before the British empire's monopoly in the mid-19th century changed to a situation in which the United States, Germany, Japan, Russia, Britain, and France being the six imperial powers vying for hegemony. It took another 40 years before the coexistence of the six big powers at the beginning of the century changed into the bipolar world of the United States and the Soviet Union at the end of the Second World War. It took still another 40 years before the Cold War between the two super powers changed into a situation of one super power with multiple centers after the disintegration of the Soviet Union. We do not know whether the three forties are a regular historical pattern or just coincidences, but we can be certain that absolute hegemonic power is sure to decline. Because of the fast development and globalization of science, technology and economics, the dispersion of world power will speed up. It probably will not take another 40 years before a world structure of multipolar coexistence comes into being. It might take 10 or 20 years to take shape. During this transitional period, the world situation might be very unstable, with outbreaks of local wars and military conflicts. We should form our national defense and military strategy within this international framework, in order to safeguard our national interests, safeguard our territorial sovereignty and ocean rights, and provide a secure environment for the construction of the four modernizations.

• Seen from the world's point of view, and especially from the superpower's point of view, there is great unbalance between the purpose and the means of war. Nuclear weapons have reached the state of oversaturation. Even if they can not be totally destroyed, they must stop within the limit of deterrence and must not leap over to become the actual means of combat. Otherwise, it would either be the end of war, or the end of the mankind. Now that the superpowers practice military interventionism, and interfere and intervene all over the place, they are the police and the arms dealer of the world. When they spread the latest model of new weaponry, and aggravate local conflicts, do they think of the future when one day nuclear weapons and other weapons of mass destruction fall into the hands of terrorist groups, or become the bombs of the hijackers of the earth, and all the people of the world are turned into hostages? At that time, they should not blame others, but blame the super power that first practiced nuclear blackmail. Anyhow, now is the time to reconsider the purpose and means of war.

• Geoeconomics will dominate geopolitics. War is the continuation of politics, and more directly is the continuation of economics. When we talk about the fundamental causes of war, it is undoubtedly the contradiction and struggle of economic interests, including conditions for survival and territorial sovereignty. With regard to the ethnic and cultural conflicts, they often appear to be the driving force behind actual wars, but are more often than not swayed by big power's economic interests. Looking back on the course of history, peace under the guardianship of big powers is totally unreliable.

• High-tech local war will gradually become the leading, mature form of war. Whenever human progress in science and technology and their applications are expanded into a new area, battlefields follow closely behind. Modern wars have become the competition of the comprehensive power of nations, symbolized by the level of their high technology. The scope of wars has expanded from the traditional battlefields of land, sea, and air into the fields of electromagnetism, space, and biology. As a result, the command, control and coordination of the different services of the army in the battlefield, and the comprehensive utilization of the fields of politics, economics, culture, science and technology and diplomacy will be a more acute problem. This will certainly cause changes in strategy, battle methods, guiding theory on tactics, and fighting methods. However, all these will not change the fundamental principle that "people are the decisive factor in the war," and weapons are but the manifestation of human knowledge.

● The new strategic situation and its development trends will require new strategic thinking. Past strategic thinking of blocs, nuclear war, and a bipolar balance has all become a thing of the past. New objective reality requires the guidance of new military theory. Creative strategic thinking is often born in a period of turbulence, historic change, and great structural change. Only when we have established new models of strategic thinking can we solve the problem of predicting and making judgments on the world strategic situation.

● People usually refer to strategy, battle methods, and tactics as the art of war. Its highest level is grand strategy, which is the art and science of utilizing and strengthening the comprehensive power of a nation to realize long-term political goals. The philosophical thinking of the art of war is military dialectics, or military philosophy. Its keys are the theory of knowledge and methodology in military affairs. Only when military dialectics have been mastered can practical experience be raised to the level of ideology and theoretical treasure. And only when this tool of understanding has been mastered can the areas of practice, guide, and study be consciously entered and current military strategic problems solved. Military science has strong application in guiding practice. We must adhere to the ideological line of seeking truth from facts and discover in the objective military field regular patterns and raise them to the level of theory and not cut objective reality and discover laws from ideology. We should not be separated from the basis of military practical experience, but we should also be ahead of the practice. Otherwise, the country might be inflicted with disasters. That is the seriousness of military science.

The Science of Strategy

The science of strategy is not satisfied by one particular historical pattern of war or by the result and viewpoint of one particular war. It constantly uses new war experiences, new war models, new technical equipment's effect on war to study and guide warfare. The Gulf War, for example, symbolizes the beginning of a new phase. The domination of the battlefield by cold weapons, hot weapons, and nuclear weapons has been changed into domination by high-tech weaponry. That is to say, the emergence of the new character of local war or military conflict a few years ago has now gradually become the leading factor on the battlefield. It will cause change in the patterns of war, and this is the rule. For instance, the use of rifles caused the change in the formation of combat teams, creating dispersed formations. Trench warfare appeared after machine guns and wire netting. When the infantry could not make a breakthrough, they expanded into two flanks. Protracted flanks appeared in the First World War, and fronts were long and unbroken. After the introduction of tanks, machine guns and wire netting were of no use, thus mobile warfare appeared. During World War I, tanks were the new weapons but not the dominant ones. During World War II, planes and tanks became the dominant weapons on the west front of the battlefield, and great depth of attack and high speed in the form of combat occurred. The United States used more than 80 high-tech weapons in the Gulf War, and these new weapons are beginning to play the dominant role on the battlefield. This form of high-tech warfare has just emerged, and its rules and regular patterns are not completely revealed yet. However, we must realize that the domination of the battlefield by these high-tech weapons will cause a series of changes in the patterns of war, forms of combat, combat command, or even in the strategic control.

In terms of the range of the battlefield, the high-tech local war battle field will include land, sea, air and space, as well as areas of electromagnetism. We can say that each wave in the development of mankind added an area of battlefield. For example, the first wave added the area of sea battle. The second wave, the industrial revolution added the area of air battle. The third wave, information, has added two new battle fields in outer space and in the area of electromagnetism. So the coming of each wave of industry and technological revolution has added a corresponding area of battlefield. We can say that the Gulf War has brought about many new changes.

It takes a long time to prepare for high-tech local war, but the process of war is short. However, it costs too much—the Gulf War cost $61.1 billion for a very short time period. This war could be divided into three phases. The first was *Desert Shield*, lasting 167 days and accounting for 80 percent of the total process of the war. This phase mainly saw the assembly and transport of forces. The second phase, *Desert Storm*, was the phase of air strikes, it lasted 38 days and accounted for 18 percent of the total process of the war. The third phase was *Desert Sword*, the phase of ground attack, which lasted only 4 days and accounted for 2 percent of the total process of the war. This reflects a rule that the preparation time for the high-tech war is long, the attack time is short, and the rhythm of the war is fast.

During the Korean War, it was mainly the armed forces of the United States and South Korea that did the fighting. Britain sent two brigades, Turkey sent one, and the other 12 nations sent only symbolic troops. During the Gulf War, the majority of the allied forces on the side of the United States sent real troops, and Germany and Japan contributed money. The combat areas of high-tech war were expanded, and although it was a local war, it involved the interests of many nations and had the character of alliance and internationality, because of money and troops contributed by the allied countries.

In the way of attack, it was very different from the past. Take the air strike for example, in the past the first strike would be at the front, and then strike behind the front line. The Gulf War was different in that it first struck headquarters, then the crucial energy and production facilities, then the transportation system, and finally the armed forces. Compared with past strikes, the sequence was turned around. It is very important for the combat commander to learn this change.

In terms of the requirements of organization and command, the Gulf War was a war of systems against systems. The C^3I system became the nerve center of the whole war. The strategic and campaign battles were often mixed together. The campaign battles became more important, and had the characteristics of the strategic battles. The first battle of a high-tech war could also be the last one. This places higher demands on the quality of service personnel, especially of commanders and commanding offices.

Of course, we must also see the limitations of high-tech local war. The Gulf War itself was not typical. U.S. Armed Forces revealed many weak points. For example, the combat consumption was too great, and it could not last long. There was great reliance on the allied countries. The high-tech equipment was intensive and its key links rather weak; once they were damaged, combat effectiveness was greatly reduced. Also, if the adversary of the United States was not Iraq, if the battle was not fought on the flat desert, if the Iraq armed forces struck first during the phase when U.S. Armed Forces were still assembling, or if Iraq armed forces withdrew suddenly before the U.S. Armed Forces struck, then the outcome of the war might have been quite different. High-tech war has not at all changed the decisive role played by the people. In the history of wars, each time when there was a revolution in military technology, it was easier to ignore at the beginning, and then when it became established, its role was often exaggerated.

The Study of Strategy

Strategy concerns the survival of a nation and the dangers of war and therefore must be handled with great care. For a nation or an army, the managing of strategy quite often decides the outcome of the war or the survival of a nation. We all know that the failure of the Soviet Union at the start of its war against Hitler was due to many factors, but it was chiefly because of strategic mistakes, and the causes can be found in Soviet strategic policies and combat theories. For instance, the Soviet Union did not seriously learn the lessons of the Spanish War and Germany's surprise attack on France. In the purges from 1937 to 1938, large numbers of senior military leaders were killed, and almost all the army corps, division and brigade commanders were changed. There was great retrogression in the Soviet Union's military. At the beginning of the war, the Soviet Union made a series of mistakes in strategic guidance. For instance, it incorrectly judged the timing of the enemy's attack, believing that war would break out in 1942 at the earliest. Additionally, it made a wrong guess about the direction of the German invasion. The Soviet Union also ignored strategic defense, pushing the areas of fortresses forward. The result was that while the old areas of fortresses had been dismantled, the new ones were not yet set up, and adjustments in deployment could not be made before Germany attacked. When the German armed forces attacked, the

227

orders from the supreme commanding office of the Soviet Union were still to launch attack into German land, which was not in keeping with reality. So the mistakes in military theory and strategic policy caused irreparable damage to the country. Of course there were political reasons as well. In the past, we used to summarize only military factors, and not political ones. For example, there were over five million Soviet servicemen captured as prisoners of war. Its army was fighting for a just cause on its own land, so how were so many servicemen captured as prisoners of war? One reason may be that the broadened scope of the movement to eliminate the counter-revolutionaries lowered the cohesiveness of the armed forces.

The safeguarding of national interests and integrity of the national territory and sovereignty is the starting point and the ultimate goal for the study of strategy. The Chinese nation has a rich heritage of history and culture. The Chinese civilization has existed for over 5,000 years and is the only uninterrupted civilization in world history. Ancient Chinese fairy tales attribute the source of this vitality to reflections of the soul of the Chinese nation, which makes unremitting efforts for self-improvement and stresses morality and respect for others and national unity. Later, there were the Confucianists, who were kindhearted and self-restrained, the Taoists, who were gentle but firm and detached, and the military strategists. All these historical forces exerted great influence on the formation of the Chinese nation's soul and strategic thinking. They became the unifying consciousness of the Chinese nation, namely, the social opinion of maintaining the unity of the country and its territorial integrity and sovereignty, formed by a history of 2000 years of unification.

In Chinese history, starting from the Qin Dynasty's unification of China in 221 B.C. and up to the revolution of 1911, there were nine dynasties under which China was unified without interruption. The Han Dynasty was the longest, 426 years. Starting from the middle of Qing Dynasty, China was invaded by foreign powers, and the country became weaker and weaker. Emperors Kangxi and Qianlong concentrated on governing the border regions and successfully maintained stability in the border areas of Tibet and Mongolia. There were nearly 100 years of stability. After the mid-19th century, China entered a period of border troubles. There were two Opium Wars and the Sino-French war. The eastern gate was knocked open, and problems on the western border grew more acute, and the threat of imperialist aggression loomed over the entire country. The strategic directions of China have always been closely related. During the Qing Dynasty, there was the argument over which was more important, the defense of the sea or the defense of the border area. Actually, whenever there was a tense situation concerning the sea, the situation on the border would also be tense. The focal point of our strategic study is our national interests, and the interests of the Party and socialism. Our socialist cause of today did not come easy, it is the result of thousands of years of the fine cultural traditions of the Chinese nation and of the hard struggles and sacrifices by countless Chinese people with lofty ideals. One precondition for the study of the science of strategy is love for the motherland and for the socialist cause.

We should also master the correct theory of knowledge and methodology. The Marxist theory of knowledge and methodology is the essence of the works by Marx and Engels. It is a theoretical system of science and consistency. The statement by Engels that technology determines the tactics and economy is the material foundation of war still holds true today. Mao Zedong's military thought guided the Chinese revolutionary war to victory and is also the focal point for our study. Mao Zedong guided the Chinese revolutionary war for over 20 years. After the founding of new China, he again led the struggle of construction and national defense. Mao Zedong, a leader, statesman and military strategist, was able to combine military practice and military theory at the highest level.

From the files of the central archives, we can clearly see from the cables and directions Mao Zedong wrote to command battles that he was a great strategist of rare gifts and bold vision. Take the war to resist the United States and assist Korea for example. At that time, New China was just founded, there was a big flood in southern China, hungry people were anxiously waiting to be fed, and China's industries were still in shambles. It took unusual strategic daring and resolution to dare to fight against the number one power in the world. When our volunteer army entered Korea, the relative military strength between the enemy ground force and our force was 1 to 1.2, but if you count the enemy's ship-carried planes and aircraft carriers, and take into consideration the actual forces and weaponry, the enemy strength was several times our own. But under those circumstances, our army with Chairman Mao and General Peng as the commanders achieved great victories and gained prestige for our nation and army. The battlefield is the fairest test ground.

To fight against a superior force and win victory is the highest honor for our army. Mao Zedong's brilliance in military strategic thought is even acknowledged by our enemy. From the end of the Second World War to the Gulf War, the United States fought two local wars, the Korean War and the Vietnam War, and in both suffered defeat. In both, its opponent was China. In the Korean War, it was the direct opponent, and in the Vietnam War, the indirect opponent. Therefore, in order to master the essential points in the study of science of strategy, we should first of all master the Marxist theory of knowledge and methodology, study Mao Zedong's strategic thought, his strategic theory and practice, and means of war, as well as Deng Xiaoping's theory of military strategy in the new period.

It is also necessary to comprehend how to utilize the method of cause and effect analysis, statistics analysis, and systematic analysis, and bring to light the inherent laws of war. We should master the history of war, not only the Chinese history of war, but also the world history of war. Kissinger was once the chief foreign policy advisor for the United States Government. He studied 19th-century European military and diplomatic history for ideas to apply to the 20th-century. History itself is the object of cause and effect analysis. Through the study of history, we gain insight into real-life problems.

We should use the method of statistics analysis. Dupuy of the United States, who collected statistical figures on the wars from 1600 to 1973, drew the conclusion that though the weapons had become more and more powerful, everyday the casualties in combat had decreased. This was because the coefficient of dispersion of soldiers had increased 4,000 times. Of course, this is just an example of statistics analysis; whether the conclusion is correct or not is another matter. The Soviet army stipulated that an artillery battalion's salvo could suppress the center of resistance by a platoon, and that infantry density of fire should be eight bullets per minute per meter in the front. These statistics from the Second World War raised the level of theoretical understanding. The statistical analysis method is obviously relative in nature, but it is an important step in the law of understanding.

We should also use the systematic analysis method. We should conduct analysis with a full, systematic, developed, high-level point of view. We should see through the appearance to the essence, studying the intrinsic links and changes of the various factors of war. For instance, the development of technology and its application in war could cause changes in military equipment, and could in turn cause changes in strategies, battles, and tactics. It could also cause changes in the forms of arrangement for the armed forces and the principles and means of command. These changes would raise new requirements for technology. In these links and changes, military rules are fully revealed.

Finally, we should adhere to seeking truth from facts. This is a very important point. The study of strategy is to raise concepts from practice, and not from concept to practice, and not from idea to idea. We should explain things from their true features of objective fact, and the rules of practice should be taken as what they are. The worst truth is still better than the perfect false. This is the least we ask for the fearless spirit of science. We should be good at thinking independently, and should encourage creative thinking. We should not rely on a walking stick and throw away our own legs, by doing so we would never be able to climb the peaks of military science.

CHINESE MODERN LOCAL WAR AND U.S. LIMITED WAR

Senior Colonel Chen Zhou

China has fought a number of local wars and built up rich experience in this area since the founding of the PRC. It has been guided by a strategy of active defense within a framework of countering possible large-scale invasions by outside enemies. While the Chinese theory of "modern local war," which has developed rapidly since the 1980s, has distinct Chinese characteristics and a distinctive Chinese style, the concept of "limited war" is a U.S. postwar [World War II] military concept that has long dominated U.S. foreign policy and military strategy. It still has a crucial influence in the United States today. The intent of this article is not to make a full comparison of these two conceptual theories, but rather only to analyze their major differences and bring them to public attention.

Historic Social Conditions

Concerning the historic social conditions in which these theories emerged, the U.S. concept of "limited war" was a theoretical reflection in the United States and the Western nations of the new international bipolar political order and the state of warfare under nuclear

A research analyst at the Strategy Department, Academy of Military Science, Beijing, Chen Zhou is the author of works such as Theory and Practice of the People's Liberation Army's Democratic Institutions. *This paper was originally published in* China Military Science, *no 4 (Winter 1995).*

deterrence. This concept developed after the Korean War and peaked in the 1960s.

In contrast, the Chinese theory of "modern local war" is mainly the product of a rational recognition by the PRC of the changed contemporary international political order, the growing conflict between war and peace, and its own most pressing security issues.

This theory started to evolve under the conditions of preparations to counter a new all-out war of aggression against China while being forced to fight a number of local wars against aggression. It developed quickly, bringing a strategic change to the guiding ideology of our defense and military establishment. The concept of limited war that emerged after the Second World War was first set forth by certain U.S. and British academics, and developed mainly out of the U.S. overseas war experience. Its key substance is its advocacy that both sides in a war need to act in line with the "politics-first principle," voluntarily and consciously setting certain limits on their war objectives, means, and scopes, thus keeping the war controlled to meet the goal of achieving the maximum effect at less cost. While the emergence of this concept was not unrelated to public aversion to the destruction caused by the two World Wars, it was essentially a theoretical reflection in the United States and Western nations of the new international bipoplar political order and the state of warfare under nuclear deterrence.

The postwar United States, as 'the only power that did not suffer from large-scale war destruction," became in one leap the capitalist world's overlord and the world's top military power. America's actions and attempts to dominate the world were quite obvious; however, the evolution of the U.S.-Soviet bipolar order sharply restricted the U.S. and left it feeling that its own strategic interests were seriously "threatened." The United States on the one hand did not want to fight a major war, particularly a nuclear war, while on the other it needed to keep a rivalry going in the "intermediate zone" between the two major camps to maintain its world supremacy.

That was the historic setting in which the concept of limited war emerged. The evolution of this concept had two key features:

- It was directly related to the emergence and use of nuclear weapons. The United States successfully tested the first atomic bomb in July 1945, and then dropped two atomic bombs on Japan in August. In 1946, U.S. strategic analyst Bernard Brody and

British military theoretician Liddel Hart clearly set forth the thinking on the need for war on nuclear terms to be limited. Once the Soviet Union acquired nuclear weapons to establish gradually U.S.-Soviet nuclear parity, the immediate significance of this thinking became even more conspicuous.

● It was closely related to the formation of the U.S. policy on the "containment of communism." George Kennan, who served successively as charge d'affaires at the U.S. Embassy in the Soviet Union and director of the U.S. Department of State Policy Planning Office, noted repeatedly in 1946 and 1947 that "containment of Russia's 'expansionist' tendencies will not require an all-out military conflict. Rather, we can use all appropriate means, including military ones, to firmly confront it at 'a series of changing geographic and political points' where it might endanger the interests of the Western nations."

This ideological viewpoint laid the grounds for the concept of limited war. At the 1951 U.S. Senate hearings on the dismissal of [General Douglas] MacArthur, U.S. Secretary of State Marshall called the Korean War a "limited war." It was precisely through reflection on the Korean War and criticism of the strategy of massive retaliation that the concept of limited war gradually developed. The 1957 publications, *Limited War: A Challenge to U.S. Strategy*, by University of Chicago Political Science Professor Robert Osgood and *Nuclear Weapons and Foreign Policy*, by Harvard University Political Science Professor Henry Kissinger, symbolized the evolution of the limited-war concept. Former U.S. Army Chief of Staff Maxwell Taylor supported the concept, setting forth a strategy of timely reaction in the book, *An Uncertain Trumpet*, after his retirement. Once Kennedy became president in 1961, he made the strategy of timely reaction the new U.S. military strategy. This showed that the limited-war concept had been officially converted into a specific military strategy. While the limited-war concept was downplayed after the Vietnam War, it was certainly not abandoned and its fundamental concepts continued to influence subsequent U.S. foreign policy and military strategy.

The U.S. focus in the 1980s on dealing with low-level conflicts through a "new timely reaction strategy," and its 1990s focus on dealing with large-scale regional conflicts through a "regional defense strategy" and a "selective timely-participation strategy," have all actually been influenced by the limited-war concept, and can be traced to the same origin.

The Chinese theory of "modern local war" has developed gradually under different historic conditions. It is mainly the product of the CCP's understanding of China's particular historic conditions, the changed international political order, the major conflicts that China needed to resolve, the most pressing security issues China was facing, and issues such as war versus revolution and war versus peace. Its evolution can be divided into two major phases:

- The first started not long after the conclusion of World War II, ending before the Third Plenary Session of the 11th CCP Central Committee. After the Second World War, although Mao Zedong made many brilliant expositions on the state of world political and military development, such as clearly setting forth in 1946 the "intermediate-zone" concept," because he was facing at the time an all-out civil war launched by Chiang Kai-shek, he was unable to consider more systematically the changed state of war related to the "intermediate zone."

  Just after the PRC was founded, it was forced to fight the War To Resist U.S. Aggression and Aid Korea (1950-1953). In the 1950s, the basic assessment of the CCP and Mao Zedong on war versus peace was that a new world war could be prevented or postponed if all the forces of peace and democracy were unified. However, because the threat of imperialist war still existed, the possibility of a third world war also still existed. Therefore, our military work needed to emphasize preparations to counter a possible large-scale imperialist invasion of China.

  The strategic policy of active defense drawn up in 1956 by the Central Military Commission to defend China proceeded from and was grounded precisely in that need. In the 1960s, because of factors such as the rapidly changing international situation and the clamoring of the Guomindang authorities on Taiwan to "counterattack the mainland," Mao Zedong started to place more emphasis on the "inevitability" of war and the ties between war and revolution. Additionally he showed great concern about the threat of Soviet supremacy, and calling for our military strategy to be grounded in fighting sooner, fighting on a larger-scale, and fighting a nuclear war.

This thinking lasted until the 1970s, so an independent theory of local war generally did not emerge during that time. Leaders such as Mao Zedong, however, did discuss the matter of local war from the perspectives of preventing or postponing a new world war and studying the new features of imperialist-launched wars. They accumulated much valuable experience in modern local war from leading the War To Resist U.S. Aggression and Aid Korea, from self-defense in the Sino-Indian border counterattack, and certain other military struggles. For instance, in the War To Resist U.S. Aggression and Aid Korea, they held that on the one hand, it was only by sending troops to fight that they could curb the war's expansion, defend Chinese security, and put us in a state of readiness for war with the United States. On the other, they made painstaking plans in all areas such as the method, time, and scale of dispatching troops, and the targets and scopes of attack in an attempt to "keep the Korean problem localized," as well as promptly drawing up after the fifth campaign the general strategic guiding principle of "full readiness for protracted war while striving for peace talks to end the war."

• The second phase was from the Third Plenary Session of the 11th CCP Central Committee to the present. Deng Xiaoping's many crucial discourses on the world trend [of peace and development] and war versus peace laid the most important grounds for the systematic evolution and all-out development of the Chinese theory of local war. Deng Xiaoping clearly pointed out that "since the Third Plenary Session of the 11th CCP Central Committee, our evaluation of the international situation has changed, and with it our foreign policy has also changed."

These are two crucial changes. We have changed our former view that the danger of war is very near because of factors such as the fact that in the Soviet-U.S. strategic balance of nuclear power, neither side has completed a global strategic deployment, and the forces for peace are growing more than the forces for war. This means that for quite a long time to come, it is possible that a world war will not occur. This adds to the hope that world peace will be maintained. It was precisely this assessment that brought about the strategic change in the guiding ideology of our defense and military establishment in 1985, and gradually shifted the focus of our military strategy toward countering possible local wars and military conflicts.

It is obvious that there have been sharp differences in the postwar views of the United States and China over their respective stances on world order, the key security issues that have needed to be resolved, the major dangers that they have faced, international politics, and war versus peace. In addition, their different social systems, ideologies, overall national power, and cultural traditions have brought obviously different features to their two conceptual theories on local war.

Concepts of Limited War

Regarding the qualities, aims, and limits of these theories, the U.S. concept of limited war is essentially an offensive theory focused on the needs of the struggle for world supremacy. It provides the theoretical grounds for launching offensives and engaging in rivalries in the "intermediate zone," and all its battlefields are in places outside of or far from U.S. territory. In contrast, the Chinese theory of modern local war is a defensive one grounded in China's self-defense realities. It is aimed at defending our national sovereignty, rights, and interests and providing a secure and stable environment for our national modernization. All its battlefields are in border regions that are dependent on China or specific surrounding locales.

The United States did not want to fight a major war, particularly a nuclear war. The standoff between the two large East-West camps restricted any use of nuclear weapons. But to contain the growth of the socialist camp, to curb the serious threat to the west of the so-called "Communist expansion," and to maintain the U.S. standing of world supremacy, the United States had to engage in rivalries in the "intermediate zone" (also called the Eurasian mainland's "border zone" or "grey zone") between the two large camps.

As certain advocates of the limited-war concept repeatedly emphasized, to meet the objective of avoiding all-out war while "containing communism," the only rational means of resolution was to "draw up a strategy that places limits on war and can win limited wars." In keeping with such political needs, the limited-war concept was actually an offensive theory with aggressive features in particular terms. It reflected the interests of the United States and the Western nations, and served the needs of U.S. imperialist policy and its struggle for world supremacy. Meanwhile, the concept of "limited war" per se was relative, as the limited wars that the United States fought were undoubtedly full-scale wars as far as their opponents in small and weak countries were concerned. The limited war theoretician Osgood acknowledged in his book, *A Review of Limited War* (1979), that "the Western definition of limited war, just like the concept per se, certainly reflects not certain general realities, but rather only the interests of the Western allies, particularly U.S. interests, at a particular stage of international conflict." World history since the Second World War shows that the United States was directly or indirectly involved in over 50 of the 182 local wars and armed conflicts that occurred in the world from 1945 to 1986. Concerning the places and limits of such U.S. involvement, most were in Third World Asian, African, and Latin American countries far from the United States, of which the majority were in the so-called "intermediate zone" outside of the spheres of influence set by the Yalta Accord. It is obvious that the U.S. aim in direct incitement of or indirect involvement in local wars and armed conflicts was certainly not to defend its territorial security, rights, and interests, but rather to struggle with the Soviet Union over supremacy and spheres of influence. The limited-war concept provided the crucial theoretical grounds and practical means for achieving that aim.

Regarding its ideological and cultural origins, the limited-war concept carried forward both the U.S. strategic tradition and ideology that emphasized attack and expansion formed in its colonial period and in its transition from laissez-faire capitalism to imperialism, as well as the balance-of-power policy inherited from British imperialism. The "containment" policy originator Kennan and limited war theorists Osgood and Kissinger all belonged to the realism school of Western international political theory. That school's founder, Hans Morgenthau, wrote in his book, *Politics Among Nations* (1978), that "international politics, just like all other politics, is also a power struggle. . . throughout history, despite the social, economic, and political terms, international intercourse always occurs through a struggle for supremacy." A fundamental means of keeping peace is "the balance of forces formed through the struggle for power in the international arena." In addition, U.S. geopolitician Spikeman's "border zone" theory—"to control the fate of the world, it is necessary to control Eurasia, the control of which in turn necessitates control of the border zone"—is also a key ideological pillar of the containment policy and the limited war theory.

The Chinese theory of modern local war is a defensive strategic theory. Either when preparing to counter all-out war or when coping with local wars and armed conflicts, the strategic policy of the Chinese military has always been one of active defense. This was determined by China's socialist system, the nature of our people's army, our basic mission of modernization, and our peaceful foreign policy. The various local wars that China has fought since the founding of the PRC were aimed not at struggling for supremacy and engaging in expansionism, but rather at defending our country's territorial land, air, and sea sovereignty and our maritime rights and interests, as well as maintaining our national unity and security to provide a secure and stable environment for our national modernization.

Our strategic guidance in local war has always adhered to the principle of "gaining mastery by striking only after the enemy has struck." Mao Zedong's states, "We will not attack unless we are attacked, but if we are attacked, we will certainly counterattack" which insists on the principle of "fighting to promote talks," with fighting being in the interests of peace. This "reasonable, favorable, and restrained" principle is absolutely not an attempt to occupy another country's territory, so our war agenda genuinely becomes a backup for and means of our peaceful foreign policy.

We waged the War To Resist U.S. Aggression and Aid Korea mainly because the U.S. Army was already in Taiwan and had advanced to our border on the Yalu River, bringing the war to China's border. The Chinese Government had issued two warning statements, which had been formally transmitted through the Indian Ambassador in Washington. After the end of that war, the Chinese people's volunteer army had withdrawn completely from Korea on its own initiative by the end of 1958.

We were also forced to launch a counterattack in self-defense at the Sino-Indian border because the Indian Army had invaded Chinese territory and repeatedly created border bloodshed. The Chinese Ambassador to India frankly and sincerely told India our strategic motives, explaining that China's main attention and fighting direction was toward the east, not aimed at India. China would not be so foolish as to make enemies with the United States on the east and India on the west, to leave us with two priorities. Once we were forced to counterattack in self-defense on our border zone, we fought and settled the matter quickly, unilaterally withdrawing 20 km from the original line of real bilateral control after our victory.

U.S. strategic analyst Michael Mandelbaum wrote in his book, *The Fate of Nations* (1988), "[China's] every combat aim has been limited. China has never in any war tried to occupy another country's territory. The People's Liberation Army withdrew from Korea after the cease-fire. Having routed the Indian Army, it did not follow up the victory with hot pursuit. It withdrew from Vietnam just a few months after South Vietnam was occupied in 1979. And once the United States stopped bombing North Vietnam, China also withdrew the troops that it had sent in 1965 to support the North Vietnamese regime."

This assessment is in accordance with historic realities. The strategic tactics of "striking only after the enemy has struck" and being "reasonable, favorable, and restrained," which China pursues in local wars, not only have a unique standing in all of our contemporary political and military thinking but also reflect longstanding Chinese cultural traditions. We can cite here the Confucian thought that "peace is precious," the Mohist idea of being "nonoffensive," the Taoist concept of "strength in yielding," and our ancient Chinese military strategy of "subduing others without a fight." Of course, defense in Chinese modern local war theory is an active, not a passive defense, one that includes both counterattack and attack. Our strategic principle of "striking only after the enemy has struck" certainly does not exclude sudden "first strikes" in campaign battles or counterattacks in self-defense into enemy territory. Deng Xiaoping pointed out clearly in 1980 that "active defense is not merely defense per se, but includes defensive offensives. Active defense also includes our going out, so that if we are attacked, we will certainly counterattack!"

As to its theoretical ways, means, and effects, the U.S. concept of limited war is grounded in a policy of strength and superior technology and equipment. It is a combat theory for fighting conventional wars with mostly an allied strategy, with its Cold War experiences showing that it was less pro than con to have weakened U.S. might to a certain extent.

The Chinese theory of modern local war, on the other hand, is based on the concepts of a people's war and follows the policy of defeating with inferior equipment an enemy with superior equipment. It is a combat theory that adopts flexible and diverse combat forms and adheres to independence and autonomy. The practical experiences gained while implementing the theory show that it safeguards national security while raising a country's international prestige. Because the realism school of Western international political theory stresses that power struggles are the crux of international politics, it puts particular emphasis on national "might." Morgenthau says that "international politics can be defined as a sustained effort to maintain and increase one's own country's might while containing the power of other countries." Such thinking has had a profound influence on the concept of limited war. While the limited-war concept called for limiting the aims, means, and scope of war to prevent an all-out or nuclear war between the United States and the Soviet Union, it also held that military might is the only arbitrator of conflicts between nations, because "the inability to use force absolutely cannot ease tense situations, rather it probably will prolong all disputes indefinitely" (Kissinger, *Nuclear Weapons and Foreign Policy*).

The limited-war concept favors sharp development of conventional forces, because it is dependent on U.S. powerful might and superior technology and equipment to win conventional war and meet its political goals. In contrast to the strategy of massive retaliation, the timely reaction strategy focuses on limited war; it regards nuclear deterrence as a "shield" against nuclear attack and treats conventional forces as a "double-edged sword" to be used for charging and attacking, particularly emphasizing preparations to fight special and local wars. The new timely reaction strategy of the 1980s once again stressed fighting conventional wars, placing particular emphasis on coping with low-level conflicts, as well as calling for the large-scale development of high-tech conventional weaponry to make up U.S. conventional-force deficiencies. In the 1991 Gulf War, the United States abandoned its Vietnam War method of "gradual escalation." It used large amounts of high-tech weaponry to achieve its limited military objectives and had an absolute superiority of conventional forces. All of which were further developments of the limited-war concept.

Another keystone of the limited-war concept is its allied strategy. All postwar U.S. administrations have pursued an allied strategy whose main essence is collective security, which means that U.S. military strategy is grounded in a powerful system of allies. Limited-war theorists go on to note that not only does the allied policy absolutely not run counter to the limited-war strategy, but it should be seen as a special operation typical of the strategy. A strategy of all-out war could weaken the allied system in two ways, by making the allies believe either that they would not have to take any military action or that it would be best not to fight because the terms were ripe for peace through surrender. Therefore, it is only an understanding of the allied policy on limited-war terms that could make the allies want to take action (Kissinger, *Nuclear Weapons and Foreign Policy*).

The limited wars launched by the United States in the postwar period, whether fought directly or through "locals fighting locals," all paid great attention to bringing into full play the role of regional allies and groups. But while the limited-war concept reflects to a certain extent certain objective realities of the changed state of war since World War II, it has been frequently foiled in practice, the most typical example of which was the Vietnam War. The U.S. defeat in the Vietnam War at once touched off a major crisis for the limited-war concept. Some said that the concept emphasized matters such as limited political objectives, the deterrence policy, diplomatic action, and bargaining at the expense of the military issues involved in this new style of war such as how to bring the military role into full play. Others held that the lesson was mainly in its irregular-war part, because it had not drawn up a strategy for Third World limited war. Since the 1980s, the United States has summed up its Vietnam War lessons and revised its "old limited-war concept," doing well in repeated low-force operations such as the invasions of Grenada and Panama and the air raids on Libya. In these actions it has achieved a fast-fight, rapid-resolution effect.

The self-defense and defensive nature of the Chinese theory of modern local war means that it cannot and never has regarded local war as a tool for pursuing any policy of strength. Additionally, the current state of China's national and military power also leaves it with less options for combat means. While the local wars that China has fought since the founding of the PRC have been essentially conventional ones involving mostly ground forces and limited weaponry, the Chinese theory of modern local war also has its own sharp distinctions:

- It emphasizes essentially a people's war based on defeating with inferior equipment an enemy with superior equipment.

243

Coping with all-out war inevitably means carrying forward the glorious traditions of our people's revolutionary war and war of national liberation, mobilizing and organizing all of our people to fight a large-scale people's war that would combine field armies with local forces and militia guerrillas, and armed masses with unarmed masses. As a well-fought local war also involves the matter of the just and mass nature of war, it still needs to be grounded in people's war on modern terms. Deng Xiaoping said that "Chairman Mao's strategic thinking was people's war." In this sense, China has always based its combat operations on defeating with inferior equipment an enemy with superior equipment. While the local wars that China has faced have never been of a single type, the most threatening one has been a local war with direct or indirect superpower involvement on modern technology, particularly high-technology, terms. So a strategy grounded in countering that type of war also works well when encountering other types of war.

• It stands for independence from any political or military grouping. While the PRC has pursued the successive strategies of "leaning toward one side" and "a united front," our basic stand has always been for independence, autonomy, and self-reliance, which was quite obvious in the War To Resist U.S. Aggression and Aid Korea, the War To Aid Vietnam Against U.S. Aggression, and our successive self-defense counterattacks. Since the 1980s, China has repeatedly declared that it pursues a foreign policy of independence and autonomy, that it is independent of any grouping, and that it does not have strategic relations with any country. Deng Xiaoping has repeatedly said that as the "community," "bloc politics," and "spheres of influence" styles can all cause conflicts and disrupt the international order, no foreign country should expect China to either be its vassal or to stand for any infringement on our national interests. China will neither play anyone else's cards or let anyone else play the China card. This thinking is also China's key strategic guiding principle for possible future local wars on high-tech terms.

• Finally, it adheres to flexible strategy and tactics. The set of flexible strategies and tactics created by Mao Zedong and based on his concept of "you fight your battles, and I'll fight mine," to play advantages up and disadvantages down, is the cream of Mao

Zedong military thought, the magic weapon that brought about victory in our all-out people's revolutionary war. As the terms of modern local wars are more complex and varied, with their war features, objectives, combat means, and many other aspects differing obviously from our successive revolutionary wars, we need to adhere even more to initiative, flexibility, and planning in our war guidance, striving for combat dominance through the flexible use of force and varying tactics. For instance, we need to do the following: adhere to a cautious policy of striking last, not fighting unless forced to and then winning if we do; stick to our traditional combat forms of mobile, positional, and guerrilla war, while flexibly using and developing them in line with varying terms and combat targets; insist on the basic guiding ideology of war of annihilation, while emphasizing on certain terms routs and wars of attrition; strive for rapid resolution and quick victory, while being prepared for protracted war; and make active war preparations, while persisting in a policy of simultaneous political struggle and military combat. As to their practical results, all the successive local wars that the PRC has fought have effectively defended our national sovereignty and security, while raising China's prestige. U.S. scholar Jonathan Pollack presents the following evaluation: China has been highly successful in using military force to defend its national interests, "with no countries on China's borders daring to either underestimate China's military actions or not seriously consider the political and military consequences of antagonism with China . . . and even the superpowers harboring evil designs toward Chinese military might also genuinely respect it" (*China and Global Strategic Balance*, 1988).

The Chinese theory of modern local war has played a key guiding role in its military operations.

PART FOUR:
The Revolution in Military Affairs

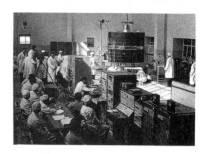

Top left: General Yang Huan, deputy commander of the Strategic Rocket Forces
Lower left: China's Long March 2 missile
Top right, top to bottom: Checking out a communications satellite; a satellite control center, Beijing; and observing a missile launch.

WEAPONS OF
THE 21ST CENTURY

Chang Mengxiong

Numerous facts show that we are in the midst of a new revolution in military technology in which electronic information technology is the central technology. This technology provides unprecedented applications for the development of new weaponry.

Information acquisition will be the main distinction of 21st-century military forces. Military battles during the 21st century will unfold around the use of information for military and political goals.

Weapons

This article looks at how weapons and military units will be information intensified, focusing mostly on the years 2010-2020. Information-intensified weapons include precision-guided weapons, (guided bombs, artillery shells, and cluster bombs, cruise missiles, target-guided missiles, and anti-radiation missiles). These are weapons

Chang Mengxiong serves on the Committee of Science, Technology and Industry of the System Engineering Institute. This paper first appeared in China Military Science *(Spring 1995).*

that can acquire and use information provided by the targets themselves to correct trajectory. These smart weapons will be able to be launched from outside the enemy firepower network and identify and attack targets. Their circular probable error of target accuracy will be close to nil. The Gulf War has already demonstrated that accurate guided weapons are the basic firepower of high-technology warfare.

The term information-intensified weapons may inspire a search for weapons that make full use of information. Foreign "smart land mines" and "smart water mines" may automatically head toward and destroy a target after acquiring information about it. Reactive armor on tanks also actually uses information acquired from attacking weapons and detonates them at once. In the 21st century, all weapons, with the exception of rifles and machine guns, will be information intensified.

Combat methods will consequently change: accurate over-the-horizon firepower attacks may become the primary form of firepower attacks; blind firing and carpet bombing will become antiquated combat methods whose cost-benefit ratio is not high; and damage outside the combat target area will also be greatly reduced.

Soldiers

In the 21st century soldiers will carry conventional rifles and hand grenades, and also use small, light-weight, multimedia electronic information equipment. This equipment will have a personal radio communications function, a global positioning system (GPS) direction-finding function, a personal computer and network function, a night-vision function, an identification (friend or foe) function, a warning function, and a launch command function for some information-intensified weapons. The soldiers will wear clothing with adjustable temperature and color; in some circumstances personal flight platforms will be used.

Information-intensified soldiers will be able to receive all sorts of information about combat—to receive highly concentrated commands and, when necessary, orders directly from a division commander. Because of this enhanced information, they will have the ability to make their own decisions about enemy bases in combat plans.

Combat Platforms

The battle platforms of the 21st century, including airplanes, vessels, and armored personnel carries, will all be equipped with large amounts of electronic information equipment. They will have various kinds of telecommunications equipment for use in exchanging combat information with higher levels and neighboring units. They will have various kinds of equipment to detect enemy targets, in order to provide information for accurate firepower attacks against enemy targets. They will have ample computer and computer-network capabilities that will be able to provide timely and effective supplementary information for combat actions.

In addition to making full use of information about one's own side and the enemy, information-intensified platforms will also be fully able to counter the use of information about them by the enemy; they will have electronic warfare equipment that has detection, jamming, and deception capabilities.

Stealth technology will prevent the adversary from obtaining information through the use of radar and infra-red detection. Stealth aircraft and surface vessels already exist, and other stealth combat platforms will also appear.

Robot troops, vehicles possessing a certain amount of information-acquisition, information-processing, and lethal firepower, are a kind of unmanned information-intensified combat platform. As electronic information technology develops, these will develop into unmanned information-intensified combat platforms. Early in the next century, robot sentries, robot engineers, robot infantrymen, and even unmanned smart tanks may appear under some battlefield conditions.

Information-intensified combat platforms are bound to bring about major changes in operational concepts. Because the distance over which these platforms can fire accurately is vastly greater than the distance their operators can see, the scale, range, and accuracy of their coordinated operation will greatly exceed the level that non-information-intensified platforms can attain in the 20th century. It is foreseeable that by 2010 the conventional combat methods of the past several decades of groups of short-range fighter planes will be rare, as will attacks by tanks and simultaneous firing of thousands of artillery pieces. It is also possible that large aircraft combat groups will no longer be useful. Robot troops will be used in real warfare in large numbers.

The C³I System

The C³I system is the nerve center for all information-intensified weapons and military units. When summarizing the lessons of experience of the Gulf War, every country concluded that the C³I system will have a tremendous role in future warfare. They emphasize that a dispersed C³I system that resists destruction is the orientation for development.

Satellite space telecommunications, reconnaissance, monitoring, navigation, and locator systems are the important component parts of the C³I. With improvement of the entire C³I system and satellite performance and widening of satellite applications, by 2010, high-level commanders may be able to know at once about events occurring on any spot on the earth. This will enable pilots and tank drivers, as well as ordinary soldiers, to know accurately their own location on the earth at all times, and it will permit contact with higher-level command organizations anywhere. It will also provide real-time, continuous, accurate guidance information for pinpoint guidance of missile to targets as much as 1,000 kms away. The use of airplanes as carriers of highly mobile radar detection, command and control, electronic warfare, and telecommunications relay equipment or systems holds many advantages. The C³I system of the future will have increased shared information among those engaged in combat, which most likely will develop into an integrated national defense information system. There are two ways to integrate the C³I system into the "high-speed information highway" of individual countries: by resource sharing on the two-way communications portion of a network, and by serving as an integral part of the latter operating in coordination with it. Because the C³I system has such an extremely important position in information-intensified weapons and military units, attacking and protecting the satellites that are an integral part of the C³I system, airborne early-warning and electronic-warfare aircraft, and ground command sites and telecommunications hubs will all become important forms of combat.

Weapons Systems and Battlefields

The weapons systems of the 21st century will be "information-intensified weapons systems" made up of information-intensified combat platforms and weapons and corresponding C^3I systems. Various kinds of information-intensified combat platforms in which information-intensified weapons form the basic firepower and carry out different missions will be logically arrayed to form "information-intensified combat groups." The overall combat effectiveness of these combat groups will show a qualitative leap, and they will be the main form of 21st-century combat systems. In combat, if just one side has information-intensified units under control of trained personnel, an "information-intensified battlefield" exists.

On an information-intensified battlefield, many events are transparent. Information about installations of major military value to both sides, such as military bases, information hubs, and command centers, will be stored in a combat data bank to provide information about possible targets against which precision guidance weapons will be aimed. Military movements will find it difficult to fool an adversary's intelligence system. These movements will be reflected in real time in the adversary's data bank. If there is a gap between the information capabilities of the two sides, many events will be transparent only to one side. A statement by Sun Tzu in *The Art of War* applies to the one who has the strongest information capability: "By knowing the enemy and knowing yourself, you can fight a hundred battles and win them all."

The strategy, tactics, and campaigns suited to the information-intensified battlefields of the 21st century will differ from those of today. The distinction among the three will become blurred, and specific ingredients of each will change.

A realistic point of view on combat methods of information-intensified troops in the 21st century can be provided only after thorough study, and this article can make only some guesses. An analogy can be made about the major changes that will come about: Information-intensified combat methods are like a Chinese boxer with a knowledge of vital body points who can bring an opponent to his knees with a minimum of movement. By contrast, non-information-intensified combat methods are like fights between villagers in which heads are broken and blood flows, but it is hard to distinguish the winner from the loser.

Information Warfare

Information warfare uses firepower and command to obtain and to deny information, to suppress and countersuppress, and to deceive and counterdeceive, as well as to destroy and counter the destruction of sources of information. It is also warfare to win people's minds and boost morale by employing television, radio broadcasting, and leaflets focused on the use and prevention of use of information.

Information warfare and firepower are closely linked. Information warfare is used to find and attack targets for firepower. Full use of information warfare is a prerequisite for full use of firepower. This is expressed clearly in precision guided weapons, as well as in the tracking, aiming, reconnaissance, and fire control of all guns. Information warfare includes countering C^3I systems and ensuring the security and accessibility of ones own lines of communications, the effective operation of ones own detection equipment, making sure that it is not jammed or damaged; and the normal operation of ones own numerous combat command computers, protecting them from damage by computer viruses. At both the strategic and campaign levels in information warfare, it is important to decipher and analyze information and to prevent information from being obtained and deciphered.

A newly conceived weapon that will appear in the 21st century is the high-performance microwave weapon that will use powerful electromagnetism to destroy the opponent's electronic equipment and electronic telecommunications systems, thereby rendering enemy weapons ineffective. This is a special kind of information-intensified weapon for waging information warfare.

"Information capability" includes information support for command, operations, precision strikes, and logistical support that military units need to carry out missions. The equipment that supports this capability is the C^3I system, electronic warfare systems, and precision-guided weapons. A military unit's information capability equals its combat capability. Like precision-strike capability or an air-defense capability, it is absolutely indispensable to high-technology warfare and may be the most important combat capability.

The term "information superiority" means the party that has the strongest information capability between two opposing parties in combat. In future high-technology warfare, not only will we have to gain air and sea superiority, but even more important, we will have to win information superiority first of all. Possibly new military terms like "contain information power," and "contain electromagnetic power" may appear.

Information warfare will be the most complex type of warfare in the 21st century, and it will decide who will win and who will lose the war.

Information Deterrence

Nuclear weapons appeared an the end of World War II. They were followed by the appearance of the nuclear deterrence concept in military theory. Owing to the appearance of large numbers of high technology conventional weapons during the late 1970s, the concept of conventional deterrence reappeared. Nuclear and conventional deterrence are not just theoretical issues, but real forces that have a powerful and effect on a potential adversary.

"Information deterrence" may appear in the future. Because all weapons used in warfare and the various branches of warfare depend closely on electronic information technology, the power that has a strong information capability and holds the electronic information technology advantage has an overall advantage over the weaker information power. Moreover, if the power with a weaker information capability can deliver a crippling attack on the information system of the power with a stronger information system, it can likewise greatly decrease the capability of the adversary's war machine. In other words, even if two adversaries are generally equal in hard weapons, unless the party with a weaker information capability is able effectively to weaken the information capability of the adversary, it has very little possibility of winning the war. Conversely, if one side can effectively weaken the information capability of the other side, even if its capability in other ways is less, the other side will dare not take any ill-considered action. These two situations constitute "information deterrence." It can prevent war from breaking out. Adroit strategic employment of one's own information deterrence capabilities constitutes an information deterrence strategy.

Combining High Centralization With High Initiative

The existence of centralized command, decentralized command, echelon-by-echelon command, transechelon command, and combined command are all recognized to be necessary, but centralized command and echelon-by-echelon command are the basic forms of command.

The Gulf War attests that Iraq's highly centralized command system was unsuited to high-technology warfare.

The former chairman of the U.S. Joint Chiefs of Staff, Army General J.W. Vessey, said: "Our command and control are based on the following principle: Make decisions at the lowest possible level. This not only gives flexibility to the on-the-ground commanders, but it also gives them resources, authority, and responsibility, thereby enabling maximum effective use."

Information-intensified weapons systems create the material conditions for highly centralized combat command at a high level. It enables theater commanders to do across-the-board planning of their tactical moves. During the Gulf War, plans for the daily 2,000-sortie aerial combat missions of the allied forces were drawn up by the U.S. Air Force information system, and assigned to each country and to each branch of service for implementation. This capability and trend continue to be strengthened. Information-equipped weapons systems enable independent combat commands. Dispersed C^3I systems will be highly resistant to destruction. They will ensure that lower level commanders receive the detailed combat information that they need. This will enable them to make on-the-spot decisions about dealing with ad hoc situations on the basis of the overall combat plans of higher headquarters, thereby gaining maximum combat results.

Combat command during the 21st century is certain to be a combination of high centralization and high independence, the number of echelons is bound to decrease, and existing command systems and doctrine are destined to be revised.

A Smooth Transition

U.S. National Defense Science and Technology Strategy, published in 1992, called for the development of seven military technology capabilities, one of which was "synthetic environment." A synthetic environment consists of a number of simulated systems that are connected to form a network. The environment being completely visual, operators can immerse themselves completely in the simulated environment. Any national defense system that has computer programs, such as various combat platforms, C³I systems, and models, can ultimately be incorporated into this environment for various kinds of network combat simulation. One can create an electronic battlefield by using this synthetic environment, which has a mixture of real and simulated targets from factories to the battlefield and can be used in widely separated locations, thereby enabling subscribers, research and development personnel, and testing personnel to communicate effectively. This environment enables both leaders and combat units to prepare for war and accompanies them to the real battlefield.

Required key technology is electronic information technology, including virtual reality technology, which employs computer technology to create a simulated imaginary world and uses computers to generate a simulated world and a three-dimensional visual environment. Operators can visually wander around in this visual virtual world, and operator actions can change this visual virtual world in real time. This world may be a weapon, a battlefield, a factory, etc. This environment is very helpful when examining a large volume of problems requiring assistance from visual thinking (including visual memories and visual associations). Virtual reality technology has broad prospects for military application.

Further development of the "synthetic environment" that Americans have conceived will provide a unified environment for virtually all military activities including setting requirements for designing and producing prototype machines and manufacturing weaponry; troop training and war preparations; drawing up joint combat doctrine; drafting emergency plans; post-mortem evaluations; and historical analysis. This synthetic environment will help create a relatively smooth transition from virtual (imaginary) weapons and virtual (imaginary) battlefields to real weapons and real battlefields and thus have far-reaching effects on military activities.

Measuring 21st-Century Military Forces

Measures of effectiveness for 20th-century military forces have often been portrayed as static, but they will not suffice for military forces during the 21st century.

Because information-intensified military units make full use of all kinds of information, the intensity concept must be introduced. So-called intensity means the number of events occurring within a certain time and space. The history of warfare shows that real military superiority really means only superiority at certain times and in certain places, or superiority in a unit of time or a unit of space. When one has this superiority, one is victorious within these limits.

Firepower and Destruction Intensity

Once an information-intensified military unit discovers the enemy disposition, it can make a judgment within a very short time and decide what to do. It can concentrate powerful precision-guided firepower to attack the enemy, its firepower figured in terms of unit of time and unit of space, i.e., its firepower intensity is unprecedentedly great. The strike accuracy of precision guided weapons is very high, far higher than the firepower intensity that non-information-intensified weapons can attain. Furthermore, although the total consumption of ammunition is very great for non-information-intensified forms of combat such as blind firing, enemy firepower suppression, and carpet bombing, when looked at in terms of the targets of attack, the intensity of this firepower is really very low.

However, the intensity of destruction is a more direct and more basic concept than the intensity of firepower. It connotes the amount of damage done to an attacked target per unit of time and space.

The intensity of firepower and destruction of information-intensified military units made up of information-intensified weapons, soldiers, combat platforms, and weapons systems tied together by a C^3I system is unprecedentedly great. The total firepower that a non-information-intensified military unit can bring to bear may also be very great, but in terms of "intensity," such a unit's firepower and the damage it causes is very small.

Mobility Intensity

Mobility intensity as applied to combat troops and combat platforms means the distance in space possible to move per unit of time (day, hour, minute, or second). Applied to military units, it means the quantity of combat troops that can move at the same time. The continued development of power technology enables continued increases in the dynamic properties of combat platforms. The continued development of electronics technology makes possible accurate coordination of movement on a large scale. By 2010, global mobile warfare by joint forces (a combination of army, navy, and air forces) may be possible. A single highly mobile army battalion may be able to defeat two or more mobile army battalions.

Information Intensity

The special feature of information-intensified military units is full use of information. Information intensity is the amount of information that an organizational unit can use, or prevent the use of, within a unit of time or space. Information intensity is an important indicator of accurate strike, coordinated warfare, command and control, and electronic warfare capacities. A military unit whose information intensity is very low cannot fight a high-technology war. A difference in information intensity between two military forces is bound to translate into a gap in combat capabilities.

Supply Intensity

Supply intensity means the amount of supplies of various kinds that an organizational unit can provide per unit of time to a prescribed area. The total amount of logistical supply for information-intensified warfare during the 21st century will likely be less than for today, but the intensity of supply will increase to meet the requirements of highly destructive and highly mobile warfare.

The Armed Forces Will Require Those Best Skilled

The human factor will be more prominent in high-technology warfare. Making the most of the combat effectiveness of high-technology weapons and application of correct strategy and tactics will depend on the caliber of military personnel.

In the future information society, everything will be affected by the extent to which society uses information. Weapons will become information-intensified weapons; military units will become information-intensified units; and combat will become information-intensified combat. The destructiveness of weapons will increase greatly, but their numbers will decrease. The combat effectiveness of military units will increase greatly, but their numbers will also decrease. Warfare in general will not only become more a mental than a physical contest in which the technology content is high, but this will also be the case in limited warfare and even in soldier-to-soldier combat. This means that the education and technical skills of military officers in the future information society will have to be higher than that those of civilians; otherwise, even with information-intensified weapons, defeat in war will be possible.

Information-Intensified Weapons and Technical Support

The contribution of electronic information technology to weaponry is manifested in the following:

- A very great increase in accuracy, meaning "they hit the mark"
- A great increase in the ability of commanders to understand their own and the enemy's situation
- A great increase in the coordinated combat capabilities of military units.

Nevertheless, "fighting fiercely" requires an increase in weapon payloads, and "fighting remotely and rapidly" requires an increase in combat platform payloads.

However, information-intensified weapons do not rule out the application of other new conventional technologies. New technical capabilities will be added. Information-intensified weapons require the support of aerospace, naval, ground, and nuclear technology. One cannot concentrate on electronic information technology to the neglect of other technologies, nor can one proceed with all equally without any particular emphasis.

21ST-CENTURY
NAVAL WARFARE

Naval Captain Shen Zhongchang
Naval Lieutenant Commander Zhang Haiyin
Naval Lieutenant Zhou Xinsheng

The war between Greece and its dependency, Corfu Island, in 664 BC was the first naval battle with a reliable recorded history. Since then, naval warfare has gone through the wooden-warship age, the sail-warship age, the steamship and large-ship cannon age, and the guided missile warfare age. The seas and oceans always having been directly tied to mankind's vital interests, they are going to be tied even closer in the 21st century. In the last decade or two, ever-growing numbers of countries have been realizing the importance of the seas and oceans as a "21st-century resource" for human survival and development. As all countries gain a stronger sense of the values, rights, and interests of the seas and oceans, disputes over matters such as maritime economic zones, continental shelves, and sea-area boundaries are likely to intensify, thus making it hard to prevent sharper conflicts and even outbreaks of war. Today, on the eve of the 21st century, we need to study naval warfare history and experience to determine the naval warfare development track of the new century.

Naval Captain Shen Zhongchang is the Director of the Research and Development Department of the Navy Research Institute, Beijing. Naval Lieutenant Commander Zhang Haiying and Naval Lieutenant Zhou Xinsheng serve as staff officers at the Navy Research Institute. This paper is from China Military Science *(Spring 1995).*

As the 21st century is also going to be an age of rapid scientific change, with certain cutting-edge technologies likely to be applied first to naval warfare, we need to forecast and explore 21st century naval warfare from the perspective of the coming trends of the scientific and technological revolution.

Naval Warfare Development Trends

More triphibious and multidimensional operations are going to develop in a battle space that integrates land-sea, land-air, surface-subsurface, sea-space, and the full electromagnetic spectrum. By now, warfare has been through the stages of cold arms, hot arms, thermonuclear arms, and high-tech arms. As we have seen scientific and technological advances steadily expand the scope of deployment of combat forces, with armed attack and destructive might growing steadily, battlefields are developing from single to multidimensional, little to greater depth, small to large triphibious operations, and relatively fixed to uncertain battle lines. The battlefield scope in the next century is also going to expand sharply, with the major fields of expansion being outer space, undersea and electromagnetic space. The use of high-tech arms will make direct attacks on naval battlefields possible from outer space, remote altitudes, and remote land bases, while improvement in long-range mobile combat capacity at sea will expand the control and striking range of naval warfare. Naval battle space is going to expand unprecedentedly.

Future naval warfare will display the following types of engagements:

- In land-sea combat, naval surface ships, submarines, carrier-based aircraft, and possibly other new service arms will generally have the capacity to conduct strategic offensive attacks in great depth and even against intercontinental land-based targets. As land-based arms will be sharply improved in reaction capacity, strike precision, and range, they will be able to powerfully strike formations at sea, and even individual warships and cruise missiles.

- In sea-air combat, electronic warfare and missile strikes, particularly long-distance strikes by warships, their carrier-based aircraft and aerial combat fighters will become the essential forms.

Submarines will be capable of making missile strikes on air targets. Sea-air combat will also develop in the direction of low- and super low-altitude engagements.

● In surface-undersea combat, as submarines resolve technically the obstacles to very deep operations, their higher capability in very deep communications and ability to monitor and reconnoiter submarines and surface ships will sharpen surface-undersea confrontations. While the submarine will rise in status to become a major naval warfare force, the development of ASW reconnaissance and combat methods will sharply restrict future activities of submarines in shallow-water zones, underwater levels, and continental-shelf zones. The appearance of underwater aircraft carriers and undersea mine-laying robots and even the construction of seabed military bases will sharpen surface-undersea combat. In sea-space combat, space based methods and forces will have a very conspicuous status in future naval warfare.

For thousands of years, the theory of "mastery of the seas" has always been praised as the infallible law of decisive naval engagement. As aircraft carriers and carrier-based aircraft have appeared, however, the theory, "Without mastery of the air, there is no mastery of the seas," has found favor throughout the world. Since the 1970s, "electromagnetic dominance" has also been held to be crucial to naval victory. By the next century, as high-tech space technology develops, the deployment of space-based weapons systems will be bound to make "mastery of space" and "mastery of outer space" prerequisites for naval victory, with outer space becoming the new commanding elevation for naval combat. All spacecraft, including military satellites, space shuttles, and permanent space-based platforms, will observe and control maritime operations from high altitudes, with space-based weapons systems probably directly attacking and intercepting warships and their cruise missiles. But ships at sea will take stronger antireconnaissance steps, probably constituting along with seabed-based weapons platforms for direct strikes against space satellites and other space systems. The electromagnetic battle will densely cover all naval battle space, penetrating all combat operations. The side with electromagnetic combat superiority will make full use of that invisible "killer mace" to win naval victory.

In short, on the 21st-century naval battlefield, undersea space, outer space, and electromagnetic space will all become complicated technical fields. Their mutual independence and limitations, with mutual impact and roles, will make future naval battlefields ones of integrated sea-land, sea-air, surface-undersea, and sea-space combat operations, putting the combat activity of sea-land, sea-air, surface-undersea, and sea-space confrontations into a state of alternating and intricate military struggle.

New Weaponry in Naval Combat

In the 21st century, the development of a host of new science and technology fields and new sciences will certainly speed up the development of naval weaponry:

- Nuclear technology will be widely used in naval propulsion systems, as means of supporting the development of larger naval ships. This will enable naval vessels to carry larger quantities and types of weapons systems and electronic equipment, providing solid grounds for making naval warships faster, larger, and more electronic, with more missiles, more aircraft capacity, and longer range.
- Microelectronic technology will make warships essentially electronic, with the next century bringing widespread consideration of electronic equipment first in warship design to make both ships and their weapons systems smarter.
- Stealth technology will grow sharply, with antivisible light, antiradar, antisonar, anti-infrared, and anti-electronic reconnaissance being widely deployed in naval ship, ship-based aircraft and guided missile equipment (including new naval service arms), and naval ships and cruise missiles becoming stealth capable.
- Infrared technology will be widely used as a naval offensive and defensive means, being able to find and distinguish targets earlier, as well as providing all sorts of data for central intelligence and command systems.
- Precision-guidance technology will sharply raise the accuracy of all naval weaponry, genuinely achieving the stage at which

"detection means destruction;" this will apply to long-range precision strikes as well.

• Satellite technology will be fully emphasized by all countries, with systems such as the satellite-based C³I and C⁴I systems, the GPS [global positioning system] navigation positioning system, remote sensing technology, space-based attack systems, and space-based, large-scale monitoring and warning systems being used by most maritime countries. Satellite technology can, in future space development, ensure better command control of naval operations.

• The development and use of superconduction technology will bring superconductor ships to the naval order of battle, enabling ships to travel faster without noise and bringing a quality leap to naval combat capability.

• New materials technology will make it possible for undersea weapons systems, particularly deep-water weapons systems, to form a complete system. Submarines will be able to go faster and deeper, with the sea bed being the ideal place to build military bases.

• Laser technology will make it possible to employ tactical laser weapons with the technology to cause personnel injury and blindness and weapons damage, which is likely to be used first in antiship missile defense systems.

In addition, marine environment technology will also be employed by the navy. In short, the new naval-warfare weaponry will have six features:

• Its reconnaissance and observation equipment will be improved, with long-range observation, precise target acquisition, and integration with guidance systems, for an improved weapons-system reaction rate.

• The lethality of weapons will be sharply higher, with a significant improvement in destructive power.

• Naval combat forces will have rapid mobility, expanded operational scope, and quicker victories.

• There will be a marked improvement in protective and survival capabilities.

• Emphasis will be placed on developing electronic jamming and attack systems.

- All-dimensional space will be brought into naval warfare service.

So it could be said that smarter, more electronic, and more lethal systems will be the basic development trends of the coming naval-warfare arms.

The appearance of this new equipment will certainly pose a grim challenge to traditional marine strategies, naval warfare campaigns, tactical theory, and naval warfare patterns. On the 21st-century naval battlefield, there will be more long-range that short-range combat, more missile combat than gun battles, electronic warfare across the whole battlefield, and both combatants making full use of smart weapons and drawing on modern command methods of fighting. In future naval warfare, the multidimensional battlefield will reveal naval targets and the marine battlefield perspective, making it impossible for surface ships without air force cover to operate in high-threat maritime zones. Deep strikes by shipboard aircraft will also be unable to do without support and safeguards in the fields of outer space, the atmosphere, and electromagnetism, with a particular need to organize thorough electromagnetic convoys. As future naval forces will be stereoscopically surrounded by air, surface, undersea, space, and electromagnetic threats, naval warfare will put more emphasis on diversified, three-dimensional, and composite service arms, which will constitute the basic form of 21st-century naval warfare. No matter how powerful the isolated service arms, ship types, and power systems, they will be victorious only by luck in the coming highly electromagnetic and high-threat environment.

In 21st century naval warfare, tactics will change sharply, with new tactical concepts proliferating and being used more flexibly and changeably. The concept of using tactical mobility of all weapons-delivery platforms to first seize advantageous positions and then attack will likely become obsolete or even disappear, with long-range battle concepts such as "remote grappling" and "over-the-horizon strikes" becoming the key forms of battle in future naval warfare (such as attacks against surface ships, missile defense, air defense, and strikes on land- or space-based targets). From the local wars since the 1980s, particularly the high-tech Gulf War, it is not hard to see that trend.

In future naval warfare, long-range battles will become the major form of battle mainly because:

- Weaponry developments will make remote warfare not only possible, but also essential.
- Remote warfare can achieve better operational results. Remote warfare more easily achieves first-strike concealment and surprise.
- Remote warfare can strike more targets on a broader and deeper scale. As the possibility of remote warfare and more powerful weapons can make conventional tactical naval strikes universally achieve their campaign-strategy objectives, future naval warfare campaigns and tactics are likely to be integrated in many cases.

New Technology is Expensive

High-tech weaponry is dozens or even hundreds of times costlier than ordinary weaponry. In 21st-century naval warfare, while the use on the naval battlefield of large amounts of high-tech weaponry will raise troop operational efficiency, the material input and expenditure will also be unprecedentedly higher. In the recent Gulf War, the multinational forces headed by the United States used over 20 new types of missiles and nearly 10 types of precision-guided bombs, with guided weapons undertaking almost 80 percent of the assault missions, for ideal combat success. The expenditures on both sides were enormous.

In the next century, as technologies such as electronics, lasers, and new materials are further improved and developed, directional weapons such as lasers, particle beams, and microwave beams will also be employed in naval warfare, so that naval warfare weaponry movement and development rates will be faster, strike precision higher, and lethality greater. With much weaponry being guided, personal, and smart, and command and control being automated, mobility and strike precision will be easier. The high input, high expenditure, and destructiveness of warfare will force coming naval warfare to be more time effective, shortening sustained time, speeding up the rhythm, and making battlefield conditions sharply changeable. The content of both sides' forces in naval warfare will change quickly, with belligerent stances also changing in a short time.

S&T developments are making the world smaller. As growing world economic integration more easily subjects naval warfare to economic, political, and diplomatic limitations, shorter battle times and controlled belligerency scales are bound to become new requirements for future naval warfare. When a naval war starts, there will be an attempt to end the fighting before the other side makes an all-out military response, in order to avoid subjecting national human and financial resources to the huge battle expenditures of sustained combat. So 21st-century naval battles will break out much faster, with suddenness likely to play a decisive role in winning wars. Lightning attacks and powerful first strikes will be more widely used in coming naval battles. As both sides will strive to make lightning attacks and raise their first-strike damage rates, while doing all possible to organize a rapid and effective counterattack, speed against speed will become the crux of future naval victory.

In the age of peace and development, the limited objectives of future naval warfare will restrict the scale of battle. The high input, high expenditure, and time effectiveness of naval warfare will all make control of the scale of future naval warfare not only possible but also essential, so it will be very hard to see in future naval battles the past grand scenes of "decisive fleet engagements." As the forms of battle change, there will be few naval engagements beyond the scale of battles; instead, there will be ever-growing numbers of medium and small conflicts with high-tech, small forces.

But that certainly does not exclude the future possibility of large-scale naval warfare. This is because the following conditions will still exist in the next century:

- In medium and small naval battles, in which both sides might be balanced, meaning no quick victory, one side might sustain great damage, causing a large-scale retaliatory naval war, or one side might be unable to achieve its war aims, yet refuse to cease fire.
- If the glaring conflicts in world maritime development and delimitation intensify, it might lead to war.
- Large-scale naval developments will provide the forces and therefore the possibility of large-scale naval warfare.

Optimized Force Structure Will Be Crucial

The history of 20th-century naval warfare is one of steadily growing force coordination. In the 21st century, with the development of operational means, and with combat forces being highly mobile, most forces will be capable of being deployed quickly to make a timely response. The joint impact of the multidimensional battlefield and force utilization will require all forces taking part in naval engagements to quickly get into a favorable battlefield stance, as well as adjust their might at any time to steadily maintain their force superiority. That will require the participating forces to have a very high coordination capacity, and pay attention to coordination accuracy and operational-time planning. In naval warfare, it will be necessary to coordinate naval surface ships, submarines, air forces, marines, and other new service arms and combat troops, as well as land, air, and space forces. As only the matched integration of naval, air, space, land, undersea, and electromagnetic fields and multidimensional participating forces can form a partial or overall advantage, coordination accuracy and response speed and quality will be an essential factor in future naval victory. In the Gulf War, the effective cooperation of the multinational naval forces with air, land, and other forces proved this point. In coming naval battles with multiple participating service arms and intricate and diverse weaponry, even small-scale naval battles will need multi-level, highly accurate, and effective coordination.

Future high-tech developments will bring a crucial change to naval composition, with the naval force structure being sharply adjusted to meet naval warfare needs:

- Streamlining will eliminate unnecessary intermediate links, ensuring command effectiveness and efficiency. For instance, the U.S. Navy's land command agency has installed many command agencies on ships, no longer using a separate shore command, to reduce command levels. This structure is very likely to become the generally used battle-command form of the future.
- The force establishment system will be optimized. With the navy being a developing service arm, the future is going to see certain new service arms, such as special naval units, deep-sea troops, rapid response and deployment troops, robot units, high-performance fleets, electronic warfare troops, flight-instrument units, and even space troops. Meanwhile, certain traditional service arms and units will have less status and a less important

role, being eliminated, shrunk, or merged. For instance, shore defense units will be incorporated into the army establishment.

• Crack-troop compositions will raise combat capability. Because of the sharp increases in future weaponry automation and fighting efficiency, relatively fewer personnel will be needed, but they will have to be of higher quality. The inevitable trend will be crack troops and weapons forming naval superiority. The future naval warfare force organization will grow ever smaller and more multifunctional. During World War II, a carrier battle fleet normally was composed of three to five carriers and a corresponding number of surface ships, submarines, and other protective ships. In contract, the modern carrier fleet is generally made up of only one or two carriers.

Systematic "Soft Casualties"

In the 1970s and 1980s, the emergence of precision-guided weapons, high-efficacy bombs, "smart" bombs, and "ingenious" bombs brought a sharp rise in the "hard casualty" capability. "Soft casualties," characterized mostly by electronic jamming, also showed new might. At present, studies and applications are developing rapidly in the use of high-tech methods such as biochemical and electronic, radio frequency, and secondary waves for "soft casualties" against weapons systems and personnel "internal organizations." Ever-diversifying "soft casualty" means in the 21st century are likely to become even more perfected, with their antipersonnel effects making it ever-harder for certain hard-strike weapons to keep up, as well as making protection correspondingly more difficult. The widespread use and efficiency of "soft casualty" weapons in coming naval warfare will have a crucial impact on war at sea.

Modern, high-tech, local wars often start with an electronic battle, and also occur in a dense, complex, and changeable electromagnetic environment. Future combat systems, especially command and weapons systems, will grow ever more dependent on electronic technology. Many international figures hold that the development of electronic technology in future wars will be no less important than that of the atomic bomb during World War II. A comprehensive overseas study weighing all S&T factors affecting overall military combat capability, which were the eight criteria of deterrence, interchangeability, economics, comprehensiveness, long-term effectiveness, possibility, technology and capacity, and adaptability, noted that electronic technology has the most impact. At present, the more advanced naval ships and aircraft are equipped with electronic warfare instruments, in some cases forming a comprehensive electronic warfare system.

Maintaining efficient communications with and effective command over troops is a prerequisite for the use of naval force. Because using guided weapons to attack enemies is a basic means of naval attack, the "electromagnetic" advantage will become the focus of rivalry between opponents. The Gulf War showed that electromagnetic dominance is a prerequisite for control of the air, sea, and battlefield. The more electronic and smarter naval equipment, combat command, and information controls of the 21st century will pose very high demands on electromagnetic dominance. Steadily developing "electronic warfare technology" equipment and new means of electronic confrontation will push electronic warfare at sea to new heights. Before long, systems such as the C^3I multi functional confrontation system, comprehensive combat ships, and enormously powerful electronic confrontation neutralization aircraft and computer "coded virus" confrontation systems will play a joint role in the electronic confrontations of naval warfare.

"Secondary wave radiation" casualties and "beam-capable weapon" casualties are "soft casualty" categories now under development. As such beam-capable weapons are now being developed very quickly, they are expected to be put into the testing stage early in the next century. With future "soft casualties" not only coming in many forms, but also being easy to use, the defensive difficulty will grow steadily. The ingenious "soft casualties" of naval warfare combined with fierce "hard strikes" is an unavoidable development trend.

Command and Control Will Grow in Complexity

Twenty-first-century naval warfare will be a coordinated operation of triphibious, comprehensive, and multiservice operations. Therefore, naval commanders will have to have an overview of the whole battle, be able to quickly learn about ever-changing battle conditions, and then computerize, analyze, and judge data to make a quick response, as well as command troop coordination in a timely and accurate way. This will tie command, control, communications, and intelligence systems into a tightly connected whole, giving it advantages such as remote operation, good communications secrecy, and fast data processing. It can then be applied to both strategic command and battle-tactics command, and even command of individual ships, planes, and troops, thus ensuring battlefield-command efficiency, continuity, stability, and flexibility. This will play a crucial role in the rivalry over naval dominance.

Since the C³I system was established in the early 1980s, it has played an enormous role in several recent local wars. In future naval warfare, on the one hand, the participating forces will be more complex in makeup, putting high demands on overall coordination, and even higher demands on better centralized command and better controlled overall command efficiency. On the other hand, the development of C³I systems has provided a powerful means for better command efficiency, thus driving battlefield command and control to develop in the direction of more automation. While this will speed up the integration of command, control, communication, and intelligence systems, along with raising command and control efficiency, it will also increase command and control complexity:

- It will make command and control activity more dependent on automated and electronic equipment, while the extent of automation and the complexity of electronic equipment and procedures will increase simultaneously.
- As the C³I system will be the "nerve center" and "force multiplier" of future naval warfare, it is bound to become a crucial item in jamming and attacking opponents. As this will give command, control, communications, and intelligence systems more confrontational capability, it will make command more complex and difficult.
- As future naval warfare will involve enormous amounts of information, putting higher demands on the effectiveness and accuracy of the C³I system, it will sharply increase battlefield command and control difficulty.

Naval Warfare Logistics Security Will Be Difficult and Complex

The enormous destructiveness of future naval warfare, with its extensive spatial limits, diversified participating service arms, and its rapid tempo, will make it more dependent on logistics security:

- Naval warfare will put extremely high demands on battlefield-technology security. Because the navy is a technically complex service arm, and future naval weapon will have higher comprehensive operational capacity, which will spur weapons to be more precise and complex, the technological aspects of naval security are going to become more evident in the next century. In addition, the higher precision, newer technology, and greater destructiveness of naval weaponry will also sharply raise the battle damage rate of naval weaponry. War will mean expending large amounts of human and material resources on weapons maintenance and upkeep, which will necessarily make battlefield technical-security harder.

- Logistics survival will face a great challenge, making logistics security harder. As high technology has given the battlefield all-dimensional awareness and deep strike capability, future maritime supply lines and logistics security bases will find it hard to survive, with a stiff challenge being posed not only to maritime security operations, but also to logistics base protection. It will be very important to organize and effect maritime logistics security, to raise logistics-security efficiency and reliability and ensure a high survival rate for logistics systems.

- The diversification of large amounts of material consumption and security will add to the difficulty and complexity of logistics security. Future naval warfare will sharply increase the load on combat logistics security. The Gulf War's daily ammunition expenditure was 4.6 times that of the Vietnam War and 20 times that of the Korean War; its oil consumption was over $26 million, for oil consumption of around 19 million gallons a day. In the several local wars prior to that, material consumption was also enormous. Material consumption in future naval wars will be not only large in volume, but also diverse in category and level. And that will put even higher demands on logistics-security, effectiveness, and comprehensiveness.

Naval warfare has developed and changed enormously in this century, and its development and changes in the next century are going to be amazing. Naval warfare in the 21st century is bound to bring about an historic change in its traditional appearance to confront the people of the next century. Today, while our forecast of the major issues of 21st century naval warfare is subject to time limitations and is not immune to mistakes, we can still forecast future naval warfare in order to proceed actively with our future naval preparations.

THE MILITARY REVOLUTION IN NAVAL WARFARE

Naval Captain Shen Zhongchang
· Naval Lieutenant Commander Zhang Haiyin
Naval Lieutenant Zhou Xinsheng

A new military revolution refers to the historical military trend in which warfare is changing from a war of mechanization to a war of information. The Navy is a force that requires high technology. The new military revolution will inevitably have an important impact on sea warfare and naval construction.

The New Military Revolution, Traditional Sea Warfare, and Future War

At present, technology groups, such as technologies of nuclear, space, shipbuilding, microelectronics, satellite, air cushion, surface effect, new materials and marine technology, are becoming the materials bases for the new military revolution to influence naval combat theory and to change concepts. Among the new technologies, electronic and

Captain Shen Zhongchang is the Director of the Research and Development Department of the Navy Research Institute, Beijing. Navy Lieutenant Zhou Xinsheng and Lieutenant Commander Zhang Haiying serve as staff officers at the Navy Research Institute. This paper originally appeared in China Military Science *1 (1996).*

information technologies are of the most profound significance in terms of improving the capacity for obtaining, processing and transmitting information of the battlefield, increasing the transparency of the war, improving the precision and reliability of firepower, and quickening the process of sea warfare. There is no doubt that during the revolution, combat theory and concepts will be largely modified.

Control of Information Is Important

Like nuclear deterrence, information deterrence is a new concept of victory without war and can even prevent escalation of sea warfare. Electronic information is needed to facilitate both naval and land operations and the command and control of vessels and aircraft. The new military revolution will accelerate the digitization of the naval battlefield, increase modes of communication, strengthen the capacity for information processing and improve the efficiency of command and control. High-speed platforms and long-range precision missiles will, to a great extent, rely on effective combat information systems in order to achieve combat efficiency. In addition, such systems will significantly improve the power of platforms and weapons, resulting in a sharp increase in the role of information, control of which then becomes a new and important deterrent. The side controlling information will be able to manipulate the beginning, middle, and end of the war, attack the enemy with advanced information weapons to paralyze enemy aircraft, vessels and various command systems, and destroy important targets with precise firepower. It will be difficult for the other side to initiate sea war against an opponent who controls information, and once a war starts, it will not be able to win. Hence, future naval warfare needs a strategy not only in the air and sea but also in information control.

Concentration of Firepower Will Replace Concentration of Force

In naval combat, vessels are usually organized in task forces or battle groups to fulfill tasks. Concentration is conveniently used for organizing effective command, using massive firepower, and forming the most favorable defense system in order to reduce enemy threats. However, in the informationized battlefield, vessels can have direct communication with the command post. Vessels can have access to each other's location and situation and have information about enemy vessels and aircraft. In addition, the capacity for long-range precision attack is also improved. Information enables dispersal of platforms. Under such circumstances, the firepower needed to attack targets can be allocated through precise information transfer and long-range attack instead of concentration of platforms. Concentrations of battle groups in future warfare will probably be replaced by small formations and single vessels. Vessels will be dispersed "evenly" at sea.

Remote Attack Will Be the Major Combat Concept

With high technology, future sea warfare will adopt the remote attack as the major combat concept. Satellites and other information platforms will provide large-scale monitoring, warning, and target information processing and transmission services. This will supply future vessels and aircraft with targeting information for launching long-range, precision-guided platforms. On the other hand, missiles and other weapons will be produced that have long-range capacity, intelligence, and precision accuracy, all of which provide remote attack. Hence, remote attack will be widely employed on future battlefields and even become the major mechanism for combat platforms to destroy the opponent's strategic targets. Such mechanisms will survive better and extend the range and number of targets that can be attacked by using stealth and sudden strikes. In November 1993, U.S. troops attacking Iraqi "restricted airspace" launched 45 cruise missiles from ships a thousand miles from the targets. In the future, when combat information is transmitted instantly during battle, it will be more common to attack targets with remote firepower from various places

Underwater Raids Will Be an Important Combat Concept

The extensive application of information technology improves the transparency of the sea battlefield and increases the deterrence of vessels and aircraft. Such deterrence is multidirectional but much less serious to submarines, because submarines are more difficult to track. Submarines can fulfill combat tasks and attack land targets according to information obtained from the command post while keeping their movement concealed, and they can move under water for a long time without being discovered. The prospect for using submarines is good, because of their covertness and power. Even without attacking targets, submarines are menaces existing anywhere at any time. Therefore, the role of submarines in future information warfare will be very important.

Digitization of Naval Warfare

Digitization is the connection of various combat platforms, units, and even arms of the services in naval combat through digital communication systems and information systems, including computer information processing systems and terminals, and establishment of a digital command and control chain to inform the units involved precisely and rapidly. In the digitized naval battlefield, information is somewhat transparent. Information about the facilities, military bases, communication networks, and command and economic centers of both sides are kept on a combat data base. Naval weapons will be long range, feature high precision, and have more power. In the future naval battlefield, a single tactical action can probably achieve the goal of the entire campaign or even the strategy. U.S. vessels are equipped with the capacity to launch both strategic and campaign attacks; such capacity will make the boundaries among strategy, campaign, and tactics ambiguous and sometimes concepts integrate to change naval combat. Such change is reflected in three aspects—fulfilling strategic missions with nuclear-powered attack submarines; long-range attack from sea to land; and joint actions of cruise missiles and aircraft carriers. With the growing changes in naval tactics, tactical concepts will be expanded tremendously. The employment of tactics will be more flexible and tactical doctrine will be enriched.

The Opponent's Information Network As an Important Target

During the Gulf War, the Iraqi troops were not overly different from the multinational troops in terms of equipment and logistics. However, the situation always favored the multinational troops. As Alvin Toffler commented, the Gulf War was a trial of strength between two military systems. After most radar and monitoring equipment of the Iraqi army was disabled, the army became a conventional military machine, which was at the Second Wave level. It was still strong, but slow. Western countries have become more restless about the shortcomings in developing information war systems. The U.S. military has examined information combat and believes that computer systems and communication networks could be easily destroyed by an enemy. The increase of information systems probably could provide an enemy with targets for attack, thus the U.S. Defense Department has invested $1 billion in establishing a network to safeguard its information system. Some military colleges have added training on computer information security. A new service arm, computer security, is under consideration. In future naval war, destroying the opponent's information network will have important significance in controlling information and taking the initiative in the war. There are many ways to destroy information systems—attacking radar and radio stations with smart weapons, jamming an enemy's communication facilities with electronic warfare and attacking communication centers, facilities, and naval command ships; destroying an enemy's electronic system with electromagnetic pulse weapons; and even destroying computer software with a computer virus.

Future Naval War Will Emphasize Joint Actions

To adapt to future war, the structure of the army, navy, and air force will become similar. Command communication among the armed forces will be more integrated. Weapons will be more interchangeable among the services, and rear services will work for various services. In addition, land, sea, air and electromagnetic space will be linked together by an information combat system, which will provide timely and precise technical support to the army. Difficulties and barriers of joint combat will be smoothed. The navy will emphasize joint combat with other armed forces because it can improve the attacks on land targets—a development trend of future naval combat actions. In addition, the navy will depend more and more on army and air forces in sea and offshore combat. The U.S. Army believes that joint combat is the key to winning. Any single arm of the service cannot implement a campaign-level operation. Each service on the battlefield should cooperate and give full play to the advantages of air, land, naval and space forces. Today, the U.S. Army has established a doctrine center for naval, army, and air forces to formulate technical and tactical command and control programs.

The New Military Revolution Will Stimulate Reforms

First, technical groups headed by information technology will accelerate the improvement of the navy's combat ability. The offensive and defensive capability of single vessels and aircraft, coordination ability of single force action, and joint combat will all be enhanced. For single navy combat platforms, quick reaction and precise delivery of firepower will be improved because of timely and accurate information. Because of the connection between the of communication systems of submarines, aircraft, and ships, the various combat platforms will be effectively combined into an integral part to attack the enemy. The communication and navigation capacity of the vessels will be strengthened to expand the scope of combat for various platforms. Combat tasks will be emphasized more on the ocean and the defense focus will shift from land to sea. Firepower will play a superb role with the assistance of information technology. Combat capabilities of informationized platforms cannot be estimated by the firepower of weapons, but by the formula "firepower + information force." It is estimated that digitized troops will possess three times the combat effectiveness of conventional troops.

Second, changes of naval combat doctrine and concepts will inevitably impel more effective use of the navy. Development of platforms and weapon systems depends both on the fusion of combat concepts and techniques and on the development of these concepts into a comprehensive combat doctrine. New doctrine will ultimately employ naval technical revisions to improve combat power. Future naval combat doctrine and concepts will abandon the old and obsolete elements and replace them with new and improved ones to suit naval combat requirements. Therefore, doctrine will adapt to the need for more effective firepower.

Third, the establishment of a high-quality navy during the new military revolution will provide a solid foundation for improvement of joint combat effectiveness. To meet the needs of information warfare, countries with a strong navy are reforming the entire naval system. The steps include:

- Downsizing and investing in high-tech weapons
- Removing or combining duplicate or worthless units, simplifying links and improving command efficiency
- Adding new joint departments, such as a joint coordination department for the navy and other services
- Improving command systems. Some command organizations can be moved from land to sea. The naval command system is networked.

- Retraining forces and allocating them to ships, air units and submarines to improve training levels and strengthen combat ability.

Naval Restructuring

Motivated by the new technological revolution, each country will no doubt reduce force sizes and improve quality. According to the principle of "being rational and sufficient," countries are downsizing and making transcentury military plans. A prominent character of force restructuring is the expansion of the navy and air force. Navy restructuring is regarded as key to military organization. Most countries are reducing the number of military personnel and stressing navy restructuring to bring about a fundamental change in the military structure.

Another character of quality navy restructuring is the emphasis on establishing rapid deployment forces, among which naval forces are an important component. The U.S. rapid deployment forces have aircraft carriers and amphibious ships; the British task force and Japanese fleet both have rapid deployment forces.

Winning Information War Combat

During the Cold Weaponry era, the major mode of operations for the navy were ships that rammed each other. In the Hot Weaponry era, the mode was artillery action within vision distance. Firepower and mobility are the most basic and decisive technical elements in such actions. Early this century, ship speed was limited, so technology focused on increasing firepower. Technical competition was focused on increasing firepower. The development of nuclear technology also brought forth a "zenith" of fire power. Currently, the military revolution is infiltrating into every aspect of naval equipment buildup. The pounding of the revolution on war format, mode, and methods of operations will eventually bring about further change in weapons. Such change is not interested in acquiring new ships and aircraft with faster speeds and higher destructive power but tries to focus on winning information combat.

One requirement of winning information combat is to strengthen the "soft" systems in vessels and aircraft, including systems of reconnaissance, monitoring, communication, navigation and meteorology. These systems can create favorable conditions in the information war to control information and help one survive. In information war, the efficiency of vessels, aircraft and equipment is largely determined by the quality of soft systems. Without the assistance of such systems, ships and aircraft cannot carry out tasks. Today, soft systems are becoming an important symbol of estimating the combat force of vessels. Consequently, during the development of modern vessels, soft systems, especially communication facilities, target- determining installations, and electronic war systems are increasing and becoming more complicated. In designing and building ships, the U.S. Navy gives priority to electronic equipment, installing electronic jamming facilities in many vessels in order to enhance their defense capability. The tactical information data system is a sound comprehensive combat system installed in large vessels. The system can not only command all weapons in the vessel, but also coordinate and command weapon control systems in other vessels in the formation through a data chain. It can integrate the entire formation into one unit. It can be foreseen that the naval C^3I system based on satellite and computer technologies will be developed as an important soft system during the military revolution and will become compatible with the C^3I system of the air and land forces.

To prepare for information war, weapons used in the navy will be produced more precisely and with advanced intelligence. These weapons include intelligent missiles, shells and torpedoes. Missiles are the main weapons not only for modern sea war but also for future sea information war. The character and rule of missile operation will dominate the developing trend of sea warfare. Today, there are more than 120 types of missiles in the world that can be used in marine operations. These missiles will be upgraded with information processing technology. Antivessel missiles will be updated to travel at supersonic speed, function at minimum altitude, be precision guided, and use anti-interference features. Air defense missiles will have air defense and antimissile features and have a combination of long, medium and short ranges. Hence, the flexibility of weapons can be improved.

Various combat platforms will be featured with new characters, one of which is the concealing technology. In digitized sea battlefield, platforms face the dangers of being monitored, detected, and attacked from space, air, land, sea, and submarine. It is thus particularly important for vessels and aircraft to conceal themselves well. It is vital to develop and apply stealth technology and upgrade the covertness of navy platforms. Navies in each country have already shown concern about this issue. Another feature is the development of submarine forces, which have higher covertness. It is difficult to determine if information technology will be developed to detect submarines effectively. Therefore, submarines will receive less impact from reconnaissance technology than other platforms. In addition, submarines have a greater attacking power under water. Accordingly, it is an important aspect of navy restructuring to develop and maintain submarine forces. Countries will choose to develop vessels according to situations in neighboring countries and national conditions—larger countries will place importance on developing aircraft carriers and amphibious ships; medium-size and small countries will increase destroyer, corvette, minesweeper and minelayer capabilities. However, each country will give attention to developing submarine forces. China's neighboring countries are already focusing on purchasing and developing submarines—for instance, Korea will buy 11 submarines from Germany. Indonesia will increase the number of its submarines from 3 to 5, and Australia plans to build 6 submarines. Malaysia, Singapore and Thailand are also establishing submarine forces. After the Cold War, Russia and the United States downsized their submarine forces but strengthened the modernization of the troops in order to maintain their operational ability. We can conclude that during the First World War, the dominant vessel was the battleship, and in World War II, it was the aircraft carrier. In future global wars, the most powerful weapon will be the submarine. In addition, the navy and other armed forces will develop some new equipment, such as directional weapons, subsonic radiate weapons, high-energy electromagnetic wave weapons and computer virus, to increase the power of weapons.

Higher Quality Personnel and Training

Future navies will consist of scientists, engineers, and technicians. Equipped with information technology, the navy needs a large group of specialists in computer, information engineering, and satellite technology.

With the development and broad application of information technology, it is necessary for navy personnel to upgrade their education and improve professional skills. The new technological revolution has doubled and redoubled the navy's combat capacity; indeed, such is the result of human talent. The navy is a special arm with intensive knowledge and techniques, and navy personnel must be empowered by updated skills. Navy officers must have the ability to command in a high-tech war, and be familiar and coordinate operations with the other services.

To narrow the gap between training and actual operation, future training of navy personnel will be conducted through computer simulated systems, which can simulate sea battles. Such simulated training can replace large-scale maneuvers, save materials and money, and effectively improve the skills and command ability of navy personnel.

21ST-CENTURY AIR WARFARE

Colonel Ming Zengfu

In the last decade of the 20th century, along with other grand changes in the international situation and patterns of war, the air battlefield will become decisively significant.

Air Warfare Weapons and Equipment

Air warfare weapons and equipment in the 21st century mainly will be smart ammunition, thinking operational platforms and integrated automatic C^3I systems.

Smart Munitions

In the course of its development, air force munitions went through three stages—unable-to-control after launching, able-to-control after launching, and, finally, unnecessary-to-control after launching. The first state of air force munitions was in the decades after aircraft came into being until World War II, when all airborne weapons were aimed by sight, which has a low-kill probability. Along with the rapid development of information technology and control technology after WWII, airborne sight weapons developed into guided target-

Colonel Ming Zengfu serves at the Air Force Command Institute, Beijing. This paper is from "New Changes in Air Defense Operations," in Chinese Military Science (Spring 1995).

seeking weapons, and the development of air munitions progressed to the second stage and then to the third. Before early air-to-air missiles, air-to-ground missiles, and precision-guided bombs were launched, information about targets was transmitted to their control section by pilots. In order to control the missiles, pilots continually transmitted information about targets to the control section after launching the missiles or bombs, in order to insure that they flew precisely toward targets. As information technology further develops and is applied to air munitions, active and passive information devices can automatically acquire information about targets after air munitions have left their platforms. Thus the munition is able to change its own flight and destroy targets precisely. "Unnecessary to control after launching" has therefore been largely achieved. According to calculations, if the kill probability remains unchanged, while precision increases by 1, 2, or 3 times, the efficiency equals, respectively, that of 4, 9, or 16 times that of warheads, or that of 8, 27, or 63 times that of ammunition equivalent. Increased ammunition performance enables air warfare to develop toward "one warhead, one target." According to relevant data, to destroy a strong underground fortification in World War II, 9,000 bombs were needed; in the Vietnam War, 600 bombs; in the Gulf War, only 1 or 2 bombs. Thus, "unnecessary to control after launching" air munitions for the 21st century are already under research, and the amount of this kind of munition is increasing rapidly. It is predicted that, with its high precision, this kind of ammunition will play a dominant role in the air battlefield of the 21st century.

Informationized Platforms

An early aircraft was only a machine able to fly in the sky. Only after it was used in war did it become an operational platform. Aircraft have undergone a development course from a mechanical platform to an informationized operational platform and finally to an intellectualized operation platform. The first generation aircraft were jet-propelled and pursued supersonic speed; the second generation could reach bi-sonic speed and a height of over 20,000 meters. On this basis, information equipment on board second generation aircraft began to hold an important position. Fire-control radars were generally used in second generation aircraft. Information equipment in third-generation aircraft holds a more important position. What are generally used on board include pulse Doppler radar, forward-looking infrared devices, night vision devices, low-light TV, navigational and digital headsup displays, etc.

Equaling 50 to 60 percent of the total cost of common aircraft (or over 60 percent of the total cost of stealth planes), information equipment aboard fourth-generation aircraft holds a far more outstanding position. For example, there are more than 700 computers on a B-2 bomber. For this reason fourth-generation aircraft have become intellectualized operational platforms, which have three apparent advantages: they can extensively collect information; they can deal with all kinds of information; and they can carry all kinds of ammunition. With the help of the fire-control system, they can automatically distribute targets and control a number of warheads to attack simultaneously. Their electronic warfare system can authoritatively judge the threatening sources and provide the pilot with conduct methods for him to select. Additionally, their operations assisting system can help drive the aircraft. Nowadays, modern aircraft has become an information-dominated weapon. Compared with that of WWII, the efficiency of the battle aircraft of the 21st century will increase more than 100 times.

Integrated and Automated C^3I Systems

Radar is an information-collecting device which was designed to adapt to aerial warfare weapon's characteristics. Its emergence made it possible to control air warfare and brought to an end the epoch when air warfare equaled blind men touching an elephant. However, in the long period ever since, because of low-level of information technology, the command system was restricted to the realm of manual operation, thus the operation or capability of air power was heavily limited. Since the 1950s, when collecting, transmitting, processing and using information were fused, the command system of air warfare has witnessed such a rapid development process—"manual operation command became semi-automatic command, which became automated command," resulting in the eventual appearance of integrated and automated C^3I systems.

Employment Concepts of Air Power

In the multipolar international framework of the 21st century, a focus of national attention will be on how to cope with local wars and regional crises. In multilevel military operations, in peacetime or in times of neither-war-nor-peace, air power will play a more important role. The employment concepts of air power will become more diversified.

Air Deterrence

Compared with actual combat, deterrence has some limitations. However, because its functions are broad, one may both launch an attack and make peace, achieving goals without sacrifice. So deterrence can be used separately or as the precursor of actual combat. In the 21st century, air deterrence will become the first-choice mode of employing air power.

High-tech conventional deterrence is a new mode of deterrence developed after nuclear deterrence. Although the effect of nuclear deterrence is very strong, its actual value has decreased because of the height of the "nuclear threshold." High-tech warfare requires deterrence strength capable not only of maneuvering rapidly in vast battle space, but also of moving about freely and quickly within hostile borders. It further requires the deterrent force to be able to attack and withdraw quickly after destroying the enemy's strategic targets. Air power happens to possess these characteristics. Air deterrence has three advantages:

- It is highly effective for a fixed period with wide coverage. Modern air forces are capable of carrying out supersonic maneuvers and intercontinental missions and can cover any target in any part of the world.
- There is low political risk. Modern air forces can attack strategic targets with precision of less than 1 meter. On the one hand, this ability can ensure target destruction and, on the other, avoid unfavorable political effects, which is the inevitable result of killing or wounding civilians or destroying civilian facilities.
- It can operate under a range of conditions. It can function both separately or jointly with the Army and the Navy, and it can

also function both in conventional conditions and nuclear conditions.

Therefore, air deterrence will become the basic employment mode of future deterrence.

No-Fly Zones

A "no fly" zone is a forbidden airspace set up in a conflicted area, using air power as its main force. In the no-fly zone, none of the opponent's air actions is permitted, nor can any opponent install ground-to-air weapons that may threaten one's own air actions. No-fly zones are a new application mode of air power in the last decade of the 20th century. For example, the United States, Britain and France set up a no-fly zone in Iraq to protect the Kurds, and the U.N. Security Council passed a resolution to set up a no-fly zone in Bosnia-Herzegovina.

Limited Air Strikes for Peacekeeping Missions

According to relevant resolutions of international organizations and at the request of peacekeeping forces, limited air strikes may be carried out by authorized countries or a group of countries against military targets that violate relevant rules; these are called limited aim air strikes. For example, in November 1994, in accordance with U.N. resolution 958, NATO's air forces bombed Udbey airport in Bosnia-Herzegovinia, which was controlled by Serbs. Soon after, Serbian military targets, such as ground-to-air missile positions and groups of tanks, were attacked by air.

Characteristics.
- It is ordered in accordance with U.N. authorization.
- Because it is restricted to attacking military targets directly threatening peacekeeping missions, it is small scale.
- It is restrained by political and diplomatic actions, thus it is strictly controlled.

Air Blockades at Sea

The sea-air blockade is one of the basic application modes of air power. It is a military action blockading a certain section of the sea, a certain coastal area, or a certain country by way of aerial mining in order to blockade seaports and sea lanes as well as attack targets trying to break the blockade. Naval blockades against Japan in World War II and against important ports of northern Vietnam in the Vietnam War were enforced mainly by aerial mining. In air battles of the 21st century, air blockades will still be important.

Characteristics.

● Sea blockade and air blockade are inseparable.

● Air blockade's role will increase further.

● Struggles between the blockaders and the antiblockaders will be more complex.

Strategic Air Lift

Strategic airlift is a large-scale operation to transport troops to warring regions by air. With the improvement of air transport, strategic airlift has demonstrated some incomparable advantages which other transport modes do not possess:

● It is high speed. Modern air transports are able to cover a distance of 800 to 900 km per hour while cruising, which is 10 times that of land transports. Because air transporters commonly take a direct route, air transport is the most rapid means of transport.

● Air transporters can cover a long distance. Modern strategic transports can travel thousands of miles. With air refueling, they are able to carry out global lift.

● Air transport is highly maneuverable and seldom restricted by geographic conditions. It can transport troops and military equipment to any airport in the world.

● Air transport has large freight volume. For example, an An-124 can carry 150 tons per sortie; the An-225, over 200 tons; the U.S. C-5, 120 tons. Modern air power is capable of transporting strategic troops. During *Desert Shield* in the Gulf War, the U.S. Army used 90 percent of its strategic transport and commandeered part of the civil aircraft fleet to air lift more than 500,000 personnel, equaling 99 percent of the total, and over 500,000 tons of material.

Precision/ Surgical Operation Air Strikes

Surgical air strikes are a growing aspect of air power employment in high-tech local wars. Its strategic objective is obtained by precisely attacking the enemy's sensitive strategic targets. Typical examples include the Israeli air force bombing both the Iraqi nuclear reactor in 1981 and the PLO headquarters in Tunisia in 1985, and the United States striking Libya in 1986. In this kind of operation, air power is the main strength, and sudden attack is the main operational principle.

Characteristics.

• It is up to the supreme authorities to make the decision to order such an air strike, so the strategic objective can be obtained directly.

• Comparably fewer troops can be used. Israel dispatched only 14 to 16 planes to bomb the Iraqi nuclear reactor in 1981 and the PLO Headquarters in 1985.

• It takes a short time to strike. For example, it took the U.S. Air Force 18 minutes to strike Libya; the Israeli Air Force took 3 minutes to bomb PLO HQ and 2 minutes to bomb the Iraqi nuclear reactor.

• Its concealed action makes it possible to do long-range strikes. To bomb the Iraqi nuclear reactor, Israeli planes made a 2,000 km round trip, and to bomb PLA Headquarters, a 5,000 km round trip; U.S. planes went more than 10,000 km to raid Libya.

Large-Scale Air Offensives

By studying the regional wars after World War II, especially recent regional wars, we can conclude that air offensives begin with massive air strikes in rather long and relatively separate phases.

Characteristics.

• It is large scale. In the Gulf War, the multinational forces used more than 2,700 planes, and 2,600 sorties were dispatched each day.

• It lasts a rather long time. The Gulf War can be divided into four stages—strategic air strikes, seizing local air dominance, battlefield preparation, and ground operations. Missions in the first three stages were done in 38 days, equaling 90 percent of the total time of the war.

• In large-scale air offensives, there is a direct confrontation for victory and domination. In the Gulf War, air operations reduced the Iraqi troops' operating capability by 50 percent, which ensured that the U.S.-led multinational forces would win the ultimate victory.

Joint Operation of Various Services

Joint operation of various services means air power joins in an equal partnership with the army and navy. This symbolizes a qualitative change from previous history. In the past, the air force assisted the army or the navy to carry out missions. In past large-scale wars, the air force's operational role was subordinate to that of the army and navy and could only share the victory of the army and navy. When air operations became decisive, a great breakthrough was made in applying air power.

Characteristics.
- Air power is in an equal partnership with the army and the navy. Air power is mainly used in strategic depth and campaign depth.
- Air power is able to function in more special fields, such as reconnaissance, warning, electronic warfare, aerial mining, artillery and anti-aircraft strike tasks, road blockades, feints, protection of supplies and communications, etc.

Basic Operational Methods

Before the Vietnam War, when air strikes were carried out by the same type of aircraft, visual coordination was the main type of strike. Air operation methods qualitatively changed during the Vietnam War, when several joint operational methods with various types of aircrafts taking part came into use. In order to cope with the integrated air-defense systems comprising fighters, surface-to-air missiles, anti-aircraft guns and air-defense C^3I systems, an operation took shape to include formations such as airborne early warning and command formations, escort and protective formations, strike formations, air defense suppression formations, reconnaissance formations, electronic warfare formations, air refueling formations, air-rescue formations, etc. Among these the strike formations are the main force, with the rest supporting, protecting and assisting.

Along with the further development of the operational mode, joint air strikes were invented. In the Gulf War, a typical daytime strike group of aircraft of the multinational forces comprised 60 aircraft, in addition to the stealth aircraft. The daytime strike formations included 24 F16-A/Cs, "Tornados," and A-10s, escort formations of 12 F15Cs and Mirage-2000s, accompanying jamming formations of EA-6Bs, EF-111As and one EC-130H, and finally hard-target electronic warfare formations of F-4Gs and A-6Fs equipped with antiradiation missiles. There were also some airborne early warning aircraft and air refueling aircraft participating in actions. Joint air strikes became the main operational mode the multinational forces used in the Gulf War.

As the basic operational mode, joint air strikes completely alter the operational state of air battle space. Thus, joint air strikes have the typical characteristics of nonlinear operations. What may be pointed out is that the way air battlefields were dominated by air power completely changed in the Gulf War. Participants in air operations also included army helicopters, navy Tomahawk cruise missiles, reconnaissance satellites, communication satellites, and global positioning systems comprising over 30 satellites. This change lifts the joint air operation to a new height, unlike previous small joint operations. While a great number of digitized troops are going to be established and a large number of digitized battlefields are taking shape, the three-dimensional air strikes that developed in the Gulf War will become a basic mode of air operations in the future.

Global Strike and Global Reach

When the operational mode of global strike and global reach is applied, the battle space is enlarged, and traditional theories and ideas about the battlefield are broken. Any target in any part of the world is within striking range of air power. After the Gulf War, the main military powers in the world decided to enhance their air power's ability to carry out global strike and all-depth operations. In May 1993, the Russian Air Force organized a large-scale intercontinental maneuver operational exercise from its European region to the Far East. According to the military strategy of "forward presence plus troop transport," the U.S. Air Force established an operational doctrine of "global reach and global operations."

Over-the-Horizon Air Combat

Air combat is the main means of air power used to annihilate the enemy air force. According to distance, it is divided into visual air combat and beyond-the-horizon air combat. The main concept of air combat has been to attack from behind at a distance of hundreds to thousands of meters. The precondition of attacking is the occupation the advantageous position at the rear of the opponent, called short-range air combat.

In the Gulf War, most planes of the multinational forces belonged to the third generation. These planes are of advanced performance, their airborne fire-control radars are capable of surveilling a distance of more than 100 km, simultaneously tracking quite a number of targets from scores of kilometers away, and carrying out attacks over a wide range of altitudes. These capabilities provide a reliable launching platform to make beyond-the-horizon attacks. According to materials the U.S. Defense Department released after the Gulf War, 38 Iraqi aircraft were destroyed in air combat, among which 28 were destroyed by Sparrow AIM-7M mi-range missiles; 10 were shot down by Sidewinder AIM-9L short-range missiles; and the rest were ruined by aircraft guns. The Gulf War was the first rather large-scale regional war in which the number of aircraft destroyed in beyond-the-horizon air combat exceeded those destroyed in visual air combat. It indicates that beyond-the-horizon air combat technology is maturing.

Deep-Strike and Stand-Off Munitions

Ever since air weapons came into being, the way to attack ground targets was to bomb right over the targets after penetrating the ground-to-air defense. In the past 10 years, this method has been used less frequently. Instead, a method that has been used more and more often is to stand off and launch munitions from a long range. This tendency is bringing great changes to air-to-ground operations. Primarily because of stand-off air-to-ground missiles, air power is capable of launching attacks from a long distance, out of range of the defense.

Stealth Penetration

In the first air raid in the Gulf War, 30 U.S. Air Force F-117A stealth fighters directly attacked Baghdad after flying beyond Iraqi air-defense troops, instead of attacking air-defense radars and neutralizing airports and air-defense ground positions to open a penetrating corridor for followup units. This new operational method is characteristic of nonlinear operations. It stops the enemy from organizing effective defenses by harassing the enemy's air-defense rhythm. Relying on stealth fighters' being difficult to be detect, stealth penetration neutralizes the enemy's old formula of air-defense operations, which can be described thusly: find incoming targets; judge the nature of the targets and degree of threat; assign targets; order air defense troops to annihilate the targets. With stealth, the enemy is attacked before they detect the incoming targets. Because it is the crucial positions of the enemy's air-defense system that are first attacked by stealth planes, the enemy's air-defense troops have been paralyzed before they are put into action, so it is impossible for them to arrange organized resistance against the air -raid. Therefore, the air raid attacks predetermined targets without facing resistance. Using this method in the Gulf War, the U.S. Army reduced the ratio of assault troops to service troops to 1:1, and kept the loss rate at 0.03 percent. More and more stealth planes will be rushing into the air battlefields of the 21st century, and stealth penetration bombing will be more commonly applied.

All-Weather and Round-the-Clock Air Strikes

The performance of airborne fire-control-radar is being improved, and night-vision devices such as infrared and low-light devices and space-based precision guidance systems are being added. Many midrange air-to-air missiles, air-to-ground missiles, infrared-guided bombs and laser-guided bombs are being used. Air power has greatly enhanced its ability to attack air and ground targets at night and in any meteorological conditions. Meanwhile, air power can perform all-weather and round-the-clock attacks. This was the case in the Gulf War. Throughout the Gulf War, all-weather and round-the-clock continuous operations were carried out by the multinational forces, in which sorties dispatched at night equaled 70 percent of the total.

Characteristics.

- Because all-weather and round-the-clock operations are widely used, the better equipped side benefits from the night and bad weather, which previously favored the less well equipped side. Because of high-technology, night battlefields become transparent. Bad weather is no longer an obstacle to the better equipped side. Meanwhile, the poorly equipped side can no longer utilize the night and bad weather to change its unfavorable situation.

- This operational mode greatly intensifies operations and speeds up the rhythm of war.

Attacking Joints and Ripping Fabric

The third generation of precision-guided bombs has an accuracy of less than 1 meter. Modern air strikes tend to be "one bomb, one target." Air power's ability in precision strike is increasing and the mode of long-range precision strike is used. It is possible through joint strikes to achieve fabric ripping.

According to systematic opinions, modern military strength is entirely composed of various services and various weapon systems with different functions. Joining various weapons is decisive in the operational system. We call this striking the seams and ripping the fabric in order to "take down" the enemy's operational system, to weaken or even to paralyze it by way of precisely attacking the system or its crucial positions with a certain number of weapons.

It was by way of attacking the seams of the Iraqi air-defense system that the multinational forces ripped the fabric of the Iraqi air-defense system in the Gulf War. The multinational forces took the Iraqi C^3I system as the main target to assault. Twenty hours before the first air raid, electronic warfare began to jam and neutralize the Iraqi C^3I system. In the first air raid, Iraqi targets such as command and communication centers were heavily attacked by Tomahawk cruise missiles and F-117 stealth fighters of the multinational forces. Because Iraq's C^3I system had been violated, even though it had preserved a great deal of weapons and equipment with the help of advanced defense systems, its anti-aircraft guns could merely fire separately, its ground-to-air missiles could only be launched without aim, and its operational aircraft could not take off. It is predicted that the operational concept of assault on the seams and fabric violation will be commonly used in the air battlefields of the 21st century.

THE MILITARY REVOLUTION IN AIR POWER

Major General Zheng Shenxia
Senior Colonel Zhang Changzhi

The new military revolution has brought about changes to the entire military sphere, particularly to the reforms in the air force. To study the impact of the revolution on contemporary air power is of momentous significance to China's defense modernization and air force development.

Air Force Development Is a Catalyst of the New Military Revolution

The fundamental cause of the current military revolution is the extensive application of modern technologies, within which information technology is the core. A modern air force is equipped by information technology, whose use in modern local war reveals the great changes in air power and its bright future. The development of air power is the most direct catalyst of such a revolution.

Since the 1950s, information technology has been developed worldwide. Automatic control and artificial intelligence technology have advanced quickly. Modern information technology was first

Major General Zheng Shenxia is President of the Air Force Command College, Beijing; Senior Colonel Zhang Changzhi is an Assistant Professor at the Air Force Command College, Beijing. Their essay is from China Military Science, *(Spring 1996).*

applied in air weapons. Because of computers, automatic equipment and artificial intelligence, weapons have been invented, such as precision-guided weapons, telemetry and remote-sensing systems, electronic confrontation technology, and automatic C³I systems. Air weapons have become the epitome of contemporary information technology. The special requirements of developing air weapons are the incentive for developing information technology. The mutual acceleration and simultaneous development of air weapons and information technology have resulted in the following accomplishments:

• The transition from nonguided weapons to precision-guided weapons. Ground-to-air missiles have been developed in four modes—high-altitude long range, medium-altitude medium range, and low-altitude and ultra-low altitude short range. Air-to-air missiles come in long, medium, and short range. Air-to-ground missiles come in two types— strategic and campaign tactical . It is predicted that by the end of the 1990s, more guided weapons will be produced with higher intelligence that can identify the enemy force, avoid interference, and attack targets selectively. Such weapons will become the most important conventional equipment.

• The transition from "hard-kill" weapons to "soft and hard kill" weapons. Radio and eletro-optical equipment has become the core of modern air weapons. The electronic equipment is 33 percent of the cost of planes, 45 percent of missile costs, and 66 percent of the cost of unmanned aircraft. The comprehensive aerospace electronic warfare system under development will even bring acoustic frequency into the weapon system, which can function to defeat radar, telecommunication, navigation and guided weapons.

• The transition from manual command to automatic command. The C³I system has become the "nerve center" of modern air combat. The U.S. Air Force established the Strategic Air Command, the North America Air Defense Command, the ballistic missile long-range warning system, and the space monitoring systems. In addition, it possesses tactical air command centers, an air surveillance center, and AWACs. The future aerospace automatic command system will retain high reliability,

confidentiality, confrontation, and information processing capacity.
- The combination of air defense, aviation and space defense and weapons. Since the end of the 1950s, the United States and the Soviet Union have developed ground-base anti-missile weapons and established layer antimissile systems. In the 1980s, military satellites, space aircraft, airships and space stations were developed. It is expected that by the end of the century, military utilization of flying machines can protect ground and air forces operations. By the early 21st century, attacks on space, air, ground and sea targets will have materialized. Air defense and space weapons will be able to fly both in the outer space and in the atmospheric layer.

The above changes illustrate that space-weapon development is in a transitional period of integrating information technology with weapon production. Space weapon systems have possessed some quasi-human functions (such as observation, memory, analysis and synthesis). Missiles have become "shells with eyes." Future air force C^3I systems and various weapons will be controlled by intelligence machines, and will have dialogue with human beings through connection with information processing and displaying working stations. The systems will not only change the air combat information process and transmission modes but also integrate humans, combat theory, and computers into a whole. Through the systems, human intelligence can be immediately released in the form of energy to obtain unprecedented combat effectiveness. Since World War II, the conventional destructive capacity of aircraft has increased by 70 percent. Specifically, modern air weapons have developed in seven aspects:

- Higher precision. Precision-guided weapon technology helps to produce space weapons that can attack various objects thousand kilometers away around the clock. The deviation of cruise missiles is only around a dozen meters, and that of various tactical missiles is 1 meter. The percentage of hits can amount to 98 percent. High-speed, antiradiation missiles can automatically shun radar inference and strike the target. Short-range missiles can fly at a speed three times faster than sonic speed. The range of precision glide bombs reaches 80 km. The highest speed of long-range air-to-air missiles is 43 Mach and the range is 110 to 165 km. Laser-guided missiles are able to go through the vents of fortifications, windows, or doors and explode inside the building. Antitank missiles, after being launched from aircraft, can search for a target automatically at an altitude of several thousand meters.

● Increased stealth. The development of stealth aircraft reduces radar determining range from a few hundred kilometers to a bit more than a dozen kilometers. Further advances in stealth aerospace weapons will make sudden attacks realistic and disable the air-defense warning system and entire air-defense systems.

● Improved night vision. The infrared observation system installed in aircraft makes it possible that a pilot can position at night, discover and destroy targets. The wide application of new technical night vision equipment will bring an end to airmen's "night shift."

● Increased long-range attack ability. Advanced aviation power, impetus technology, and new materials have greatly improved the mobility of aircraft. Accompanied with in-flight refueling and space technology, an air force can realize the legend of combat at the global range.

● Increased destruction power. High-tech equipped weapons have more power to attack and destroy targets. Ordinary aircraft, when equipped with new weapon systems, are doubled and redoubled in combat ability. An operational assignment that needed 230 B-17 bombers during World War II can now be accomplished by eight F-16 fighters.

● Increased command and control capacity. Infrared, laser, telemetry, and remote-sensing technologies have greatly improved the function of air and space reconnaissance systems. The side with technical advantages will take the initiative of the war by controlling information, and use the highly automatic C³I to control air operations effectively. The prewarning command aircraft can improve the combat effectiveness by a few dozen times.

● Increased electromagnetic confrontation capacity. Electron confrontation technology provides air electromagnetic combat with high efficiency, complete coverage, and strong power.

The development and application of air information weapon systems immediately resulted in revolutionary changes in the war field. A lot of concepts only imagined or developed a few years ago became reality in Operation *Desert Storm*. To a great extent, information combat has been enlightened by the Gulf War, in which multinational troops captured all the high-frequency and ultrahigh frequency radio signals of the Iraqi army and stored the numerous amounts of information gathered by the 34 reconnaissance satellites, 260 electronic reconnaissance planes, and 40 prewarning aircraft. Then, the multinational troops used various information systems and high-tech weapons to destroy the Iraqi communication system and take control of the war. The Iraqi command system, radar, and command systems of missiles, aircraft, and artillery were at a standstill. This demonstrates that information is the key to victory. The side that controls information can give full play to the materials and energy possessed, and thereby increase combat power.

After the Gulf War, the U.S. military gradually increased research centered on information combat. U.S. Defense Secretary Perry put forward the proposal of "military revolution" in early 1994, which officially confirmed the existence of the revolution. A special group was organized to conduct research on how the Pentagon can obtain and maintain decisive military superiority within the next two and three decades. Therefore, modern high technology, the key to the new military revolution, has caused the development of contemporary air power. The application of air power in *Desert Storm*, on the other hand, is the "trigger" of the new military revolution. It is predicated that future air strength will have much greater development under the influence and acceleration of the revolution.

The Buildup of Air Strength

The Gulf War displayed not only the embryonic form of information combat but also the advantages of air power and revealed the importance of air power in bringing about satisfactory operational effectiveness in information combat. Therefore, each nation has prioritized the development of air strength under the principle of upgrading the entire defense system and developing all forces:

- Acknowledge that air power is the dominant force in contemporary local war.

- Maintain a stable or increasingly growing air force.
- Keep a relatively higher input of military expenditure in the air force. Emphasize the role of the air force as the nucleus in the theory of war as a breakthrough of reforming the contemporary military.
- Strengthen the buildup of ground forces and naval air forces.

The reasons why each nation lays stress on the buildup of the air force are:

- The demands of the information age. The Gulf War revealed the power of information combat. Western countries, particularly the United States, are keen in their preparing for information combat to consolidate their military positions through highly efficient military construction during the new military revolution. Although various military forces will play different roles in future information war, air strength will possess a unique superiority that is more adapted to modern war.

  In battlefield command, gaining the upper hand in information confrontation can help commanders make decisions and work out strategies. Hence, information superiority is becoming a tremendous combat strength. The C^{3}I system is important to winning information superiority in battle and to improve the flexibility of the army and navy. Under the influence of modern high technology, the ability to obtain battlefield information from air and space has witnessed fundamental changes. Outer space itself becomes a battlefield of monitoring to provide reliable information with the assistance of reconnaissance, communication, navigation, and orientation systems and early-warning systems. Information gathered can be used for strategic command, for campaign and combat command and even by single vessels, vehicles, and soldiers.

  From the viewpoint of electromagnetic combat, armed strength in ground and marine battlefields will be greatly heightened by electromagnetic domination obtained through integrated electronic combat. Air and space are the major fields of electromagnetic confrontation in modern war. Air electronic confrontation equipment, compared to that on the ground, can cover a wider space and have a higher fighting efficiency. The U.S. Army has developed more than 600 electronic combat devices, of which 70 percent is installed in aircraft. Electronic combat in air raids can use electronic devices to reconnaissance, interfere, search, position and monitor an opponent's targets, as well as to cope with enemy electronic mechanisms, in combination with automatic command system and electronic suppression and deceiving devices. Thus, enemy communication will be cut off and radar and guided weapons disabled. Losses on one's own side will be reduced to minimum.

As for firepower, the destruction power has seen great improvement because of the combination of space electronic measures, firepower, and application of weapons with high precision and coverage. One prominent change is the *growing proportion* of air firepower in modern war. According to statistics, the U.S. Army's air munitions have increased dramatically. Today's stockpile is four times that of WWII, three times that of the total ammunition used in the Korean war, twice that of the Vietnam War, and a fifth more than that used in the Gulf War. In addition, 70 percent of casualties and injuries to enemy troops in the Vietnam War was caused by U.S. air firepower. Half the Arab tanks damaged during the fourth Middle East War was destroyed by the Israeli Air Force. During the Falkland Islands war between Britain and Argentina, 90 percent of the 29 vessels that were lost was due to air strikes. All the above indicates that with the rapid development of air weapons, the focus of modern war is gradually shifting to the air. Air firepower is becoming the backbone of joint military forces.

An important feature of information combat is the speed. Strategic air transport serves as the key to releasing and expanding the operational potential of strategic mobility. Speed and strength are the two core elements of measuring the combat effectiveness of strategic mobile force. In contemporary conditions, the contrast of strategic strength is not determined by the military force in a certain area but by the strength of strategic mobility. In modern times, partial wars break out quickly in a vast space, which allows very limited time to carry out an effective reaction. Only through speedy delivery of combat forces to favorable positions can decisive impact be exerted. Among various delivery measures, air transport is the most effective action because of its strong mobility, fast speed, and less restrictive geographic conditions. Air transport in modern times has a greater effect because of its capability of delivering force in large freight size, over a long distance, and at a fast speed between continents. To a certain extent, air transport is the amplifier of the combat strength of the strategic mobile forces of military powers and is an important condition in winning an information war.

• New and higher demands for air force are needed with the change of war format in the information era. Strategically, the focus of international military struggle in the information era has been changed from actual combat to menace. To be able to threaten other nations, one should possess a powerful attacking force. Currently, each country has some kind of means to threaten others. However, air threat takes a predominant position owing to its features of high technology, large capacity, multifunctions, all levels, and speed. Air intimidation shortens the distance between the antagonistic parties, although physically they might be thousand miles apart. Each action will arouse the opponent's vigilance. An air force can facilitate speedy and effective attacks on the enemy. Modern strategy enhances the need of air combat capacity and its function of achieving the strategic goal. This is inevitably a great impetus to develop air force.

On the other hand, military combat strength in the information era is relatively reduced. Coping with local war and controlling crises becomes the strategic concern. Local war, which restricts operational goals, time, and space, puts forward new requirements for air combat ability. To achieve the strategic goal, ground operational measures are greatly restrained and air operations enhanced. Air operations often become the major or even the only force to be used. On the other hand, the air force, which can avoid direct contact with the opponent and quickly deliver strategic proposal, can start and stop operations easily so they will not result in territorial disputes and a cease-fire agreement. This is definitely what military decisionmakers want to apply in today's conflicts, in which no one wants to escalate the conflicts but everyone is eager to restrain the other. The standard of winning and losing is changed to a great extent. The ultimate goal of the parties involved is not to occupy the other's territory but to check the enemy country and take initiative at the negotiation table.

Because an air force can achieve such a goal without escalating the conflict, it has more opportunities to be employed. In addition, the attacking side places more importance on reducing human casualties by increasing material loss. As a former U.S. Air Force Chief of Staff said before the Gulf War, the only way to avoid excessive bloodshed by the army was to use the air force.

• The limitation on use of nuclear weapons in the information era also provides opportunity to develop air force. Since the 1970s, the United States and the former Soviet Union have made fundamental changes in designing future operational conditions. This is because the quantity and quality of the strategic nuclear weapons of both sides was increased quickly, and both parties have had the nuclear capacity to destroy the other. Therefore, they believe that using nuclear weapons surpasses the purpose of war. In nuclear war, there is no winner. On the other hand, the conventional operational ability of air force has been greatly improved with the materialization of information technology. The number of weapons with comparable strength to small nuclear weapons has been increased. Currently, a heavy bomber's fatal efficiency index can reach 207 million, compared to 170 million of a 1,000-ton equivalent nuclear warhead. This means that informationized air weapons not only can replace nuclear weapons to a certain extent, but also have larger application in war. As individual weapons, most aircraft cannot compete with nuclear weapons in terms of power. However, the gap between the added effect of multiple use of air weapons and small nuclear weapons is narrowing.

Because of the strict restriction on use of nuclear weapons and the air force's replacement of nuclear force, nuclear-possessing countries have started to shift their attention from preparing for nuclear war to conventional war. The production of nuclear weapons is slowed down. The principle of using nuclear weapons has been changed from "using in the first place" to "using at the last stage." Strategic rockets are in a declining position and the air force enjoys a rising importance. Both the United States and the former Soviet Union have re-emphasized the role of air force to make up the gap in fire structure caused by restrictions on the use of nuclear weapons.

This analysis shows that strengthening the air force is an inevitable outcome of the development of the new military revolution, and the changes in war format and the world nuclear situation. Further development of the air force will eventually increase the struggle among nations in fighting for air superiority. Future information war will rely more and more on air superiority. The air force will no longer be an important independent strategic force but an effective conventional campaign force that all services will depend upon. Each service will own a troop of airmen. Such a trend will further spur the conventionalization of high-tech equipment, development of information war and nonlinear operation of combat modes, therefore, strengthening the polar position of air force in modern military strategy.

Quality Restructuring of the Air Force

After the Gulf War, each key country adjusted its military strategy and the structure of its armed forces to adapt to the transformed military threat and to ease the tension between demand and possibility of armed force establishment. The core of the adjustment is to promote quality military establishment. As a high-tech-equipped service, the air force will be given these considerations:

- Consensus on a small but high-quality army. To adapt to new military strategy and tasks, large countries have adopted the policy of reducing the size of their air forces. The U.S. Air Force has taken a large step in this regard. Within 5 years, the U.S. Air Force has reduced its service staff from 600,000 to 400,000 and the number of aircraft in service has been cut from 7,000 to 5,000. The Russian Air Force has been cut by half because of the collapse of the former Soviet Union and the downsizing of troops (its military force was cut to 250,000). Both the British and German Air Forces have been reduced by one-fourth and their aircraft by 20 to 50 percent.

In the meantime, these countries have strengthened the establishment of key troops. The U.S. Air Force has sped up the establishment of a mobile speed reaction force, which includes two components—the global force, with 20 operational units and bombers, and the air transport troops, which can reach every corner of the world.

• Seek quality through restructuring. To adapt to the new military strategy, the U.S. Air Force has undergone the largest system adjustment after the war. In order to guarantee its strategic tasks, the U.S. Air Force eliminated the command headquarters of the strategic air force, tactical air force, and military air transport and reorganized air operation and air mobility command headquarters, which is responsible for all combat aircraft and provides global operational force. The air mobility command headquarters also manages weapon development and procurement for the entire air force. The air force training command headquarters and the air force school were merged into the air force education and training command headquarters, which administers the air force training programs. In accordance to the needs of partial war and speed reaction, a composite formation unit was established to support speed deployment of ground forces and implement multiple tasks.

• Promote quality establishment by applying high and new technology, which has become an increasingly important material foundation and combat strength for the modern air force. Each country pays great attention to modernization of weapons. Because of different technical and material conditions, each country takes different steps to reach their goals. The United States and Russia basically sped up the replacement of old weapons by new ones, strengthened renovation of key weapons, and developed key high-tech equipment. Western European countries choose to develop and produce a new generation of weapons. India, Korea, and Japan imported some modern weapons and, concurrently, improved their self-reliance. The common goal of each country was to modify their development plans for high-technology weapons and accelerate the quality establishment of air force.

The model of the fourth generation fighter of the U.S. Air Force, the F-22, has been chosen and is undergoing flight trials. It is planned to be manufactured in the mid-1990s. The EFA, which was jointly developed by Britain, Germany, Italy and Spain, the JAS-39 of Sweden, and the followup of the M-29 of Russia are all under development. Some Asia and Pacific nations have also joined the trend. Japan has sped up development of its FSX attackers to replace the current F-1 attackers.

Regarding weapons installation, all countries will focus on developing and applying precision-guided technology. The United States and Western European countries are jointly developing the AIM-120 medium-range, air-to-air missile and the AIM-132 short-range, air-to-air missile. The AGM-129 air-launch cruise missile has a range of more than 10,000 kilometers. The new generation of antiradiation missiles will have more intelligence that will allow it to search, trace, and attack targets automatically. Antitank missiles will feature improved attacking power beyond vision and precision.

● Link air and space force together. Under the strategic principle that the one who controls outer space can control the Earth, super powers and military giants are expanding their strength in outer space and the function of air force. The United States points out that their air force is a major arm of its national strength, and it is and will remain a key force to protect the nation and threaten potential invaders. It also says that maintaining air superiority is necessary to control outer space. In 1979, the U.S. North America Air Defense Command Headquarters set up a space defense operations center. In 1982, the U.S. Air Force organized an Air Combat Command Headquarters, which replaced two prior air force commands. In addition, the United States has modified the space and C^3I plans in order to improve the quality establishment of its air force through developing projects to assist operations:

- One substantial step is to enhance the functions of space and C^3I systems to support combat activities and prioritize the development of a military communications satellite system, which provides highly confidential and reliable communication services for U.S. commanders throughout the world.

- The second initiative is to emphasize the global prewarning system to provide prewarning support for defense in North America.

- The third action is to emphasize development of air prewarning aircraft in the monitoring system to provide timely information for commanders. The core is to develop an E-8A ground target-monitoring system, an E-3 air prewarning and command system, and an RC-135 electronic signal monitoring system aircraft.

- The fourth initiative is to develop a space navigation system to provide precise navigation and position services to the U.S. Army. In 1993, the United States launched a new global navigation and position satellite to provide quality service for the U.S. Army. All the above indicates that a future air force must integrate space, air, and air defense forces into one. Following the struggle for air control, space control will become a decisive component of strategic initiative.

- Fifth is to stress the quality of personnel. Along with equipment, personnel is the most important component of the military. The improvement of soldiers needs strict and scientific training. The U.S. Air Force uses the combination of technology development and practical training to maintain combat strength. To further improve training, the U.S. Air Force takes measures to modify the training content, reform the training system and focus on comprehensive and module training.

21ST-CENTURY LAND OPERATIONS

Colonel Xiao Jingmin
Major Bao Bin

From the very beginning of the 20th century to the end of 1980s, one of the most remarkable features of military revolution was the application of the results of the industrial revolution. With a beginning marked by the appearance of tanks, aircraft, and other weaponry, military firepower and its mobility have created a relatively perfect combination. They provide a powerful assault ability to forces and give rise to various theories on mechanized or mobilized operations such as the "surprise attack" of the Germans, the "deep strike" of the Soviets, and the "joint air and land operation" of the U.S. Army. By the end of 20th century, the arrival of the information revolution and the application of computers, sensors, and other information techniques in the command and control activities of the armed forces, together with long-range guided weapons and automatic, informational and intelligent weapons that have been developed will lead to profound changes in the operational concepts, fighting, and command methods of the 21st century.

Colonel Xiao Jingmin and Major Bao Bin work at the Strategy Department, Academy of Military Science, Beijing. This paper appeared in China Military Science *(Spring 1995).*

Future Land Battles Will Be
Multidimensional and Multidirectional

The fighting capabilities of modern weaponry have been greatly increased, making it possible for armed forces with modern weapons to fight in great depth, in multidimensions and in multidirections. Operations can be carried out against an enemy target not only from a short range, but also from a long range, super long range or even from any corner of the globe. An important developing trend for the land battle is the interlacing of fighting in the far and near distances. Operations will be carried out on the land, on the sea surface, under the water, in the air, or even in space. The attacking weapons at different levels of altitude will be able to strike land targets from optimum altitude. Air strikes and mobility have become the main methods of cooperation with land operations.

The differences of front, rear, and side will be mitigated, the front and rear of the battle field will be attacked simultaneously, and important facilities of the strategic rear area might be the first target of attack. The battle front will not be fixed, the fight will be waged in all directions, and outer space will be a battlefield. All spaces will be full of intense combat. The expansion of land battlefields has greatly surpassed the firing range of guns and attacks by infantry and tanks. Bombers and tactical missiles can cover a fighting radius of several hundred or thousands of kilometers. Confrontation in outer space can be elevated to tens of thousands of meters or even kilometers high. The interlinking of battlefields far and near, or high and low in space, is unprecedented and will make people rethink land-battle concepts, and strategy for future land operations.

Time and Speed Will Have
New Meanings

Modern science and technology have greatly improved the fighting capabilities of weaponry, and the concept of time and speed on the land battlefield has greatly changed. Time equals force, and speed is power. Time on the battlefield has been shortened, and operational activities will become faster. Modern weapons make the speed of the operational activities much faster. Armed forces use the high efficiency and high-speed mobile transportation tools not only for fast tactical and campaign mobility, but also for strategic mobility. Various kinds of weapons will shorten the time of reaction and in very short time will carry out fire power mobility and support and transfer, replacing manpower to a large degree. The C³I battle command system can have quasi real-time and fast analysis of all kinds of information and will increase the level of command control of the battlefield, armed forces, and weapons systems.

Operational activities will become all-weather, all-time, and continuous activities. Modern optics, electronics and other sensor equipment have become popular and are widely used, which greatly increases the fighting capability of weaponry and forces at night or in unfavorable weather conditions. Different army corps and their main weapons systems will have high-level and continuous fighting ability at all times and in all weather conditions. Operational activities will proceed at an unprecedented speed over all battle areas. In future land warfare, those who have gained time will have the upper hand on the battlefield, and those who have increased speed will have gained more power.

The Power and Accuracy of Strike

The operational activities of the army have always been restricted by time and other conditions, seeking the unity of the battle objective and efficiency. In the industrial era, the fighting capability of the army was manifested mainly in huge armed forces and mechanized weapons, and the objective of the battle was to destroy enemy forces and weaponry in large numbers. The destruction of the enemy transportation system and supply line was to create better conditions for the destruction of the enemy forces. It was through continuous and intense fighting and large consumption of materials that increased our own strength and decreased the enemy's, and finally led to the defeat of the enemy. During the process of operational activities, the objectives of the battle moved with the battle. The latter part of the industrial era found changes in this strategy. With the development of electronics technology, armed forces can interfere with an enemy's command system through electromagnetic jamming and can destroy the coordination among enemy forces, creating even better conditions for their destruction. In future 21st century land warfare, the primary objective of the battle will mainly be the destruction of enemy command, control, and weapons systems through the combination of counterinformation and fire power attack, and not the destruction of the enemy forces. Increased firepower range and accuracy make the choosing of battle objectives more flexible and more threatening. This kind of fight will be low in consumption of supplies but highly efficient. The destruction of enemy command and control systems means the disintegration of the enemy fighting forces. Though smart weapons carry a small strike load, they are highly accurate and destructive, which makes small-scale operational activities highly efficient. The concept of achieving high efficiency at a relatively low cost has become the basic goal of modern warfare and will be even more so in 21st-century land operations.

Information Superiority Will Become the Focal Point on the Battlefield

The wide application of electronic information technology in the military sphere will integrate information with firepower, resulting in a new type of warfare. The competition for information in future 21st-century land operations will be based on computer technology. With digital communication as the means, the information network collects and processes the data on the battlefield and utilizes these data in the weapon system to ensure efficient attacks against enemy forces, realizing automated, informationized, and intelligence capabilities to the greatest degree at every stage of operations. Under the conditions of information warfare, armed forces will use satellites, high-altitude aircraft, helicopters and unmanned flying equipment, and sensors to collect and process information; use digital communication techniques to transmit computer data within the information network; and use digital modulators and demodulators to retrieve various information and command or control information, which it will display on the information complex with many forms like graphics, data, sound and images, so that the various command organs and units of the armed forces will have relevant intelligence regarding the fighting task. In future land operations, the main activities will be the collection and processing, transfer and utilization, and competition for and countering of battle information. This will be the case during the whole process of the battle. The supremacy of information will replace the supremacy of forces and weapons and will be the key in winning the upper hand in the land operations and the guarantee for defeating the enemy. The side with information supremacy will—from the collection of information to command decisions, from detection and positioning to guided strike—proceed with automation and at high speed, achieving quasi real-time or even real-time battle results and, discovering the enemy first, will strike first. The traditional concept of "hard kill" and the negligence of "soft kill" apparently will not be suited to the future new situation on the battle fields.

Land and Air Operation Integration and Joint Operations

The integration of fighting forces in the 21st century will not be a simple adjustment in the structure of the army and the multigroupings of the fighting forces. Instead, it will require a new combination of land fighting forces as a result of the development of army weapons and changes in the methods of warfare. The combination of land fighting forces with the air and sea forces will become an integrated fighting force connected by a battle information network and formed by special units of the various army corps. Land fighting forces will be part of integrated forces in battle. Under the circumstances, the role of the army land fighting force will obviously change and become part of the network formed by the land, sea, air and space forces. It will be possible to destroy important military and economic facilities of the enemy without contact with the enemy at the front, and make the enemy lose its ability to resist. At the same time, the land fighting force will continuously receive all-round, all-depth, and all-time support from air and space fighting equipment as well as from fighting forces on the sea. The integrated operations by various army corps will be able to comprehensively use different fighting methods and striking means, thus avoiding the shortcomings of fighting by a single force coordination.

Digitization in the Future Land Operation

On the digital battle field, the units of the armed forces, through a digital information network, will receive orders and decisional information from the commanding organization, feed back the situation on the battle field, exchange information with other units, and carry out a close cooperation. The various units of the armed forces will not only be able to use their own weapons systems but also will be able to use different support weapons systems flexibly and in a timely fashion within the network. They will be able to carry out long-range and accurate attacks, and every unit or even every single soldier will have the information and fire power support of the whole digital information network. In past warfare, attention was focused on the same battle area, and close coordination of fighting activities in different time frameworks. On the digital battle field, more attention will be focused on the close coordination of different fighting areas in the common time framework. Different fighting units will, according to the unified time and objective, strike different battle targets, and achieve coordination of the whole campaign or battle with active fighting activities of their own. For the digital fighting force, every unit will be in contact with the enemy force on the battle field, and there will be no frontline.

THE CHALLENGE OF INFORMATION WARFARE

Major General Wang Pufeng

A ndrew Marshall of the Pentagon believes the information era will touch off a revolution in military affairs, just as the cannon in the 15th century and the machine in the past 150 years of the industrial era touched off revolutions. U.S. Army Chief of Staff General Gordon Sullivan holds that the information era is changing the army and will change the means of war fundamentally. U.S. Secretary of the Army Togo West says, "We place the stakes of winning a victory in the next century on digitization." The U.S. Army believes that the assessment of an army's combat capability used to depend on how good its munitions were, but in the 21st century, it will depend on the operational capability of the C^3I system based on information technology. The U.S. Army has presented the concept of Force 21 and makes it clear that it should be armed for information warfare and become a digitized army. Its plan is to build a digitized brigade in 1996 and expand it to a division in 1997. The U.S. Army has taken these actions to prepare for future information warfare.

Major General Wang Pufeng is a former Director of the Strategy Department, Academy of Military Science, Beijing. His paper was excerpted from China Military Science *(Spring 1995).*

In the near future, information warfare will control the form and future of war. We recognize this developmental trend of information warfare and see it as a driving force in the modernization of China's military and combat readiness. This trend will be highly critical to achieving victory in future wars.

Establishing Concepts of Victory in Future Information Warfare

Looking at the current situation, it can be seen that the authorized strength and equipment, strategy, tactics, and military theory of China's military are still basically the products of the industrial era and are far from satisfying the demands of information warfare. We have much work to do to shrink this gap, and our first task is to clarify our war preparation concepts. We have already made it clear that the basis of war preparation is to achieve victory in modern warfare, especially high-tech warfare, and this is quite correct. High-tech warfare, however, has already developed from an emphasis on guided missiles to an emphasis on information. Firepower superiority depends on information superiority. This has been a phased transition. In keeping with the demands of information warfare, we must base our war preparations on achieving victory in this area and use it to plan China's military and national defense modernization. When we engage in war with strong enemies in the future, we will face comprehensive and powerful information suppression.

There is a question of how to use weakness to defeat strength and how to conduct war against weak enemies in order to use information superiority to achieve greater victories at a smaller cost. It must be confirmed that information and weapons are all controlled by people. People are the main factor in combat power. However, it must also be confirmed that the functions of people and weapons will primarily be determined by the control of information, because information can play an important role in warfare. Hence, the flow of information, under the control of people, is injected into the flow of manpower, capacity, and materials, and will influence the form of warfare and determine victory or defeat. During the industrial age, the combat power of a military was measured primarily by how much capacity that military held and could utilize. During the information age, the efficiency of capacity utilization is even more important. Generally speaking, a military with capacity but no means to use it cannot become a true combat power. If capacity is used to no effect, it will only cause unnecessary damage and waste and will not have practical significance to victory or defeat in the war. A military can become a truly effective combat power only if it can use its capacity effectively. Capacity utilization controlled by information technology can successfully solve this problem. In this way, the thrust of China's military construction and development of weapons and equipment will no longer be toward strengthening the "firepower antipersonnel system" of the industrial age, but toward the strengthening of information technology, information weapons systems, and information networking. Our sights must not be fixed on the firepower warfare of the industrial age, rather they must be trained on the information warfare of the information age. This must be the starting point from which to propel China's military construction forward and raise that construction to a higher grade and standard.

Theory is the new guide to action, and information warfare theory is a new warfare theory. We must understand it, study it, and use it to guide military construction and combat. China's military, which has always had advanced Marxist and Maoist warfare theory, absolutely must not fall behind the times. We must use a practical combination of information warfare and Marxist and Maoist military thought to guide information warfare and issues in military construction. In light of the fact that the military lags behind its strong enemies in information technology and information weapons, the military must emphasize the study of ways to use inferior equipment to achieve victory over enemies with superior equipment. "Using the inferior to overcome the superior" is a tradition of China's military. However, "using the inferior to overcome the superior" in information warfare is definitely much different in content and form from the techniques of war used in the past. The question of how to conduct a people's war in information warfare also requires study. The people's war of the past was conducted in tangible space, but information warfare, in addition to occurring in tangible space on the ground, on the sea, and in the air, is conducted even more in intangible space, such as in electromagnetic fields. It is not only a battlefield in which guns and bombs proliferate, but also a "computer battlefield" in sheltered laboratories and control rooms. There are many new issues here we need to explore.

Improving Weapons and Equipment Through Information Technology

We must put effort into information technology, information weapons systems, and information networking. These are the important aspects of hardware construction for the military when adapting to information warfare. Information is a material good, and information sources, information channels, and information storage are all material goods. The gathering, transmission, processing, and use of information and the development of information into combat power all depend on certain material goods, energy, and technology carriers. Information technology itself is a pinnacle of high technology. The key technologies are remote-sensing technology, communications technology, and computer technology. Key information weapons include precision-guided weapons systems and electronic warfare weapons systems as well as C⁴I systems (communications, guidance, control, computers, and intelligence) which form the central nervous system. These hardware items are necessary and essential to adapt to and achieve victory in information warfare, and we must make efforts here. Developing this hardware, however, is not easy. It will be restricted by the level of our information technology base and funds. Hence, comprehensive consideration must be given to the direction, goals, and emphases of this development. The overarching demand, for long-term planning as well as short-term arrangements, is to consider fully the threat faced by China, the possible warfare tasks of the near future, the battle regions and battlefield conditions, the state of China's defense technology development, as well as the possible support for military funding. Thus, it appears that we should emphasize in our development the following aspects of information technology.

A Reliable Reconnaissance and Remote-Sensing System

The goal is to obtain timely information, to understand the enemy and ourselves, and to achieve clarity about our situation with great determination. It is especially necessary to establish a strategic reconnaissance warning and air defense system to achieve a capacity for early detection of enemy movements, in order to be forewarned and ready.

Information Weapons Systems

The most important of these are air defense weapons systems, offensive tactical guided missile attack systems, landing and touchdown operations equipment systems, electronic warfare equipment systems, and underwater minelaying systems. These will give China over-the-horizon, high-precision, concealed, sudden defensive attack capability and a stronger survival capacity and make the enemy terrified and worried, providing an effective threat.

Computer Technology and Battlefield Information Networks

First, we should establish battlefield information networks and battlefield databases for the battlefields in priority strategic directions. By bringing all branches of the military into an information network, information may be shared on the network. Near-real-time communication can be gained in all directions and a better solution can be achieved for the problem of vertical and horizontal coordination in warfare.

Firm Control of Battlefield Information

To achieve victory in information warfare, the central issue is control of information.

Preparation and Defense with Attacking and Fighting

In comparison with the strength of potential enemies, the information technology and information weapons of China's military may all be inferior for quite some time. When China's enemies mainly use their air forces and navies to conduct strategic information warfare, China will be in the strategic position of engaging in defensive warfare along interior lines. The progress and outcome of the war will be determined by the state of China's advance preparations and defensive situation during the war. In defensive warfare, China should still thoroughly implement an active defensive strategy. In addition to hiding and concealing forces, in combat, especially during key phases in key areas, we must engage even more actively in air defense warfare and intercept and attack enemy weapons as they arrive in surprise attack. When conditions permit, we should also engage in counterattacks against the enemy and interfere with or misguide their guided weapons, thus damaging or destroying their equipment. Strategically, we should use preparation and defense, and in combat we should use attacking and fighting to achieve victory.

Organize Offensive and Defensive Information Warfare

Information warfare includes engaging in an active offense of information suppression and attack, as well as in the reactive defense of information counter-reconnaissance, resistance to interference, and defense against destruction. The issue of an information offensive can only be discussed if one has superior technology for information suppression. In a strategic defense situation, sometimes information offensives can be undertaken during warfare actions in limited areas. In that case, information technology suppression superiority must first be achieved in warfare actions in that limited area. Under the conditions of modern high technology, an information offensive is often a prelude to a strategic offensive. Take, for example, the surprise attack on Libya by the United States. Before the attack, 18 electronic-warfare aircraft were sent to Libya to engage in powerful interference. Fighter aircraft were then sent to launch counterradiation guided missiles to destroy Libya's air defense radar stations, then fighter aircraft were sent to launch precision-guided bombs to attack five important targets. The information offensives in this raid included: 1) information reconnaissance to gain information on targets of the raid and to study the target in detail; 2) electronic interference to paralyze the opponents's communications and blind the opponent's air defense guided missiles; 3) information suppression by using counter radiation guided missiles to destroy air defense radar stations, and 4) information attack by using precision-guided warheads to attack pre-set targets. During the Gulf War, the information offensives of the multilateral forces were even more representative. In addition to the four types listed above at least the following should be added: 1) Computer viruses were used to destroy the computer systems of Iraq's air defense system and thus paralyze it, and 2) stealth aircraft were used to launch precision-guided bombs against the communications building and the command center, thus achieving information suppression.

In situations of information defense, we must strive for an active approach in a reactive situation and use every means possible to destroy the opponent's information superiority and transform our inferior position in information. We must pay attention to:

- Counter reconnaissance to prevent the opponent from obtaining information about the true situation. For example, secret falsification can be used to plant false intelligence and false targets in the place of true intelligence and true targets to confuse the real and the false and muddle the opponent's perceptions and inspire false assessments. When conditions exist, active methods may be used to engage in interference to blind or even destroy the opponent's reconnaissance instruments.
- Resistance to interference to maintain one's own channels of information. By using defense advantages, multiple-communication methods can be used to weaken the impact of the enemy's interference.
- Resist viruses to protect the normal operations of information processing in computer systems.
- Information counterattack. This is an important action to be carried out according to the general strategic plan and in coordination with strategic and combat counterattacks. The specific content and form is the same as that of information offensives.

The information offenses and defenses outlined above, in addition to using information technology extensively, also use information weapons extensively. Thus, during the process of a war, these do not exist alone but accompany strategic offenses and defenses and are consistent with the overall situation of strategic offenses and defenses. Before and after war, information hassling never stops for a moment but usually does not involve the use of information weapons.

"You Do Your Fighting and I'll Do Mine"— Using Strengths to Attack Weaknesses

This is the basic warfare style which Mao Zedong taught us, and it is an excellent tradition of China's military. Strengths and weaknesses are in comparison with those of the enemy. What then will China's strengths be in future wars? What will be China's weaknesses? Politically speaking, China's military has the advantage of justness, which is conducive to gaining international sympathy and support, and it has the support of the people domestically. In terms of warfare space, when China's military engages in war on China's soil, it will have the advantages of topography and position. In air, sea, space, and electronic warfare, however, the enemy will have the advantage. In terms of the choice of timing for warfare, because the enemy will have more advanced night-vision instruments, the advantage will not be China's, especially in air and sea warfare at night. The enemy will have advantages in instrumentation. China will have advantages in familiarity with the topography. Each will have half the advantages. In terms of warfare techniques, China's military has a tradition of flexible fighting methods and is more adapted to nonlinear warfare, but lacks practical battle experience in information warfare with high technology. In terms of weapons and equipment, generally speaking the enemy will have the advantage, but in some areas, such as guided missiles and submarines, China can still shock the enemy to a certain degree. China is strong in close warfare; the enemy is strong in distant warfare.

In wars of the future, China will face the enemy's more complete information technology with incomplete information technology. Because sometimes superior tactics can make up for inferior technology, China will still carry out its traditional warfare method of "you fight your way, I'll fight my way," and use its strengths to attack the enemy's weaknesses and adhere to an active role in warfare. To do this, it appears that we must pay even more attention to:

- Fully utilizing the advantages of national territory and front information facilities to carry out reconnaissance on the enemy's situation and protect ourselves and attack the enemy
- Developing, improving, and utilizing China's information weapons in a concentrated way to carry out raids on enemy operation platforms and bases and damage and foil the enemy's offensive
- Emphasizing mobile war in the context of information warfare
- Conscientiously organizing sabotage operations by the Army, Navy, and Air Force, grasp exploitable opportunities, and make continuous raids to exhaust and wear down the enemy
- Organizing specialized combined special warfare troops and equip these with information technology weapons to carry out powerful special warfare.

In summary, our warfare methods must adapt to the needs of information warfare. We must use all types, forms, and methods of force, and especially make more use of nonlinear warfare and many types of information warfare methods which combine native and Western elements to use our strengths in order to attack the enemy's weaknesses, avoid being reactive, and strive for being active. In this way, it will be entirely possible for China to achieve comprehensive victory over the enemy even under the conditions of inferiority in information technology.

Cultivating Talent

In the final analysis, information warfare is conducted by people. The basic great plan is to cultivate talented people suited to information warfare. One aspect is to cultivate talent in information science and technology. The development and resolution of information warfare can be predicted to a great degree in the laboratory. Information science and technology talent is the forerunners of science and technology talent is the forerunner of science and technology research. The achievements and practical use of their research will play a key role in the development and advancement of society and military construction and warfare. The second aspect is talented people in command and control. They especially need to have the ability to conduct comprehensive analysis and policy-information processing, to understand themselves and the enemy, as well as the battlefield, and also to have a capacity for scientific strategic thinking and a comprehensive point of view. Senior command personnel especially need to have information knowledge and the ability to control information warfare and must be adept at using information technology to organize and command warfare. They must be very knowledgeable, brave, and talented people.

Combat personnel must also be familiar with the technical and strategic aspects of the weapons and equipment in their hands and must be very well versed in the operation of those weapons and equipment. They must be able to understand accurately the combat plan and resolutely and flexibly utilize weapons and equipment to wipe out the enemy. The combat personnel of information warfare are not only the warriors who charge enemy lines for face to face struggles of life or death, but sometimes are the operating technical personnel who sit before computers and instruments. They stand at the first line in electronic warfare and in the resistance against C4I systems and on the front line in information technology conflicts.

Rear support and technical support are very important in information warfare. Information technology relates to a number of high-technology groups of people and touches on new energy, new materials, artificial intelligence, space travel, marine engineering, systems engineering, and other high-technology subjects. The demands for the technical level of support personnel are quite high. They are required to be able to guarantee that weapons and equipment are always kept in excellent condition. While carrying out rear and front-line support, the use of information technology is a support method just like other methods. In information warfare, the support of information technology penetrates the contents of information resistance and is also one method of warfare support.

The main methods of cultivating talent are study and training. In addition to conducting training in politics, ethics, and psychology, there must also be study of high-tech knowledge and the fundamental knowledge of and warfare techniques related to information warfare. If conditions permit, we want to create as much as possible the conditions necessary for implementing simulation training. We can first consider creating stimulated battlefields with information in key areas of the army, navy, air force, and artillery, and, second, conducting rotational training of cadres and key troops. Colleges and universities should also establish curriculae in information warfare. Scientific research institutions should also engage in research on information warfare.

The large-scale importation of information technology deep into the field of warfare will inevitably bring about a military revolution. This revolution has actually already started. Those who perceive it first will swiftly rise to the top and have the advantage of the first opportunities. Those who perceive it late will unavoidably also be caught up in the vortex of this revolution. Every military will receive this baptism. This revolution is first a revolution in concepts, then it is a revolution in science and technology, equipment, troop strength, strategy, and tactics as well as a revolution in training. Thus, the issue of how to adapt to and achieve victory in the information warfare which we will face from now on is an important question which we need to study carefully.

INFORMATION WARFARE

Senior Colonel Wang Baocun and Li Fei

While the military officials of all countries have not yet defined information warfare (IW) authoritatively, military experts in many countries have delimited its implications. While such definitions may be imperfect and even somewhat biased, they are certainly of great benefit to our understanding of the innate features of information warfare.

In *Army* magazine (1994), Lieutenant General Cerjan, former U.S. National Defense University President, notes, "Information warfare is a means of armed struggle aimed at seizing the decisive military superiority and focused on the control and use of information." General Sullivan, U.S. Army Chief of Staff, holds that "information is the most crucial combat effectiveness," with the essentials of "battlefield information warfare" being to "collect, process, and use enemy information, and to keep the enemy from acquiring and using our information." A U.S. combat theory analyst sums up the substance of information warfare in six points:

- To obtain intelligence on enemy military, political, economic, and cultural "targets," and to keep the enemy from acquiring intelligence on one's own similar "objectives."

This paper was excerpted from articles in Liberation Army Daily, *June 13 and June 20, 1995. The authors work at the Academy of Military Science, Beijing.*

- To destroy or jam the enemy's C³I system, and to protect one's own C³I system.
- To ensure our use of outer space information and to keep the enemy from using space information.
- To establish a comprehensive data processing system that covers everything from sensing to firing.
- To establish a mobile and flexible information and intelligence data base.
- To use simulated means to help commanders make decisions.

Chinese experts who are studying high-tech warfare have also defined information warfare thusly:

> Information warfare is combat operations in a high-tech battlefield environment in which both sides use information-technology means, equipment, or systems in a rivalry over the power to obtain, control, and use information. Information warfare is a combat aimed at seizing the battlefield initiative; with digitized units as its essential combat force; the seizure, control, and use of information as its main substance; and all sorts of information weaponry [smart weapons] and systems as its major means. Information warfare is combat in the area of fire assault and operational command for information acquisition and anti-acquisition; for suppression [neutralization] and antineutralization; for deception and antideception; and for the destruction and antidestruction of information and information sources.

We hold that information warfare has both narrow and broad meanings. Information warfare in the narrow sense refers to the U.S. military's so-called "battlefield information warfare," the crux of which is "command and control warfare." It is defined as the comprehensive use, with intelligence support, of military deception, operational secrecy, psychological warfare, electronic warfare, and substantive destruction to assault the enemy's whole information system including personnel; and to disrupt the enemy's information flow, in order to impact, weaken, and destroy the enemy's command and control capability, while keeping one's own command and control capability from being affected by similar enemy actions.

The essential substance of information warfare in the narrow sense is made up of five major elements and two general areas. The five major elements are:

- Substantive destruction, the use of hard weapons to destroy enemy headquarters, command posts, and command and control (C^2) information centers
- Electronic warfare, the use of electronic means of jamming or the use of antiradiation [electromagnetic] weapons to attack enemy information and intelligence collection systems such as communications and radar
- Military deception, the use of operations such as tactical feints [simulated attacks] to shield or deceive enemy intelligence collection systems
- Operational secrecy, the use of all means to maintain secrecy and keep the enemy from collecting intelligence on our operations
- Psychological warfare, the use of TV, radio, and leaflets to undermine the enemy's military morale.

The two general areas are information protection (defense) and information attack (offense). Information defense means preventing the destruction of one's own information systems, ensuring that these systems can perform their normal functions. In future wars, key information and information systems will become "combat priorities," the key targets of enemy attack.

Information offense means attacking enemy information systems. Its aims are: destroying or jamming enemy information sources, to undermine or weaken enemy C&C capability, and cutting off the enemy's whole operational system. The key targets of information offense are the enemy's combat command, control and coordination, intelligence, and global information systems. A successful information offensive requires three prerequisites: 1) the capability to understand the enemy's information systems, and the establishment of a corresponding database system; 2) diverse and effective means of attack; and 3) the capability to make battle damage assessments [BDA] of attacked targets.

Information warfare in the broad sense refers to warfare dominated by information in which digitized units use information [smart] equipment. While warfare has always been tied to information, it is only when warfare is dominated by information that it becomes authentic information warfare. Information warfare in the broad sense has many manifestations, as follows:

- Computer virus warfare. Sharven [as translated] claims that: While the major 20th century weapons were tanks, the key 21st century weapon will be the computer. In future wars, operations against military computers will become a key type of information warfare. That will mean computer virus warfare. Computer viruses are special software programs that can alter or destroy a computer's normal operating programs. They are characterized by detection difficulty, rapid contagion, longstanding latency, and active and continuous encroachment, and can severely disrupt the C^3I system, smart weapons, and combat potential. Some countries are now considering the organization and establishment of computer virus warfare platoons.
- Precision warfare. The advent of smart weapons was bound to cause the appearance of precision warfare. Precision warfare means precision in reconnaissance (spying) and advance warning, in information transmission, in command coordination, in mobile positioning, in target strikes, and in damage extent. Precision warfare is characterized by less destruction and fewer casualties, less "combat fog" and fewer troops, less logistics support, and better troop mobility.
- Stealth warfare. Stealth aircraft, ships, tanks, and missiles will flood future battlefields. In future wars, as target detection will mean immediate elimination, future warfare will be a confrontation between the "stealthy" and the "detectors." So stealth and counter stealth warfare will not only arrive in the battle arena as an independent and crucial type of warfare, but will also be conducted very intensely.

Innate Features of Information Warfare

While information warfare in the true sense has not yet arrived in the battlefield arena, the repeated live-troop maneuvers and simulated drills of the armies of Western nations such as the United States, as well as the Gulf War, have enabled us to determine certain innate features of information warfare:

• Battlefield transparency. While "battlefield fog" used to be a major problem troubling battlefield commanders, with digitized units, the battlefield is transparent. All belligerent troops will have the battlefield situation at their fingertips both day and night, and be able to see clearly on computer terminal display screens both their own and the enemy's positions, postures, concentrations, and movements. Sullivan says that the transparency of coming wars will be "a quantitative step higher than in the Gulf War."

Battlefield transparency will be the result of digitized technology. Digitized technology can transmit battlefield intelligence to commanders quickly and accurately in a noiseless and graphics-plus-words form. Digitized cameras on reconnaissance planes can send, in 30 seconds, a 24-power photo that was shot in the morning to an operational command center as far as 315 km away. Frontline troops using digitized infrared sights can detect maneuvers by over 100 enemy tanks, immediately reporting them to their superiors with digitized information equipment. Digital compression technology can determine enemy detection distance, raising information processing capability, and transmitting intelligence in real time to all units (subunits), even to individual soldiers, for joint information sharing.

• Overall coordination. Overall coordination is another feature of information warfare. The building of the battlefield information superhighway will mean that all operational systems such as combat forces, combat support units, and combat logistics support units, as well as all operational functions such as battlefield intelligence, command, control, communications, and assaults, will be linked into an organic whole. Coordinated actions by all units of this whole can raise combat effectiveness. For instance, coordinated firepower can raise fire assault effectiveness. Air and land sensors detect enemy target activity, which is immediately displayed on screens at the support arm operational center, with the target positioning system accurately converting enemy target coordinates; the target assignment system then assigns suitable targets to the weapons-launching platforms (such as cannons, helicopters, and tanks) that are most suited to attack.

• Operations in real time. Real time is defined as the time of dealing with a certain event being almost the same as the real time of the occurrence of the event. Real-time operations mean immediate responses to all events that occur on the battlefield between ourselves and the enemy and involves the taking of countermeasures such as timely target detection, timely command, timely mobility, real-time strikes, and real-time support. The advantage of this is that missions that used to be hours or even longer can now be completed in minutes or even seconds, making decisionmaking and the course of battle nearly simultaneous.

• Precision strike. Long-range precision strikes without collateral damage will become the essential fire-assault form of future information warfare, making carpet bombing and area fire part of history. Future warfare will be as accurate, clean, and neat as a scalpel cutting out a brain tumor, because future wars will use smart weapons on a large scale. Such weapons include guided bombs, guided shells, guided shrapnel, cruise missiles, no-tip guided missiles, and antiradiation missiles. Their sensors will be capable of capturing all useable direct or indirect target information, such as sound waves, electric waves, visible light, infrared waves, lasers, and even odors and gasses, which information computers will be able to differentiate and analyze. Such smart ammunition not only can hit targets 100 percent of the time, but can also hit predetermined target positions. To conduct and win information warfare, two major supports will be needed.

A Digitized Battlefield

A digitized battlefield is a composite network system covering the whole operational space. It is made up of a communications system, a command and control system, an intelligence transmission system, a computerized battlefield database, and user terminals, all of which can provide users with large amounts of operation-related information in real time or nearly real time. This network system's function is to use information technology to acquire, exchange, and use digitized information in real time, promptly meeting the information demand of commanders, combat personnel, and combat support personnel, so that they can clearly and accurately grasp all battlefield conditions needed to draw up and apply operational plans. This system can transmit information such as voice, graphics, text, and data, and can also provide users with a battlefield image portrayed by a common database and the supreme battlefield command knowledge-base (including substance such as one's own posture, the enemy's posture, combat readiness, logistics conditions, and operating environment). This picture is dynamic, changing with the movements of both combatants and changes in terrain and weather. A digitized battlefield is a prerequisite for information warfare. The establishment of a digitized battlefield has many advantages. For instance, information sharing clarifies the position of the enemy and one's own units, sharply lowering accidental injuries; it enables battlefield commanders to amass key units at crucial sites at critical times; it can effectively coordinate short-distance, in-depth, and rear operations, providing intelligence support for all-out, in-depth, simultaneous offensive operations. As all come to know the battlefield conditions, subordinate commanders can bring their initiative into play, acting promptly at their own discretion in line with their superiors' intentions; it makes logistics support "very accurate," for such activities as material provision variety and quantity "accuracy," logistics support provision-time "accuracy," and wounded treatment "timely accuracy."

The establishment of a digitized battlefield is a sort of systems engineering. Many U.S. military specialists claim that this project is more challenging than the Manhattan Project. To carry out this project, the United States is taking many steps.

In line with Clinton's Presidential Order #29 issued in September 1994, the U.S. Defense Department has set up the National Security Policy Commission and the National Information System Security Commission. The former is charged with formulating military security policy and digitized battlefield establishment principles, while the latter is responsible for controlling the security and secrecy of classified and sensitive information on the military information superhighway and the digitized battlefield. The U.S. Army set up in January 1994 the Army Digitized Special Taskforce under the direct leadership of the Army's first deputy chief of staff. In June 1994, that taskforce was expanded into the Army Digitized Office, and charged with the design and establishment of the digitized army battlefield. In July 1994, the U.S. Navy set up the Theater of Operations Information Warfare Center; in January 1995, it established the Fleet Information Warfare Center. Their joint responsibilities are to study and design the technology and software needed for the digitized naval battlefield. The

U.S. Air Force Information Warfare Center was set up in October 1993, and charged with establishing a digitized air battlefield.

To build a digitized land, sea, and air battlefield, the computer system structures, operating programs, program design languages, software applications, database languages, and communications rules of all information systems must be standardized and interchangeable throughout all branches of the military. Thus the U.S. military is now pursuing two information resource standardization plans: 1) the all-service command, control, communications, computer, and intelligence system standardization plan, which will set up a global military information database and a global joint network system, thus deploying throughout the world global information sharing for the U.S. military; and 2) the defense information control standardization plan, which is aimed at upgrading the interchangeable software technology of all Defense Department information systems, to eventually make information control and usage standardized and interchangeable.

To achieve battlefield digitization for all arms of the service, the U.S. military is now pursuing a diversified C&C digitized joint-network plan. For instance, the U.S. Army has seven plans:

• The "composite unit C&C, a high-tech demonstration" plan aimed at improving and developing the computer assisted C&C system

• The "joint ground station" plan to provide rapid operational intelligence information to brigade commanders

• The "global network grid" plan to bring many combat units into a single working network

• The "survival adaptation system demonstration" plan that uses multi-media technology to transmit information such as voice, graphics, and data to combat troops

• The "21st century ground warrior" plan to achieve a free battlefield dialogue between man and machine

• The "brigade and below unit (subunit) C&C plan" to provide battlefield information to units (subunits) at the brigade level and below

• The "battlefield combat friend and foe recognition demonstration" plan.

An Informationized Military

The second major support for information warfare [IW] is an informationized military. While many developed Western nations are now considering the establishment of technology-intensive informationized armies, the United States is the only one that has drawn up and started to implement plans for an informationized military establishment.

An informationized army is a brand-new "information-based" military category, with its combat theory, system establishment, personnel quality, and weaponry being completely suited to IW needs. The U.S. informationized military establishment plans are in two stages, which are estimated to be completed by the mid-21st century.

In the first stage, the U.S. Army will first be digitized. While digitized units will be essentially the same in authorized strength and structure as units with ordinary equipment, they will be units with digitized communications technology; integrated command, control, communications, and intelligence; smart weaponry; and networking of all operating systems. The major signs that a unit is digitized will be that its main outfits will be equipped with digitized communications equipment, second-generation forward-looking radar, identification friend-and-foe [IFF] equipment, and the global positioning system [GPS]. Such equipment will include M1A2 tanks, M2A2 fire support vehicles, M2A3 fighting vehicles, Black Eagle command helicopters, Apache attack choppers, Kiowa Brave reconnaissance choppers, M109A6 Warrior self-propelled guns, and M106A2 mortars. The U.S. Army now has a digitized battalion and will have established a digitized army by 1999, with all Army units digitized by 2010.

To test the combat capability of digitized units, the U.S. Army has conducted repeated simulated tests and live-troop confrontation exercises between digitized task forces and nondigitized units. The simulated tests show that digitized technology can shorten the time of choppers going into action from 26 minutes to 18 minutes, while raising the hit rate of antitank missiles from 55 percent to 90 percent. The live-troop exercises show that using conventional communications means to send on-site reports to battalion headquarters takes 9 minutes, while digitized communications means takes only 5 minutes; that the repetition rate is 30 percent for (telegram) text sent by conventional means, but only 4 percent for that sent by digitized means; and that the completion rate of on-site reports is only 22 percent by phone, but as high as 98 percent by digitized means. Through repeated demonstrations the U.S. Army has reached the initial conclusion that "digitized units have enormous combat potential," with their combat effectiveness being "about three times that of ordinary units."

In the second stage, the U.S. Army will grow more informationized on that digitized foundation, as well as build the entire U.S. military, including the Navy and Air Force, into a fully informationized force. After 2010, the U.S. Army will probably be the first to draw up "IW theory," as well as act in line with that theory to reform its system establishment, carry out military training, and develop weaponry, to informationize its units. For two reasons this will probably take about three decades, with completion by 2040:

- The shortage of money for military expenditures dictates that, only once its key combat equipment is digitized, can its related combat support and combat logistics support equipment be gradually digitized. Also, it will have to develop a batch of new smart weapons. So projected from an arms development cycle of about 15 years, it is estimated that its equipment will be completely informationized by 2030.
- The conversion of a military establishment from one structure to another that can operate effectively will take roughly two decades. The U.S. military that can begin to adjust its troop structure after 2010 will still need around two decades to establish the mechanisms suited to fight an information war. Also, as weaponry informationization and military establishment reform cannot be completely synchronous, with an approximate time lag of at least a decade, it is projected that the U.S. Army will be fully informationized only by 2040. The U.S. Navy and Air Force are now also informationizing. By about 2040, once all services are informationized, it will still take more than a decade to get the entire military into a digitized joint network. So it is obvious that by mid-century, the United States probably will have built the world's first completely smart military.

While IW has not yet occurred or at most has only started to show up, as it is an exceptional and new form of warfare with milestone significance, it will have an enormous impact on all aspects of the military arena.

The IW Impact on Combat Concepts

The IW proposition will have an impact on many aspects of combat concepts:

• It will make the rivalry over "information dominance" particularly intense. Certain experts note, "information dominance can be defined most easily and accurately as knowing all enemy information, while keeping the enemy from learning one's own." In future wars, most participating troops in most situations will be dealing not with material, but rather with information. The formation and development of troop combat effectiveness will rely mainly on information collection, processing, transmission, control, and usage. A superior force that loses "information dominance" will be passive, beaten, and in trouble, while an inferior one that seizes the information advantage will be able to win the battlefield initiative. As future combat actions will all be dependent and focused on information, the struggle to wrest information dominance will permeate everything and will be exceptionally fierce and intense.

• It will expand the implications of warfare. This will be manifested mainly in two areas. 1) It will make it harder to win wars. In the agricultural age, it was necessary only to exterminate the enemy's armed forces to win the war. In the industrial age, in addition to wiping out the enemy country's military, it has also been necessary to destroy its military-industrial base. However, in the information age, it will be necessary not only to eliminate the enemy country's war making "material base," but also to control and destroy the enemy's information systems, which will be the primary assault targets. 2) It will expand the limits of war into outer space. That is because the key IW systems—space monitoring, positioning, guidance, and communications systems—will all be deployed there.

• It will shorten the time of battle. The institution of IW will shorten future wars for two reasons: 1) On one hand, attack means will be highly precise, with the strike targets also being key enemy military positions such as "brain centers," which can be forced to submit very quickly. 2) On the other, in the information age as compared to the industrial age, the combat objectives pursued by both belligerents will be more limited, not total surrender or extermination of the other side, but rather limited political objectives.

• It will make combat more integrated. As information will flow more quickly and not be subject to service branch or time-space limitations, future wars are going to be unprecedentedly integrated.

—Land, sea, air, and space warfare will be highly integrated, which will be the case not only in large-scale wars, but also in small-scale armed conflicts.

—The combat lines among service arms will be hard to distinguish. For instance, the weapons that destroy enemy tanks may not be one's own [friendly] tanks, but rather smart missiles fired from friendly naval submarines.

—War zone combat operations will be integrated. As information-age units will have real-time information for rapid mobility both day and night, "the decentralized campaigns developed in the industrial age will no longer exist, being replaced by integrated combat operations in the entire theater of operations."

—The lines among the strategic, campaign, and tactical levels will be blurred. As smart weapons will provide effective means of meeting combat objectives, it will be possible at times to meet strategic and campaign objectives without losing large units.

• It will change the substance of force concentrations. As the use of precision-strike and stealth weapons will make it possible for force concentrations to meet campaign and even strategic objectives, the force-concentration priority will change from the tactical to the campaign and strategic level. A concentration of mostly personnel will change to a concentration of mainly firepower and information, and a concentration of mostly troop and weapons quantity will change to mainly quality. Force concentrations will occur faster, more precisely, and more often during operations.

The IW Impact on Military Organizational Structure

Wars during the industrial age have had military structures determined by the "firepower casualty system" base, but wars in the information age will require an "information-based" troop organization. With a changed base, the military system establishment will also be bound to change significantly.

Alvin Toffler noted recently that in the information age, "as the winning of wars will rely on military quality, not quantity, the military will shrink in size." Therefore IW in a certain sense is "precision warfare," with objectives achievable without using large amounts of troops or arms.

The military makeup will change. To adapt to IW needs, changes in military makeup will experience the following trends: In the balance of army, naval and air force might, the ratio of army troops will decline, while that of naval and air force troops will grow; in support units, technical support will grow, while logistics support will decline; in the officer-to-men ration, there will be more officers and less men; in the officer makeup, there will be more technical officers and less commanding and ordinary staff officers. Also, there are likely to be new service arms such as a space force and computer soldiers.

The unit establishment will tend to be smaller, more integrated, and more multifunctional. While Western nations have not yet determined the IW unit establishment, they hold that these units will have the following features: "The best combination of men and machines," with quality personnel and high-tech arms both being as efficient as possible; flexible mobility suited to command, control, and information flow; light equipment that is easy to deploy; high combat effectiveness, fewer command levels, multifunctional commanders, and crack commanding organs.

There are two implications for smaller units. 1) Unit might at all levels will be smaller. For instance, U.S. Army divisions will be cut from 18,000 to 12,000 troops each, with British and French Army divisions likely to be reduced from 12,000 to under 10,000 troops each; 2) The status and role of units at all levels will be obviously higher. For instance, the U.S. military plans to raise the role of the army in campaign planning to the group army level, replacing the division with the brigade as the basic tactical operations unit equipped with all sorts of combat and support platoons. The Russian military is also planning to institute an "army brigade system." The factors in the appearance of such a situation include higher-quality officers and men, weaponry advances, and robot-equipped units.

Unit integration means that composite units will reach new heights, with a transition from composite service arms to composite armed forces. For instance, the U.S. military is considering the establishment of two units, one being a composite army-air force unit—the "flying tank" or "air mechanized unit,"—and the other a land, sea and air "joint task force." This latter unit will be made up of an army brigade task force, an air force fighter squadron, a naval fleet unit, and a marine expedition platoon, suited to countering low-force conflicts and breakouts overseas.

Multifunctional units will mean that units at all levels will have to fulfill diverse combat missions in wars on all combat terms and all degrees of force, including "noncombat operations." Meanwhile, army, navy, and air force combat units are also likely to break the traditional service arm operating limits, and perform the combat operations of other service arms. For instance, land units will fight naval and air battles, with naval and air force units fighting land battles. Therefore, some Western military experts predict that as units diversify, unit establishment categories will decrease.

The IW Impact on Organizational Structure

Because of the "effects" of IW and military spending shortages, developed nations are adopting an equipment establishment policy of "more research and new technology, and less production and arms purchases." To implement this policy, they are taking three steps:

- Terminating and adjusting preset unit development projects and purchase plans. For instance, the United States has eliminated over 150 arms production plans, and delayed over 20 equipment purchase plans; Germany has eliminated and postponed over 40 arms purchase plans.
- Increasing their research input. In the past decade, the defense research outlays of Japan, the United States, France, and Germany have increased, respectively, by 120 percent, 67 percent, 66 percent, and 56 percent. Most of this outlay is going to develop the "crucial technologies" of smart ammunition, smart weapons platforms, and the C^3I system.

- Upgrading their existing weapons. While the Western nations are slowing their rate of production of new weapons, they are paying more attention to the use of electronic information technology to modernize and upgrade their existing equipment. For instance, the U.S. Air force is planning to upgrade its B-52 bombers by outfitting them with high-tech systems such as new radar, global positioning systems, and cruise, missile launching units, to keep them in service until the year 2000.

To be able to fight IW in the next century, developed nations such as the United States will place priority on the development of equipment such as the C^4I system (command, control, communications, computers, and intelligence system), personal digitized equipment, and stealth weapons.

FUTURE TRENDS OF MODERN OPERATIONS

Major General Wu Guoqing

Ever since the 1970s, when new high technology began to be rapidly developed and widely applied in the military field, the international strategic situation has undergone a series of great changes. Regional wars, especially those under high-tech conditions, have resulted in the profound reform of concepts, modes, and tactics in modern operational doctrine. The traditional doctrine of operations since the World War II has been seriously challenged. Some of it gradually has lost significance. Therefore, new relevant doctrine must be explored and developed for future warfare.

Operational Concepts

The Limitation of War Scale

One significant feature of regional war is its limited scale. Conventional weapons will be applied to achieve operational purposes at low cost in military actions by limiting the war's scope. The new edition of *Operational Outlines* by the U.S. Army puts forward operational concepts of the early 21st century. It emphasizes limiting future war and requires controlled actions. The concept of limiting the scope of war has now been accepted by a number of Western powers and many underdeveloped countries.

Major General Wu Guoqing is the Director, Department of Operations and Tactics, Academy of Military Science, Beijing. His paper was originally published in China Military Science *(Summer 1994).*

Limiting war scope and controlling its effects are possible with new technology and are actually required by the international environment and modern warfare. Operational purposes can be better realized with precision conventional weapons. On the other hand, the high consumption rates of high-tech regional wars require their scope to be limited and that combat remain within the limits a country's economy is able to endure.

New Implications of Joint Warfare

Operations with several services, where the air force and the navy will play even more important roles, will change past patterns where the army played the main role with other services only assisting it. Operational range will increase because joint air force/army actions will gradually be replaced by jointness of the army, the air force, the navy, and the missile force. Battlefields will increasingly depend on outer space. Encouraged by the strategic concept that "whoever controls outer space dominates the world," great powers regard the opening of outer space battlefields as the essential component of military strategies. Development of space weapons will be a critical means to seize hegemony in outer space. An important military part of being a superpower will be military space systems with high performance and multiple purposes. Future wars must be joint with different combat arms throughout the entire battlefield including air, land, sea, and space forces.

The integration of military actions, politics and diplomacy will increase. Military actions will be subordinate to politics and diplomacy. In turn, political and diplomatic struggles will make full use of military success to achieve victory in regional war. All this is subject to the strategic conceptual enrichment of military operations in regional wars. With the deepening and perfection of joint operations doctrine, from now on, is most likely to develop into essentially operational theory early in the next century. By then, though, the doctrine will be further enriched with newer meaning.

The Concept of Quality First

Putting quality first means that the qualitative advantage of an army will be crucial in operations, and particularly superiority in any equipment that helps to achieve victory.

With the rapid spurt of science and technology and its extensive applications in military fields, military equipment has become the key to operational competence for modern forces. An army's fighting competence will largely be affected by its combat equipment. Among the many factors affecting the decisive victory in wars is the increasingly important role of the technology of military equipment. Troops using weapons no longer depend principally on their bodily strength as a standard, but on skillfully mastering and applying equipment, and adapting themselves to high-tech warfare. Quality first and technology first will become more fully embodied in the operational doctrines and practices of the armies in the world.

Operational Principles

Operational principles are developing in three ways. The first is just adding the new to the old. For example, the operational principles in the new edition of U.S. Army Field Manual 100-5, *Operations*, add "multipurpose" forces to the original "initiative, agile, profound, and coordinated." Further, "operations other than war or non-wartime actions" now have a set of formal theoretical principles. The Russian army has also augmented its operational principles for suddenness and independent operation in defense. Second, principles that have lost significance have been abandoned. For example, there used to be 13 phases of campaign principles in the former Soviet army, but now they have been recomposed into only eight. Those dropped mainly concerned operations under nuclear conditions. Third, new subjects have been added to former operational principles. For example, *Operations* has added "non-wartime actions" to the operational principles of "initiative, agile, profound, and coordinated." The Russian army's principle of "achieving sudden action" now emphasizes military planning and counter reconnaissance.

High-Speed and Flexible Reactions

After the Cold War, many countries are now confronted with realistic problems such as uncertain operational regions and unpredictable targets. Additionally, the emergent regional actions have become the main task for armies in future fighting. Such actions that frequently result from sudden incidents are characteristic of suddenness. With the high-tech scouting and monitoring system widely applied, it is more difficult to achieve suddenness of actions. However, the sudden actions in operation are much more favored by the improvement of the assault, mobile capabilities, and the technology of camouflage in high-tech weapon systems along with the successful. Therefore, only when an army possesses the strong capability of high-speed and flexible reactions, able to arrive at whatever areas in whichever circumstances to fulfill any task, can it meet the demands of future high-tech operations in a regional war.

Principle of Quick Decision

In order to reach the operational purpose, a war of quick decisions endeavors to shorten the duration and to end a campaign early with increased fighting force. This is chiefly decided by the limitations of high-tech regional war and other factors such as high input, high consumption and high efficiency. The high-tech regional war, whether large or small in scope, is closely related to policies of politics, economy and diplomacy, and to the fundamental interests of a country. Either side of the war, therefore, will inevitably send a high-tech weapon system and picked troops into the decisive campaign and do their utmost to win. The fundamental feature accounts for the limitation of the operational purpose, duration, and range. High-tech weapons are very destructive and can cause great loss; they are also quite expensive to produce, even for large and stronger countries, which may find it difficult to fight a prolonged war of this kind. Ever since the Gulf War, the U.S. Air Force has forwarded the new concept of the so-called "oversleeping war," which would attempt to end a regional war within the shortest period of time through repeated attacks of high intensity. With the development of military technology and combat doctrine, such operational doctrines as "twinkling war," and "brief assault" are likely to be put forward or enhanced.

Hitting Vital Parts of the Enemy

The systems engineering and the experiences of the modern war prove that in the systems of military forces and weapon equipment, there are vital parts or crucial links that can affect the whole situation, e.g., the C^3I system that links the operational forces, the supply system that helps maintain strong operational forces, and the operational platform on which high-tech weapon equipment depends. Once these targets are damaged, the fighting capabilities as a whole will certainly be affected, and the functions of the weapons system will be in disorder. Hitting the vital parts of the enemy is quite effective in an operation and is favorable to winning greater victory with little costs. The high-tech systems of scouting and surveillance, the accurate guidance weapons, and the equipment for electronic war all provide advanced measures for hitting the vital parts of the enemy effectively.

Battlefield Dominance Will Change Meaning

Battlefield dominance, the prerequisite in gaining the operational initiative, has long been regarded as a very important operational principle by many armies of the world. To control future battlefields does not mean only control over land, air and sea, but also over electromagnetism, information, and even outer space. The control of the latter three is vital to the former. In a sense, only after dominance over electromagnetism, information, and outer space is achieved can control over land, air, and sea be effectively obtained. This is interrelated and interactive, forming the new meaning of dominance over battlefields. Therefore, only in these ways can dominance and initiative in high-tech local war be really possessed.

Operational Modes

Operational modes are the manifestation of operational concepts. Operational modes in the past, offensive or defensive, were usually mobile warfare, positional warfare, and guerilla warfare. Many factors are reshaping operational concepts, so the traditional three modes are being gradually replaced by high-tech mobile, positional and special warfare.

The Importance of Mobile Warfare*

As an operational concept, mobile warfare has a long history. It is, however, only after the 1970s that it began to be recognized as an independent operational mode and was adopted by more and more armies. The application of high technology improved mobile and

---

Editor's note: Mobile and maneuver warfare are interchangeable in Chinese; "jidung" is used for both English terms when translated from Western articles.

reconnaissance capabilities, which laid the foundation for mobile warfare. With the end of the Cold War, the probability of high-intensity warfare decreased, and nations focused on how to deal with regional conflicts and wars. Since local war is characterized by multiple threats, uncertain battlefields, suddenness and quickness, the side good at mobile warfare is more likely to be successful. Those who stick to traditional methods and fight along fixed fronts are bound to lose opportunities, be passive, and be defeated. U.S. and Russian armed forces, accordingly, particularly emphasize research on mobile warfare. They even view it as the best mode of operation for the beginning of the next century.

With the development and extensive application of military high technology, the side possessing superiority in high-tech weapons may adopt mobile war tactics, such as launching surprise attacks, laying siege and outflanking over long distances, "frog leaps" by air, and penetration in depth and width. New tactics such as mobile warfare over air and land and over-the-horizon and amphibious mobile warfare can be used one by one. Owing to the greater variations of future battlefields and front lines, uncertain fighting areas, irregular and frequently changing battlegrounds, any operation must act according to the changing situation. Meanwhile, with the substantial advancement of the devastating effectiveness of precision-guided, long-distance weapons, it will become even more difficult to use fixed battlegrounds and fixed positions for covert actions and to protect personnel. The traditional linear positional operation will hardly meet the demands of future military actions. It can be estimated that new mobile warfare, nonlinear operations, unbalanced dispositions, and mobile actions will be adopted by more and more armies of the world.

Special Warfare

Special warfare is an irregular operational action in which special troops adopt special tactics. In its 40 years, special warfare has developed from the original so-called "counterinsurgency" into the actions of special reconnaissance, sabotage and attacks in the enemy's rear area, search and rescue, and psychological war. In the Gulf War, the multinational forces headed by the United States were organized in special units and thousands of servicemen were sent into the rear area of the Iraqi troops to perform special warfare such as reconnaissance, jamming, sabotage, deception, and feint movements, supporting the main attack and assaulting units from the sky.

From now on, every country may strengthen the study of special warfare by determining war purposes by special warfare; coordinating special warfare with mobile and position warfare; and enlarging the content of special warfare. Traditionally, special warfare is an irregular operation. It may in the future include the content that originally belonged to regular warfare, involving political and diplomatic struggles and aerial combat. Currently, studies on special warfare are in their development phase, and their contents will inevitably be enriched and enlarged through practice and theoretical research.

Operational Methods

New Operational Methods

Large quantities of high-tech weapons on battlefields pose serious challenges to traditional methods of operation and also accelerate a series of revolutionary changes in concepts. On the one hand, new methods adapting high-tech tactics will be created one after another, e.g., advances in highly precise and long distance powerful signs may make it possible for remote fire to become important. With this method, operational forces can, instead of entering the battlefields at the front, directly start their actions from bases far from battle. Opposing sides may not necessarily face each other in battles. Instead, they will launch attacks hundreds or even thousands of kilometers away by fully employing air assaults and missile weapons. Even if a campaign starts within a battleground, attacks are as likely to be launched from outside of the enemy's defense area and actions will occur with opposite sides "never meeting each other."

On the other hand, traditional methods will be reinvigorated and adapted to new operational conditions. With technical development of precision all-weather targeting, stealth weapons, precision guidance, and night fighting, traditional warfare can also be enhanced. Further, night fighting will no longer be confined by the range or parts of a battlefield. Large-scale night fighting in depth and width with combined arms coordination may be extensively adopted in high-tech operations in the future.

Modes and Patterns of Operations Will Be Synthesized

Battle space has drastically increased with the rapid advancement of military technology. Interdependence of operations will strengthen day by day. Any military actions under future high-tech conditions, large or small in range, will be characterized by comprehensive antagonism between the two sides in various battlefields with multiple forces and forms. All military means in the conflict will tend to be synthesized, emphasizing the superiority of some modes and patterns in order to seek maximum system effectiveness. This means that operations will most likely become "combination boxing," the combination of various operational modes and patterns.

Operations of Joint Services Will Increase

Operations will well exceed the range of a single service or battle ground in high-tech conditions. The operations of various services will be further merged, and a basic feature of future operations will be joint operations with integrated services. For example, air strikes are no longer only attacks by the air force. Naval and army air forces can also play very important roles. Missile attacks can be either from aircraft, cruise missiles, or land; information war, electronic wars and psychological war are usually combined actions of all services together. Because of this, operational method must tear itself away from the reach of a single service. The substance of developing operational methods is the pattern of joint trans-service action.

Technology and Art in Operational Methods

Operational methods have never been just the passive adoption of new technology, but are created by new operational art. Applying new technology in the operational field means that instead of rejecting or degrading the role of operational art, conditions are created for combining military technology and operational art. For example, the advancement of simulation will even more forcefully stimulate the merging of deceiving technology and art in operations, thus having better effect in deception warfare. Future methods of operation will be the product of closer combinations of military technology and operational art. More emphasis will be laid on the methods of "attaining high quality with low cost." That is to say more efficient results will be achieved with fewer personnel wounded or killed and minimum loss of high-tech weapons in the shortest time.

Operational Command

The phenomenon of war will fundamentally change with the development of modern science and technology and its extensive application in the military field. This profound change will also occur to the basic elements of operational command with respect to organizations, skills, and patterns.

Highly Synthesized Command Organizations
Future fighting formations will integrate the army, the navy, and the air force, resulting in more and more operations of combined services. Not only will campaigns require multi services and weapon systems, but all combat units will need to be cooperative. The complexity of operational forces determines that the command structure must meet the requirement of integrating the operations of many services. Synthesized command organization with various combat arms, shared information, and compatible communication will certainly emerge, along with development of command theory involving integrated operations.

Intelligently Automated Command
In past decades, operational command efficiency has been greatly improved since the highly automated operational command system was integrated with command, control, communication, and information by computers. This has enabled commanders and staff officers to get rid of much of their complicated manual work and helped to break through the human limits of physical and mental abilities. On the basis of automated information collection and processing, and operational calculation, further improvement of command decisionmaking will enable the artificial intelligence simulation systems to mimic commanding officers' mental activities and be extensively used in command activities in the near future.

In the Gulf War, the multinational forces had their means of command intelligently automated to some extent. The appearance of intelligently automated command will bring about changes in the command doctrines of the armed forces. With the use of intelligently automated command in operations, scientifically determined operational doctrine will be gradually perfected.

Command Concepts Will Synthesize Doctrine

Future high-tech regional wars will provide the platforms for numerous command forms—including command and autonomy, centralized and decentralized, hierarchical and overstepping, stable and movable, those on land, in the air and at sea, and even those involving outer space facilities—to play their parts based on the situation of the battlefield. These command forms will be flexibly used and make up for each other's deficiencies to raise command efficiency and keep command constant, so that continuous command can be achieved in any circumstances. This is the trend of command doctrine in study and practice.

Defensive Theory

Nowadays, the armed forces of the world are confronted with the contradiction between the increasing dependence of operational activities on defense and the increasing difficulty of defense. A common topic is how to develop defense theory for high-tech regional wars in the future.

Studies on Stereoscopic Defense Theory Will Deepen

In future wars, defensive technology will become more and more advanced and defensive patterns be continuously increased, particularly with outstanding stereoscopic defense protection. As range has been enlarged, range of protection will also increase. The range of operation will quickly expand into the air and outer space along with the stretch towards the two sides and depth of the battlefields. In operational protection, forces will more extensively use various platforms in the air, including reconnaissance and surveillance systems and communication systems based on those in outer space to perform reconnaissance over the enemy. Command centers in the air and outer space will be developed so that mobility, high speed and secure communications will be improved. Logistical protection will be increased, and troops will depend more on airplanes, even space carriers for the protection of materials, technology, and medical service. In future battlefields, combat to safeguard ourselves and destroy the enemy's defenses will take place in the air and outer space, on the ground, on the surface of and under the water, and even under the ground. Winning or losing combat in larger stereoscopic range will decide the success of the defensive forces.

A Mobile Defense Doctrine Will Emerge

Future high-tech regional wars characterized by suddenness, uncertainty of the operational areas, and the rapid shift between attacks and defense, will be more mobile than ever. Unitary fixed defense can hardly meet the requirements of highly mobile future battlefields. At present, therefore, the main military powers have laid great emphasis on the study of mobile defense doctrines. For example, in dealing with the new situation under amphibious mobile operations, the U.S. Marine Corps has proposed that most fixed or semifixed defensive facilities be at sea for mobile protection. Under the condition of remarkably improved operation mobility, the traditional connection of fixed defenses will probably be replaced by a combination of mobile with fixed defenses, taking mobile defense as the dominant factor.

A New Structure for the Defense System

Future defenses will vary with the changing of requirements and the increase of means. The structure of traditional defensive systems will be destroyed. The main features of the new structure will include:

- Some new defenses will emerge such as the protection of high-tech weapons by special weapons and the special warfare.
- The position and functions of some defenses will rise from the ordinary to become the chief defense. For example, in high-tech operations, many technical weapons will be used in battlefields, greatly increasing their role. Defense will be separated from protecting logistics to form an independent category of defense parallel with the protection of logistics and government.
- The content of some defenses will change, say, into the protection of reconnaissance and surveillance.
- There will appear the trend of interchangeable defensive and offensive operations. Some activities that used to be within the defense category will be changed into that of offense, while some activities belonging to the offensive field may change into that of protection.

- The protection of government will require more attention to psychological warfare designed to destroy the cohesive force of the enemy, in addition to strengthening the encouragement of our fighting capacity. The combination of psychological warfare and combat operations will become an important topic for research on protecting government.

Integrated Protection and Operations

In future warfare, the gap between the front line and the rear area will be greatly reduced. Modern protective facilities and their functions, most of which have the double function of protection and combat operations, will become more advanced so that a closer connection between defensive protection and combat operations will gradually fill the gap. This tendency may bring about the following results: on defense, the original function of mere protection will change into both protection and combat operations; in combat operations, the idea that protective troops are just for protection and operational troops are just for combat operations will be replaced by the concepts that operational troops will take responsibility for self-protection while performing their main task of fighting, and that protective troops should share the task of some operations.

Under today's comparatively peaceful environment, the armed forces of many countries are now paying attention to the shift from the traditional formula of "technology pushing" tactics to that of "doctrine pushing," which means that the progress of military technology and development of weapons will be guided by thinking about future operations. The interactive function of "technology pushing" and "doctrine leading," will bring forth scientific ideas and theoretical principles compatible with our era.

FUTURE TRENDS IN
STEALTH WEAPONS

Cao Benyi

This article sets forth the important function of stealth weaponry in modern warfare, as well as domestic and foreign research and development in this field. It also points out the crucial technological problems that have to be overcome in research on stealth weaponry in view of Chinese conditions, and offers some recommendations. The purpose is to draw the attention of relevant Chinese specialists to the problems connected with stealth weaponry research.

The powerful capabilities and special characteristics of stealth weaponry enable evasion of detection by sensing equipment on the ground, breaking through a great variety of the enemy's defensive systems, and penetrating deeply into enemy territory to attack all strategic objectives. As a consequence of the very rapid development of stealth technology, the survival potential and the rate at which stealth weapons will successfully break through enemy defenses in modern warfare have been remarkably enhanced. This has attracted worldwide attention. This article elaborates on four aspects of the functions and future trends of stealth weaponry.

Cao Benyi contributed this article to the Commission of Science, Technology and Industry, Modern Weaponry, *no. 11 (8 Nov 1992).*

Stealth Weaponry in Modern Warfare

It is characteristic of modern warfare that it stakes everything on technology. Following the rapid development of radar, infrared, laser, and millimeter wave detector and guidance technologies, every kind of weaponry is almost immediately monitored by concentrated radar and photoelectric detectors. It is for this reason that every country is now expending great energy on stealth weaponry research to enhance the operational effectiveness and survival potential of weaponry in modern warfare. Stealth technology is part of high technology; stealth weaponry is extremely important in modern warfare. Several countries have by now developed various kinds of highly efficient stealth weaponry, such as stealth planes, stealth missiles, stealth naval vessels, stealth tanks, etc. Some have indeed already been transferred for use by the armed forces and successfully tried out in actual combat.

F-117A stealth fighters, developed by the United States, were used in the armed invasion of Panama on December 20, 1989, when they successfully evaded the radar network of the Panamanian defensive forces and unloaded two almost laser-guided bombs on the Rio Hato airfield, 90 km southwest of Panama City. This made it very easy for the U.S. paratroopers to accomplish the great military achievement of occupying the Rio Hato airfield. When the Gulf war erupted on January 17, 1991, F-117A stealth fighters were the main formation in the attacking air force, and they dropped the first bombs on Baghdad. These laser-guided bombs of the "Bao-shi-lu" III type, weighing one ton each, were dropped with unerring precision on the large communications building that housed the information services of the Iraqi armed forces, scoring a remarkable hit. One F-117A stealth fighter dropped two 2-ton laser-guided bombs right into the entrance to the Iraqi Scud Missile storage hangar. Another F-117A stealth fighter dropped one bomb into the air shaft of the Baghdad air defense headquarters, and yet another made a very destructive attack against the Baghdad air force headquarters, bringing this huge building down in a big cloud of fire and smoke. In all these air attacks the F-117A fighters maintained a record of zero losses.

Used as a strategic and tactical attack weapon, a stealth-guided missile makes it impossible for the target to defend itself. During the Falkland War of 1982, the Argentines used the French-made Exocet guided missile to sink the British destroyer *Sheffield*. In the Gulf War, the U.S. Navy used 100 highly effective Tomahawk cruise missiles with stealth characteristics to attack Iraqi strategic targets in the early morning of January 17, 1991.

The great importance of stealth weaponry in modern warfare has gradually been realized by China's scientific and military experts. China has vast territories, vast territorial skies and waters, and long shorelines. To protect its territorial rights over its land, air, and sea against any future aggression, it is necessary for China to make every effort to develop stealth technology, to develop stealth weaponry, and to do what is necessary to enable China's stealth technology to catch up with the world's most advanced level of such technology in a short time.

Domestic Developments and Critical Technological Problems

In China, research on stealth weaponry was started in the 1980s, and great progress has been achieved, particularly in aspects of theoretical research on active and exterior stealth applications for entire aircraft and for components. Microwave tests, in dark rooms and in the open, have by now been completed in the case of a number of entire aircraft and a large number of components.

During the last few years, some units have started research on stealth materials. For example, the research institute of the Beijing Iron and Steel Complex has developed a coating material of superfine metallic particles with radar wave absorption properties. Other relevant units have developed other coating and structural materials.

Because China was late in starting research on stealth weaponry, it has technically not yet nearly reached the level of such countries as the United States and the former Soviet Union. To offset its underdevelopment, to narrow the disparity with the rest of the world, and to be in control of the initiative in any future war, it is certainly necessary from now on to intensify research in stealth weaponry.

The following are some of the critical technical problems that will have to be resolved in China's research on stealth weaponry:
- Expand the stealth waveband. Stealth technology is an important component of electronic warfare, and development of stealth technology must be conducted with full consideration for

the peculiarities of modern warfare. The main emphasis on research of stealth weaponry in the various countries is currently placed on centrimetric wave, submillimeter wave, infrared, laser, and metric waveband expansion. The stealth waveband will therefore have to be expanded.

● Meticulous design of the external contours of stealth weaponry. It necessitates streamlining of the exterior of stealth weaponry, eliminating angular reflections and mirror reflections, and the rational design of the exhaust and air intake system of the power unit, to provide minimal surface area for radar reflection.

● Use of the most modern types of radar wave absorption and permeable materials. Exterior coating of the stealth weaponry with wave absorptive material and the use in structural components of wave absorptive and permeable materials can effectively reduce the surface area for radar reflection.

● Selection of power units with limited heat radiation, combined with the cooling of the exhaust fumes will reduce infrared and heat radiation of stealth weaponry and will make it infrared indiscernible.

● Use of electronic countermeasures and increasing the outer impedance load of the stealth weaponry. Installing on stealth weaponry electronic interference mechanisms and various kinds of equipment that would signal out false targets.

● Developing and installing accurate measuring devices. We should place main emphasis on setting up radar testing plants that are consonant with the environment of modern warfare, develop newly structured radar, taking as our principal research objective measurement of the reflecting surface area of the radar targets under wideband conditions, and should thoroughly research the reaction in the targets of the radar waves.

Suggestions for Development of Stealth Weaponry

● In light of the world's modern testing technology, and giving overall consideration to China's financial, material, and geographical conditions, it is necessary for China to start research on stealth weaponry, and to develop as quickly as possible stealth weaponry that is attuned to China's national conditions and that is also up to worldwide advanced standards.

• In the development of stealth weapons, China must firmly adhere to the principles of independence, initiative, complete self-reliance, and must in technological matters take the road of integrating what has already been developed with activities of own independent creativity. At present, China must set up as quickly as possible various research projects. Those projects that have already been set up should be considered as models and research topics to be brought to fruition in the research units.

The radar-indiscernible structure of the stealth weaponry is an important research topic. It comprises primarily research on the external structural contours and structural research on power units, power unit installations, exhaust and air intake, directional guidance installations, installation platform for the armament system, and the antenna system. The rational structural composition of stealth weapons is extremely important for a reduction of its radar-reflecting surface area and for enhanced radar-indiscernibility.

Radar-indiscernible material is one of the key items in stealth weapons; application of indiscernible material and the outer stealth structural contours are of equal importance. Research abroad has already produced various kinds of highly effective radar-indiscernible coatings and structural materials. At present, as far as materials technology is concerned, mixed materials for increased wave absorption have very good prospects. The appearance of such new technologies as sandwich-intertwined wave-absorbing materials and self-programming materials have opened new roads for the development and manufacture of radar-indiscernible materials. Superfine metal particles also have great potential as a radar-indiscernible coating material. It is necessary for China to develop through various technological methods a series of structural and coating materials with radar-indiscernible properties.

• Costs of stealth weaponry must be reduced and production must be made economically more acceptable. Abroad, costs of developing various types of stealth weaponry have been excessively high. For instance, the cost of one single American B-2 Stealth bomber is in excess of $500 million. China's economy is still very backward, and its financial and material resources are extremely limited, which makes it even more necessary to reduce the costs of developing stealth weaponry and make its production economically more acceptable.

• In light of China's backwardness in stealth technology, if we are to fill as quickly as possible the present stealth weapon gap that exists in China, we must make use of every opportunity that is offered, import from abroad advanced technologies and equipment, establish as quickly as possible a research organization in the country. Thus we can speed up development of China's stealth technology.

• At the same time as the development of stealth weaponry is going on, research must also be undertaken in antistealth technology. Stealth technology as well as antistealth technology are parts of the key projects in high technology that are currently being pursued by the various countries of the world. For the period from 1990 to 2000, the U.S. Defense Department ranks stealth technology second among its 17 technology projects of highest importance. Among the 22 key technology projects for preferential development in 1990, three dealt with antistealth technology. This makes it very obvious that in future warfare stealth technology as well as antistealth technology will both be indispensable.

CHINA'S NATIONAL DEFENSE DEVELOPMENT CONCEPTS

General Mi Zhenyu

Competition

In today's era, filled with various contradictions and complicated interweaving of interests, development of anything is necessarily competitive. The differences in the development of objectives between national defense and politics, economics, science and technology is that the form that the development of national defense objectives must take to be competitive is external competition. This is especially true of our country with our kind of socialistic characteristics where our national defense development is not production methods to meet our own needs but to counterbalance threats from the outside. So, the selection of our national defense development objective must include the following aspects of competition.

Structure of a Competition

There is structure to competition. From the point of power, there is total national defense power competition and military power competition, there is actual power competition and potential power competition, there is actual combat power competition and deterrent

General Mi Zhenyu is a former Vice President of the Academy of Military Science, Beijing. These excerpts are from China's National Defense Development Concepts *(Beijing: PLA Press, 1988), 50-53 and chapter 9.*

power competition. From the perspective of form, there is the competition of superior over inferior, of the inferior over the superior, and also the competition of sitting as equals at the same table. From the perspective of attributes, there is the competition of material strength and the competition of spiritual strength, obstinate competition and flexible competition; there is the competition that draws one into a war and the competition to accept actively a challenge. There are multilevels in each competition. For example, the competition at a lower structural level of military power could be divided into competition with nuclear power and conventional power; at a level below the nuclear level could be competition of strategic nuclear power, battlefield nuclear power and tactical nuclear power. Lower levels of conventional power competition could also be divided into land, sea and air services competitions. In a word, the competition aspects of national defense development strategy objectives requires that one enter into it with an analysis of the specifics of the competition and use the overall competition objective to determine each of the subsystem's competition missions, using the competition functions of each subsystem to assure the competition results of the whole. The basic tactics that competition objectives force us to adopt are to attack the weakness of the enemy and avoid his strength, and to develop our strength and avoid our own shortcomings. If we cannot attain these then we ought to raise competition to a new sphere where the enemy and we are on the same plane, and where we strive to gain the initiative and have the ability to change before the enemy.

Predicting Competitions

National defense development strategy is a mentality that we hope to achieve in the future. Thus, its competition possibilities do not deal only with what is before our eyes. We must direct our attention globally, direct our attention toward modernization and find ways to deal with the sciences of the future. It is even more urgent to get a foothold on the capabilities to deal with future threats and planning for the future, especially under the historical conditions where there are no possibilities of a world war being fought. However, to predict the future does not mean to ignore the practical. It means to keep an eye on its development and, based on the revelations of the laws of development of objective reality, scientifically take control of the trends of the future. Think about the potential development in terms of competition in the year 2000, predict the possible ways that the national defense strength can be used, analyze its strong and weak points and, on this foundation, determine the challenges and opportunities that would be faced. We must focus the selection of our strategy objective with the aim of attaining the competition results set by that objective and not just the general efficiency of that objective. For example, the discrepancy in standards between the weapons and equipment we now possess compared to those of advanced countries is 20 to 25 years. If our objective for the year 2000 is merely to shrink this discrepancy to 10 to 15 years, then from the point of view of effectiveness, it would seem to be high, but from the point of view of competitive effectiveness, it would only be an impractical increase in quality, perhaps even a decrease. Indeed, when we compare the discrepancy of one or a half generation of weapons in the year 2000 with the two- to three-generation discrepancy today, the difference in competitive effectiveness could prove even greater. Thus, although it is necessary to close the gap, focusing only on setting objectives to close this discrepancy gap and not set a competition objective could turn out to be useless even if the objectives are reached. This should be of extreme concern to us. Today is the starting point of our future and only when we come up with a competition objective to project the future will it be possible for us to be less sidetracked and gain time. If we do not start today to plan to be better, to be ahead of everyone, how can we possibly make use of the opportunities and become latecomers that surpass the old timers?!

Elasticity of Competition

Because the development of objective reality undergoes myriad changes in the twinkling of an eye, especially for competition predictions, and when potential actions and intentions of the enemy are constantly changing, it is not possible for us to entirely understand all his actions and intentions. This, inevitably, brings with it some level of unpredictability and danger when we base our national defense development objective on these projections. Therefore, when we select our development objective, we should do so with a certain amount of flexibility to guarantee that in situations of complex changes, the adaptability and efficaciousness of competition objectives are preserved. This would require that when we formulate our objectives, we must first of all focus on the compatibility of the very best and most satisfactory objectives, most satisfactory and feasible objectives, and the most feasible and possible objectives. Even though there will be changes in this kind of situation and although it may be impossible for us to completely realize our predetermined competition objectives, we will still be able to achieve some benefits from this competition.

We must build and complete effective feedback loops, change static projections into dynamic projections, continuously make use of feedback information, promptly come out with new assessments and selections, and make timely and necessary adjustments, refinements, and amendments to predefined objectives to ensure a subjectively and objectively unified state. We must also focus on the relationship between the positive flexibility and negative flexibility of the objectives. In terms of its totality, strategy objectives must be sought with keen determination, with an eye towards ensuring positive flexibility and not "holding back a trick or two" but "giving the extra effort" when something comes up. With scientifically based predictions, we must prepare beforehand various plans for selection and be prepared for the enemy changing and our own changes, as well as our changing before the enemy can change. From the partial perspective, even though we may strive to of our own accord to influence change, there are times when we will definitely be forced into a position of reacting to change, hence, we must concentrate on maintaining enough latitude to deal with especially serious key elements so as to ensure the stability of the overall predefined objective. There are times when we must use some negative flexibility to ensure that a positive system can quickly move toward the general development of a predefined objective.

Strategy for Weapons and Equipment Development

Weapons are tools used to carry out armed conflicts. It is an important component of the military's combat power. It is the major element that determines the success and failure of a war. The development of modern weaponry, contained and controlled by national defense science and technology and national defense economic realities, have affected a succession of military scientific theories.

The Development of Modern Weaponry and National Defense Science and Technology
On June 7, 1981, the Israeli Air Force sent out 14 aircraft and bombed a nuclear reactor 20 km southeast of the Iraqi capital of Baghdad. "The bombs landed precisely on the main building where the nuclear reactor was located." On May 2, 1982, during the Falklands War between England and Argentina, England's SSN *Conqueror* fired two wire-guided TIGERFISH torpedoes and sank the only 13,000-ton large cruiser, *General Belgrano*, in the Argentina Navy. Two days later, the Argentina air force flying the French manufactured SUPER ETENDARD fighters needed only one EXOCET AM39 air-to-ship missile to sink the large, superbly equipped and costly ($200 million) SHEPHERD class destroyer from a distance more than 45 km away. On May 25, Argentina sank the British Navy's 18,000-ton troop transport, an ATLANTIC SEA TRANSPORT [Daxiyang Yunsongze] class ship. In June 1982, in the air battle above Syria's Bekka Valley, the Israeli Air Force won an important battle by using all types of jamming methods and precision-guided weapons like air-to-surface missiles and television and in 2 days completely destroyed all the surface-to-air missile sites in the Bekka Valley. In the surprise attack on Grenada on October 25, 1983, the United States used many surveillance methods and sent out an E-2C high-altitude, early-warning aircraft with antijamming capability, and hi-tech F-15s and F-16s, which had been remodeled and equipped with infrared sighting equipment, laser-guided bombs, and radar-guided self-seeking air-to-surface missiles, to achieve its predetermined military objectives with very little cost. During the military conflict over the Gulf of Sidra between the United States and Libya between March 24-25 , 1986, and in the air attack on Libya by the United States on April 15, the United States used hi-tech weapons such as laser-guided bombs, "Rockeye" cluster bombs, TRIDENT radar-guided, self-seeking air-to-surface missiles and for the first time, used its high speed antiradiation missile "HARM" as well as other hi-tech equipment such as new infrared sighting equipment. The United States lost only one F-111 fighter-bomber and in turn sank and seriously damaged two Libyan cruisers, destroyed one missile launching site, destroyed about 5 to 12 Soviet made MIG-23s and 3 to 5 IL-76 transports, and achieved combat successes on 5 predetermined targets. Since the 1980s, several local area conflicts have vividly shown, and people have clearly understood

even before the smoke cleared, that modern weapons have assumed some new characteristics under the impetus given them by the advances made in national defense science and technology.

One is electronics. With the development of microelectronics, computers, satellite communications, lasers, and other technologies and greater improvements seen in communications, navigation, radar, telemetering, remote control, remote sensing, and modern electronic command, control, and communications systems because of electronics and the radio, various kinds of weapons systems are extensively using electronic equipment and technology. From the perspective of the cost accounting of weapons systems, the percentage of the costs of the electronic equipment within each of these weapons systems is relatively sizable. In aircraft, it is 33 percent; in missiles, 45 percent; in space vehicles, 66 percent; in military vessels, 22 percent; and in combat vehicles, 24 percent. Electronic equipment has already become an indispensable component of modern weapons systems. It has also become the nerve center of modern weapons systems.

With the development of the fifth generation of computers, artificial intelligence, and robotic technology, it is possible that troops could be equipped with simple artificial intelligence weapons systems in the future.

Second is the change in guidance systems. Since the 1950s, along with the development and discovery of new technologies like wireless, television, infrared, laser, microwave, inertia guidance, photoelectricity, acousto-electronics, sensors, and precision measuring and automation, precision-guided weapons systems (cruise missile, surface-to-air missile, air-to-surface missiles, air-to-air missiles, surface-to-surface missiles, ship-borne missiles and antitank missiles) have appeared along with terminal precision-guided weapons warheads for guided artillery shells, guided bombs, and guided torpedoes. The guidance system changes in these weapon systems have greatly increased their capabilities for automatic searches and identification and attack, and have increased tenfold the precision of these weapons systems, to the point of near perfect accuracy.

Third is covertness. Weapons are tools for the destruction of the enemy but at the same time, they are also the major target of offensives by the enemy. The new technological revolution has searched for and provided advanced equipment, ways, and methods for the modern battlefield, and together with troops, weapons have now become a serious threat. In the history of combat, to increase battlefield survivability of weapons, man has thought of many kinds of decoys and camouflage. With the development of invisible light technology (like infrared, ultraviolet, laser, microwave, and others), surveillance technology and various anticamouflage technology, original camouflage mechanisms have lost a great deal of their effectiveness. To increase their battlefield survivability, weapons systems have begun moving toward the direction of concealment. "Concealment" is the use of various types of scientific technology to decrease detection by radar, infrared, photoelectricity, and weapons sighting systems. It is the adoption of a specialized technology through systems research and design. Major "concealment" methods include:

- Having the weapons system's structural distribution and design be scientifically rational and still be able to decrease the effective reflecting surfaces of radar, electromagnetic spectrum, and laser.
- Decreasing infrared radiation and the noise level of engines within the propulsion system in the weaponry.
- Selecting coatings that will absorb and shield radar waves and infrared radiation as well as effectively reduce radar reflecting surfaces. For coating on surfaces of the weaponry, new wave-absorbing structured materials made of composite materials and electromagnetic spectrum "absorbing material" are now being selected. There is also the use of different kinds of concealment technology and use of different methods for different weapons systems, such as missiles, aircraft, ships, tanks, vehicles, and artillery. The U.S.'s B-1B bomber is a weapons system that uses rather advanced stealth technology. Structurally, it uses swing-wing. The outer shape of the body and wings are designed for radar reflecting surfaces. It uses a turbofan engine and a bypass culvert that dispenses the mixed hot and cold air to decrease the heat radiation strength of the jet. It uses the radioactive isotope polonium 210 and curium 242 as well as ferrite as its surface coating. Cover coating the aircraft surface with these substances decreases the radar reflecting surfaces and will furthermore absorb and shield radar, electromagnetic spectrum, and laser radiation. From what we have seen in localized wars during recent years, covert technology has raised the survivability of weapons systems in close concealed contact with the enemy and in surprise attacks.

It has also played a role in decreasing wastefulness in terms of consumption.

Fourth, focused energy, is different from radiation mass destruction weapons like chemical, atomic, and nuclear weapons. A focused-energy weapon directs energy into beam power that kills the enemy or destroys a target directly. (It is also called a directed energy or directed beam energy weapon.) The rapid rise of laser technology, particle beam technology, microwave technology, and plasma technology has provided the foundation for the creation of focused-energy technology. In recent years, there has been rapid development in focused-energy weapons, and at present, the phase of theoretical experimentation has largely been completed and has entered the prototype stage of research. According to reports, the Soviet Union is in the process of researching three kinds of high energy laser weapons for its anti-air defense. It could complete the research work for a practical model against a star wars weapon in the 1990s and deploy a small quantity of them. There is intense research going on for various kinds of tactical laser artillery and guns and the coming of directed- energy weapons in theaters of war are not far away. The combined use of these and conventional weapons systems will result in greater casualties and destruction.

War and the need for the development of weapons power are the motivations for weapons development. As long as war, an abnormal development of mankind, persists, the military will strive to find more sophisticated weaponry and suggest the need for development of weapons. With this "demand as an incentive," opposing sides, all wanting victory, will initiate national defense construction "monitors" for "military expenditures" for large investments in national defense science and technology and support for research work in the leading edge of technology and advanced weapons systems. The greatest "investment returns" in weapons development for national security and arms superiority would be a pioneering spirit in new ideas, exploitation, and creation of new technologies. In other words, national defense science and technology could apply all kinds of new technologies to both the research of weapons and their production, thus acting as "technology boosters." In this way, the research disciplines within national defense science and technology could become the "breeding grounds" for high technology development;

furthermore, the new achievements of science and technology would most appropriately find their first applications within the military.

Weapons Development and the National Defense Economy

It is common knowledge that modern warfare is not only the competition of weapons on the battlefield but is also, at the same time, an all-out competition of the total strength of the opposing side's politics, economics, military, and science and technology. During the development of weaponry, the four aspects of politics, economics, military and science and technology are completely brought into play. In today's climate of rapid development of national defense science and technology and the daily emergence of new weapons, the material base of the actual national defense economy should be not only strong but also exceptional.

- With the upgrade in the tactical and technical performances of weapons, manufacturing costs would correspondingly be also more expensive. Since the end of WWII, science and technology development has flourished. There has been a multitude of achievements in science and technology that have continuously increased weapon precision, its powers to cause casualties, and its military effectiveness. The explosive power of a small atomic bomb has the same effectiveness as 100 bombers from WWII. The fire power of today's tank is tenfold greater than that of WWII. A mission to destroy 60 percent of the equipment of a tank division would today require only 1 percent of the aircraft used 40 years ago. During the Falklands War between England and Argentina, the EXOCET missile, which cost only $200,000, fired by the Argentinean Air Force was able to sink a British SHEPHARD missile destroyer that costs $200 million. The ratio of the two costs effectiveness is 1:1,000. The precision of precision-guided bombs and artillery shells is 2 to 3 times better than that of non-guided bombs and artillery shells. However, the upgrading of weapons performance has also brought with it the consequence ofmore expensive manufacturing costs. The cost of scientific research and technical components compared to the cost of a system with microcomputer technology, new materials, and new techniques imported in great quantities would appear to be prominently greater. Each of the U.S.'s HELLFIRE antitank missile costs about $28,100 to buy, but the scientific research to produce it costs $310 million. Each of the LEOPARD-II tanks of the Federal Republic of Germany costs $3.58 million to buy, yet the scientific research cost was $360 million. The research cost of Japan's MODEL 61 tanks cost ¥500 million to research and develop in the 1950s, its MODEL 74 tanks cost ¥2.5 billion to develop in the 1960s, and the MODEL 88 tanks that currently are under research and development have a budgeted cost that could reach ¥25 billion. The research and development expenditures of three generations of tanks seem to have increased geometrically. According to statistics, the costs of fighters and tanks increase about tenfold every 20 years and the costs of aircraft carriers increase by tenfold every 30 years. Weapons development has come to rely more and more on the national defense economy, causing great burdens for many countries.

• The increase in weapon power has also created battlefield situations where the consumption of battlefield material and economic losses are immense. It requires a huge quantity of material reserves. The 4th Middle East War lasted only 18 days and both sides, Egypt and Israel, suffered economic losses of over $5 billion. The loss of aircraft by both sides was comparable to the combined loss in aircraft in a year by all of the participant countries during WWII. In the first 3 days after the war started, the total number of tactical missiles launched by both sides was equivalent to the combined total of all the reserves of the countries in NATO. The loss of tanks was equal to one-third the number of those in the possession of NATO countries at that time. Both sides strategic reserves and materials were exhausted a week into the war. We can infer the amount of economic loss that could be created by modern warfare from this. In the Falklands War, the English spent a total of $2.16 billion, about $1.2 million every hour. This kind of consumption, to fight one mid-size modern war, is difficult for even an economically great power to support.

In addition to the above, research and production of weapons, ammunition, technical facilities and engineering equipment all consume large amounts of metal and various kinds of nonferrous metals. They also need the support of the chemical industry and energy resources, as well as military industrial products. According to the statistics from affiliated departments at the

United Nations, 15 to 16 percent of the world's copper output and 10 percent of it tin, nickel, lead, and zinc outputs are used for weapons production and toward the building of other national defense installations. The consumption of energy resources is even greater. During WWI, the consumption of fuel by each soldier for each day averaged about 6 kg. During WWII, it was increased to 20 kg for each person each day. In the several local area wars fought in recent years, the fuel consumption of each man each day increased to 90 kg. The consumption level is shocking! This not only raises problems for logistics support, it also increases the economic and energy resources burden.

● The rapid increase and shorter intervals in the updating and replacement of weaponry have sharply increased military expenditures and expenses. The advancements of science and technology have caused new weapons to emerge in an endless stream and greatly accelerated replacement and updating of weaponry. Before and after WWI, the time period for a weapons system to go from research and design, through trial tests and production to its deployment within the service required about 20 to 30 years. At present, this procedure requires only 10 to 15 years or an even shorter period. According to the analysis of a Soviet economist, Maj. Gen. Guluofu, a new weapons system for the Soviet military from research to its deployment in the services requires 10 - 15 years. Since the 1960s, Soviet missiles have already been updated three generations. The majority of its aircraft, submarines, and surface ships underwent updating long ago. Its anti-air defense missiles, radar, command equipment, communications equipment, and other equipment have also been through several generations of updating. The research of new weapons and the updating of existing weapons have greatly increased the military expenditures and expenses of every country. According to an analysis by western observers, "The world economy is already shouldering a burden of massive destructive weapons, poverty, and debt. Militarization will further sap its strength." Since the 1960s, the global expenditure for weapons has been about $14 trillion. In 1985 it was about $800 billion, in 1986 about $900 billion. Every second of every year about $1.7 million are spent. Immense military expenditures have become serious economic problems for each of the world's countries.

- The research and production of modern weapons have made even greater demands on the national defense economy and national defense industries. Since WWII, especially during the 1960s and 1970s, the unceasing discovery of new technology has led to a great revolution in weapons and military-use equipment. In 1945, the atomic bomb appeared. The research of computers for weapons use came in 1946. In 1952, the first transistorized computer was developed. In 1953, the world's first hydrogen bomb was exploded. In 1955, the first nuclear-powered submarine was launched. In August 1957, the first intercontinental ballistic missile was fired, and in October of that same year, the first manmade satellite was orbited. In 1960, mankind recovered its first satellite. In 1961, the world's first manned satellite did an orbit around the earth and returned to the surface. In 1967, the first integrated circuit was successfully developed. In 1969, man had his first landing on the moon. In 1977, the neutron bomb was researched and developed. In April 1981, the world's first spacecraft flew. The research and production of all these new weapons and equipment and a large portion of the new technology that entered into the sphere of the national defense economy not only greatly changed the production and industrial structure of the national defense economy, it also added a series of new production and industrial sectors. These changes helped to restructure the traditional national defense industries, moving them in the direction of technological improvement, and development of a technological reserve. The diffusion of a large quantity of high technology made it possible to turn a consuming national defense economy into a propagating field of national defense economy.

Weapons development is reliant on the development of the national economy. It also encourages the growth of national defense science and technology. Military high-technology also gave impetus to the development of the economy. Looking at this from two-dimensional space, this big "O" cycle could possibly expand further. Analyzing it from a three-dimensional space, this kind of spiraling trend is perfectly suited to the objective laws of material development.

Weapons and Equipment Development and Military Scientific Theory
"Technology determines the tactics." The appearance of large
quantities of technical equipment inevitably brings about great
transformations in military theory and tactics; this in turn leads to
great changes in strategic thinking, patterns of combat, combat style,
and military structures:

- Weapons development enhances man's strategic consciousness,
deepens his strategic reflections, and increases the emphasis on
strategic projections. In today's world, strategic research is
extremely dynamic. With the development of strategic rockets and
various spacecrafts, as well as the gradual development of energy
beam weapons, kinetic energy weapons, and other space weapons
systems, war has extended from the surface, air, and sea toward
outer space. The areas of man's activities have already extended
beyond the earth and moved into space. This has opened up man's
field of vision and expanded his modes of thinking. In the
wideness of space, the earth is no longer "boundless and limitless,"
but has become one of the "global villages" in the universe. In the
eyes of the strategist, the earth has become small and man's
strategic reflection is becoming more profound and his strategic
consciousness has been greatly enhanced. Man's heart embraces
the whole of the universe. The development of strategic research
is even more important than at any time in history and has become
an especially important issue for all countries globally. What is
coming will be conflicts in space. One of the conflicts will be the
military struggle for "control of the high ground in space." The
other will be exploitation and use of space, the struggle for the
resources of space. For this reason, every country in the world is
busily formulating and developing strategic plans. In March 1983,
the United States became the first to formulate a "Star Wars Plan."
This caused global commotion in strategy research. The Soviet
Union responded with "defensive measures" to the "Star Wars
Plan." Western Europe came up with the "Eureka Plan." Each of
the COMECON countries announced a "Plan for the integrated
advancement of science and technology by the year 2000." Japan
had its "Policy outline for science and technology;" China had a
"Policy for a new technological revolution;" India came out with
"Policy statements for new technology;" South Korea had its

"Conceptions for long range national growth;" and Yugoslavia had its "National science and technology development strategy." To rank within the world's family of nations, to live and survive in the "global village" in this universe, each nation must come up with ideas for a "grand strategy." "To stand shoulder to shoulder with the giants" one must intensely fix one's eye on the growth of national defense construction and weapons in the next century.

• Modern weapons are not only direct combat strengths between opposing combat opponents, they are also strategic deterrents and tools for international political struggles. The appearance of offensive strategic weapons like missiles, atomic bombs, nuclear-powered submarines, and long-range bombers has caused great changes in military strategy. The research, production, and large stockpiles of strategic weapons are already more than needed to seek out and kill an enemy. It has turned into a tool for political and diplomatic struggle. The large-scale arms race have caused the United States to stockpile over 9,400 nuclear warheads with a total nuclear weight equivalent of over 4 billion tons. The Soviet Union's stockpile of over 8,000 nuclear warheads has a total nuclear weight equivalent of over 5 billion tons. The quantity of nuclear warheads possessed by these two nuclear powers comprises above 97 percent of the global total. Both have the capacity to destroy the other several times over. Living under these conditions, the military strategy of both sides has gone through many changes; strategic ideologies have been revised about every 10 years. However, pressure from the threat that "destroying the enemy doesn't necessarily mean one's own survival" has kept them from crossing the "nuclear threshold" and taking the next step of pressing the button to launch those nuclear missiles. England, France, and China have independently and on their own developed into national nuclear powers. The limited power of these countries is not enough to compete with the capabilities of the United States and the Soviet Union, but they do play a role in the even development of political, economical, and military affairs within the world. This power is entirely a symbol of a country's independence and its existence within the world of politics, economics, military affairs, and science and technology.

In addition to nuclear weapons, the emergence of strategic weapons has definitely caused reforms within the military, changing past combat theories that we must go through war and campaigns to achieve strategic objectives to the possibility that strategic weapons could directly attack the opponent's strategic targets and achieve the strategic objectives. The development of various space weapons has not only intensified military struggles in space, it has also increased ways in which strategic objectives could be directly achieved.

• Today's weapons systems are very mobile. They also have long range, high accuracy, and great power, causing the time and spatial aspects as well as the intensity of war to change greatly. The development of these weapons and the great number of these weapons being deployed within the services have caused the arenas of war to be extended into deep sea and space, the length of war to shorten, and the suddenness, destructiveness, savageness, and mutation to increase unprecedentedly. In the "blitzkrieg" of the German armored troops during WWII, they could advance only about 30 km daily. Today, under normal circumstances, the Soviets could do 50 km and under nuclear conditions it could reach above 100 km. When the Soviet Union invaded Afghanistan, its push towards Kabul, a distance of 900 km took only 6 days. The time it takes for an intercontinental ballistic missile to travel its whole distance is only slightly more than 30 minutes and there is no more than 20 minutes of early warning for its defense. During the Falklands War, England's SHEFFIELD class missile destroyer did not even have the opportunity to react before it was hit by Argentina's EXOCET missile. With this short span of time, it is very difficult to react. This has made even greater demands on command and control. The largeness of the battlefield and the number of troops involved have given rise to immense increases in technical weaponry and specialized technology and have caused even greater problems in the coordination of operations and commands. According to reports, there were only 20 different military specialties during Word War I. It grew to 160 during World War II, and at present, the number of military technologies and specializations exceed 2,000. During combat, the army, navy, air force, and the other different service branches are all involved at the same time. The types of weapons used are never less than a dozen and usually are in the hundreds. This alone would demand that the commander prepare detailed plans and coordinate his commands well. There must be no mistakes in differentiating missions, allotting time, and coordinating activities. Any small error could lead to major mistakes and even greater disasters.

First strike has always been the combat phase that militarists attach greatest importance to. The success or failure of the first strike impacts the whole battle. In modern combat, because of the short time needed for combat, the phases of combat are no longer clearly delineated. The long range surprise attack or the counterattack during the preliminary period of the combat has become the main combat model for first strike. Thus, every nation has given special attention to studying the first strike phase of a war. The United States emphasizes that "every preparation must be made to win with the first strike." The Soviet Union also believes that "surprise attacks are the most effective combat opening moves to implement in future wars. . . . Victory can basically be determined in the first phase of a war." This will demand that commanders make complete preparations for first strikes. Intelligence, reconnaissance, personal observations with automatic and rapid analysis, processing and judgment, decisionmaking, formulating careful plans, and even reactions must be quick and accurate because only then could the "first strike win" objective be achieved.

• The extensive use of modern weapons has caused great changes in military structures. Before WWI, the military was basically composed of land forces that included the infantry, artillery, calvary, and navy. Before WWII, there was a great deal of aircraft and tanks in the military, thus the air force, armored troops and motorized troops came into existence. The air force itself was divided into bomber, fighter, and attack aircraft forces. There were surface vessels, submarines, naval aviation forces and marines in the navy. After WWII, strategic rocket forces, army airborne forces and other service branches were formed. With the development of space technology and the successful development of various spaceflight vehicles as well as the development of various space weapons, the militarization of space will possibly strengthen the military deployment of a new independent military service branch—"Space Forces." In 1982, the United States established the Air Force Spaceflight Command (a command comparable to the Strategic Air Force and Tactical Air Force

Commands combined), and in 1983, the United States established the Naval Spaceflight Command. In 1985, the two commands and affiliated army commands were combined to form the U.S. Spaceflight Command. Not long after the United States had established the Air Force Spaceflight Command (1982), the Soviet Union appointed Lt. Gen. Sadaluofu as the "Aeronavigation Forces Commander." Some reports have said that "it is possible that the Soviet Union had already established a military spaceflight command like the U.S. Air Force Spaceflight Command and that the aeronavigation force was nothing but a subforce of that command." Various evidence has shown that the growth of the militarization of space has brought about the birth of the "Space Forces." With the advancements made in microelectronics, computers, and artificial intelligence technology, multipurpose robots could soon be used more and more in military applications and in those work areas where the labor is heavy and environmentally dangerous; thus a "robot force" would have to be deployed. The influence of weapons development on military administrative systems and deployment and on the overall structure can be easily seen. At present, the strategic course for overall military development is: a reduction in the overall personnel strength, a rise in the proportion of technical military personnel in the overall structure, a decrease in the proportion of personnel directly involved in combat, and a different scale for the increase in the proportion of logistic personnel (including technical support personnel).

The impact of modern weapons on military theory has been profound and extensive. The various sophisticated tools, means and methods of modern policy decision studies, projection studies, and futures studies have scientifically given impetus to and provided directions for military theories and strategic growth. It has allowed the military to grow scientifically so that it can completely anticipate conflicts and play a better leadership role.

Weapons and Equipment Development Strategy Research

The weapons development strategy is dictated by the *realpolitik* of politics, economics, national defense and science and technology. These situations suggest comprehensive ideas for the development of weapons. Weapons development hinges between the needs of combat and military construction, and what is possible economically and in science and technology. At the same time it is also determined by a country's political system, its national defense strategic policies, and its fundamental appraisal of the international condition. Thus, different countries have different weapons development strategies.

China is a socialist country and a part of the Third World. This is the political basis from which China formulates its national defense development strategy. China espouses a foreign policy of independence and self-determination. It is against all expansionism and aggression. It supports all struggles and movements for justice. China, together with the rest of the Third World, is a major force for the preservation of world peace. This demands that China have the necessary military strength and an appropriate weapons development program to defend itself against outside aggression. It also demands that it have the ability to completely protect its territory and rights, to protect its country's unity, legitimate rights, interests and self-respect, to prevent the breakout of world wars and to protect world peace. China is a country that is still economically, scientifically, and technologically undeveloped. This in itself imposes a limit on the amount of money it can possibly commit to weapons development and makes it even more impossible for it to be involved in an arms race. Thus, the development of China's weaponry must be based on the needs of national defense and military construction and economic strength, the level of potential in construction and its economic strength, the level of potential in the development of its science and technology, and the independent, self-determining and self-reliant road it takes toward developing weaponry. In the near future, our actions must be firmly directed toward transforming our present weaponry, so that our military weapons will be improved by the end of the century and they will have the ability to meet the demands of a localized conflict. We must also face the future by developing weapons systems for our country, striving to reach world advanced standards in weapons in the next century and carrying out the modernization of our weapons. In order to realize the objectives of the above-mentioned weapons development strategy, our military must develop suitable strategic nuclear weapons and tactical nuclear weapons, strengthen its research for precision-guided weapons and electronic and technological equipment, and work even more toward modifying various conventional weapons.

Strategic nuclear weapons are not only a combat tool of immense destructive power; they also serve as powerful deterrents and an anti-deterrent force. After our country had successfully exploded its first atomic bomb on October 16, 1964, it went on to successfully explode its first hydrogen bomb in June 1967. With every step China takes in the development of its strategic nuclear weapons, the strength of world peace is also increased by those steps. China's development of its limited nuclear capability is completely for the purpose of defense, for breaking up the nuclear monopoly and nuclear threats of the United States and the Soviet Union, and for preserving long-lasting world peace. To win time for the world to stabilize within this nightmarish nuclear situation and to provide our socialist modernization greater security in the international environment, to completely destroy the nuclear blackmail of the U.S. and the Soviet Union, to strive for the thorough destruction of nuclear weapons, to proceed toward preventing a world from exploding into war, and to increase the strength for world peace over war so that China and Third World countries can play a greater role in international affairs, China must continue to develop proper strategic weapons and move toward upgrading their precision, lessening their weight, and increasing their mobile combat capability.

Field tactical nuclear weapons are an effective antipersonnel weapon. The extent of their destructive area is above 300 km. This weapon not only has the superior tactical technical capabilities of long range, fast firing rate, high accuracy, and great destructive power, but it could also be used as a surprise weapon in major field operations to strive for and grasp the field initiative. In its tactical use, in an offensive situation it could directly break up the effective fire power of the enemy and destroy the defense points of the enemy from a distance, or it could attack the depth defenses of the enemy and cut off the enemy's retreat. In a defensive situation it could attack the enemy rear echelon troops, stop the continuous assault of the enemy, and defend against the enemy making a direct deep push. Coordinated and complementary field tactical nuclear missiles used with various other conventional weapons systems could give the military greater military benefits and battlefield power. In a situation where, temporarily, no global wars are being fought, localized wars will be the major forms of combat for a period of time. In localized wars, the possible use of field tactical nuclear weapons by the enemy cannot be dismissed.

Thus, China appropriately and within reason must develop field tactical nuclear weapons in order to further break down the various kind of nuclear threats of the hegemonists and restrain the use of field tactical nuclear weapons by the enemy.

After the implementation of the strategical changes in the guiding ideologies of military construction, the serious research of various weapons systems for localized wars will become the major tasks of our country's weapons system development for a period of time. The effective use in recent years of conventional precision-guided weapons in several localized combat theaters of operations has been followed with general interest by various countries around the world. Our national socialist characteristics have also determined that the major combat form of our military will hereafter still be that of defending our national territory. In a defensive war, the major missions assumed by our military will be defending against the enemy's surprise air attacks and stopping a mass invasion by the enemy's tanks. In our military's conventional arms buildup, the development of different precision-guided weapons for anti-air and antitank defense will be of special importance.

The level of modernization of our weapons directly corresponds to how sophisticated our electronic technology is and this will have a direct impact on victory or defeat in modern warfare. After our forces are equipped with a large quantity of electronic equipment and computers, not only will the electronic command, control, communications and information systems (C^3I) within our combat and control become highly automated, and simple platforms and partial electronic equipments of warfare like reconnaissance and antireconnaissance, jamming and antijamming, destructive and antidestruction devices be completely transformed for "electronic wars;" they will also allow electronic technology to spread and permeate into all of the other weapons systems until it becomes the mainstay of our modern weaponry. The energetic development of our country's military use of electronic technology is of utmost importance to upgrading the modernization level of our military weapons and closing the weapons gap with advanced countries.

For a long time, our military had summarized a complete set of combat methods and experience on how to gain victory with inferior equipment over a superiorly equipped enemy. Facing a strong opponent, our military would be inferior in terms of weapons. Our country's economic strength is still very weak, our science and technology is still not very developed and compared to a strong enemy, the gap in our weapons will be difficult to overcome immediately. After our country implemented the strategic change of "transferring the work emphasis towards economic construction," there has been little possibility that military expenditures will be increased greatly and also little possibility that more money will be forthcoming for the research of sophisticated weapons. Thus, we must begin exploring new ways to develop weapons that possesses Chinese characteristics. On the one hand, we can track the development of global high technology, build a good technological reservoir, and actively research new weapons systems in order to lay a foundation to close the gap with the advanced standards in foreign countries. On the other hand, we can use what we currently have and what high-technology results we have already achieved to change the low-tech conventional weapons system in our military, and upgrade the tactical technological capability of our present weapons so that with these slightly improved low-tech weapons systems we can still win a victory over our enemy's hi-tech weapons.

A weapons development strategy is an important component of our national defense development strategy. In the historical situation where our guiding ideology for military buildup is undergoing grave strategic changes, the somber formulation of a military weapons development strategy, the development of military weapons in a planned, focused, and measured way, and the acceleration of the pace of development of our military weapons will all have practical and long term impacts on encouraging our military's modernization and standardization.

TACTICAL STUDIES

Yang Wei

Military Forum recently called a "Pen Meeting on Tactical Studies" at the Shaanxi Military Command. Guided by Mao Zedong's military thinking and Deng Xiaoping's thinking on Army-building during the new historical stage, participants at the meeting aired their views, which have provided us with much food for thought, on battlefield environment and basic tactics of modern warfare under future hi-tech conditions, renewing military concepts, and strengthening the study of tactical changes from a technological angle.

An Era of Tremendous Change

We believe that the two industrial revolutions took place in the 1760s and the 1870s which brought about qualitative changes in military weaponry and equipment, thus changing the basic form of military confrontation. The current of the new technological revolution that began in the 1970s has led to a sudden change in the arena of military technology. The effects of these changes on the modes of war will be even more profound and far reaching.

Today, some people believe that the economic arena has been most affected by the technological revolution and has seen the greatest changes. This is true. However, as long as we study closely the

---

Yang Wei serves at the Shaanxi Military Command. This essay originally appeared in the Liberation Army Daily, *28 May 1993, 3.*

several limited wars that have taken place in the postwar world, it will not be difficult to see that the technological revolution has had similarly powerful effects on the military arena. Military technology has undergone changes with each passing day. However, the basic law that the military absorbs and utilizes scientific and technological results the fastest and the most has not changed a bit.

The PLA enjoys a good reputation in the world after overcoming very strong enemies on several occasions. For the PLA, refraining from remaining satisfied with past glory and being brave enough to stand at the new starting point are key to overcoming one's self. To show indifference and apathy toward changes in weaponry, while being intoxicated with the glorious history of the past, is an great ideological roadblock. Since the 1980s, the powerful message relayed by hi-tech weaponry has resulted in drastic changes in operational methods. We must shift our point of interest and stimulus to high technology. Should we stick to the traditional train of thought, or study medium- or low-tech operations when we are aware of hi-tech weapons, we would be making an error. Under such circumstances, we would become our own enemy and would have defeated ourselves before any action had taken place.

To overcome the enemy in ourselves, we must seek out our own weaknesses. Compared with the armed forces of industrially developed countries, the PLA is used to studying tactics from the strategic rather than the technological angle. This is chiefly because PLA weapons and equipment have lagged behind those of the enemy for a long time, and there was no other choice; on the other hand, it is undeniable that it was quite beyond PLA ability to study tactics from a technological angle because of knowledge limitations. Obviously, such conditions must be changed today.

We should never evade our shortcomings; the result of evasion can only be a widening of the gap. It is imperative for us to pursue our glorious tradition of overcoming an enemy with superior weaponry and equipment with our inferior ones and to seek ways of dealing with hi-tech warfare through high-tech study. Meager hi-tech knowledge or even ignorance would be like trying to catch a sparrow when blindfolded, and new tactics would become outmoded even before they were applied. Only by renovating our knowledge and absorbing the results of technology studies done by foreign armed forces will it be possible for us to go deep into modern hi-tech warfare to seek out the laws governing things at a deeper level, while refraining from letting our studies stay at some superficial level characterized by "being extensive in scope for a short period with a quick tempo."

The PLA has implemented a great change in its strategic guiding ideas since 1985, which was a first step made in transcending the self. However, we cannot expect transcending the self to be completed by a single change. We said long ago that we should not study "minor warfare" with the concept of "a major war"; however, as soon as a study begins in depth, the "major war" train of thought would dominate academic study. From another angle, this shows that the degree of difficulty in overcoming the self can be very great and that there is still a long way to go.

The impetus for overcoming the self originates from sober judgment and scientific analysis. For example, in hi-tech warfare, tactical effectiveness no longer depends on the size of forces or the extent of firepower and motorized forces, but more on control systems over the war theater and efficiency in utilizing information from the theater. "Superiority in numbers and strength" no longer plays a decisive role. The amount of time modern hi-tech warfare can be sustained is already leaning toward "a quick decision," some even call it "second-count warfare," and great changes have taken place in the relationship between a traditional "quick decision" and protraction. The goal of war has changed from attacking cities and strategic locations regardless of the cost, as in the past, to obtaining maximum result with minimum cost, thus paying greater attention to seeking a favorable strategic state. War is now becoming "clean," a demand that hi-tech means are capable of meeting. That "war begins only after a declaration has been made" is now a historical concept, and the traditional "three steps" has been replaced by a new "three steps," namely, "low-altitude, night action, and electronic warfare," and so forth. We should resolutely do away with our outdated "Panorama" of war, broaden our vision, and find a new path for overcoming the self.

Combine Tactical Studies With Studies in "Shaping Tactics"

The Army should be built today according to how future hi-tech warfare will be fought. First, tactical studies can lead directly to the development of weaponry and equipment. Successful 20th-century examples are noteworthy. In 1929, when the German military did not have any tanks, a young officer, Heinz Guderian, broke through the bondage of traditional thinking and initiated the theory of lightning tank warfare based on the historical experience of the British use of tanks during World War I. His theory lead to the production, organization, and founding of operational corps with tanks as the main body, which then swept across Europe 10 years later. President Roosevelt accepted Einstein's theory to develop the atomic bomb, and turned a new leaf in the history of war and mankind. Stalin consulted the great and talented aircraft designers Ilyushin and Yakovlev and discussed various issues related to improving aircraft technology; consequently, the air force of the former USSR enjoyed a great global reputation. Mao Zedong, the soldier who introduced the proletarian military theories of people's war and guerrilla warfare to the world of military thinking, saw the far-reaching historical significance of developing the "atomic and nuclear bombs and satellites." The fulfillment of this goal has greatly elevated China's position in the world and has made historic contributions to peace for scores of years.

Today, high technology is an important support for a country's military strength and war potential. It is a sign of comprehensive national strength, as well as the material basis for creating new tactics. There is no time to lose in developing hi-tech weaponry and equipment to comply with the needs of our specific tactics. We must seize the opportunity and link it to China's national conditions.

Second, tactical studies should guide reform in military training. Presently, explorations and discussions of the Gulf war are being approached at a deeper level to seek "new" characteristics and revelations. The tremendous energy released by hi-tech operational forces on the battlefield originates from the long-term accumulation of an army's peacetime building; such quantitative accumulation is precisely the result of strict training aside from breakthroughs in tactical studies and the impetus of technological development.

The requirements of hi-tech warfare on our army's training are that training should be implemented according to a program, but it should not go round and round at a low level characterized by achieving "certain scores in shooting, certain times in obstacle clearance operations, certain distances in grenade throwing, and certain skills on the horizontal bar." Military training should not be limited to the traditional repetition and extension of the experiences of officers and men from one generation to the next. High technology should be regarded as the extension of the arm and the expansion of the brain to war as well as the main content of training. An army with low-level intelligence training will be eliminated in war. This has been proven time and again in recent limited wars. If we believe that the ways and principles of traditional military training remain useful, they should not stay in the simple form of whether or not the army's forces are concentrated and whether or not coordinating actions are implemented. Military principles and predetermined operational plans could possibly be "included" in computer software for future operations through the "starter" of military training in peacetime operational studies, joint exercises, the finalization of weapon designs, army formations, seeking optimum tactics, and building automated systems. Such military training is "war behavior" in a higher sense and has unfolded "war" in a comprehensive way in peacetime, where war is but a final solution through one or several contentions.

Tactical studies may provide new trains of thought or goals for army building; however, how we should combine "tactics" with "the way of building" eventually depends on man's dynamic role. The limited wars of the 1980s and 1990s provide us with a clear picture: the two major factors of arms and man are merging with each other, and man's decisive role is not only embodied in the employment of weaponry, but runs through the weapons systems. In the Gulf War, the multinational air force controlled some 30 airfields, 122 in-flight refueling lines, 660 no-fly zones, and 220 air corridors, involving scores of computers working around the clock. Because computers simulate man's thinking, the extent of its dependence on man is far greater than other technological equipment. What differs from the past is that intelligent weapons systems possess certain thinking "functions," whereas man's intelligence and wisdom is realized through making weapons intelligent. Passing judgment while relying solely on the direct perception of the commander is a long way from complying with modern warfare.

Modern trained soldiers are the leaders and organizers of a new hi-tech revolution. Many strategists with vision have stated that the next century will be a time for the combination of soldiers and high technology, and soldiers should be the ones who blaze new trails at the forefront of science and technology. Military technology is entering the forefront of military development with a faster development rate, higher practical value, and still greater military and economic results. Should we hesitate to take into consideration the issue of training qualified people until we come across a new technology on the battlefield, we will undoubtedly be doomed to defeat.

It is not too difficult to play a musical instrument; however, he who plays a musical instrument is not necessarily a musician. An outstanding musician must have a perfect command of musical theory, while having a good knowledge of every single piece of the musical instrument under his baton. Likewise, on a hi-tech battlefield, an accomplished commander should have a perfect command of basic tactics, while being familiar with the use of various technological means in conducting war. Only then will it be possible for him to perform one scene after the other full of the power and grandeur of the arena of war. It is precisely in this way that hi-tech warfare has set such a severe historical requirement.

THE THIRD MILITARY REVOLUTION

Ch'en Huan

Up to the present, there have been three military revolutions:

- Before the 1930s, the large number of units equipped with airplanes, tanks, and radios touched off the first military revolution, proclaiming that mankind had passed from the era of "cold weapons" into the era of "hot weapons."
- From World War II to the 1960s, the development of nuclear technology and the use of guided missile technology on the battlefield brought about the second military revolution, proclaiming the arrival of the "nuclear-hot weapon" era, followed by the development of nuclear strategy and the theory of nuclear deterrence.
- Following the rapid development of information technology, stealth technology, and long-range precision strike technology, the Gulf War, which occurred at the beginning of the 1990s, opened the curtain on the information war era and marked the sudden appearance of the third military revolution.

Without the slightest doubt, like all previous military revolutions, the third will have far-reaching effects on military practice and theory.

This article is from Contemporary Military Affairs, *March 11, 1996.*

The Challenge to Traditional Operational Principles

Concentration of military force is an operational principle universally followed by strategists in ancient and modern times, in China and abroad; it is mainly achieved by increasing the density of unit-space military force. Following the rapid development of technology and its increasingly widespread application in military affairs, the ancient military principle of concentration of military force must be reconsidered and viewed from a new angle:

- First, from a look at the object of concentration, we see that military force concentration in the traditional sense is no longer effective; it has been replaced by the concentration of striking efficacy, including firepower, electromagnetic energy, photo energy, information energy, and other energy forms. Because of the development of information technology and its widespread application in weapons and equipment, all the methods of information warfare create conditions, under modern circumstances, that allow concentration of combat-effective energy without needing to concentrate large units. Provided these weapons are deployed in a dispersed manner, they can attain the operational objective; deployment in a concentrated manner, on the contrary, leads to trouble.
- Second, from a look at the component parts of concentration, we see that the position and role of "software" is constantly rising. Armed force "software" (including the level of intelligence of officers and men, the level of armed force control of information energy, and other invisible factors) is gradually occupying the dominant position in warfare and its role is becoming larger day by day.
- Third, regarding the methods of concentration, a "soft" strike force is even more important than a "hard" strike force. If we liken military force and weapons to a "hard" strike force, then electronic countermeasures and other information war measures are a "soft" strike force. The application of high technology makes electronic and information technologies widely permeate all weapons and equipment, all operational measures, and battlefield commands, so that information warfare technology permeates every important measure in the operational domain and runs

through the entire course of a war, directly influencing the course and outcome of the war.

From a look at the object of concentration, we see that striking the other side's effective force is no longer the main starting point, and the focus is now on interfering with and destroying the other side's information and cognitive systems. By striking at one point one can achieve the operational objective of paralyzing the entire body. "Destroy the enemy and preserve oneself" is another operational maxim that all armed forces, in ancient and modern times, in China and abroad, have always followed. However, in warfare in the information era the tendency is for military forces to be deployed in a dispersed manner, the demarcation line between the front and the rear to disappear, and weapon systems to reach over the horizon and cross national boundaries.

The method of the past in which a decisive battle with the enemy's main force was sought makes it difficult to grasp the opportunity for battle and also makes it difficult to achieve ideal results. However, provided the enemy's information system and his command and decisionmaking system are destroyed, countered, or interfered with, thereby destroying his capability to obtain, process, transmit, control, and use information, we can paralyze the enemy's entire operational system and thus he will lose his operational capability. This has more results in actual combat than continually killing or wounding many troops, and continually destroying many ordinary weapons. That is to say, the meaning in the traditional sense of "destroy the enemy and preserve oneself" should be extended to "strike the enemy's information system and ensure our side's capability for information warfare."

From Physical to Cerebrum Countermeasures

In the "cold weapons" era, armed forces mainly depended on the physical ability to use weapons when waging war, and their overall combat effectiveness was only the multiplication of the individual combat effectiveness of their soldiers. Even in the "hot weapons" and "hot-nuclear weapons" eras, armed forces were skilled armed forces; among operational units there existed a relationship of a clear division of work and coordination; the overall combat effectiveness was the square of the sum of the collective combat effectiveness. In armed forces with information weapons, rank-and-file soldiers, who originally depended on their physical skill in using mechanized weapons and equipment, will be replaced by specialized software that mainly depends on intelligence in using weapons and equipment that has been transformed by information. This "multiplier" effect of intelligence and information almost leads to a limitless expansion of the combat effectiveness of conventional weapons and equipment.

In a certain sense, for armed forces in the information era the test of strength is between intelligence capabilities, and the core of the third military revolution is the development and use of information capability. Therefore, some people say: If we say that in the two previous military revolutions, because of the use of chemical, thermal, and nuclear energy, man's physical capability was extended and man's four limbs were liberated, then the third military revolution, which develops and uses information capability, will extend man's intelligence capability and liberate man's cerebrum. The armed forces of the future will be "high-tech forces" with photoelectric specialists, information specialists, aviation specialists, and other outstanding specialized talents as its core.

Lines Between Front and Rear Will Blur

In a future war there will be nonlinear attacks on enemy objectives. The concepts in the "hot weapon" era of a battle front and an operational depth will lose meaning. The main reasons for this are:

- First, all kinds of information-transformed platforms and information-transformed weapons have sprung up like bamboo shoots after a spring rain; operational capability has reached the global level, and five-dimensional operations—air, land, sea, space, and electromagnetic—have become the main operational forces in high-tech warfare. Battle lines of the past, like the "Maginot Line" and the "Bar-Lev Line" are no longer terrifying shields, and they are also not chasms that cannot be crossed. The conventional one-by-one breakthrough tactic of first going to the forward position and afterward to the in-depth position is no longer effective. The operational sequence could be going first to the in-depth position and afterward to the forward position, and the objects of strikes could be first the support and technical units and afterward the combat units. The way to achieve victory is not necessarily occupation but rather the destruction by firepower of information capability. The disappearance of the battle line causes the front and the rear to lose their support conditions dependent on differentiation.

• Second, the operational objectives of the two sides on attack and defense are neither the seizing of territory nor the killing of so many enemies, but rather the paralyzing of the other side's information system and the destruction of the other side's will to resist. The enemy's command centers, communication hubs, information-processing centers, high- tech weapon control systems, and supply systems could become priority targets of attack. The scenes in the past of close- combat fighting have become history, and where the front and the rear are located is no longer an issue of concern to commanders and units.

Rapid Rise of New Operational Concepts

The vigorous development of information-transformed weapons will make fundamental changes in the traditional operational concepts, thereby causing many new operational forms to appear in future wars.

Long-Range Combat

Previously, because the performance of weapons and equipment was limited, quite a few strategists were fond of the tactic of "close combat." Now, there has been a great increase in the types of long-range antipersonnel methods. Among them, the air arm, the over-the-horizon precision strike force, and the large amount of equipment of electromagnetic units will replace the face-to-face ground attack units of the past and become the main strike forces in future operations. The further development of long-range strike weapons will make long-range combat an operational form in future wars. There will be three main forms of long- range strikes in the future: the first form is the one in which the air arm independently carries out long-range strikes; the second form is one in which the long-range strike combines with the long-range rapid movement of troops transported by land and sea with the vertical airdrops of airborne forces; and the third form is five-dimensional—air, land, sea, space, and electromagnetic— long-range combat.

Outer Space Combat

Under the impetus of information technology and other high and new technologies, satellites, space shuttles, manned spaceships, and space stations have appeared in succession. The following new-concept weapons will come forth in a continuous stream—all these weapons will make outer space the fifth dimension operational space following land, sea, air, and electromagnetism:

- Laser weapons
- Ultra- high frequency weapons
- Ultrasonic wave weapons
- Stealth weapons
- Mirror-beam weapons
- Electromagnetic guns
- Plasma weapons
- Ecological weapons
- Smart weapons
- Logic weapons
- Sonic weapons.

Because the efficacy of these new-concept weapons depends on the hard-shell support of a space platform, once the space platform is lost their efficacy will be weakened and they will even become powerless. In this way the two sides in a war will focus on offensive and defensive operations conducted from space platforms in outer space, and these operations will certainly become a new form in future wars. In the U.S. Armed Forces a new service—the Space Force—is being discussed, showing that the idea of outer space combat is close to moving from theory to actual combat.

Paralysis Combat

This tactic does not make the elimination of the enemy's effective forces its objective, but rather takes as its starting point the destruction of the enemy's overall structure for combined arms operations and the weakening of the enemy's overall efficacy in combined arms operations. Under high-tech conditions, all subsystems of combined arms operations are mutually replenishing and inseparable operational groups. If there is no unified command and control monitoring and early warning by the information- transformed C^3I system, then it is difficult to obtain timely, reliable intelligence. Additionally, when there is an assault it is also impossible for the subsystems to coordinate without electromagnetic superiority, assaulting units become "blind persons," and even if they have more troops and weapons than the enemy they are nothing but a pile of trash. Therefore, by striking at the "vital point" of the enemy's information and support systems one can at one blow paralyze the enemy and collapse his morale.

- *Computer Combat*: The computer has infused powerful vitality into modern military machines, but it also has unavoidably been reduced to an object of attack. Once a computer system is damaged so that it cannot operate normally, cruise missiles and other precision-guided weapons become arrows without targets; and high-tech performance aircraft, tanks, warships, radar, and activated command systems will be totally in the dark about what to do. Engaging in computer combat can be compared to borrowing on the battlefield the principle of "Sun's understanding that boring a hole in the Iron Fan Princess's belly causes internal damage." Relevant data show that, before the outbreak of the Gulf War, American intelligence organizations put a virus into Iraq's air defense system, which led to the destruction of 86 percent of the Iraqi forces' strategic targets in the first 1 or 2 days of the war. This also shows that making the computer an operational means of attacking the object of a strike has already become a reality. One by one, many armed forces have now put an enormous amount of funds into research on the types, methods, and results of computer virus invasions and attacks, and they have come up with all sorts of ideas, e.g., concealing a "virus source" in the integrated circuits of enemy computers and, when necessary, activating the virus by electronic measures, propagating, and duplicating it. Again, for example, with the aid of electromagnetic waves, a virus can be injected from a long distance into the enemy's command and communication systems and into the computers on his aircraft, tanks, and other weapons, causing "nonlethal destruction."

- *Radiation Combat*: In wars of the past, the power to inflict casualties mainly depended on the effects of kinetic energy and thermal energy, but the weapon systems produced by the third military revolution mainly use sound, electromagnetism, radiation, and other destructive mechanisms. Operational actions in which armed forces use radiation-damaging energy to strike at the enemy's electronic equipment, weapon systems, military equipment and personnel, and other military targets are called "radiation combat." The main radiation weapons are laser weapons, microwave weapons, particle beam weapons, and subsonic wave weapons; they possess enormous military potential.

- *Robot Combat*: The latest advances in information technology, artificial intelligence, virtual reality, and computer control have already provided the necessary conditions for developing functional robots. The main type of military robot on active service or about to be put on active service in the armed forces of various countries of the world are vehicle emergency robots, minelaying robots, minesweeping robots, reconnaissance robots, transportation robots, electronic robots, and driver robots. Later there will appear engineer robots, chemical defense robots, patrol robots, and even unmanned intelligent tanks, unmanned intelligent aircraft, and other "robot soldiers." In essence, a robot soldier is an unmanned antipersonnel firepower carrier that possesses a certain capability for obtaining and processing information. It can complete many operational missions with a high degree of efficiency, and it can also avoid unnecessary casualties to the effective strength. In view of its strong points, there could appear armed forces with intelligent robot officers and men in primary roles. Once two belligerents put them on the battlefield at the most dangerous places and the most critical times, and they charge into battle, like the tank combat and missile combat before them, and similar to the robot wars in science fiction films, they will mount the stage of war.

"Thin and Flat" Command Systems

The armed forces command system in the "hot weapons" and "hot-nuclear weapons" era was a horizontally unconnected "tree-shaped" structure, which from top to bottom was in line with the units in the military arm and branch establishments. This structure was convenient for centralized command, but it had a fatal weak point— its survivability was poor. If a branch of a tree-shaped structure is cut, that branch is affected, but if its trunk is cut, the entire structure is paralyzed. When the information-weapon era arrived, because of the large amount of use of the computer and the great improvement in its capability for searching, processing, transmitting, and displaying information, the various command and control systems could form an integral, mutually connected network connecting in one body the state's command authorities to the individual soldier, all of them sharing information.

Formation of the mutually connected system allows a front-line commander to directly obtain intelligence from general headquarters or space information centers, and the middle-level commander loses the reason for his existence. This will make the command system of future armed forces, because of the reduction in the number of levels, a thin and flat structure that is wide horizontally and short vertically. Therefore, this kind of command system is called a "thin and flat" command system. Its main characteristics are: all the network's nodal points are connected vertically and horizontally, thereby both maintaining the strong point of the past vertical connection between the upper- and lower- level units, which is convenient for centralized command, and have the capability to make direct connections between parallel units, which is convenient for dispersed command. The "thin and flat" command system will lead to a change in the form of command, which will shift from the former centralized command to dispersed command, and, under a unified plan, the lower-level commanders will have a primary role in decisionmaking. This thin and flat command system will be able to reduce the amount of information flow, shorten the line of information flow, ensure that the lower-level commanders obtain real-time battlefield intelligence, improve the capability for decisionmaking response, and fully display subjective capability.

Operational Simulation Will Play a Major Role

Modern operational simulation uses an especially large amount of computer operational simulation, applying it to simulate tanks, battle vehicles, artillery, surface ships, submarines, and many other weapons.

It will also apply to different levels of strategy, campaigns, and tactics, thereby providing a scientific basis for decisionmaking.

Operational simulation—this "laboratory" for war—no matter whether in the domains of military science, armed forces system and establishment, weapon development, and military training, or in the aspects of selection of long-range delivery of military force and firepower, force composition, plan formulation, logistics and technical support, and tactical application, is playing an increasingly important role. For example, in unit training, by providing an operational simulation system that is sufficiently scientific and rational for tanks, armored vehicles, portable weapons, aircraft, helicopters, ground combat units, and other systems, training costs can be reduced, thereby greatly improving the beneficial results of training and increasing its safety. As of now, the U.S. Armed Forces have set up six laboratories for simulation techniques and methods. These six laboratories, by putting all arms and branches of the service on line with computers, can combine in one form the units, weapons and equipment with simulation equipment, and if necessary can conduct large-scale combined arms exercises. Britain, Russia, Japan, France, Sweden, and Israel are vigorously exploring the use of laboratories similar to those mentioned above.

"Smaller and Divisible" Structures

Following the development of information technology, any armed force will certainly tend to become smaller. At present the group army- and division-level scale structure widely used by the armed forces of various countries could become obsolete and be replaced by crack, intelligence-type small units that possess the capability for a high degree of mobility. In future operations, the attacking and defending sides will put more emphasis on being economical in the use of their operational strength, only throwing into the operations the essential units. A prominent characteristic of this kind of establishment is that it possesses "divisibility," i.e., based on the nature and need of an operational mission, units can at will be "divided" and combined.

MILITARY CONFLICTS IN THE NEW ERA

Major General Zheng Qinsheng

The end of the Cold War has added many uncertain factors to the international situation. In our efforts to make a greater contribution to the development of our country and nation during this major historical transition period, we should first gain a clear idea of the following two issues concerning military struggle: One is the need to carefully analyze changes in the international strategic setup in our age and be clear about the tasks of military struggle, with a view to keeping to the correct orientation of the struggle; the other is the need to profoundly grasp the law of military struggle in the new period and provide correct strategic guidance, with a view to gaining a sound grasp of work methods.

Tasks of Military Struggle

In our study of military struggle in the new period, we should first take a look at "major events throughout the world" and gain a clear idea of the features of our age. Marxists believe that an historical era serves to be the foundation of our decisions. Lenin stressed repeatedly that "only when we make a correct assessment of the international environment, or the basic features of our times, can we correctly formulate our own strategies." In an effort to base the situation

---

This article is from Liberation Army Daily, *July 16, 1996, 6.*

analysis on the features of our age, we should pay attention not only to the local situation of our neighboring areas, but also to the strategic setup of the whole world, and not only to changes that have taken place during a recent period, but also to the historical vicissitudes over a considerably long period of time. During the mid-1980s, basing on his correct assessment of the situation then, Comrade Deng Xiaoping vividly summarized the highly complicated international situation into a four-word idea of "East, West, South, and North," with "East and West" referring to the issue of seeking peace, while "South and North" refers to the issue of seeking development. Meanwhile, he also expounded the dialectical relationship between peace and development. This summarization not only identified the major contradictions of today's world, but also analyzed the two sides of these contradictions, thus putting forward the idea of seeking peace and development. Centered around the two major themes of peace and development, in recent years, the central authorities have readjusted the country's diplomatic strategy and foreign relations, and have attained major victories in our diplomatic struggles. When trying to gain a correct understanding of peace and development as the features of our age, we need to grasp the following several basic points:

- First, relaxation is the general trend of our age. The force of opposing war and seeking peace is growing on a world-wide scale, and major wars have become avoidable.
- Second, countries under different social systems and with different ideologies are allowed to coexist in our age, though such coexistence is naturally characterized by competition and contention.
- Third, economics and science have become the two major competitive fields in our age, and competition in comprehensive national strength among different countries has taken the forms of both global trade wars and ascendence in the scientific and technological fields.
- Fourth, seeking peace and democracy has become an irresistible general development trend in the human society of our age, and the relationship between East and West has always been characterized by simultaneous confrontation and dialogue.

In short, seeking peace and development is a great banner for mankind in our age. We need to regard it as the basic ground for our observation of the world trend, and also for our resolution of major problems during the future historical period. In today's world, the main forms of military struggle share the following two distinguishing features: One is the shift from violent confrontation to deterrence based on actual strength; the other is the exercise of effective control over war behavior.

Ever since the time when countries first appeared, war has always been a major way to seek national rights and interests. The evolution of human history, as well as the rise and decline of countries, are mostly a historical record of war. That is why historians have noted: "War is the normal behavior of mankind." However, during the past 50 years, in the wake of World War II, considerable changes have taken place in the forms of war, unprecedented, savage intercontinental wars have occurred, and the past nearly half a century has witnessed a sustained period of relative stability. During this period, "cold war" has to a great extent, taken the place of the "hot war" of violent confrontation. Instead of causing worldwide turbulence, the over 200 local wars and armed conflicts that have taken place during this period have been effectively limited to a certain scope and intensity. Deterrence has become a prominent component of modern national strategy, yet it is not a strategy for staging wars but for avoiding wars. It can be said that every formulator of war strategies will have the same thought: On the one hand, he should try his very best to prevent his country from being drawn into a modern war; and on the other hand, he will also try his utmost to enable his country to win an advantageous strategic position and to realize the ideal of "winning a war without actually going into it." As a result, plans to win wars have been turned into efforts to contain war. Such changes, which have been brought about by the special features of military struggle, are not only a reflection of objective material conditions, but a selection of subjective will and behavior as well. The former is based on the fact that the military revolution facilitated by scientific and technological advances has provided the objective material means for deterrence; while the latter gives expression to a distillation in the understanding of wars shared by strategists.

Military Strategy in Peacetime

Demands for survival and development constitute the eternal interests of a sovereign country. Today, the space and resources needed for survival and development remain the focus of contention between all countries, and military struggle is a major expression of such contention. The turn of century witnessed extremely acute competitions for survival and development among different countries in the world. Amidst the rapids of such international competitions, we will inevitably encounter severe challenges in our effort to realize the strategic target of "unifying the motherland, promoting the economy, and safeguarding peace." At present, major countries in the world are vying with each other to readjust their own strategies. Under the new strategies, they will:

- Give first priority to the development of science, technology, and the economy
- Enhance their comprehensive national strength
- Strive to occupy a superior strategic position in the next century.

As Chairman Jiang Zemin pointed out in "China's Declaration of the 21st Century," China should first turn itself into a powerful country if it intends to make a greater contribution to both the progress of mankind and world peace. This is the strategic thought of our leaders as well as the voice of all our nationals and comes from the bottom of their hearts. The present relatively stable period of peace is still fraught with many destabilizing factors. The challenges result from competition in comprehensive national strength, which is a pressure in reality, while struggles centering on national reunification, territorial disputes, and arguments over maritime rights and interests may lead to local wars and sudden changes. What merits our special attention is that with the increase in the world's population and the ongoing trend of tighter supplies of natural resources and a relatively smaller space for subsistence, the tasks of military struggle currently facing us have not yet been totally separated from the nature of taking cities and seizing territory.

With the economic growth of the Asia-Pacific region and the future arrival of the Pacific age in the 21st century, hegemonists have stepped up their economic, scientific and technological, cultural, and military infiltration into the Asian-Pacific region, thus giving prominence to a number of hidden contradictions. In our efforts to attain the strategic targets of economic take-off and national rejuvenation, we hope to have a peaceful international environment in order and a stable neighboring environment; to explore and make use of more resources for the purpose of promoting the economic, scientific, and technological development of the country; to gain greater shares in international markets and successfully practice an export-oriented economic strategy; to arouse the self-confidence and enterprising spirit of our nationals; and to safeguard the integrity of our country and nation. External challenges are unavoidable, and what counts is how we are going to meet the challenges and take countermeasures.

To fulfill the tasks of military struggle in the new period, the most important issues are those of military strength and strategic guidance. In ancient times, military strategy was called the "principles of commanding generals." In modern times, military strategy was summed up as the "art of wars and battles," a belief shared among Napoleon, Clausewitz, von Moltke, and Schlieffen. Contemporary strategists believe, however, that traditional military strategies dealt only with what an army must do during wartime and failed to make clear what they should do during peacetime. We must be aware that with the rapid development of science and technology in the world today, the issue of the peacetime building and the development of military strength is becoming the focus of attention among military strategists. Defense experts in western countries have stressed that today's military strategy is no longer the "science of military victories." This means that under a longstanding peaceful environment, the emphasis of military strategies has been shifted from wartime to peacetime; and peacetime strategies will not be limited to the planning and guidance of wars, but will also cope with the issue of how to build up and develop military strength during peacetime.

The Military Revolution

The Central Military Commission has put forward a military strategic principle for the new period, which calls for efforts to base military struggle on winning local wars, which employ modern technologies, especially wars under high-tech conditions. Meanwhile, stress has been placed on the need to accelerate the modernization building of our Army, contain and win wars, and fulfill the army's major missions in the military struggle of the new period. This new strategic principle embraces both the realistic employment and the long-term building of military strength. Today, the employment of military strength by major countries generally shares the following features:

- First, they have adopted a prudent approach toward wars and taken steps to avoid wars. When employing military strength, we should act in accordance with the needs of the national strategy; adapt it to the needs of political, economic, and diplomatic struggles; adopt a prudent approach towards wars and take steps to avoid wars; and strive to attain the highest strategic realm of "deflating the enemy's arrogance without actually going to war."
- Second, they have resorted to the demonstration of armed forces. Centering on the experiments of new and high-tech weapons and equipment, they have organized major military exercises and other demonstrative activities concerning major strategies and the direction of campaigns. They have displayed the full status quo of their military strength and the will of sovereign states, in order to attain the goal of deterring the enemy and stabilizing the strategic environments that are beneficial to themselves.
- Third, they have adopted the practice of putting an end to war by means of war. Basing a longer and more stable peaceful environment on deterrent forces is one aspect of the principle of "winning a war without actually going into it." However, because war is the ultimate reason for the existence of an army, we still need to consider the issue of "winning victory in all wars."

We should maintain the modernization and alertness of our military forces at a high level so that we can make rapid responses to contingencies and gain the strategic initiative in any place at any time. To win local wars under high-tech conditions, we need all the more to adhere to the Confucian ideology of "winning victory in a war before actually going into it." If we say that the idea of "winning a war before actually going into it" adhered to by militarists in the past was concerned only with the stage of pre-war preparations, then the idea of "winning a war before actually going into it" held by today's militarists means, more importantly, the design and building of military strength during peacetime.

The Americans have claimed that victory in the Gulf War was the outcome of 20 years of hard effort. In a sense, the "20 years of hard effort" refers to the whole process of rebuilding their military strength. In the wake of the Vietnam War, the U.S. Armed Forces suffered from low morale and army building remained in the doldrums. To put an end to such a situation, they carried out a series of reforms in such fields as military theory, military technology, military training, cultivation of military officers, and operational formations. The 20 years of of hard effort have brought new life to the armed forces. This is a typical example of "winning a war before actually going into it."

In a local high-tech war, the first battle is the decisive battle, which will decide the outcome of the entire war. Generally speaking, there will no longer be any chance for wearing down the enemy's effective strength. In view of this, experts have pointed out that most victories on future battlefields will not be "decided by the war itself" but "decided by pre-war building." Therefore, to fulfill the tasks of military struggle in the new period, we must plant our feet on the reform and the quality building of our army. To reinforce the quality building of our army, we must persistently carry out theory-trailed policies. A global review tells us that in the past, the blueprints for army building were mostly drawn up on the basis of experience gained in previous wars. Today, they are designed in accordance with the demands of future wars.

What are the demands of future wars? We can only gain a clear idea through theoretical thinking, and can only complete such a design through the theoretical study of science. With the emergence of the technology of "virtual reality," the military theories guiding future wars will be produced in combat laboratories, and the inspection of the "product" quality of the army will also be conducted in combat laboratories. This tremendous change has provided new ideas for military development.

A military revolution is now in the ascendant in today's world. Thoughts on reinforcing the quality building of our army should be conducted against this general background. "After going through the stages of bare-handed battles, cold steel weapons, hot steel weapons, and mechanization, military operations are now entering the information age. These five major military revolutions corresponded with five industrial revolutions."

What we need to do now is to study the information war under nuclear deterrence; the well-known scientist Qian Xuesen laid bare the essence of the military revolution with one remark. "The world has entered a period of new military revolution, which is a reflection of social, economic, and scientific and technological changes in the military field. Information technology is the nucleus and foundation of this military revolution."

Information and knowledge have changed the past practice by which military capacities were simply measured by numbers of armored divisions, wings of the air force, and aircraft carrier combat groups. Today, we also need to count invisible strengths, including:

- Calculation capability
- Volume of telecommunications
- Reliability of information
- Real-time reconnaissance ability.

The well-known scientist Zhu Guangya profoundly pointed out these criteria for judging the quality of today's army.

In recent years, our troops have attained considerable results in implementing the military strategic principle of the new period, learning high-tech technologies and knowledge, and in studying wars under high-tech conditions. However, where shall we place the nucleus of high-tech development? Where shall we put the main emphasis of local high-tech wars?

A consensus on these issues has yet to be reached throughout the army. People still tend to place greater emphasis on hardware instead of software, and on the present instead of the future. Such a transitional "optical parallax" is hindering us from gaining a correct grasp of major contradictions.

In our consideration of the quality development of our military in the context of a world military revolution, we need to appropriately handle relations between universality and individuality and between generality and particularity. Armies have always had a role in the international arena. Therefore, the modernization building of our army will naturally follow the common law guiding the world's army modernization, yet it also needs to maintain its "Chinese characteristics" at the same time. It should not copy indiscriminately the patterns of Western developed countries, yet cannot cut itself off from the general trend of the military revolution. From the strategic change in its guiding ideology to the formulation of a military strategic principle for the new period, our army can be said to have completed the change in its strategic guidance only, and needs to make further efforts to facilitate a change in its overall building.

In view of this, we have called for the efforts of all officers and men of our army to conduct a conscientious study of

- The new changes taking place in the world's strategic setup since the end of the cold war
- The recent military revolution which is producing a most profound and lasting impact
- New ideas on military development
- "Magic weapons" that can really serve our purpose.

A philosopher once said: "At the back of the tremendous tension of traditions is an inert force of history." During this important cross-century period, we should conform to the trend of our times, renew our military concepts, and accelerate the quality building of our army amid reform, with a view to adapting ourselves to the needs of the military struggle during the new period.

INFORMATION WAR:
A NEW FORM OF PEOPLE'S WAR

Wei Jincheng

A future war, which may be triggered by a disruption to the network of the financial sector, may be combat between digitized units or a two-man show, with the spaceman (or robot) on the stage and the think tank behind the scenes. It may also be an interaction in the military, political, and economic domains, making it hard to define as a trial of military strength, a political argument, or an economic dispute. All this has something to do with the leap forward of modern technology and the rise of the revolution in the military domain.

The technological revolution provides only a stage for confrontations. Only when this revolution is married with military operations can it take on the characteristics of confrontation. Some believe that the information superhighway, the Internet, computers, and multimedia are synonymous with commerce, profit, and communications. In fact, this is far from true.

Thanks to modern technology, revolutionary changes in the information domain, such as the development of information carriers and the Internet, are enabling many to take part in fighting without even having to step out of the door. The rapid development of networks has turned each automated system into a potential target of invasion. The fact that information technology is increasingly relevant to people's lives determines that those who take part in information war are not all soldiers and that anybody who understands computers

---

This article was excerpted from the Military Forum column, Liberation Army Daily, *June 25, 1996.*

may become a "fighter" on the network. Think tanks composed of nongovernmental experts may take part in decisionmaking; rapid mobilization will not just be directed to young people; information-related industries and domains will be the first to be mobilized and enter the war; traditional modes of operations will undergo major changes; operational plans designed for information warfare will be given priority in formulation and adoption; and so on and so forth. Because other technologies are understood by people only after they are married with information technology and because information technology is becoming increasingly socialized, information warfare is not the business of armed forces alone. Conditions exist that effectively facilitate the participation of the public in information warfare.

Ideas Guide Action

In the information age, an all-new concept of operations should be established. Information is a "double-edged sword." In the information age, information is not only a weapon of combat but also the object sought after by the warring parties. The quantity, quality, and speed of transmission of information resources are key elements in information supremacy. That is why information is not just a piece of news and information weapons do not refer only to such information-based weapons as precision-guided weapons and electronic warfare weapons. The most effective weapon is information itself. Information can be used to attack the enemy's recognition system and information system either proactively or reactively, can remain effective either within a short time or over an extended period, and can be used to attack the enemy right away or after a period of incubation. Therefore, good information protection and launching a counterattack with information weapons when attacked will become the main subjects of preparation against war during the information age.

Information is intercommunicative and therefore must not be categorized by sector or industry. It is very wrong to think that information in only the military field is worth keeping secret and that information for civil purposes does not belong to the category of secrecy. In fact, if no security measures are taken to protect computers and networks, information may be lost. Similarly, if we think it is the business of intelligence and security departments to obtain the enemy's information and that it has nothing to do with anyone else, we would miss a good opportunity to win an information war.

In March 1995, Beijing's Jingshan School installed a campus network with 400 PCs, an "intelligent building" design, and multimedia technology. The school runs 10 percent of its courses through computers; students borrow books from the library through a computerized retrieval system; and experiments are conducted with demonstrations based on multimedia simulation systems. This illustrates in microcosm the many information networks that our country has built with its own resources. More than one million PCs were sold in China in 1995, and the figure is expected to reach 2.7 million in 1996. Faced with the tendencies of a networking age, if we looked upon these changes merely from a civil perspective and made no military preparations, we would undoubtedly find ourselves biased and shortsighted.

Information War Depends on the Integrity of the Information System

Information warfare is entirely different from the conventional concept of aiming at a target and annihilating it with bullets, or of commanders relying on images and pictures obtained by visual detection and with remote-sensing equipment to conduct operations from a map or sand table. The multidimensional, interconnected networks on the ground, in the air (or outer space), and under water, as well as terminals, modems, and software, are not only instruments, but also weapons. A people's war under such conditions would be complicated, broad-spectrum, and changeable, with higher degrees of uncertainty and probability, which requires full preparation and circumspect organization.

An information war is inexpensive, as the enemy country can receive a paralyzing blow through the Internet, and the party on the receiving end will not be able to tell whether it is a child's prank or an attack from its enemy. This characteristic of information warfare determines that each participant in the war has a higher sense of independence and greater initiative. However, if organization is inadequate, they may each fight their own battles and cannot form joint forces. Additionally, the Internet may generate a large amount of useless information that takes up limited channels and space and blocks the action of one's own side. Therefore, only by bringing relevant systems into play and combining human intelligence with artificial intelligence under effective organization and coordination can we drown our enemies in the ocean of an information offensive.

A people's war in the context of information warfare is carried out by hundreds of millions of people using open-type modern information systems. Because the traditional mode of industrial production has changed from centralization to dispersion and commercial activities have expanded from urban areas to rural areas, the working method and mode of interaction in the original sense are increasingly information-based. Political mobilization for war must rely on information technology to become effective, for example by generating and distributing political mobilization software via the Internet, sending patriotic e-mail messages, and setting up databases for traditional education. This way, modern technical media can be fully utilized and the openness and diffusion effect of the Internet can be expanded, to help political mobilization exert its subtle influence.

In short, the meaning and implications of a people's war have profoundly changed in the information age, and the chance of people taking the initiative and randomly participating in the war has increased. The ethnic signature and geographic mark on an information war are more pronounced and the application of strategies is more secretive and unpredictable.

Information-based confrontations will aim at reaching tangible peace through intangible war, maintaining the peace of hardware through software confrontations, and deterring and blackmailing the enemy with dominance in the possession of information. The bloody type of war will increasingly be replaced by contention for, and confrontations of, information.

The concept of people's war of the old days is bound to continue to be enriched, improved, and updated in the information age to take on a new form. We believe any wise military expert would come to the same conclusion.

NANOTECHNOLOGY WEAPONS ON FUTURE BATTLEFIELDS

Major General Sun Bailin

History shows that today's scientific dreams can readily become tomorrow's scientific realities and today's scientific explorations can become sources of development for tomorrow's socially productive forces and military combat power. Therefore, people who are concerned about future social development trends inevitably are also concerned with current scientific exploration. While advancing toward a macro world, people are also engaging in unremitting exploration of the micro world. Having undergone the "catalysis" of modern science and technology, certain notions that used to be viewed as wild tales are now approaching mankind "as if coming to "life." Some of man's fancies are to manufacture extremely small-scale electrical machinery that can only be seen under a microscope, an "intelligence chip" that could be transplanted into the brain of an insect, a "remote controlled submarine" that could freely navigate the human circulatory system, small-scale spacecraft and satellites the size of a thimble, an actuator that could respond to a single atom, and so forth. These are microscale electromechanical system technologies that have been discussed with increasing frequency during the 1990s.

This article by Major General Sun Bailin of the Academy of Military Science is excerpted from National Defense, *June 15, 1996.*

The term "microscale electromechanical system" principally refers to controllable and movable microscale electromechanical apparatuses that have exterior dimensions of less than a millimeter and the components of which have dimensions that are in the micron to nanometer range. They are the inevitable result of man's pursuit of the miniaturization of high-technology apparatuses since the advent of microelectronic technology. As early as the beginning of the 1970s, exploratory research into microscale electromechanical systems had already begun, but this field saw substantial development only by the end of the mid-1980s. At that time, it was realized that by using advanced manufacturing technology for large-scale integrated circuits, one could develop microscale prototypes of large-scale mechanized systems. Hence, a "technological revolution" was initiated advancing toward microscale electromechanical systems. The essence of this "technological revolution" was that in the course of transforming man's relationship with nature, we have progressed from the material millimeter-micron stage to the molecular-atomic nanometer stage. It could possibly bring about a leap forward in unit material storage and information processing capabilities. Its basic characteristic is, through precise, perfect control and accurate, subtle discrete forms, to configure molecular or atomic structures rapidly and, according to a person's intent, to control atoms and molecules or atomic and molecular clusters to manufacture microscale devices with a specific function, thereby raising materials processing technology to an unprecedented level.

Because this revolution's latent prospects for application and its extremely rapid development, and also because of its having opened up several new high technologies of great significance to the national economy and defense, including nano-electronics, the study of nanomaterials, nanomechanics, nanobiology, nanomanufacturing, nanosurveying, nanocontrol, and nanomicrology, it is ushering in the "nano-era" of the 21st century. Experts commonly believe that technology on the micron-nanometer scale is military-civilian dual-use technology that contains extremely great promise. At present, its application in military affairs consists primarily of two aspects: microscale electromechanical systems and their micro-electric connected specialized integrated microscale apparatuses.

Rand Report

In 1993, the U.S. Rand Corporation submitted to the U.S. military a research report, "Military Applications of Microscale Electromechanical Systems," which portrayed the latent military applications of microscale electromechanical systems, attracting attention from relevant quarters. The possible military applications of the microscale electromechanical systems conceived of in this report include the following:

Microscale Robot Electrical Incapacitation Systems

The microscale electromechanical systems typically conceived for development usually include six sub-systems: sensor systems, information-processing and auto-navigation systems, maneuvering systems, communications systems, destruction systems, and drive generators. These microscale electromechanical systems have a certain automatic capability and mobility. When there is a need to attack enemy electrical systems, one can utilize unmanned aircraft to disperse these microscale electromechanical systems in the vicinity of a target. When the target goes into operation, the systems sense the target's location and move in its direction until they permeate the target's interior, thus causing the enemy's electrical systems to malfunction. When releasing microscale electromechanical systems, one should be as close to the target as possible. In this way both time and equipment can be saved. After release, the systems can automatically seek the target and permeate its interior, thus causing it to wholly or partially lose its ability to operate. Microscale robot electrical incapacitation systems have an additional potential use, which is an economic blockade or embargo of the enemy. For example, by slipping into "information superhighway" apparatuses and preventing unimpeded flow along the "information superhighway," these systems could severely harm a modern, information-intensive economy. In addition, strategic targets that are vulnerable to attack by microscale robot electrical incapacitation systems include electrical power systems, civilian aviation systems, transportation networks, seaports and shipping, highways, television broadcast stations, telecommunications systems, computer centers, factories and enterprises, and so forth. Of course, there are those who worry that, were this kind of apparatus ever to used by an international terrorist organization, it could very possibly become a "double-edged sword" that threatens social stability.

Ant Robots

These microscale electromechanical systems can be controlled with sound. The drive-energy source of ant robots is a microscale microphone that can transform sound into energy. They can be used to creep into the enemy's vital equipment and lurk there for as long as several decades. In peacetime, they do not cause any problems, but in the event of war, remote control equipment can be used to activate the hidden ant robots, so that they can destroy or "devour" the enemy's equipment. In addition, there are at least 25 specialists who have done many years of research on nanotechnology and microscale electromechanical systems. Speaking from the latter stages of a great deal of scientific investigation, within the next 10 to 25 years, manufacture of these microscale electromechanical apparatuses of molecular dimensions will be possible and may actually sport "changeable hair," like that of Sun Wukong.* These ant robots would "self-replicate" and have ultrasensitive reconnaissance apparatuses and remote-control mines for a combat platform. Were the need to arise, ant robots could be released against an enemy and used to search out sensitive military areas that must be controlled. By means of a control program, microscale reconnaissance apparatuses and microscale mines could "self-replicate" to the required density, thereby creating a "strategic threat" or decisive blow against the enemy. It can be conceived that, once ant robots that can "self-replicate" appear on the future battlefield, a "sudden paralysis" of the enemy's macroscopic combat system will occcur by means of the tremendous combat force emitted by microscopic apparatuses, to the extent that the enemy must submit to the combat pressure created by microscopic electromechanical systems.

---

*Editor's note: Sun Wukong, the Monkey King of the Chinese novel, *Journey to the West*, could pluck a handful of his own fur, which would metamorphose into hundreds of other monkeys that would assist him in battle.

Blood Vessel Submarines

Microscale electromechanical systems can be made yet smaller, being manufactured into "blood vessel submarines." Such devices can undertake patrol missions within the complex human circulatory system, and upon discovering a "focus of infection" or an "abnormality" somewhere within the body, they can both send a warning signal and also undertake activities under the direction of a doctor or engage in mortal combat with bacteria and viruses within the body. If this concept is realized, doctors will be able to call upon microscale electromechanical systems to perform "molecular or atomic surgery."

Distributed Battlefield Microscale Sensor Networks

In modern warfare, in order to accurately reconnoiter enemy combat deployments and troop movements in a timely fashion, opposing sides have invested financial, material, and personnel strength to research, produce, deploy, and employ reconnaissance systems and apparatuses throughout the world. However, the solemn facts of the Gulf War tell us that, when hunting the highly mobile and wideranging "scud" missiles, the area covered by existing reconnaissance systems is limited. However, microscale electromechanical systems could solve the problem of crucial areas that must be kept under continuous surveillance.

One possible case would be to use unmanned aircraft or other methods to distribute a large number of low-cost, use-on-demand microscale sensor systems over a combat zone. High-altitude unmanned aircraft would employ an onboard coded laser of a modulated double-angle reflection communications system to record the position of every microscale sensor. Then, the sensor systems begin to collect, process, and store information, until another unmanned aircraft uses an identical coded laser to send out an inquiry. Each sensor again employs modulated double-angle reflectors to transmit its data back to the unmanned aircraft. This type of microscale electromechanical system has clear advantages in terms of deployment, endurance, and vulnerability. Compared to existing theater long-range monitoring systems, microscale sensor systems are more rapidly and conveniently deployed, and they are more complete. Existing sensor equipment, when in the open, can be seen with the naked eye within a range of 200 meters. However, microscale electromechanical systems, which are measured in millimeters, cannot be distinguished with the naked eye when dispersed in the air and are also difficult to identify with instruments. Certain materials reveal that microscale electromechanical systems are not confined to use in the military arena. They also provide impetus for man's efforts to understand and alter his environment in the fields of information technology, the study of materials, environmental science, biology, and medical science.

In the application of specialized integrated microscale apparatuses, such apparatuses currently being developed can acquire environmental information on the local area or in remote areas and, through the specialized integrated microscale apparatuses' gene-fragment communications system, transmit the information to nearby microscale apparatuses. They can also transmit to a central processor. The uses of specialized integrated microscale apparatuses with the most vitality are the infield of space navigation. They will be able to gradually replace all sorts of subsystems on current spacecraft and carrier rockets, and then develop further into independent space systems, thus leading to the advent of microscale satellites and "nanosatellites."

Nanosatellites

"Nanosatellites" represent a revolutionary breakthrough in future satellite development. They are a type of distributed satellite structural system. Such distributed systems, in contrast to integrated systems, are able to avoid the damage that follows the malfunction of an individual satellite, and thus will increase the survivability and flexibility of future space systems. The best application of nanosatellites is their deployment in local satellite groups or in distributed constellations. For example, if we launch nanosatellites in solar stationary orbits, with 36 nanosatellites placed evenly into each of 18 equally spaced orbits, then there would be a total of 648 nanosatellites in orbit. Thus, we could ensure that at any given time, there would be continuous coverage and surveillance of any spot on the Earth. Currently, there are already a few western countries that are researching "microscale" satellites.

Japan Making Greatest Investment

Since the beginning of the 1990s, the topic of microscale electromechanical systems has been raised many times in scientific publications, and this field's specialized deliberations have attracted attention. A few experts in Japan, Western Europe, and the United States believe that with the rapid development of science and technology, microscale electromechanical systems will be a research topic of the utmost importance over the next 10 years. According to the Rand Corporation report, Japan is the nation making the greatest investment into research and development of microscale electromechanical systems at present. Japan's Ministry of International Trade and Industry has formulated a 10-year plan for developing microscale electromechanical systems; furthermore, it has already built a "molecular assembler." At the end of 1993, the Hitachi Corporation announced that it had, under room temperature conditions, built a working single-electron memory chip. Just like current chips, this type of chip can store one bit of information, but the newer memory devices only require 1/1,000,000 of the power consumption of older memory devices, and they require only 1/10,000 of the surface area.

U.S. Military 3-Year Plan

According to the Rand Corporation, the investment of the United States in research into microscale electromechanical systems is probably an order of magnitude lower than that of countries such as Japan or the Netherlands. In order to turn around this lag in the area of microscale electromechanical systems, the United States has already included such systems in its "U.S. National Critical Technologies" plan, and the U.S. military has especially drafted a 3-year plan for developing and applying microscale electromechanical systems.

Of course, whether one discusses microscale electromechanical systems or specialized integrated microscale apparatuses, their research and development are not easy to accomplish. For microscale electromechanical system technology and specialized integrated microscale apparatus technology to move from the laboratory into engineering practice, and finally into application, there are still quite a few difficulties that must be overcome. However, a variety of indications show that "nanotechnological weapons" could well bring about fundamental changes in many aspects of future military affairs. "Nanotechnology" will certainly become a crucial military technology in the 21st century!

ABOUT THE AUTHOR

Michael Pillsbury is currently an Associate Fellow at the Institute for National Strategic Studies, National Defense University, and a Senior Fellow at the Atlantic Council of the United States, where he is sponsored by the Office of Net Assessment, Department of Defense. During the Reagan administration Dr. Pillsbury was the Assistant Under Secretary of Defense for Policy Planning; under President Bush he was Special Assistant for Asian Affairs in the Office of the Secretary of Defense, reporting to Andrew W. Marshall, Director of Net Assessment. Previously he served as an defense analyst for the Rand Corporation and on the staff of several U.S. Senate Committees. He has taught graduate courses in Chinese foreign policy at Georgetown University, UCLA, and USC.

Dr. Pillsbury studied Mandarin Chinese for 2 years at the Stanford Center in Taipei, Taiwan, under a doctoral dissertation fellowship of the National Science Foundation. He earned a B.A. from Stanford University and a Ph.D. from Columbia University.

421